The Eucharistic Prayers of the Roman Rite

Enrico Mazza

The Eucharistic Prayers
of the Roman Rite

Translated by: Matthew J. O'Connell

Pueblo Publishing Company

New York

Design: Frank Kacmarcik

Originally published in Italian as *Le Odierne Preghiere Eucaristiche* © 1984, Centro Editoriale Dehoniano, Bologna

The English translation of *The Roman Missal* © 1973, International Committee on English in the Liturgy, Inc. All rights reserved.

The English translation of the *Eucharistic Prayers for Masses with Children* © 1975, International Committee on English in the Liturgy, Inc. All rights reserved.

The English translation of the *Eucharistic Prayers for Masses of Reconciliation* © 1975, International Committee on English in the Liturgy, Inc. All rights reserved.

Scriptural pericopes quoted from the Revised Standard Version.

Printed in the United States of America.

ISBN: 0-916134-78-4

Contents

Foreword   ix

Introduction   xxv
    I. *The Situation*   xxv
    II. *A Historical Study*   xxvi
    III. *Sources and Pastoral Theology*   xxvii
    IV. *Content and Method*   xxx

CHAPTER ONE
The Eucharistic Prayer Between Past and Present   1
    I. *Description*   1
    II. *Characteristics*   4
    III. *Developments in Theocentric Orientation*   5
    IV. *Literary Genre*   12
    V. *Origin and Development of the Anaphora*   16
    VI. *The Account of Institution*   22
    VII. *Excursus: Concelebration and the Anaphora*   29

CHAPTER TWO
The Preface   36
    I. *Meaning*   36
    II. *Theological Value*   41
    III. *Text of the Sanctus*   47

CHAPTER THREE
The Roman Canon   49
    I. *Translations of the Roman Canon*   49
    II. *Introduction*   53
    III. *The Text of the Canon*   59

CHAPTER FOUR
The Second Eucharistic Prayer   88
    I. *Translations of the Second Eucharistic Prayer*   88
    II. *The Source*   90

III. *Departures from Hippolytus*   91
IV. *Analysis of the Text*   100

CHAPTER FIVE
The Third Eucharistic Prayer   123
    I. *Introduction*   123
   II. *The Author of the Text*   125
  III. *Vere Sanctus es, Domine ("Lord, you are holy indeed")*   125
  IV. *First Epiclesis*   128
    V. *Anamnesis*   131
  VI. *The Sacrifice*   134
 VII. *Sources of the Text*   137
VIII. *Epiclesis*   140
  IX. *Intercessions*   142
    X. *Appendix to Chapter Five*   149

CHAPTER SIX
The Fourth Eucharistic Prayer   154
    I. *Structure of the Anaphora*   158
   II. *Anaphora as a Profession of Faith*   158
  III. *"Holy Father"*   160
  IV. *Celebration of God*   161
    V. *Sanctus*   162
  VI. *Anamnetic Narrative of the History of Salvation*   164
 VII. *Epiclesis*   170
VIII. *Account of Institution*   173
  IX. *Anamnesis*   177
    X. *The Paschal Mystery*   178
  XI. *The Offering*   179
 XII. *Epiclesis for Unity*   180
XIII. *Intercessions*   186
XIV. *Doxology*   189

CHAPTER SEVEN
The Anaphoras of Reconciliation and the Anaphora for the Swiss
Synod   191
    I. *The Anaphoras of Reconciliation*   191
   II. *The Anaphora for the Swiss Synod*   213

CHAPTER EIGHT
The Eucharistic Prayers for Masses with Children   225
    I. *Introduction*   235
   II. *The Problem*   236
  III. *Anaphoras for Children: A New Direction*   237

IV. *Meaning of the "the Latin as a Model"* 239
V. *Examination of the Three Anaphoras* 240
VI. *Prospects (in Lieu of Conclusions)* 248

CHAPTER NINE

Theology of the Anaphora: Prayer of the Lord and Proclamation of the Passion 250

I. *Introduction* 250
II. *Some Data from the Fathers* 252
III. *A Historical Problem* 255
IV. *Theory of Antoine Chavasse* 262
V. *The Supper, Sign of the Cross* 266
VI. *Analysis of the Relation Between Supper and Cross* 273
VII. *Conclusion* 280

Abbreviations 281

Notes 285

Select Bibliography 355

Index 361

Foreword

Twenty years ago, although the Second Vatican Council had not dealt directly with the eucharistic prayer, I ventured the following observation:

"One of these days the eucharistic prayer of the Roman Mass will change. Whether this comes about by way of radical revision of the Roman Canon or by the addition of several alternative anaphoras, the change will come."[1]

Happily, the radical revision of the Roman Canon, perhaps impossible and not truly desirable, was rejected. Instead, three additional anaphoras were soon put into liturgical use throughout the Roman rite (1968); later five other anaphoras, for somewhat more limited use but still for the entire rite, were formally approved (1974). And, even today, the process is hardly at an end, given the conciliar commitment to open-ended liturgical development and also the instances of a few other eucharistic prayers officially approved in a number of countries.

As the process goes on—and especially as we catch up with what has already happened in the liturgical reform—there is a desperate need for all who celebrate the eucharistic liturgy to understand the central prayer of praise and thanks, of memorial and offering. The Constitution on the Liturgy stated the goal of reform clearly but idealistically:

"The rites should be marked by a noble simplicity; they should be short, clear, and unencumbered by useless repetitions; they should be within the people's power of comprehension and as a rule not require much explanation (no. 34)."[2]

Whether much explanation or little explanation is required is a matter of judgment, but some explanation is needed. Certainly it is needed to understand the complex function, structure, and meaning of the eucharistic prayer. And needed not only for the people at large who celebrate the eucharistic mysteries, but equally for those who preside and minister at the celebration. The conciliar goals of simplicity and comprehensibility have to be supported by study and reflection.

An admirable nucleus for such exposition, by way of sound liturgical catechesis, was provided in the General Instruction of the Roman Missal (1969; nos. 55 and 56) and earlier, after the promulgation of the first three new eucharistic prayers, in an important set of guidelines (1968).[3] This was supplemented by circular letter (1973), to be considered below, although the letter was marred by a cautionary stance and by an effort to forestall further development by suggesting alternatives to new anaphoras.[4]

Official Church documents, however useful, however significant, are seldom read. Much less are they translated into popular liturgical catechesis. The lack of direct, intensive commentaries on the eucharistic prayers, in English and in other languages, is apparent.

Enrico Mazza fills the gap through the present volume. It is a commentary of depth and quality. Background and development, theory and analysis, from historical notes to the fine excursus on concelebration, all will strengthen understanding by the presidents of the eucharistic assemblies who pronounce the words of the anaphora and, still more important, understanding by the members of Christ who hear the words and invest them with their faith and devotion.

Among the suggestions agreed upon by the Synod of Bishops at its extraordinary session in late 1985 were some generalizations about the liturgy, made two decades after the completion of the Second Vatican Council:

"The bishops should not merely correct abuses but should also clearly explain to everyone the theological foundation of the sacramental discipline and of the liturgy.
"Catecheses must once again become paths leading into liturgical life (mystagogical catecheses), as was the case in the Church's beginnings.
"Future priests should learn liturgical life in practical way and know liturgical theology as well."[5]

Mazza's insights come then as an ideal response to the plea for an explanation of the "theological foundation" of the liturgy, a path to mystagogy, a tool for learning the liturgical life practically and doctrinally. The scope of the book is restricted, but restricted to the central act and expression of the Eucharist itself.

In 1973, the new Roman Congregation for Divine Worship studied the question of more anaphoras and reached a rather negative conclusion: "At this time it is not advisable to grant to the conferences of bishops a general permission to compose or approve new eucharistic prayers."[6]

The hesitation at that time was perhaps understandable (although it was soon followed by the introduction of five more eucharistic prayers: two for reconciliation, and three for children). Certainly the privately produced eucharistic prayers of the 1960's and 1970's were not always encouraging: some were highly idiosyncratic, personalized, and particularized; some lacked biblical orientation; others had little basis in the traditions of (diverse) functions, structures, and meanings of anaphoras. And often official interest in new projects foundered on occasional and thematic approaches to anaphoras, with the danger of suffusing the entire eucharistic prayer (and not merely its preface or embolisms) with a particular concern: marriage, funeral, ordination, pastoral gathering, eucharistic congress, etc.

The 1973 reaction of the Congregation was partly a matter of stopgap suggestions, good enough in themselves but no answer to the underlying issue. Certainly it is possible and desirable to supplement the existing prayers with embolisms appropriate to a particular festal observance or ritual celebration. It is possible and desirable also to achieve some of the purposes of new eucharistic prayers in other ways: choice of diverse Mass formularies and texts, discreet introductions (*monitiones*), or comments, homilies, and general intercessions.

These were sound proposals in the document, but in the context they looked like devices to put off the troubling question of additional eucharistic prayers that were then being sought, especially by conferences of bishops. The Congregation, however, did put the matter candidly. It listed the very reasons why new anaphoras would be appropriate: unity and variety in liturgical prayer; the opportunity for the one mystery of Christ to be proclaimed in a variety of ways; a more effective share in the celebrations; the needs of different groups, regions, and peoples; compositions in accord with the contemporary mentality and idiom; the fact of the publication of privately composed eucharistic prayers as theoretical models.

The English edition of Mazza's work appears most opportunely at a time when there is a growing desire for additional anaphoras, over and above the nine studied in this book, for it exposes the basic principles of anaphoral structure.

The Apostolic See made a remarkable statement in reference to the translation of the latin texts of the Roman rite in general, and the development of new texts in particular:

"Texts translated from another language are clearly not sufficient for the celebration of a fully renewed liturgy. The creation of new texts will be necessary. But translation of texts transmitted through the tradition of the Church is the best school and discipline for the creation of new texts so 'that any new forms adopted should in some way grow organically from forms already in existence' " (Constitution on the Liturgy, art. 23).[7]

Perhaps the strongest statement from an official Roman source occurs in the 1968 guidelines already mentioned. The reasoning valid for the three eucharistic prayers added in 1968 is just as valid today for further growth:

"The Holy See has introduced three new anaphoras into the Roman liturgy . . . in the interest of making possible in the central part of the eucharistic celebration a better proclamation of God's blessings and a better recollection of the history of salvation. . . . "Why this new departure? To consider the variety of anaphoras in the tradition of the universal Church is to realize that one anaphora alone cannot contain all the pastoral, spiritual, and theological riches to be hoped for. A multiplicity of texts must make up for the limitations of any one of them. This has always been the course taken by all the Christian Churches, the Roman alone excepted; they have all had and continue to have a variety of anaphoras, sometimes a great variety. In adding three new anaphoras to the Roman Canon, the Church's intent here too has been to enrich the Roman liturgy pastorally, spiritually, and liturgically."[8]

A significant and indeed unique commentary like Mazza's on the existing, approved anaphoras is a valuable contribution to the continuing process. The hesitations about new anaphoras that were expressed in 1973 are no longer applicable more than a dozen years later. In fact, a logical sequence may be set up: first and most important, a deeper understanding of the nine eucharistic prayers, to which this book is directly addressed; second, greater use of the neglected anaphoras, especially Eucharistic Prayers I and IV and the two prayers of reconciliation; third, the creation of new texts.

The contribution of existing, privately prepared models should not be denigrated. Their weaknesses may be great. Their unauthorized use may be deplored. But their contents should be examined and judged on their own merit. More important still, the continuing experience of the other Christian Churches of the West needs to be respected and explored for their valued insights. Their new liturgical books (many influenced by the Roman efforts), offer an invaluable wealth of new anaphoras. And, for the English-speaking world, the current enterprise of some twenty-six conferences of Catholic bishops is promising.

The agency of these conferences of bishops is of course the International Commission on English in the Liturgy (ICEL), since 1963 a joint commission of Catholic bishops' conferences: eleven member or sponsoring conferences, fifteen associate member or participating conferences.

As part of its mandate, ICEL has prepared one original eucharistic prayer and study translations of two ancient prayers in contemporary English suited to the liturgical assembly. At this writing, it has projected one or two other texts, in particular those that would function as do Eucharistic Prayers I, II, and III, that is, permitting the use of the restored corpus of Roman prefaces. From a pragmatic and pastoral viewpoint, the latter seems most needful now, since Eucharistic Prayers II and III have been vastly overused and stand in danger of becoming almost as routine as was the Roman Canon in Latin before the reforms.

"Eucharistic Prayer A" was first issued by ICEL in 1984 for extensive consultation, which included as always the bishops of the twenty-six episcopates. A definitive edition was completed in early 1986 and submitted to the conferences of bishops, which alone can determine its possible liturgical use.[9] Already a number of conferences have approved the text and await the confirmation of their decision by the Roman Congregation.

The text of Eucharistic Prayer A is notable because it survived a lengthy screening process to uncover a suitable contemporary anaphora, during which many texts commissioned by ICEL and by individual conferences of bishops were examined. In structure and in substance it is traditional—some might even object because it does not offer alternative versions of the institution narrative and the doxology; it is strongly biblical in inspiration, concrete in imagery, elevated and poetic in style, universal as opposed to particular, contemporary in simplicity of idiom, authentic and original. While, if officially incorporated in the liturgy, it will surely not satisfy everyone, it can still be a major contribution, certainly deserving to rank with other twentieth-century compositions that have found their way into official liturgies.

The other two ICEL productions are translations of ancient anaphoras, done in contemporary and proclamatory language, but respecting the originals so far as possible.

One of these is a new English version of the anaphora of Hippolytus, now familiar in general because of the relation of Eucharistic Prayer II to that ancient text.[10] In the definitive reworking of the translation after full and public consultation, no attempt is made to incorporate all the elements of the later Roman tradition. On the other hand, none of the original is omitted nor is the theology developed—both adaptations which were introduced in Eucharistic Prayer II.

The ecumenical implications of this work (which are an important dimension of ICEL's mandate) are evident, even if the ICEL text is formally for study purposes. The interest of the other Churches is clear from their incorporation of various versions or adaptations of Hippolytus in their new service books. The appropriateness of this ancient source for the Roman rite is clear not only from the adaptation now in use as Eucharistic Prayer II, but also because the Roman revision had already (1968) borrowed the consecratory prayer for the ordination of bishops from the same *Apostolic Tradition* of Hippolytus. (In the context of Mazza's commentary, moreover, the ICEL version may be a useful counterpoint for study of Eucharistic Prayer II, since it provides contemporary liturgical language for the ancient anaphora itself, without omissions or adaptations.)

The other ICEL study project is similarly ecumenical in potential value, since it gives a contemporary English version of the Alexandrine anaphora of Saint Basil—a prayer still used, in various forms, by several Eastern Churches.[11] Its venerable character, purity of doctrine, and profound liturgical and spiritual beauty are attested to by its use over many centuries in the Eastern Churches, including of course those in full communion with the Roman See.

Although not immediately or directly intended for incorporation in the Roman rite, the ICEL study text is as suitable for that purpose as is Eucharistic Prayer IV. The latter, unlike the traditional Roman Canon, also includes the proclamation of the whole economy of salvation, as does Basil.

In 1966 and 1967, the inclusion of the anaphora of Saint Basil in the Roman sacramentary was under active consideration by the Consilium for the Implementation of the Constitution on the Liturgy.[12] The proposal barely failed of acceptance for various reasons—although hardly because of any incompatibility with the

Roman liturgical tradition, which already embraces the most diverse inheritances.

Two decades later, the proposal to add the anaphora of Saint Basil to the Roman liturgy on occasion may or may not be acceptable, but it is certainly worthy of the most serious reconsideration: in itself, as enriching the Roman rite, and in its ecumenical possibilities. (In the context of the present book, the ICEL text may provide a helpful parallel for the study of Eucharistic Prayer IV.)

The point is worth making again. Mazza's study, valuable primarily for pastoral, catechetical, and scholarly purposes, comes opportunely also in relation to the continuing call for additional anaphoras in the reformed Roman rite.

The 1963 Constitution on the Liturgy did not contemplate the use of the vernacular in the eucharistic prayer, aside from the introductory dialogue and the Sanctus, but it did not preclude such a development. Chapter I of the document, on general principles, had envisioned the likely extension of the vernacular "in the first place to the readings and instructions and to some prayers and chants" (no. 36:2). Chapter II, on the Eucharist, permitted the vernacular for "the readings and 'the universal prayer' [general intercessions]" and "also, as local conditions may warrant, those parts belonging to the people" (no. 54). But the same decree classified "a more extended use of the mother tongue within the Mass" as among the more radical or profound adaptations which conferences of bishops might "propose" and which might be introduced with the "consent" of the Apostolic See (nos. 54 and 40).

In 1967, the decision was made and the consent given, so that the Roman eucharistic prayer (and those alternative anaphoras not then available) might be proclaimed in the several mother tongues.[13] These versions would be every much as official and liturgical as the original.

At the time, there were about fifteen popular hand missals in the English language, each with its version of the Roman Canon, and perhaps as many more English versions in other devotional books. Some were of high quality, others not. Some reflected recent scholarship concerning the meaning of the Roman Canon. Some were deliberately archaic; others were contemporary in vocabulary, but rather stilted and even slavish.

The pastoral need was answered by the preparation and adoption of the ICEL translation of the Roman Canon, later somewhat revised in the light of experience with its actual use. Similarly, the new anaphoras, which were largely contemporary in composition despite their evident organic relation to liturgical traditions of the past, were translated by ICEL and adopted for liturgical use in the countries where English is spoken.

In this edition of Mazza's study, each of the eucharistic prayers appears in its official English form—canonically approved by the respective conferences of bishops, with their approval confirmed by the Apostolic See—and each is also given in a more literal version that better illustrates some points of the commentary. The differences between the two English versions of the several anaphoras bear examination and study; they illustrate problems of both translation and celebration.

An endless number of books and articles and an equally endless number of arguments have been devoted to problems of translation from one language to another. In matters religious, it is principally a question of biblical translation and liturgical translation, to a lesser extent a question of the translation of the Fathers and later church writers. In setting up criteria or in making judgments, the greatest pitfall is to assert or deny "fidelity" too quickly. Every translation, including that done by machines, is interpretative and explanatory, incomplete and imperfect.

The task is complicated when the translation is from an ancient language like Latin, carrying the burden of its own period(s), culture, development into modern languages, etc. The complexity is the greater when the stages of development of the modern language into which it is rendered are taken into account or when a contemporary composition in a dead language is the starting point.

The English language has its own characteristics, which do not make the task any simpler. Its breadth and diversity may be greatly esteemed and valued: as "a vernacular of vernaculars," it has both "fixed" and "free" modes of existence and use. It is almost uninflected and without genders; it has an interchangeability of parts of speech, a wealth of prefixes and suffixes, a unique number of prepositions; it enjoys unlimited freedom in assimilating words from other languages; and the meaning of its words may change almost overnight. It can boast of subtlety and creativity; an extraordinarily large vocabulary, including words with a dozen meanings and complexities of nuance and synonym—not to mention its literary figures of speech, from metaphor to metonymy.[14]

A translation into English may range from rigid proximity, to which pejorative terms such as *slavish* or *literal* may be applied, to a loose but felicitous relation to the original, which may then be wrongly labeled *inaccurate*. If it goes without saying that the purpose of translation is to convey in another tongue what is or was said in an original, then within this range there may be various degrees of closeness and remoteness.

In the two sets of translations provided for the purposes of this commentary, one series is relatively close. It is sound, accurate, and faithful. These texts serve an important purpose for anyone attempting to understand the original texts of the anaphoras or, more important in the context, Mazza's commentary.

It is the other series of official and liturgical translations which require some explanation, particularly where they may appear to exceed reasonable bounds of proximity to the original. They also are sound, accurate, and faithful versions, but their translations are governed by broader principles.

A recent popular discussion of the subject of translation in the field of religion, and specifically in the field of biblical translation, sums up the principal criteria or concerns: how well the translations convey the *full meaning of the original* to the *widest* audience of speakers of English *today*. The writer goes on to specify further concerns: the primary criterion must be the faithful translation of the meaning—by which he means "meaning for meaning," not word for word, much less figure of speech for figure of speech. Next, the use of the twentieth-century English is demanded, by which is meant natural English that is at a "relatively common level" of the language as opposed to simplified or "literary" English, much less un-English vocabulary or un-English grammar.[15]

How much of this approach may be transferred to the language of the liturgy in English translation? How much more need be said? The answer seems to be that these criteria—and other criteria which might be more thoroughly developed—are indeed applicable to liturgical as well as biblical translation, but with at least one important, crucial addition.

The language of the liturgy, whether Greek or Latin, English or French, is meant to be proclaimed aloud in the worshiping assembly of Christian believers. With the very slight exception of a few prayers said inaudibly by the presiding celebrant, every liturgical text of the Roman rite is sung or said aloud. In the case of the eucharistic prayers, the acclamations are sung by the assembly; the dialogue and concluding doxology are in exchange between the assembly and its president; and every other word, phrase, clause, and sentence is to be said aloud or sung for all to hear and for all to affirm with the Amen of faith.

This criterion or, better, this demand for liturgical translation does not necessarily prevail over other requirements and expectations—but it does color and even explain them. If the meaning of an original in Latin (or perhaps the meaning of the underlying Greek or other language) is to be conveyed, it must be done in such a way as to be heard by the worshiping community and understood by the members of that community when it is heard. Again, if the language of translation is to be contemporary, natural, or at a relatively common level, this too is at the service of the hearers (as well as of the speaker or singer) so that the text may be understood, attended and responded to, accepted as the articulation of their faith and devotion.

This criterion may be looked at negatively. It excludes the needlessly complex and certainly the un-English. It may exclude the syntactical and rhetorical peculiarities of the original language, some of the special figures of speech, elaborations that may occur in the original without significant change of meaning, and elements that are largely oriented to or conditioned by a particular culture.

This criterion may even require a choice between the primary and the secondary in the original, if the inclusion of every last nuance, real or conjectural, in a given text has to be transferred to the second language. This possible omission of something that is certainly secondary and incidental is a sensitive matter, but the choice may be necessary: perhaps the original has several possible meanings; the integral transfer may require a didactic paraphrase more appropriate to a footnote or a catechism; the new version may become so overburdened or overtranslated as to distort the purpose of the original or, much worse, compromise or invalidate its actual use in the eucharistic assembly.

The demand that the text of the eucharistic prayer, like other presidential prayers of the celebration, should be recitable or singable so as to be heard and comprehended brings with it all the elements of rhythm and phrasing, of assonance and concern about homonyms, that may be expected, in varying ways and degrees, in every utterance from a song to a speech.

One way of summing up this matter, going beyond the evident need to convey meaning and to convey it in contemporary idiom, is again somewhat negative. Liturgical translation is not the translation that is intended for, or can be tested by, the quiet reading of a student or scholar.

The specialist in the original language has his or her essential role to play. Similarly, those who know the liturgical history and weight of a particular element of the liturgy—in this case the anaphora—have a critical role. The expert in the literary style of the language of translation is more important in the process than the specialist in the original language. And still more important is the expert in the very practical art of reciting and singing in an assembly: in this instance, the words are uttered not to a theater or concert audience but, quite the contrary, within and for a community of faith, so that they may be the authentic affirmation of that community.

This line of reasoning suggests why it was hardly possible to choose even the best of the existing English versions of the Roman Canon for liturgical use in 1967, when the possibility of vernacular for the eucharistic prayer was opened up. In 1949, for example, a new and elegant version of the Roman Missal had appeared, the work of J. B. O'Connell and H. P. R. Finberg, both highly qualified scholars; the edition was enhanced by the brilliant biblical translation of readings by Ronald Knox.[16] The liturgical texts, including the Roman Canon, were done carefully, accurately, in a most acceptable English style—for reading, for study, for "following the priest" during Mass. Even today, aside from its studied use of archaic forms, the translation stands up. It was and is totally unsuitable for liturgical use, nor was it ever designed for public recital or singing by the priest who presides at the eucharistic celebration.

A parallel may be drawn. A classical polyphonic Sanctus may be a masterwork of religious music, inspired and moving. It may be—and probably is—totally unsuitable for inclusion within the eucharistic prayer of an actual celebration, where it may overwhelm the principal elements of the anaphora and destroy its integrity and unity.

The primary and formal purpose of translation is to convey meaning from one tongue to another, but in doing so these other considerations may not be neglected, at the risk of weakening the liturgical act itself. Drawing the line is difficult and nowhere more so than in making the translation suited to the communal assembly. The liturgical reform of the Roman Mass was directed by the Fathers of the Second Vatican Council to the Sunday eucharistic assembly, not to small gatherings on weekdays or sophisticated communities, not to religious institutes or university congregations. Judgments will always differ when the level of language is at issue, because of the reasonable fear that the language will become commonplace rather than common (in the good sense of suited to the largest number of hearers and speakers), or that it will be puerile or flat rather than dignified and eloquently simple.

Fortunately, in English there is a strong sense, almost incompatible with a false notion of ecclesiastical or religious English, that simplicity and clarity can themselves be strong, dignifed, and eloquent. This is the sense of those experts in English style who caution against the needless word or phrase:

"Vigorous writing is concise. A sentence should contain no unnecessary words, a paragraph no unnecessary sentences, for the same reason that a drawing should have no unnecessary lines and a machine no unnecessary parts."[17]

The same source offers another caution: "Avoid the elaborate, the pretentious, the coy, and the cute. . . . Anglo-Saxon is a livelier tongue than Latin, so use Anglo-Saxon words."[18] The context of these observations and injunctions is nonliturgical and not directly concerned with the spoken word. What is said, however, is all the more applicable to the spoken word and to the language of liturgical celebration.

The Constitution on the Liturgy did not speak directly to the style or mode of liturgical translation. Its basic norm for ritual change, however, has a providential applicability to liturgical translation. It even serves to sum up much of what has been suggested here. The paragraph already quoted calls for "noble simplicity," for rites that are "short, clear, and unencumbered by useless repetitions," for rites that are "within the people's power of comprehension and as a rule do not require much explanation."[19] Among the elements of rite, this norm is nowhere more applicable than in the case of language.

What has been said thus far is the theoretical background of the actual English translations approved for official liturgical use, which in this book accompany those which are intended for study purposes and for the purpose of the commentary. The historical background of the official texts is also worth stating briefly.

Concomitant with the issuance of the Constitution on the Liturgy, the joint or mixed commission on English liturgical translations came into being. Its formal establishment by the interested conferences of bishops was announced in October 1963 after a year of discussion and planning by bishops designated to represent the several episcopates.[20] Similar bodies came into existence, at least for the major language groups, as conferences of bishops began to exercise their authority to prepare or approve liturgical texts for the local churches of their territories.

As early as January 1964, the Apostolic See began issuing a series of documents and statements related to the vernacular and its own responsibility, in accord with the conciliar decree, which was to confirm the decisions of conferences of bishops in this matter. The collection of conciliar, papal, and curial documents includes twenty-six, of varying weight and significance, which deal exclusively with the question of translation, another fifteen in which it is treated along with other questions.[21]

In the light of discussions at a congress on liturgical translation, held in Rome during November 1965,[22] and in consultation with the commissions from the several language groups which had their own experience, the postconciliar liturgical commission or Consilium was able to issue a broad and substantial instruction in January 1969.[23] This useful and significant document sums up what had been reflected upon in the first few years after the Council; it opened up the potential of liturgical translation within the Roman rite.

Of the thirty-three paragraphs of the instruction devoted to general principles and "some particular considerations," at least twenty-three positively support and encourage more open, free, or creative translation forms. Although understandably cautious about the principal euchological texts, such as anaphoras, consecratory prayers, and sacramental formulas, the document is remarkably appreciative of the problems of contemporary vernaculars.

It is clear, for example, that the "unit of meaning" is not an individual word but the whole passage. Repeatedly, the instruction rejects verbatim translation. Instead it favors cautious adaptation, substitution of metaphors, use of the concrete in place of the abstract, retention of essential elements either intact or in equivalent terms. It espouses explicitly the points made above: a "common" language, not in the bad sense that might mean unworthy language, but language "suited to the greater number of the faithful who speak it in every day use . . . normally intelligible to all, even to the less educated"; and, obviously enough, the instruction recognizes the demands of "spoken communication" and singing.

With direct reference to the translation of the Roman eucharistic prayer, some of this had been anticipated, simply and briefly, in a Roman circular letter two years earlier. This had noted how, in the translation of the Canon, "the language is to be that normally used in liturgical texts, avoiding the exaggerated classical and modern forms" and that "the style is to display a certain rhythm, making the text easy to speak and sing."[24] Add to this the 1969 instruction with its reflections on the freedom necessary for liturgical translation, and one can discern the guidelines for the translation of the nine Latin eucharistic prayers into English. Now, as will be mentioned below, the English translations are subject to a general revision. (Only Eucharistic Prayer I was revised as a whole after an initial period of use.)

The degree of closeness to or remoteness from the original Latin—or in certain instances an underlying text in Greek or a modern language—differs in the nine prayers. Eucharistic Prayer I may be used as an example. The Latin text of the Roman Canon, given its venerable character and long use, had not been radically changed except for the institution narrative and minor optional omissions. The English version called for much more, in particular the avoidance of what is in modern ears, at least in the ears of English speakers, a measure of floridity or even pomposity; the limitation of some repetitions of words not needed for the meaning of passages; the pragmatic resolution of some difficult or uncertain phrases (as had to be done in all modern languages); and above all, the creation of a text that might authentically express the faith and devotion of the people assembled for the eucharistic celebration here and now.

Opinions will differ about how well these goals are achieved in Eucharistic Prayer I or in the other eucharistic prayers in their official form. But the judgment should be made in the light of the principles enunciated by the Apostolic See or by the corporate body of translators. The latter acted as the agent of the conference of bishops, which made the canonical decision in each case.

In 1980, ICEL proposed a few slight revisions in the translations of the anaphoras, as a temporary expedient in response to special problems.[25] These were approved by several conferences of bishops but still await Roman confirmation. Most of the revisions were designed to eliminate instances, especially from Eucharistic Prayer IV, of exclusive language referring to humankind, that is, words which are masculine in form and which, previously understood as generic, are now understood as masculine in intent, to the exclusion of women. This problem, experienced not only in North America and the British Isles but also in other parts of the English speaking world, is worth noting. It is an example, and a very serious one, of the change of idiom and of meaning itself, which rapidly overtakes liturgical translation as much as it does common speech.

Much broader is the current general revision of the English translations of the anaphoras, as part of the revision of the Roman Missal translation. In March 1986, the usual form of widespread public consultation on the Order of Mass, including the eucharistic prayers and their variable prefaces, was initiated. Some twenty-five hundred individual persons and commissions, among them several hundred bishops, have been invited to propose emendations of the liturgical texts—in the hope of a complete revision of the sacramentary by the year 1991. Again, Mazza's commentary appears in English most opportunely as the process goes on.

In the survey instrument or consultation booklet of 1986, a refined and slightly elaborated set of guidelines for translation (and, in this case, revision) of vernacular liturgical texts is included. It repeats a few of the central principles of the Roman instruction of 1969 and adds some others especially pertinent to the English language and the present task:

"Liturgical texts (with rare exceptions) are meant to be sung or said aloud in the liturgical assembly. Their intelligibility and effectiveness when heard is of crucial importance. The process of translating these texts will therefore differ fundamentally from what is required when translating texts which are intended to be read from the printed page by someone reading alone either silently or aloud.

"Translators of the liturgical texts must use to advantage the native qualities of the English language that are effective for oral communication, among them: clarity, directness, concreteness, and logical coherence. They should also take into account the resources of the language that move and enlighten: rhythm, alliteration, assonance.

"The syntax of the Latin cannot usually be transferred to English. For example, whatever their effect in Latin, elaborate subordinate clauses and participial phrases are often unsatisfactory in translation. They may weaken the force of the text that is meant to be sung or proclaimed."[26]

From what has already been said, the translation of liturgical texts—and, for that matter, the composition of original liturgical texts—is truly critical, certainly in the case of the anaphoras. Mazza's study is an invaluable contribution to the entire process as well as to the essential, continuing task of catechesis and understanding.

Frederick R. McManus

NOTES

1. From the preface prepared for Cipriano Vagaggini, *The Canon of the Mass and Liturgical Reform* (London: Geoffrey Chapman, 1967), preface, pp. 9–12.

2. For the English translation of this and other official texts, see International Commission on the Liturgy, *Documents on the Liturgy 1963–1979: Conciliar, Papal, and Curial Texts* (Collegeville, MN: Liturgical Press, 1982). Cited below as DOL, with the number of the document in the collection.

3. Consilium for the Implementation of the Constitution on the Liturgy, guidelines *Au cours des derniers mois,* June 2, 1968: DOL 244.

4. Congregation for Divine Worship, circular letter *Eucharistiae participationem,* April 27, 1963: DOL 248.

5. December 8, 1965. Translation from the Vatican Press Office.

6. See note 4, above.

7. Consilium, instruction *Comme le prévoit,* January 25, 1969, no. 43: DOL 123. Issued by the Apolstolic See in six major languages, the instruction used examples taken from the respective language.

8. See note 3, above.

9. *An Original Eucharistic Prayer: Text I* (Washington: ICEL, 1984). This and the other texts to be described next appeared in booklet form, published by ICEL with limited distribution to the conferences of bishops and to consultants. "Text I" was issued, after the completion of the consultation and revision as *Eucharistic Prayer A* (1986).

10. *Eucharistic Prayer of Hippolytus: Text for Consultation* (Washington: ICEL, 1983).

11. *Eucharistic Prayer of Saint Basil: Text for Consultation* (Washington: ICEL, 1985).

12. For an account of this proposal, see Annibale Bugnini, *La riforma liturgica 1948–1975* (Rome, 1983), pp. 451–453.

13. The use of the vernacular in the Roman Canon was allowed as an experimental concession by Pope Paul VI dated January 31, 1967 (DOL 117) and incorporated in the "second instruction" of the Congregation of Rites on the implementation of the Constitution on the Liturgy, *Tres abhinc annos,* May 4, 1967, no. 28: DOL 39.

14. See Robert Graves and Alan Hodge, *The Reader over Your Shoulder: A Handbook for Writers of English Prose,* 2d. ed. (New York: Random House, 1979), esp. Chapter I, "The Peculiar Qualities of English."

15. Alan S. Duthie, *Bible Translations and How to Choose between Them* (Exeter, Paternoster Press, 1985), esp. Chapter VII, "Meaning for Meaning."

16. *The Missal in Latin and English* (London: Burns Oates, 1949; New York: Sheed & Ward, 1950).

17. William Strunk Jr. and E. B. White, *The Elements of Style,* 3d. ed. (New York: Macmillan, 1979), esp. pp. 23–24.

18. Ibid., 76–77.

19. See above, at note 2.

20. Frederick R. McManus, *ICEL: The First Years* (Washington: ICEL, 1981).

21. DOL 108–133, in the section "Languages in the Liturgy."

22. Proceedings in *Le traduzioni dei libri liturgici. Atti del Congresso tenuto a Roma il 9–13 novembre 1965* (Vatican City: Libreria Editrice Vaticana, 1966). For a description of the structural and programmatic plans of ICEL, see Frederick R. McManus, "L'organizzazione del lavoro di traduzione," pp. 231–241.

23. See note 7, above.

24. Consilium, communication of the secretary, August 10, 1967: DOL 118.

25. *Eucharistic Prayers* (Washington: ICEL, 1980).

26. *Consultation on Revision: The Roman Missal, Order of Mass* (Washington: ICEL, 1986). See also Helen Kathleen Hughes, *The Language of the Liturgy: Some Theoretical and Practical Implications* (Washington: ICEL, 1984).

Introduction

In 1966, L. Bouyer published a book, in French, on the origin and development of the eucharistic prayer; it was translated into English two years later. Though the discussion was based on historical and philological data, the real character of the book emerged in the title: *Eucharist. Theology and Spirituality of the Eucharistic Prayer.*

Meanwhile, Consilium (the Commission for the Implementation of the Constitution on the Sacred Liturgy) had begun its work and was bringing to a successful issue the renewal of the celebration of the Eucharist in the Roman Church. Father Bouyer worked on the committee assigned to compose the new eucharistic prayers and was therefore in a position to see how radically unprepared most Christians were for this reform. A second French edition of his book on the eucharistic prayer appeared in 1968[1]; he added a chapter on the renewal which the Roman Church was experiencing with the adoption of three new eucharistic prayers. His brief commentary dealt with the essentials; it awakened a desire for a more extensive discussion of the subject.

Other authors, however, did not go much further. The best known commentary was provided in the series *Assemblées du Seigneur*,[2] but here again the explanations were overly brief and succinct.

These two works have been the principal ones published. T. Schnitzler's little German book has some good commentaries.[3] On the other hand, articles published in various reviews devoted to liturgical studies have found no echo except among the specialists who follow these publications; they form a very limited readership. As a result, the faculties of theology and the theological institutions that reflect at all seriously on religious subjects and attempt to apply scientific methods to them have, for practical purposes, been left without the necessary tools.

Even the recently published third volume of the collective work

Anamnesi. Eucaristia: Teologia e storia della celebrazione (Casale Monferrato, 1983) has only a few pages on the new eucharistic prayers and, for the rest, refers its readers to the periodical literature. Nothing is said of the texts published after the Sacramentary of 1970.

There is, then, a need for a careful inquiry into and commentary on the eucharistic prayers in use today so that those concerned can study and understand them. Or, to put it differently: so that readers may grasp the extent to which the treasures of ancient tradition are present in even the most recent texts, for example, the eucharistic prayers for Mass with children, which are usually regarded as without value from the standpoint of the careful construction proper to liturgical texts.

This book attempts to meet this need. It provides a study of the sources of the new texts so that these may be understood in light of the historical development of the eucharistic prayer.

An investigation of sources is necessarily a work of history; the book's findings will, therefore, depend on an application of the historical method, with all the consequences this entails. The history of the present stage of development is studied so that we may understand it through its roots in antiquity.

II. A HISTORICAL STUDY

When we speak of historians, we quite naturally think of individuals occupied with the past. Some regard such an occupation utterly useless since the past no longer exists and we must live in the present. It is present-day problems that call for solutions; the problems of the past have already found their solutions since the past is gone, gone for good.

That is surely a naive view of history. Every human being, every society, every movement is the child of its past, and the past continues to act despite appearances. The past is never over and done with. Yesterday continues to live a hidden life in today.

In the study of the liturgy, there is a further reason for emphasizing this connection between past and present. Vatican Council II set it down as a principle that any new liturgical forms must be in close continuity with the already existing forms which tradition has entrusted to the Church. In a sense, it required that the new forms be inspired by and modeled on traditional forms. "Today" is to be born of "yesterday" and emerge organically from it: this is a law of liturgical reform.[4]

If the liturgy of today is thus closely bound up with the liturgy of yesterday, it follows that to know the Church's liturgical past is to know its present as well. The history of the liturgy as studied with the aid of the liturgical sources brings understanding of our contemporary liturgy.

Such is the thought of H.-I. Marrou[5] who defines history as knowledge rather than narration and thus makes the history of Christian worship a proper theological discipline. The study of the sources of the contemporary liturgy is therefore not superfluous, since to do history in the manner indicated is to do theology as well.

This book is, and is meant to be, a historical study, but, given its subject, it ends up being a theological study as well.

III. SOURCES AND PASTORAL THEOLOGY

The primary sources are the early anaphoras or eucharistic prayers and the new texts produced by the current reform.

Another primary source is scripture. The biblical renewal that occurred in the Roman Church after the Second Vatican Council led to a new lectionary and conditioned every other reform. It required that all prayer be based on sacred scripture.

The early eucharistic prayers were likewise dependent on scripture, but not as massively and directly as the new ones, especially the eucharistic prayers for the Swiss Synod. The history of Christianity cannot but register this important fact: it is the scriptures that have had the greatest influence on the contemporary renewal of catholicism.

In studying the ancient liturgies as sources of the modern liturgies, we are obliged to take into account as well the writings of the Fathers, though to a lesser extent than might be expected. At no period have liturgical texts been the creation of single writers. On the contrary, varied, often anonymous, contributions and influences come together in these prayers. Currents of thought and mentalities play the dominant role, rather than individual authors whose writings may be checked for comparison.

Liturgical texts are prayers of a people with their culture and their good and bad traits. In the past, a text became liturgical by reason of the use made of it and not by reason of the author who wrote it or the authority that imposed it.

Liturgical means celebrated and, in fact, celebrated by all the people. It is not mere rhetoric to say that the real author of liturgical texts is the people, that is, the people of God or the Church. Nor is it a mere play on words, since the people, while being "of God," do not cease to be a people.

The Church, moreover, is not identical to the ecclesiastical hierarchy. Rather, it is an assembly called together into God's presence and therefore a cultic (worshiping) assembly. The assembly has a hierarchical leader as its president, but at the same time it will always be a gathering of the people of God, since the hierarchy too is part of that people.

Liturgical texts, then, are texts of the people, and we find embodied in them the faith and life of different periods. As a result, we also find in them the theology of these different periods, but it is not the theology developed by professional theologians. It is that which entered into the Church's life, a theology that became the pastoral guide of the Church and thus affected the very life of the community. This theology holds for the earliest texts.

In later texts (from the fourth century on in the East), the situation changes. The texts acquire set forms that are venerated and regarded as sacred by reason of their antiquity; the part played by the Church in the sense of the people progressively diminishes. Henceforward, it is the Church in the sense of the hierarchy that determines the content and form of the texts.

Such a shift was both logical and necessary. The problem of heresies and the need of an orthodoxy as the basis of ecclesial unity imposed new cautions and new concerns which inevitably had an impact on the anaphora. Theological disputes and dogmatic definitions appeared in the eucharistic prayers and made their presence felt. We need only think of the epiclesis in the Greek Anaphora of St. James, where the doctrine of the Holy Spirit is developed with a logical coherence that owes everything to the theological discussions on consubstantiality.[6] Or we may recall the Anaphora of John of Bostra, which in its Christological section is a real treatise on the ontological constitution of Christ.[7]

There would have been nothing wrong in all this if the text had not become so heavy and complex that the assembly as a whole had difficulty in following it. As it is, when we study that kind of text, we see that the liturgy of every Church in every age is in need of reform. The historian's activity does not necessarily alienate and isolate him from the period in which he himself lives. On the contrary, the fact that he is a historian can render his sensibilities more keen.

We said that a historical study of liturgical texts is in a sense also a proper theological study. But does this theology have pastoral relevance? An answer comes from the Second Vatican Council. Active participation in the liturgy is certainly of pastoral importance, and Vatican II set it down as a principle that this participation should find expression in those important rites and prayers[8] that are the object of the present study.

To appreciate this principle, we will briefly review the history of the redaction of the conciliar text on this point. The text originally presented in the Council hall differed from the one later approved. It said: "The Church earnestly desires that the faithful not be present at the mystery of faith as strangers or silent spectators but that through a good understanding of the rites and prayers they should take part in them actively, consciously, and devoutly."[9] It is clear that the faithful are to do two things: first, to understand the rites and prayers; second, to take part in the rites and prayers.

At the tenth general session, on October 30, 1962, Cardinal Bea spoke and asked that the text be amended so that participation would refer "not only to the rites and prayers but also to the mystery of faith itself; therefore not just to the external action."[10] The aim then is to participate in the celebration of the mystery of faith as such and not just in the external rites and prayers.

The amendment was accepted, and the official text reads:

"Christ's faithful, when present at this mystery of faith, should not be there as strangers or silent spectators. On the contrary, through a good understanding of the rites and prayers they should take part in the sacred action, conscious of what they are doing, with devotion and full collaboration."[11]

Two points are made here: the object of our understanding is no longer the liturgical text or the rite, but the mystery of faith or sacramental reality itself; on the other hand, our understanding of this mystery comes not directly but through the rites and prayers. "The rites and prayers are therefore not ends in themselves but means that should lead to a full understanding of the eucharistic mystery. In fact, this mystery finds admirable expression in its rites and prayers."[12]

The assertion of this principle by the Council was of historical significance. It has a simple consequence: the text of the anaphora with its structure and the faith and piety expressed in it provides all we need for a conscious, devout, and active celebration. The text should give us an understanding of the eucharistic mystery that leads to a fruitful participation in it.

None of this is possible, however, unless the liturgical texts also convey correct teaching. Texts and rites speak to us not of themselves but of the eucharistic mystery; if they are adequate and suited for conveying such an understanding, they are vehicles of a formal and complete doctrinal orthodoxy.

It is important to observe, however, that the doctrine in question is directly ordered to the celebration. Consequently, it is the actual celebration itself, rather than any prior theological understanding, that gives us a knowledge of the mystery of faith.

The theology is a pastoral theology. In other words, a theology based on texts that guide active participation and provide norms for this participation is necessarily a pastoral theology. It follows that, properly understood, a historical study based on the texts of the liturgy can be relevant even from the pastoral standpoint.

IV. CONTENT AND METHOD

In this book, we shall examine all the eucharistic prayers now approved and in use, analyzing them with the help of three different reading grills. The first is historical and textual; we shall inquire into the origin of the texts in the tradition represented by past anaphoras. The second is an understanding of the text in light of the theology to which it, or its source, gives direct expression; we will see what evolutionary line the contemporary liturgy is following and whether there has been real progress in the quality of the texts. The standard of measurement will be the liturgical functionality of the anaphora or eucharistic prayer. The third grill is a theological commentary based in most instances on the biblical source on which the text draws.

Though we shall not offer a criterion for reading, we shall pay special attention to problems of translation and point out either the value of the choices made by the translators or the difficulties these choices create. The translation often makes actual theological decisions that distance it from the theology of the Latin original. What assessment is to be made of all this? Only a careful discussion will provide the basis for a more than hasty judgment.

You may think that we have given disproportionate attention to the Roman Canon, especially since it is practically not used today. There are three reasons for this attention. First is the objective importance of this text; it is the principal source of the Third Eucharistic Prayer, which is the one most used, since with few exceptions it is said on all the Sundays and feasts of the year. Second, we must note that the various themes of the Roman Canon occur at some point in all the new anaphoras. The Canon is a source from which the composers of the new prayers felt obliged to derive the sacrificial themes proper to the Roman liturgy. The third reason is precisely the fate that has befallen the Roman Canon. Though theoretically in use, it has become marginal in practice; its use today is so minimal as to be statistically irrelevant. The Canon, whose text was most characteristic of the Roman liturgy from the fourth century on, is now practically unused.

When the reform began, the Roman Canon seemed untouchable. The most that was thought possible was the introduction of another eucharistic prayer that would play a subsidiary role while the Canon would remain the principal text. In fact, history moved in another direction. Can this shift be explained? Can it be justified? In practice, a variety of alternatives has been offered. Only a careful examination of the Canon will permit a judgment on whether the new practice is objectively justified.

This subject is of interest even from the more general viewpoint of the history of the Church. This whole episode involving the Canon may be seen as a return to the ancient principle that in matters of discipline the norm is created by use or custom. Norm does not determine use, but vice versa. It will be interesting to see to what developments this rebirth, however timid, of the value of custom will lead.

Let us hope that we continue to live in interesting times.

Chapter One

The Eucharistic Prayer Between Past and Present

I. DESCRIPTION

The eucharistic prayer, which is the high point in the celebration of Mass,[1] begins with the dialogue that introduces the preface and ends with the Amen which the congregation says at the end of the final doxology. In all the eucharistic prayers, this doxology is always the same as that of the Roman Canon: "Through him, with him, in him, in the unity of the Holy Spirit, all glory and honor is yours, almighty Father, for ever and ever."

In the course of liturgical history, the eucharistic prayer has been given various names, each emphasizing a particular aspect of the prayer in keeping with the theology of the period. The various names, although not synonyms, designate the prayer that runs from the dialogue before the preface to the Amen after the final doxology.

The oldest and most classical name is also the simplest: *Eucharistia* or "Eucharist." This name refers directly and immediately to the prayer of praise and thanksgiving that is addressed to the Father during the Lord's Supper.[2] Only secondarily and as a result does it apply to the bread and wine which are the sacrament of the body and blood of the Lord Jesus.

In the Greek speaking world, the prayer became known as the *anaphora* or *prosphora;* both words mean "offering," but anaphora (literally "a carrying up") emphasizes the ascending movement. In the last decade or so, anaphora has also won acceptance in the West as a technical term for the eucharistic prayer. The reason is clear, since the new texts in the Roman liturgy are based on ancient texts which are called anaphoras in the Antiochene liturgy.

In the Latin West, the eucharistic prayer was at one time known simply as *prex* (prayer) or *oratio oblationis* (prayer of offering). Eventually, however, the term "Canon" (*canon missae*) prevailed.

We shall not discuss the terminology for the eucharistic prayer from the standpoint of its historical development and variety.[3] The

1

short discussion given is to simply let you know that many names for the same reality have existed and do exist. In accordance with current usage, we shall give preference to anaphora, since this already has a very precise meaning: it refers to the eucharistic prayer as having the characteristics of structure and content that are peculiar to the Eastern liturgy as a whole, whatever the liturgical family and rite.

Therefore, we shall say without distinction either "third anaphora" or "Third Eucharistic Prayer." In referring to the Roman Canon, however, we shall speak only of the "First Eucharistic Prayer" and not of the "first anaphora," since the structure of the Roman Canon bears no relation to that of the Eastern anaphoras.[4]

The eucharistic prayer is both a concrete text and a literary genre. Moreover, it is made up of various units that in turn are both concrete texts and literary genres.

As literary genres, these units are autonomous in relation to the more inclusive genre known as the eucharistic prayer. For example, we can find epicleses and intercessions outside the eucharistic prayer; on the other hand, we will never find a eucharistic prayer that completely lacks, for example, the element of invocation. As concrete texts, these units must be in harmony with the other units making up the anaphora and with the anaphora as a whole.

An anaphora comes into being when these various parts or units are harmoniously coordinated among themselves. It is not, however, the simple sum of these parts.

The various parts of an anaphora are the opening dialogue; the preface or thanksgiving, which lists the great works of God that are the reasons for our thanksgiving; and the singing of the Sanctus, which is preceded by an introduction describing the heavenly choirs and angelic congregation that are the primary celebrants of this hymn. After the Sanctus comes the Post-Sanctus, which links this hymn to the account of institution. The Post-Sanctus may continue the thanksgiving and praise offered in the preface or it may be simply epicletic in character; in this case, it bears the name of first epiclesis. This first epiclesis calls upon the Father to send the Spirit and thereby transform the bread and wine into the sacrament of salvation.

The Post-Sanctus is followed immediately by the account of institution, which briefly tells of Jesus' last meal that originated the celebration of the Eucharist. The account contains the explanatory words over the bread and wine and the jussive words with which

2

Jesus ordered his disciples to eat and drink and to repeat the liturgical action in his memory. Inseparable from the account of institution is the anamnesis (in the narrow sense), which sums up the mystery of salvation in its basic elements, namely, the death and resurrection of the Lord. The anamnesis may, however, undergo fuller development in a more detailed description of the work of salvation, to the point of including even the second coming. The anamnesis is connected with the offering of the sacred bread and the chalice of salvation; the offering is sometimes accompanied by a prayer for acceptance of the sacrifice. Next comes the second epiclesis, which in general is an invocation of the Spirit for the unity and sanctification of those who receive communion. The intercessions close the anaphora by asking God to remember all those who have been named and indeed all human beings. The anaphora is now complete and can end in the summary and synthesis that is the doxology or trinitarian proclamation of the name of God.

Not only is the doxology the high point of the anaphora insofar as the latter is a proclamation and profession of faith, it also climaxes the sanctificatory movement of the anaphora, since in it the divine name is formally proclaimed in its fullest and most explicit form.

In the Old Testament, the proclamation of the divine name has power to sanctify. The clearest text is in Exodus: "In every place where I cause my name to be remembered I will come to you and bless you."[5] Inasmuch as "proclaim" and "invoke" are equivalent terms, the theme is continued in Joel: "All who call upon the name of the Lord shall be delivered; for in Mount Zion and in Jerusalem there shall be those who escape."[6]

The verse of Joel was taken up in the New Testament and expressly linked with "believing in him," which is a theme in the profession of faith and the proclamation of the name. "For man believes with his heart and so is justified, and he confesses with his lips and so is saved. The scripture says, 'No one who believes in him will be put to shame.' For there is no distinction between Jew and Greek; the same Lord is Lord of all and bestows his riches upon all who call upon him. For, 'every one who calls upon the name of the Lord will be saved.' "[7]

This Old Testament theme is not only explicitly taken over into the New Testament, but in the latter it even finds its supreme application since in Jesus the holy name is manifested to the fullest extent. In Christ, this name has in fact come to dwell among human beings: "There is salvation in no one else, for there is no other name under heaven given among men by which we must be saved."[8]

It follows from this that in the time of the New Testament the announcement and proclamation of the name still brings salvation. This assertion creates no theological problems.

We can conclude that the anaphora has an intrinsic sanctifying function precisely because it is a proclamation of the name. Furthermore, this proclamation reaches its high point in the doxology. From this we also see the meaning of the solemn elevation of the bread and wine during the doxology: it is a proclamation of the name by a gesture.

The component parts of the anaphora have now been listed as they appear in the three new anaphoras of the 1970 Missal. There are indeed variations in this order in some other texts we shall be discussing (for example, the anaphoras for children), but, with the basic structure in mind, it will not be difficult to situate ourselves in other structures that may depart somewhat from the norm. In the Eastern Churches, the structure described is verified only in the Antiochene anaphora, with the exception of the first epiclesis, which is of Alexandrian origin.

II. CHARACTERISTICS

The eucharistic prayer is always and at every point directed to the Father; it is, therefore, intensely theocentric. No part of the anaphora is exempted from this rule; only by carelessness, therefore, is it possible to speak of the epiclesis as an invocation of the Holy Spirit or, worse, a prayer to the Holy Spirit.

In the anaphora, the assembly addresses the Father through Christ in the Spirit. This is a basic fact that must always be kept in mind. This is not to deny that for various reasons exceptions have appeared in the course of history. In fact, we know of some eucharistic prayers that were directed to the Son, but the cases are so exceptional that they call for a suitable explanation, which in fact has thus far not been worked out fully.

The best known of the texts addressed to the Son is the Anaphora of Gregory of Nazianzus,[9] a text composed of material from the writings of Gregory. It dates from the late fifth century, long after the saint's death; in it the president speaks in the first person singular and expresses a profound religious spirit. When examined closely, the document proves to contain various elements that create problems which are still far from being solved.[10]

4

Another well-known text containing passages addressed to Christ is the Chaldean Anaphora of the Apostles Addai and Mari.[11] This anaphora is made up, it seems, of three clearly distinct units, each of which ends with a doxology. W. Macomber's painstaking analysis of the text and his reconstruction of its hypothetical original state show that at least the third of these units is addressed to the Son.[12] This document, too, raises problems, as can be seen from the analysis by Macomber who tries to restore the original text that was deliberately altered in the seventh century by Išo'yahb III (649–659).

With the exception of these two well-known texts,[13] the entire tradition is in agreement: the anaphora is addressed to the Father.

This characteristic is not simply a matter of literary convention, for a clear theological principle is operative. The basis for it is readily seen in the instruction which Jesus himself gave on prayer. He never taught us to pray to anyone but the Father, and the anaphora is a prayer. Furthermore, at the last supper, Jesus prayed by thanking the Father; then at the end of the celebration, he told his disciples to repeat this liturgy in memory of him. This liturgy, and not another; the liturgy performed by Jesus himself. His prayer to the Father remains the model of how we are to pray, namely, by giving thanks in a certain order and by doing what he did. Not only his celebration as a whole but his very prayer of thanksgiving was to serve as exemplar for the liturgy which the disciples celebrated in his memory. This point is well taken by John Chrysostom in his eighty-second homily of the gospel of Matthew (on Mt 26:26): "This (celebration) is a symbol of that. He gave thanks before giving (his body) to the disciples, in order that we too might give thanks. He gave thanks and then, after doing so, sang a hymn, in order that we might do likewise" (*Hom.* 82, 30 [PG 58:740]).

We may conclude that the eucharistic prayer should always be addressed to the Father because the archetypal model given us by Jesus requires it.

III. DEVELOPMENTS IN THEOCENTRIC ORIENTATION

The principle that the Father was to be addressed in the anaphora suffered some exceptions because of the way the text of the prayer developed.

The clearest of these exceptions is the trinitarian address introduced in the latter part of the eucharistic prayer. We are referring not to the trinitarian structure of the anaphora, but to the trinitarian address used. At certain points in some anaphoras, the prayer is directed no longer to the Father alone but to the Trinity, either in a global way or with specific mention of Father, Son, and Holy Spirit.

We can see, for example, that while the address is strictly theocentric in the Post-Sanctus of the Alexandrian Anaphora of Basil, some later anaphoras address the Trinity at this point. How did this happen?

In both James and Basil, the Sanctus is a later insertion, introduced after the anaphora as a whole had been composed. We can confirm this by simply removing the Sanctus; we will see that the excision leaves the text completely satisfactory in itself and even improves its coherence and internal logic. The section before the Sanctus is in perfect harmony with what follows the Sanctus, and we do not even notice that the entire passage containing the angelic hymn has been omitted. Nothing suggests that anything has been removed from the anaphora; nothing calls for the presence of the Sanctus.

Once the Sanctus was introduced, it became necessary to link it to the rest of the anaphora so that the angelic hymn might have a real function therein and share in the dynamic movement of the prayer as a whole. This required an introduction to the Sanctus that would serve as a transition between the praise expressed by the Church in the preface and the praise chanted by the angels in heaven.[14] Once the Sanctus was finished a further transition was needed to ensure the connection of the Sanctus with the ensuing text which lists the works for which God is being praised. The link was established by means of the word "Holy."

Let us give first the text of the Alexandrian Anaphora of Basil. It will help us better appreciate the development that has occurred when we turn to the Anaphora of James. In the Basilian anaphora the Post-Sanctus begins: "Holy, holy, holy are you, Lord our God, who formed us and set us. . . ."[15]

The reason may have been that the doctrine of the Trinity was now developed; it may have been simply that the time was ripe for a new prayer form. In any case, in the Anaphora of James, the term "Holy," a title for God, is applied to each of the three divine persons: "Holy are you, King of the ages, Lord and giver of all holiness. Holy, too, is your only-begotten Son, our Lord Jesus Christ, for whom you created all things. Holy, too, is your most holy Spirit, who searches all things, even your impenetrable depths, O God and Father. You are holy, almighty One. . . ."[16]

6

It is clear from this passage that the anaphora is still addressed to the Father. On the other hand, the term "Holy" is applied to the entire Trinity in a way that looks forward to an address which is no longer theocentric but trinitarian, as in the following: "You alone are holy, you alone are good, you alone are free, O God whom we confess to be Father, Son, and Holy Spirit in tri-unity."[17] The passage continues with a thanksgiving that suggests the Anaphora of James.

The evolution in a trinitarian direction was not restricted to the Post-Sanctus. It also occurred in formulas of offering and in doxologies. It can be seen still more clearly in the offering formula of *The Testament of the Lord:* "We offer you this thanksgiving, O eternal Trinity, Lord Jesus Christ, God the Father. . . ."[18]

Another example is the doxology in the thanksgiving of the Anaphora of Mark. That the trinitarian element here is a later insertion is clear from the disturbance in the sentence structure. If we remove the words in italics, we have the original text: "You made all things through . . . our Savior Jesus Christ, through whom, *giving thanks with him and the Holy Spirit*, we offer to you . . ."[19]

In the final analysis, the same can be said of the doxology in the Anaphora of Hippolytus: "through your Child (*puerum*) Jesus Christ. Through him glory to you and honor, *to the Father and the Son, with the Holy Spirit*, in your holy Church, now and for ever and ever!"[20]

Here is a final example, the Chaldean Anaphora of the Apostles Addai and Mari: "Worthy of praise . . . is the adorable and praiseworthy Name of the glorious Trinity, Father and Son and Holy Spirit, who created the world."[21]

Another point in the anaphora that sometimes is an exception to the theological orientation of the eucharistic prayer is the anamnesis when it acquires not a trinitarian character, as in the instances seen thus far, but a Christocentric character. The anamnesis is then addressed to the Son. The explanation for the shift may be psychological, given the centrality of the figure of Christ at this point in the anaphora. The account of institution has just told us that Jesus broke the bread and said the very words which the presiding priest has now faithfully repeated. All present have been gazing on the same scene as at the Supper: the protagonist is Jesus, here present in the assembly; he is a companion at table, and the bread and wine are now the sacrament of his body and blood. It is thus natural to change the direction of the anamnesis and address it directly to Christ. Here again the *Testament of the Lord* provides an example: "Mindful therefore of your death and resurrection, we offer you the bread and the cup."[22]

The acclamation of the faithful at the anamnesis in the Alexandrian Anaphora of Basil is likewise addressed to the Son, even though the preceding words of the celebrant are addressed to the Father.[23]

The Third Maronite Anaphora of St. Peter the Apostle (twin to the Anaphora of Addai and Mari) is living evidence of a eucharistic prayer offered to the Son, for it continues to address to the Lord Jesus the entire account of institution and the anamnesis: "as we commemorate your body and your blood which we offer to you on your living and holy altar as you, our hope, taught us and bade us to do in your holy gospel."[24]

Having viewed these examples, we can now ask what the state of the problem is in the Roman liturgy. Throughout the entire history of the Canon of the Mass, the Roman rite has remained faithfully and rigidly theocentric; the only formula it has recognized and maintained is "to the Father, through the Son, in the unity of the Holy Spirit." Because the Latin liturgy has been so extremely conservative, it has never admitted the formula "to the Father and to the Son and to the Holy Spirit all glory and honor" into the Canon.

The development of the doctrine of the Trinity did not affect the Canon. It did, however, influence the personal piety and devotion of Christians to such an extent that the trinitarian formula used in the Canon disappeared everywhere else and was replaced by the egalitarian formula "to the Father and to the Son and to the Holy Spirit."

One element that entered the Canon did, however, represent a Christocentric development comparable to that seen in the texts cited above. It was not a textual element but a gesture; we refer to the genuflections during and after the account of institution. We might also describe the elevation of the consecrated bread and wine during the account of institution as a Christocentric development within the eucharistic prayer.

In its historical origin, this last named rite was certainly a Christocentric development. The elevation of the host came into existence as a way of professing faith in the real presence of the body of Christ, inasmuch as the showing of the host stimulated adoration of the sacrament. This historical interpretation is confirmed by the fact that the elevation of the chalice was not introduced until a century after the elevation of the host. The reason for the delay is that

8

the elevation of the chalice gives a glimpse not of the blood of Christ but only of the metal cup, whereas the elevation of the host makes the body of the Lord visible to the congregation.[25] The testimony of William Durandus (d. 1296) shows that the elevation of the chalice was not yet a universal practice in his day: "The elevation of the chalice is not without its advantages, even though the blood cannot be seen."[26]

The contemporary practice of elevation can be regarded as Christocentric, since the gesture of elevating host and cup is increasingly identified in people's minds with the gesture of "taking bread" and "taking a cup," which necessarily involves some lifting of the bread and chalice from the altar. We shall, therefore, limit ourselves to the genuflection.

The ritual is made up of actions, or gestures, and words; the two are linked together and obey the same logic. The words are addressed to the Father: words of praise and adoration.[27] If gestures are made, they should have the same orientation, that is, be directed to the Father. Thus, as is quite clear in the Roman Canon, the gesture of raising the eyes is directed to the Father.

If, then, a gesture is directed to the sacrament itself, it ought to be part of a larger plan in which the words are also addressed to the sacrament. Thus, if the anaphora were addressed to the Son, there would be no difficulty in explaining the genuflections during and after the account of institution. In fact, however, the anaphora is addressed to the Father; it is to him that we relate what Jesus did at the Last Supper.

The account is made up of words and actions; we tell the story with words and we tell it with actions as well. Jesus took bread and therefore we too take bread; he raised his eyes to heaven and so do we. We tell of how he gave the bread and wine—his body and blood—to his disciples, but we do not at this moment break and distribute because we are still imitating his act of prayer and can imitate his other actions only after we have completed the prayer; the prayer is not yet finished and may not be interrupted. While we are giving thanks in imitation of the thanksgiving of Jesus, there is no room for doing something other than what he did.

In the perspective adopted here, which is that of the account of eucharistic institution, it is difficult to understand how we can interrupt the flow, to cut short the dialogue and prayer of adoration to the Father in order to genuflect to the sacrament. The action simply does not fit in. The words addressed to the Father involve the whole person of the minister and, through him, those over whom he is presiding. It is not easy to explain why he should interrupt this theocentric movement, this thrust of words and gestures, body and spirit; why he should break up the prayer with a genuflection to the sacrament.

It is not possible to introduce into the words of the anaphora an ejaculatory prayer addressed to the sacrament or an exhortation to the faithful urging them to adore. Given the equal status of verbal language and gestural language, it should likewise not be possible to introduce a genuflection to the sacrament into the actions of the anaphora.

The issue here is not faith in the sacrament. The disagreement is on an exclusively liturgical point: the coherence and homogeneity of gesture and word. We can take some comfort from the fact that the genuflection became obligatory only with the Missal of Pius V in 1570.

The post-Vatican II reformers had to decide whether to retain or eliminate the genuflections during the account of institution; there were four in the Missal of Pius V, two for the host and two for the chalice. A complete removal could not be expected; it would have been too abrupt a departure from previous practice. It was proposed, therefore, to keep the genuflections in principle but to retain only one at the end of the account of institution and eliminate the others during the account so as not to break up the unitary movement of the narrative. The pause created by the genuflection should be allowed only when the account of institution had been completed.

This was still the plan in Schema no. 218 of March 19, 1967.[28] A reading of this document makes it clear that the only point in issue was the number of the genuflections and not the theological and historical framework in which the genuflections were to be set. The final decision, however, restored the genuflection after the words of institution over the bread; now, therefore, there are two genuflections, one after the elevation of the bread, the other after the elevation of the chalice.

In making such decisions, the Church weighs the timeliness of one change rather than another; it is motivated by pastoral needs, and at times these are far different from the reasons that move the historian or theologian. But, it is not up to the historian of the liturgy to settle such questions and make such decisions. What is theologically or historically correct can be pastorally inappropriate. The task of historians is not to conduct reforms but to provide the data that explain the origin and causes of phenomena; in so doing;

10

they make possible an understanding of facts that is proportionate to the research tools, methods, and sources available, and nothing more.

Let us return to the theocentric orientation of the anaphora. There is a final factor that characterizes it, namely, the trinitarian structure of the anaphora.

We are not saying that every eucharistic prayer must have a trinitarian structure; the Roman Canon, for example, does not. All of the new anaphoras, however, do obey this rule because their structure is based on the anaphoras of the Antiochene liturgy, and these have a trinitarian structure. What is meant is briefly this: the anaphora falls into three parts, each of which focuses attention on the Father or the Son or the Holy Spirit, in that order. The eucharistic prayer begins with praise and thanksgiving to the Father for all that he has done in creation and redemption. In some eucharistic prayers, for example, the fourth of the new Missal, this praise opens with a description of the greatness of God in himself; he is praised in and for himself, independently of his works and before any mention is made of them. God himself is thus the protagonist in the first of the three parts that give the anaphora a trinitarian structure.

The second part consists of a description of the works which the Son has done and especially of his death and resurrection; this brings us to the anamnesis. This section includes the account of institution, which is the high point of the part of the anaphora devoted to the Son.

The third part begins with the epiclesis asking that the Holy Spirit might come and sanctify the bread and wine. Such a prayer celebrates the work of the Spirit, which is precisely the work of sanctification. In the epiclesis of the Anaphora of James, for example, we are given a real treatise on the Holy Spirit. In keeping with the profession of faith, the Spirit is described as the one who "spoke in the Law and the prophets and your New Testament, descended in the form of a dove on our Lord Jesus Christ at the Jordan and remained upon him, and at Pentecost descended on your holy apostles in the form of fiery tongues in the upper room on holy and glorious Zion."[29] Other divine attributes of the Spirit are also listed: consubstantial, co-eternal, co-regnant, seated on the throne with (synthronon) the Father and Son. In short, a real treatise on the Holy Spirit, as we remarked before.

Lastly, there is the closing doxology which has always been trinitarian and therefore brings into focus and sums up this aspect of the anaphora.

The first example of this trinitarian structure is the eucharistic prayer of Hippolytus[30]; we are speaking, therefore, of something very ancient. Trinitarian faith and doctrine are clearly present in the anaphoras after Hippolytus; the result was that binitarian anaphoras gradually disappeared. The more developed the doctrine of the Trinity became, the more it influenced the themes of the anaphora in the East where the eucharistic prayer remained open to further growth and absorbed new elements rising out of the development of theology. At Rome, on the other hand, the Canon resisted any and all new themes, which were thus forced to exist apart from the eucharistic prayer. As a result, the Roman Canon remained binitarian with the exception of the doxology and some prefaces.

What we have been saying about trinitarian structure needs to be read carefully. We have not claimed that the entrance of the doctrine of the Trinity into the anaphora created a structure with three blocks of material, each dedicated to one of the divine persons. We do not think the text of the anaphora can be schematized in such a way—not even the Anaphora of James, the Antiochene text that displays the clearest trinitarian structure. This warning is even more necessary in reading the contemporary Roman formulas, inasmuch as these have two clearly distinct epicleses, each speaking of the Spirit as sanctifier.

IV. LITERARY GENRE

We said earlier that the eucharistic prayer is not only a concrete text but also and above all a literary genre. Discussion of the eucharistic prayer as a literary genre began with an address of J.-P. Audet, O.P., to the patristic congress at Oxford in 1957,[31] in which he discussed the literary genre of the Jewish blessing (*berakah*), its origin, and its laws. According to Audet, this literary genre was the progenitor and cradle of the literary genre we call the eucharistic prayer.

Audet begins his study with a consideration of two Old Testament passages which have since served as the classic examples for the argument: Genesis 24:26–27 and Exodus 18:9–12.

The first tells of Abraham's servant going off to look for a wife for Isaac. A divine sign leads him to Rebecca, and he blesses God: "The man bowed his head and worshiped the Lord, and said, 'Blessed be the Lord, the God of my master Abraham, who has not forsaken his steadfast love and his faithfulness toward my master.

12

As for me, the Lord has led me in the way to the house of my master's kinsmen.' " We are in the presence of a spontaneous and unmediated act: when faced with the sign from God, the man recognizes it and blesses the Lord. His response is a spontaneous reaction of the heart; his state of mind produces the outward act in an immediate but conscious way.

The short text has two parts: (a) the initial address to God which contains the word "bless"; and (b) the motivation for the blessing, that is, a description and proclamation of the reason for blessing God, or, in other words, an account of that which God has done and thereby elicited gratitude. Such is the structure of the Jewish blessing as a prayer addressed to God.

The blessing is always a human reaction or response to God because of the latter's intervention. In a prayer thus structured, there is always and necessarily a first moment or stage in which the protagonist is God who intervenes in behalf of human beings. Realizing this intervention, the human beings are filled with joy and wonder; wonder and admiration are constitutive of the state of mind[32] in which they find themselves in face of God's interventions. It is not simply emotion or feeling, but acknowledgment and appreciation of God's deed that moves the heart of Abraham's servant and compels him to bless the Lord. He blesses him because he has discovered that God's action is a sign of his steadfast love and faithfulness to Abraham. The servant's response in the face of God's action is spontaneous and immediate; it is the result not of emotional impulse but of a conscious understanding of the divine sign. It is very important that we realize this, lest we empty the Jewish blessing, a blessing directed to God, and turn it into a general sense of wonder before the numinous.

This last point emerges even more clearly from the second passage cited by Audet:

"Jethro rejoiced for all the good which the Lord had done to Israel, in that he had delivered them out of the hands of the Egyptians. And Jethro said, 'Blessed be the Lord, who delivered you out of the hands of the Egyptians and out of the hand of Pharaoh. Now I know that the Lord is greater than all gods, because he delivered the people from under the hand of the Egyptians, when they dealt arrogantly with them.' And Jethro, Moses' father-in-law, offered a burnt offering and sacrifices to God" (Ex 18:9–12).

Moses has just told how God acted in favor of Israel and freed it from the Egyptians. Jethro's response is to acknowledge God's action and to bless his name. He thus makes explicit the internal dynamics of the prayer of blessing and achieves a formal profession of faith: "Now I know that the Lord is greater than all gods."

The Jewish blessing is itself already a profession of faith because the second part contains a list of God's works, which it commemorates and proclaims. Jethro in this instance makes the internal dynamics formally explicit by altering the narrative style in the second part. His understanding of what God has done leads to a profession of faith. It is in this sense that, as a famous theological dictum has it, "faith is a gift." In the same sense, the prayer of blessing is a gift: it is God's action that generates this response. The divine blessing that comes down from heaven elicits from the devout Israelite a response that ascends to heaven in return. God saves his people by thus placing in their mouths the response that is a blessing of his name.

The following passage from the *Book of Jubilees* (ca. 100 B.C.) is important for the theme of the prayer of blessing as a gift from God to a human being.

"At this she [Rebecca] looked up to heaven and spread out the fingers of her hands, and opened her mouth, and blessed the Most High God who created heaven and earth, and gave him thanks and praise. And she said, 'Blessed be the Lord God, and may his holy name be blessed for ever and ever, he who has given me Jacob as a pure son and a holy offspring; for he is thine, and thine shall his offspring be continually and in every generation for evermore. Bless him, O Lord, and put in my mouth the blessing of righteousness, that I may bless him.'

"And at that very moment, when the spirit of righteousness came down upon her mouth, she placed both her hands on Jacob's head and said, 'Blessed art thou, Lord of righteousness and God of the ages; and as for you, Jacob, may he bless you more than all the generations of men.' "[33]

This passage shows that the word "bless" is not the only one that can convey the meaning of the prayer of blessing. It can be accompanied with or replaced by other verbs, such as "praise," "thank," "confess," etc.

The critique of T. J. Talley[34] shows that this is the weakest part of Audet's work on the literary genre of the Jewish blessing. Audet regards all these verbs as practically synonymous. If they did indeed all have the same meaning, it would be of little relevance that

14

eucharistia rather than *eulogia* (blessing) prevailed in the Christian liturgy. Nor would there be any particular relevance in the difference between the two types of account of institution that we find in the New Testament, where the Markan-Matthean type uses *eulogein* (bless) for the bread and *eucharistein* (thank) for the wine, while the Pauline-Lukan type uses only *eucharistein*. A blessing is spoken over the bread, a thanksgiving over the wine. Is there a difference, or are blessing and thanksgiving the same? Audet replies that the two have the same meaning.

According to C. Giraudo, who accepts the critique just outlined, there is a certain difference between them. Giraudo adds a further criticism. According to Audet, the literary genre and structure of the *berakah* are primary in the institution of the Eucharist. Giraudo shows, however, that the *berakah* genre is secondary, since it derives from another, the Old Testament *todah*.[35] The real source of the Christian Eucharist is therefore not the *berakah* but the *todah*. The change in source has implications, as we shall see.

For the moment, let us follow Audet's analysis of the development of the *berakah*. The original structure, he says, is bipartite and spontaneous. The first part contains the opening thanksgiving (opening blessing) with its invocation of the divine name. The second part contains the motive for the praise, namely, the account of God's action. The two parts are closely connected; in fact, the second emerges from the first by way of a simple amplification of the divine name. It follows that the first part already implicitly contains the second part, and it is easy to see why: the first part contains the divine name, and we know that name signifies everything known about God, that is, everything he reveals about himself in and through his saving acts. "God" is the God of Abraham, Isaac, and Jacob, or, per our example, "he" is what he has done for Abraham, Isaac, and Jacob. The works he has done in behalf of the three patriarchs have made known his name; his name is connoted by these works and it sums them up. That is why the first part generates the second part by a process of amplification and explicitation of the divine name.

Audet speaks of a further development of the *berakah* from spontaneous blessing to cultic blessing. The blessing undergoes explicitation because of public worship. In this process there is added to the two parts already described a third that is closely connected with the account of God's works. This third part is the petition, invocation, or, to use the Greek, *epiclesis*. God is asked to continue to act in our behalf, to continue the works he has already done for us. "Thy will be done" captures the logic of this part of the *berakah* as adapted to public worship.

There is still another part to be found in the cultic version of the blessing, namely, the doxology. The doxology is a conclusion in which God is praised as though he had already heard the request which the devout Jew makes in the cultic blessing. It returns to the opening praise or glorification, so that the cultic blessing forms an inclusion (opening praise matched by concluding doxology).

Audet's explanation has not gone uncriticized. Both Talley and Giraudo object that this ingenious construction is based on data from the rabbinic codification of worship. This codification, however, is too late to explain the origins of the Christian *eucharistia*. According to these critics, the schematization of the prayer of blessing was accomplished by the rabbis at a period subsequent to the institution of the Christian Eucharist.

As we indicated, Giraudo points to the structure of the Old Testament *todah* as source even of the *berakah* itself. The *todah* comprises two coordinated parts: an account of the works of God and a petition (epiclesis) that the prayers of Israel may be heard. This literary genre also underlies the formulas for the renewal of the covenant and, through development, the formulas for thanksgiving at table and the texts accompanying sacrifices.

The basic structure, then, is bipartite: account and invocation. All texts deriving from the *todah* will necessarily have these two parts. The Christian Eucharist will have to have them as its original constituents. And, in fact, it is undeniable that the earliest eucharistic texts quite evidently display this structure: a richly developed thanksgiving and an equally developed prayer for the Church.

There is a perfect balance between the two parts, which must obviously be regarded as equally important. This parallel importance of the two parts is the most persuasive reason for accepting Giraudo's thesis.

V. ORIGIN AND DEVELOPMENT OF THE ANAPHORA

It is impossible to trace the origin and development of the eucharistic prayer with any completeness, if for no other reason than that these studies are far from being acceptably concluded. We shall, of course, use our own researches, if only because they cover an area left untouched by others.[36] These researches, too, have not yet all been completed and published.

The Church's celebration of the Eucharist originated in its obedience to Christ's mandate at the Supper: "Do this in memory of me." We do not know for sure whether or not the Last Supper of Jesus was a Passover meal,[37] though it was certainly a meal taken in a paschal ambiance; in any case, the answer to this question is not determinative for our purpose here.

On the other hand, whatever the particular kind of meal it was that Jesus celebrated with his disciples, in its general outline it certainly followed the pattern of the Jewish ritual meal. Jesus took this pattern and transformed it so as to make it "his" Supper.

For the Jews, every meal was a religious event. No special rites were needed to turn a meal into a religious celebration; it was already such by its nature, antecedently to any ritual. The ritual came into being as a result of the religious character inherent in the taking of food; it did not create this character. For this reason, it is not accurate to speak of a ritual meal, but we have no other way of making our point, since for us Westerners a meal is always a secular event and any religious character it may have depends on added ritual.

The religious character of the Jewish meal found expression in the prayers that accompanied it. In festive meals, there were also opening prayers that introduced the meal. In this instance, there was a rite in the true and proper sense; it was known as the *Kiddush*.[38]

The most important prayer, however, and one that could never be omitted, was the thanksgiving after the meal: the *Birkat ha-mazon*. This prayer was regularly spoken over a cup, the one that Paul calls the "cup of blessing."[39] The *Birkat ha-mazon*, or the prayer of thanksgiving at meals, is regarded as the source of the Christian eucharistic prayer. Let us see how this came to be.

A. Structure of the Birkat ha-mazon
The *Birkat ha-mazon* has three parts: two sections of thanksgiving and one of petition.

The first thanksgiving is concerned with the food God gives to the people of Israel (*Birkat ha-zan*), the second with the good and desirable land God has given to Israel (*Birkat ha-aretz*). The third section is a prayer for Jerusalem (*Birkat Yerusalayim*).[40] It is frequently difficult to say where the first thanksgiving ends and the second begins.

This scheme, usually directed to an analysis of Christian liturgical texts, has its risks. If the difference between blessing and thanksgiving resides in the length of the formularies, we would have two *eulogiae* in *Didache* 9, whereas the text itself speaks of a *eucharistia*. The structure of the Jewish blessing as just outlined is evidently a schematization that can help us get into the subject, but the matter proves much more complex once we discuss the actual texts.[41]

Given the logic that controls the Jewish prayer, we are not dealing with set formularies that must be used unconditionally. The prayer is not a formula; rather, it develops a theme imposed by circumstances, and does so in accordance with set norms.

In other words, the prayer of Israel does not consist of formulas to be repeated verbatim, but of outlines or plots that serve as models and call for creativity by the individual. The theme, logic, and structure of the prayer are strictly determined, but the individual can exercise personal creativity within the framework. For this reason, the only texts we have of the *Birkat ha-mazon* are late[42] or are accidental finds[43]; these were texts from everyday life, where they functioned as the regular patterns for prayer and not as official texts that had to be followed. Of the texts gathered by Finkelstein,[44] the one of greatest interest to us here is from the *Book of Jubilees.* It is especially of interest because of its relation to the future development of Christian texts[45]:

"And he [Abraham] ate and drank, and he blessed the Most High God, who created heaven and earth, who made all the good things on the earth, and gave them to the sons of men so that they might eat and drink and bless their creator.

"And now, he said, I give thee thanks, my God, because thou hast let me see this day: behold, I am a hundred and seventy-five years old, an old man with a long life-span, and I have prospered all my days. The enemy's sword has never at any time prevailed against me, nor against my children. My God, may thy mercy and thy peace be upon thy servant, and upon his descendants, that they may be to thee a chosen nation and a possession out of all the nations of the earth, now and in every generation on the earth for evermore."[46]

Finkelstein compares the *Birkat ha-mazon* and *Didache* 10 and comes to a positive conclusion: the prayer of thanksgiving after meals in the *Didache* is a Christian text that has transformed the *Birkat ha-mazon* into a Christian prayer. Giraudo very aptly calls the prayer in the *Didache* "the Christian *Birkat ha-mazon.*"[47]

Finkelstein's comparison is irrefutable, even if it is open to criticism for not having used more effective devices that would make it possible to avoid the inversion of the first and second parts of the Jewish blessing.

B. Christian Development of the Birkat ha-mazon

The Jewish blessing at the end of a meal was the source of the Christian thanksgiving as found in *Didache* 10, 1–7. The only point not yet definitively settled is the character of the passage in the *Didache:* Does it reflect a Christian ritual meal or the sacrament of the Eucharist? We have argued for a sacramental interpretation, but our work is incomplete.[48]

In this review of the genesis of the eucharistic prayer, there is a factor which externally confirms the interpretation of the *Didache* that we propose. That factor is the influence which this passage had on later eucharistic texts. Thus, Hippolytus uses the *Didache* but subjects it to a bold alteration: he abandons the theme of thanksgiving in *Didache* 10 and replaces it with themes derived from the literary genre of "Easter Homilies."[49]

We believe we have succeeded in proving: (a) the connection between the Anaphora of Hippolytus and the *Birkat ha-mazon;* (b) that this connection is mediated through chap. 10 of the *Didache;* (c) that the material provided by the "Easter Homilies" acquires a place in the anaphora and turns the thanksgiving into a telling of the history of salvation; (d) that the account of the Last Supper enters the anaphora because it is drawn in by the material from the "Easter Homilies"; and (e) that as confirmation and fresh proof we can cite two anaphoras—the Coptic Anaphora of Basil[50] and the so-called Clementine Anaphora[51]—which revise Hippolytus with the aid of material from his own sources (i.e., *Didache* 10 and the "Easter Homilies").

When we speak of the *Didache,* we mean to include the document directly dependent on it, namely, the "mystical eucharist" in Book VII of the *Apostolic Constitutions,*[52] which shows *Didache* 10 being developed in a non-eucharistic direction. In this new context, the prayer of the *Didache* has already become a prayer of thanksgiving after communion. At a stage intermediate between these two texts but very close to both, the "witness" that is *Didache* 10 becomes a source for the Anaphora of Hippolytus; through Hippolytus it influences in turn the entire line of Antiochene anaphoras and therefore the second part of the Alexandrian anaphora as well.

Let us dwell for a moment on the Alexandrian anaphora. The Anaphora of Serapion, in its second part, is explicitly linked with the source in question. The Anaphora of St. Mark, in its second part, shows a direct link with the Anaphora of James which, via Basil, depends on Hippolytus. We turn now from the influence of *Didache* 10 to *Didache* 9.

Didache 9 represents a Christianization of the Jewish *Kiddush*.[53] It is not to be regarded as an early anaphora; it acquires this character only through its connection with chap. 10, inasmuch as both chapters are concerned with the same celebration and both contain prayers referring to the same bread and the one chalice.

The text of chap. 9 underwent development: in Book VII of the *Apostolic Constitutions*, it has become an early anaphora, since in addition to other elements it now includes a direct citation of 1 Corinthians 11:26, which really functions here as an account of institution. It is not a true, proper, and complete account of institution in the sense of describing the supper in the upper room at which Jesus instituted the Eucharist. Nonetheless, it has the same function, since its purpose is to say that the Church's celebration takes place because the Lord so appointed. This is evident in that it repeats the Lord's mandate in the form this has already taken in the account of the Lord's Supper as transmitted by 1 Corinthians 11:23ff. Here is the formulation: "(body and blood) whose very (*kai*) antitypes [= sacraments] we celebrate because he so appointed for us who announce his death."[54]

Chapter 9 of the *Didache* begins the eucharistic meal and, like the *Kiddush*, shows the order cup-bread. At the Last Supper as narrated by Luke, the order is the same: cup-bread-cup (Lk 22:14–20). In *Didache* 9 we have only cup-bread, and the document does not mention a second cup, even though *Didache* 10, as a Christianized *Birkat ha-mazon*, could of itself have included a cup. The parallel with Luke would then have been complete. It is clear that if the second cup ever had a place in the *Didache*, it had already been removed by the time of the *textus receptus*.

We find the same situation in Paul; that is, the order cup-bread in *Didache* 9 is matched by the order in 1 Corinthians 10:16, where the cup is mentioned first and then the bread. The cup is the "cup of blessing." The allusion is to the great prayer of thanksgiving, the *Birkat ha-mazon*, that was pronounced over the cup. But the prayer belonged with the cup that ended the meal, not the cup that began it. It is therefore permissible to think that here again the second cup (the one that ended the meal) has been eliminated so that the celebration includes only one. The characteristics proper to the second cup have been transferred to the first, which is now called the "cup of blessing."

The liturgy celebrated by Paul is attested in 1 Corinthians 10:16ff., since he uses the first person plural ("which we bless," "which we break"), and not in 1 Corinthians 11:23ff., which narrates the final meal celebrated by Jesus in the upper room as a norm for Christian behavior at the Eucharist. The order bread-cup in this second passage shows that the *narrative tradition* of the Last Supper had already evolved in the direction of the short account in Luke or, if you wish, of the Mark/Matthew redaction. This was not true, however, of *liturgical usage*, since the liturgy for which Paul gives a mystagogical catechesis has the order cup-bread, which corresponds to the long redaction of the Lukan account.

We may therefore conclude: (1) that there is no contradiction between the two descriptions of the Eucharist in Paul; and (2) that Paul is witness to the order cup-bread which matches that found in the *Didache*.

Let us return to the *Didache*. We will recall that in *Didache* 9 there are three literary units: (1) a prayer (a *eucharistia*) over the cup, (2) a prayer (a *eucharistia*) over the bread, and (3) a prayer (of petition) for the Church. Subsequently, the cup that here precedes the bread was moved to a position after the bread, giving the structure attested in *Apostolic Constitutions* VII, 25: (1) *eucharistia* over the bread, (2) prayer for the Church, and (3) *eucharistia* over the cup.[55]

You may feel somewhat disoriented in this maze, but the facts are simpler than they appear; all that is needed is to compare the texts cited. It is not easy, of course, for us to determine the development of the early anaphora in *Apostolic Constitutions* VII, 25, with its thanksgiving after communion in chap. 26. Not to be lost sight of is that chap. 25 is introduced into the account of institution in the Anaphora of Serapion and into the consecratory epiclesis in the Der-Balizeh Papyrus,[56] that is, into the center of the eucharistic prayer.

C. Conclusion

We have tried to show the connections between the earliest texts of the Church. With the Anaphora of Hippolytus, we are already in the ambit of the Missal of Paul VI, since the former is the direct ancestor of the second anaphora. Hippolytus is also the source of the Anaphora of Basil which, along with the Anaphora of James, is the direct ancestor of the fourth anaphora.

The third anaphora, for its part, is inspired by the Roman Canon, but this in turn is linked to the Alexandrian anaphora, that is, to the Anaphora of Mark and its witnesses.

As you can easily see, this very short historical survey of the origins of the anaphora contains all the elements needed to explain the genesis of the texts that are the direct sources of the anaphoras in our present Missal.

VI. THE ACCOUNT OF INSTITUTION

The account of institution plays an increasingly important role in the history of the eucharistic prayer, until it finally becomes the center of the anaphora. This is especially clear in the Roman Canon, but it is no less clear in the Anaphora of John Chrysostom[57] which, for example, reduces the element of thanksgiving to a minimum. In this case, the important part played by the epiclesis does not prevent great interest in the account of institution. The origin of the role played by the account of institution in the anaphora has not yet been fully explained. We shall sketch a hypothetical line of development.

What Jesus "did" at the Supper was to celebrate a Jewish ritual meal, into which, however, he introduced a radically new element. At the Supper he was the central figure, the unrivaled protagonist. Consequently, the Supper commemorated not so much the great works which God had done under the old covenant, as it did the works by which Jesus had effected the fullness of salvation:

"When the Messiah appears in earthly form, He goes about among His people as a man of piety. He adopts its customs and especially its religious practices. When He sits at table, e.g., when He feeds the 4,000 or 5,000, He acts like a normal Jewish host or head of the house. He follows faithfully the accepted form. He takes the bread in His hands, pronounces the blessing, breaks the bread and distributes it (Mk 6:41 and par.; 8:7 and par.).

"The only new feature is that in the prayer He does not look downwards as prescribed, but looks up to heaven. . . . It is also possible that in virtue of His sense of mission and the inner freedom which this gives He is infusing into the rigid formulae of dealings with God something of what made His own relationship with the Father so vital. Perhaps He also rendered the benedictions in a freer form approximating, e.g., to the Lord's Prayer. He must certainly have introduced something of His own into the simple, everyday process of blessing and breaking bread, since otherwise the two on the way to Emmaus would not have recognized Him by this action (Lk 24:30)."[58]

In our opinion, this analysis is quite correct. As we know, the *Birkat ha-mazon* was a text that made room for the creativity of the person pronouncing it. This was so not only because the exact words were not prescribed, but also and above all because its structure made it possible to introduce embolisms (insertions, development) for commemorating particular saving events (on specific feasts) or the particular situation in which the individuals using the text found themselves. This is the case with the blessing in *Jubilees*: the passage contains the parts proper to the *Birkat ha-mazon* and then shifts to direct discourse in which Abraham speaks in the first person, thus introducing his own embolism into the prayer.

To the joy of scholars, the author of *Jubilees* here transmits a most valuable embolism spoken in the course of a sacrificial meal which was also a meal of farewell, of leavetaking from earthly life. Now the thanksgiving of Jesus at the Last Supper was likewise uttered in the course of a sacrificial meal which was also a meal of farewell. The two prayers share the same literary genre (sacrificial and testamentary). The prayer of Jesus to the Father must certainly have reflected the real situation; that is, he must have given voice in the prayer to his own very special relationship with the Father.[59] In the other prayers of Jesus which the New Testament reports, we see a Jesus able to bring out fully this unique and unparalleled situation before God. Why would he not have done the same in his prayer at the Last Supper?

In reading John 17, we see that at the Last Supper Jesus prays in his customary manner, celebrating and living out in prayer his unique situation before the Father. We must take this passage as evidence of how the disciples remembered the special prayer of Jesus on this occasion, a prayer which they shifted into the genre of discourse.

Jesus asks the gift of unity for his disciples (Jn 17:21–23), and every Eucharist of the Church, from the *Didache* to the anaphoras in use today, has led and now leads to the same petition. Jesus confesses the divine Name and makes it known (Jn 17:3–8), and the *Didache* gives thanks for the Name that has been placed in our hearts, and for faith, knowledge, and immortality.[60] In both John and the *Didache*, the rather rare address used for God is "holy Father." If the later anaphoras derive from the *Didache*,[61] we can say that, via the connection between the *Didache* and John, they too in a sense have their roots in the New Testament.

The disciples understood the command of Jesus to do *this* celebration in his memory. Consequently, they offered their own prayers of thanksgiving by combining the commemoration of Jesus with the classic themes of Jewish prayer, for the kind of commemoration that was characteristic of Jewish prayer led to Jesus and culminated in him. In so doing, they obeyed the command of Christ; for this reason, they took the prayer of Jesus at the Last Supper as the model for their own thanksgiving.

They thanked the Father for the great things he had done in Christ. They realized, however, that the prayer of Jesus reflected his own special status before the Father. His prayer was not simply the same as theirs but was that of an envoy who was one with the Father (Jn 17:21). Therefore, they took the prayer that was Jesus' final testament but applied it to their own ritual meal. They did not copy it but rather reworked it so that their obedience might be authentic.

Similarly, they did not celebrate the Lord's Supper in exactly the same way that he did. Precisely, in order to be faithful and obedient to his command, they revised and interpreted it. The specifically new element which he had introduced into the Jewish rite was retained, but this rite itself was not repeated[62] with material fidelity to the model. In fact, they took as normative for themselves only that part of the rite which was specifically new and proper to Jesus in his celebration of it. In other words, the disciples retained that which distinguished the Last Supper from all other Jewish celebrations, not that which it had in common with them.

This is the logic that explains the four New Testament redactions of the account of institution. They report only the essential new element which Jesus had introduced into the Jewish rite at his final, testamentary meal, and omit everything that was a regular part of a Jewish meal (it made no difference whether or not the meal was a Passover supper). The accounts are, therefore, necessarily incomplete as accounts of the Last Supper, since they simply presuppose everything that a Jew would have taken for granted, and retain only that which transformed the Supper so that it now centered on Christ. This was the element that alone had to be kept in their own future ritual meals.

When Christianity came in contact with Greek culture in which meals did not embody the theology of the covenant, it faced new problems. It had to abandon the Jewish ritual meal, which could have meaning only for Jews, in order to preserve the new Eucharist which Jesus celebrated and commanded at the Last Supper.

This shift exemplified what is called the process of inculturation. We do not mean that Jesus said the Eucharist should or should not, could or could not be separated from a meal. As a man who was truly a Jew, he announced the new covenant in his blood at a ritual meal, and the disciples continued along the same line. But, once confronted with the fact that the logic of the meal threatened to take precedence over the logic of the covenant and of the Christological content of the covenant mystery, the disciples had only one choice: to separate the Eucharist from the Jewish ritual meal.

The shift began as early as the apostolic age, as can be seen from 1 Corinthians 11:17ff. and it continued to the point of such a complete separation that any restoration of the nexus between the Eucharist and a ritual meal seems unthinkable. And, yet in the New Testament theology of the Eucharist, the connection is essential. The four accounts of institution are to be regarded as summaries of what was done by Christ as he brought Judaism to its completion, and not as excluding the Jewish element. Only the evident difficulties in exporting a Jewish ritual meal into a non-Jewish environment make it possible to understand the gospel accounts of the Last Supper as having an element of the forever-past in them.

The thanksgiving which Jews offered at their ritual meals was in commemoration of the great deeds of God, with the gift of the land having the foremost place. For the disciples of Jesus, the situation had changed. God's action had, of course, manifested itself also in the gift of the land and in the formation of Israel as the chosen people; but for the disciples, God's work had now reached its high point in Christ. If Christ is the true bread that has come down from heaven and if he is the true vine, then it is no longer for the land and for the vine of David that thanks must be given. The disciples therefore realized from experience that the Jewish meal of thanksgiving had been imperfect and incomplete. It had to develop and change so as to become above all a commemoration of the work of Christ. That is why the Christian Eucharist represents the "truth" of the Jewish meal: because it goes beyond it and replaces it. That is the message conveyed in the four New Testament redactions of the story of the Supper.

In every eucharistic celebration, the Church must renew its awareness of this message and learn again the reason for the celebration, its meaning, its center, its nature. It is precisely in this sense that the New Testament account is the "form" of the eucharistic celebration and not simply one short passage among the many that make up the anaphora.

When read during the anaphora or, better, when narrated to the Father, the account shows our fidelity to the mandate that established the Eucharist. It shows God that the community intends to do precisely that which Christ left to it as his legacy, and to do it with the same meaning and values that he associated with it. In repeating the account of God, the *ecclesia* repeats to itself the form of the celebration. It repeats it to actualize it successfully, that is, to render the reality present and active. This successful actualization is a gift for which it petitions God.

In the anaphora, the account of the Supper is not simply a piece of ritual; even if only implicitly, it is a vibrant petition that God would enable his Church to obey in a wholly truthful way the command of Christ: "Do this in memory of me." It is the Church's *sequela* (following) of Christ that makes the celebration truthful. If this had been kept in mind, the Christian liturgy would never have turned in on itself and become primarily a matter of ceremony, still less a matter of rubrics.

That same principle is the basis on which the Roman Church today is confronting history with its liturgical reform. It has struggled back from its decline into ceremonialism and turned its rites once again into signs of Christ who, after having borne witness by his death, rose and ascended into heaven whence he will come in glory.

"Signs" is a perplexing word, since its meaning varies according to period and culture. It is nonetheless a classical term in the Christian tradition and has only recently become suspect. But it is immediately necessary to add that the whole development of modern semiology is bringing a recovery of the term "signs" together with the concepts connected with it.

No movement that has any sense of history can avoid a confrontation with the culture of its own time. If the movement seeks to be integrated into history as Jesus was, it cannot escape the confrontation with culture, with values, and with the religious philosophy which the human beings of every age have in one or other form.

Our culture is a culture of "signs," and semiology is becoming a discipline in its own right; its aim is to define human beings as "signing animals." On the other hand, we are seeing a major crisis in the area of the sacraments. In theory, such a crisis ought not to be possible since Catholic theologians have always defined sacraments as "located in the genus of sign."[63] Human beings ought not to lose sense of the sign character of the sacraments, especially the eucharistic meal. If this does happen, it is because insufficient attention has been paid to the sign character of the Eucharist; Christian thinking on the subject has too often been superficial and lacking in any solid historico-cultural analysis of the problem.

Before advancing to that stage, we must first carefully ascertain the content of the eucharistic celebration by the concrete elements that make it up; only then will the analysis of the sign coincide with an analysis of the event itself. It is impossible to speak properly of a sign without having first analyzed the phenomenon whose sign character we want to understand. The first step, then, is to ascertain and isolate the phenomenon; semiological reflection by those competent in the subject comes second.

Our intention is simply to clarify the internal content of the eucharistic prayer; it is a preliminary step, but absolutely necessary if there is to be a datum on which to exercise semiological reflection. This is so because the anaphora is one of the "functives" of the "sign-function"[64] that is the eucharistic celebration.

Every literary text is located in the genus of sign; every sign function requires a code and every functive follows coding rules. In the following chapters, therefore, we shall try to understand the texts of the various eucharistic prayers, considered both diachronically and synchronically. In so doing, we shall be trying to ascertain where the decoding of the sign is to be done. We shall thus not be going directly into the question of the Eucharist as sign, but simply preparing the material on which others can reflect.

We will say a brief word on the subject as we end this introduction. As the last chapter of this book will make clear, the entire content of the Church's Eucharist is identical with the content of the Last Supper as a *proclamation through action* of the passion and resurrection of the Lord. That is the datum that must serve as the starting point for semiological reflection. Both the Church's Eucharist and the Last Supper of Jesus are a sign of the cross and the final glory of Christ. But, what is the relation between the Last Supper and the Church's Eucharist?

We may exclude in advance a relation of purely external mimicry and imitation as in a play on a stage; such a conception of the Christian liturgy is alien to the sources and can be imposed upon it only by the use of allegory. On the other hand, the Church's Eucharist is not a sign of the Last Supper in the same way as it is a sign of the cross. No source treats the Eucharist as equally a sign of the Supper and a sign of the cross. At the same time, however, there is some ontological relationship between Eucharist and Last Supper, for otherwise the command: "Do this in memory of me" loses its meaning. It seems that modern semiology can clarify the relationship between Eucharist and Supper as a sign of the cross.

The theory to help here is the theory of the code: there is no sign without a code.[65] In our present case, the Supper can be viewed as the code which contains the relation to the cross and which is at the same time internal to and present in every eucharistic celebration. In this approach, the Last Supper is the institutive and foundational event in the sense that it supplies the code for our eucharistic celebrations. The code is in the concrete event of the Last Supper and is really identical with the latter: in history, two thousand years ago. At the same time, it is also really present, internal, and inherent in every eucharistic celebration today and in the past. If the Last Supper is the code, then it is actualized and realized in every Eucharist. When we say "actualized," we are not referring to something coming from outside; since the code for the sign-function correlates the various functives, it is internal to the sign-function itself.

If the Last Supper is the code, then it is in the Last Supper that we look for the truth of our present-day eucharistic celebrations, that is, their identity with what Christ did or, in short, their sacramentality.

All this is notably consistent with the theory of A. Chavasse, which we shall expound in chap. 9. In brief, Chavasse argues that there has been historically only one consecration, that of the Last Supper. If the Last Supper is the code for our eucharistic celebration and is really internally present in this celebration, it follows that the one consecration which Christ effected once and for all, the one consecration which took place at the Supper, is present in every Eucharist of the Church.

We do not know how it is more effectively possible to maintain the oneness of Christ's work of salvation as efficacious, once and for all, for the whole of human history. For if that oneness is to be ensured, the sacraments cannot be a repetition of Christ's work and therefore inevitably a derogation from that oneness and an attack upon it. At the same time, the theory also maintains sacramental realism, since our present-day liturgical celebration is nothing else than Christ's own celebration of the Supper. The realism is that

28

which is elsewhere expressed in the formula *"in persona Christi"* ("in the person of Christ").

What of the eucharistic prayer? It is to be looked upon in the same way as the Last Supper itself. If the Last Supper is the code of the present-day eucharistic celebration, the same applies to the thanksgiving. That is, the *eucharistia* which Jesus spoke at the Last Supper is the code for the eucharistic prayer which the Church speaks today. Inasmuch as it is a code, Jesus' prayer of thanksgiving is really present, internal, innerent in our eucharistic prayer today.

This theory of the code for a sign is not alien to the main object of the present book, since historical analysis shows that our present-day eucharistic prayer derives from that which Jesus spoke at the Last Supper. Historical research into the genesis of the eucharistic prayer is, in the last analysis, another way of developing the theory of the code as supplying the internal logic and organization of the sign-function that is really identical with the sign itself: the sign is its own code.

Moreover, the foundational event, which serves as code, is clearly distinct from every subsequent accomplishment of the sign and can never be ranked as simply the first in a series of the same signs. Nor can it be called simply the remote origin of the sign, in the sense that the sign can henceforth live a life of its own independently of and separated from that remote origin, which would then exist only in the past and have ceased for good to influence the sign it once generated. To create the code is to institute the sign; the Last Supper is the efficacious institution of the Church's Eucharist. Such a conception of institution will not allow us to interpret the institution of the sacraments as a purely juridical act. Understood as a code, the foundational event lives on in the sign which it has generated; it can even be said that the relation to the foundational event, or code, brings the sign-function into being. Without a code, the various functives are not even functives, since they cannot generate the concrete occurrence of the sign-function.

VII. EXCURSUS: CONCELEBRATION AND THE ANAPHORA

In its Constitution on the Sacred Liturgy, Vatican II restored the practice of eucharistic concelebration,[1] using a ritual that assigns the various parts of the anaphora to the president or to individual concelebrants or to all the concelebrants together (chorally).[2]

Concelebration has always been practiced in the Church. The same cannot be said, however, of the present ritual, which does not have a similar constant attestation in the tradition. Actually, the current practice with its joint recitation of some parts of the Canon originates in *Ordo Romanus* III[3] which in turn supplements *Ordo Romanus* I.[4] It is difficult to say with certainty just when this practice began and how long it continued, but we do have some criteria which give us our bearings, even if only in a general way.

A concelebration of this kind presupposed that the text of the eucharistic prayer had already been fixed and that it enjoyed a special degree of immutability despite repeated copying. This fact gives us some indications of a date insofar as that there could be no common recitation of the Canon as long as the president was still free to improvise the eucharistic prayer. That kind of freedom marked the Anaphora of Hippolytus, which is described for us at the beginning of the third century. Here a newly ordained bishop receives the gifts of bread and wine from the deacons and improvises a eucharistic prayer. He alone pronounces the anaphora, but the entire body of priests takes part, as is clear from the fact that all, while remaining silent, extend their hands over the gifts with the bishop.[5]

This was a concelebration; the priests concelebrated or associated themselves with the celebration by the imposition of hands. The practice of silent participation is further attested as late as the early eighth century in *Ordo Romanus* I, which describes a solemn concelebration of the cardinals with the pope four times a year. The concelebrants do not join their voices to the pope's; they do not pronounce any of the Canon. In fact, they do not even extend their hands as in the Anaphora of Hippolytus; their participation is expressed by their holding the gifts in their hands on corporals.[6]

A change came a few years later in *Ordo Romanus* III; here the cardinals say the Canon with the pope.[7] We must note, however, that the change occurs without any special meaning assigned to it. The rubric neither stresses nor explains the change; it simply states it. In other words, the joint recitation of the Canon in *Ordo* III does not represent a special change or a special theological novelty in relation to *Ordo* I. The two documents are identical except in their ritualization of a point (concelebration) that is more implicit in *Ordo* I, more explicit in *Ordo* III.

But, even if there had been a theological change, the same documents present us with another fact that serves as a criterion for judging their value for the establishment of authentic tradition. The fact is that for the redactor of the short recension, the Canon includes the preface and its introductory dialogue, while for the redactor of the long recension of *Ordo* I, it begins with the *Te igitur.*[8] This notion that the Canon begins only at the *Te igitur* must be judged a complete novelty in liturgical history, and one that was made possible only by ignorance of the Church's tradition.

This argument regarding *Ordo* III is confirmed by examining *Ordo* IV,[9] a Gallican adaptation of *Ordo* I (a Roman composition). In this new document, the pontiff alone says the Canon, while the bishops and priests stand behind him, heads bowed, and holding in their hands the corporals with the gifts: "The pontiff recites the Canon so that they can hear him and so that the gifts which they hold in their hands may be sanctified."[10] Here, then, there was no joint recitation of the Canon. Thus, in a period later than *Ordo* III,[11] there was an unproblematic return to the practice attested in *Ordo* I; the rubric does not suggest any awareness of a theological change.

We may conclude that a purely ritual change had occurred without any doctrinal implications. It follows that the three *Ordines Romani* just examined represent the same theology of concelebration, one unaffected by the ritual change that had occurred. The concelebrants are such because they associate themselves with the action of the presiding bishop and participate in it. In *Ordo* III, the association and participation are made more explicit by having the concelebrants recite the Canon with the bishop. However, we conclude that this common recitation is not theologically different from the imposition of hands attested by Hippolytus.[12]

The new rite, attested only by *Ordo* III, reappears in the concelebration at episcopal ordination in the Pontifical of the Roman Curia in the thirteenth century: "The pontiff continues the celebration of Mass as usual. When he raises his voice for the preface, the newly consecrated bishop pronounces the same words in a low voice (*submisse*) and reads everything else as well (*cetera*) and does everything that follows in the Canon down to the end of the communion rite."[13] At the ordination of priests it is different: "After the offering the priests advance to the altar; they stand on the right and left sides of the altar with their Missals and say everything in a low voice, as if they were concelebrating."[14]

From that time on, concelebration in which all recited the Canon was the only kind known throughout the Middle Ages. The theologians, however, were strongly critical, at least those cited by E. Dekkers.[15] Dekkers has no great love of the present-day rite of concelebration; A. Franquesa's summation of his opinion is accurate: "It follows that the present rite must be regarded as purely transitional."[16] The judgment may be a pitiless one, but it is not without justification. We need only recall the judgment passed on the new rite as early as 1965 by A. Franquesa, the secretary of the commission that produced the ritual for concelebration. His appraisal is still valid:

"As I said, while this rite may not be the oldest or the most authentic, it does have a venerable tradition behind it in the Roman liturgy; it accords with its present theology; and it does not by any means exclude future possible adaptations, if ecclesiastical authorities some day come to think that they can do greater justice to a more communal and hierarchic vision of the Eucharist."[17]

The problem is not a recent one. Concelebration had already been discussed for some time when a meeting on it was held at Mont César, Belgium, in 1954. Dom Botte, a member of the organizing committee, has told us of those interesting events.[18] The time had come for decisions, since first-rate historical studies now existed, as could be seen from the articles published in *La Maison-Dieu* in 1953.[19]

According to the unanimous conclusion reached at the meeting, Church history and tradition do not require that all the concelebrants pronounce the words of consecration. The tradition of the early Church certainly supports this view; so, on the whole, does the more recent tradition of the various Eastern Churches, with the exception of the Russian. In all cases, the presiding bishop alone recites the anaphora; the other concelebrants take part in silence. Dom Botte tells us that this was precisely the problem discussed at the meeting:

"At meetings and congresses attended by numerous priests . . . the priests would assist (at Mass) wearing surplice and stole. The Germans maintained that these priests were real concelebrants and that it was not necessary for all to recite a sacramental formula. I believe that from the historical standpoint the Germans were right. It was just as clear, however, that Rome would never accept this solution. . . . If the Germans had yielded, concelebration would probably have been restored ten years sooner. . . . I learned subsequently that the Assisi Congress ended with an address at Rome in which Pius XII condemned silent concelebration."[20]

All this makes it clear that the present-day rite reflects tensions and misunderstandings between the scholarly world and the magisterium. The present rite is the only allowed after the address of Pius XII.[21] According to E. Lanne, it is the same rite as is used in the Russian Church, where it was organized by Peter Moghila (Metropolitan of Kiev, ca. 1595–1647), who was influenced by Latin eucharistic theology.[22]

There is another datum to be considered. In the East, concelebration has always been practiced and is even the normal form of the eucharistic celebration: to celebrate is to concelebrate. "There is no technical term for describing it, no term suitable for distinguishing it from a nonconcelebrated Eucharist. . . . Whenever more than one priest is present, Mass is normally concelebrated; 'Mass,' when not further qualified, is concelebrated Mass. Nor does the rite change in any way when concelebrated."[23]

Like the rite, the meaning of concelebration also differs in East and West: "For Easterners the ecclesiological meaning of concelebration has always been foremost, while for Latins concelebration has with the passing of the centuries become increasingly associated with the ordination of a new priest."[24]

In restoring concelebration, the Constitution on the Liturgy says that it manifests the unity of the priesthood[25]; in the language of Dom Lanne, it manifests the "horizontal" unity of the concelebrants who join in a single priestly action. For the Eastern Churches, on the other hand, concelebration is essentially a manifestation of the "hierarchic," or "vertical," unity of the Church.[26]

If we limit ourselves to Latin theology, the eucharistic celebration is closely linked with the power to consecrate. From this standpoint, concelebration manifests above all the unity in ministerial priesthood that finds expression in the one consecration. But, if we turn to liturgical tradition, we find a richer body of thought. Since the eucharistic celebration is here seen as the celebration of the entire Church, concelebration "is above all a manifestation of the local Church."[27] And again: "Above and beyond the unity of the priesthood, concelebration manifests in a special way the unity of the Church: the hierarchical unity of that Church which is also the body of Christ."[28]

We have cited the statements of Dom Lanne because they enable us to gauge the development that took place between the Constitution on the Liturgy of 1963 and the *General Instruction* in the Roman Missal of 1969. The latter now says that concelebration manifests not only the unity of the priesthood and the sacrifice but also the unity of the entire people of God.[29] The development that took place in the period between the two documents is clear, since the Missal brings the faithful into the theology of concelebration. Here the theology of concelebration passes beyond the presbytery and embraces the whole eucharistic assembly.

After this mention of the role of the faithful in the theology of concelebration, it is worth citing an important observation of R. Taft: "Presbyterate is a common ministry whose purpose is service, not a personal privilege entailing individual prerogatives and designed to satisfy personal devotional needs."[30]

If concelebration manifests not only the unity of the priesthood and the sacrifice but also the unity of the entire people of God,[31] then we are dealing not with a collective (synchronous) celebration of as many Masses as there are celebrants, but with the celebration of a single Mass that is performed jointly by all the concelebrants under the lead of a single president. But, if there is only one Mass[32] and not as many Masses as there are concelebrants, then there is but a single consecration. Thus, it is theologically irrelevant whether all the concelebrants or the principal concelebrant alone pronounces the words of consecration. History and theology provide reciprocal corroboration.

Another point is that in concelebration there is no choral or collegial presidency of the Eucharist. Even the present-day rite makes this explicit when it prescribes that some parts are reserved to the principal concelebrant and when it says of the parts recited jointly that the concelebrants are to say them in a low voice while the principal celebrant is to say them aloud and clearly. There is but a single president over all the other participants. All—laity, ministers, and concelebrants—are alike under his presidency. There was not in the past nor is there now in the present rite a perfect parity among the concelebrants in the sense of a complete horizontal equality between concelebrants and president in the recitation of the anaphora.[33]

In a concelebrated Eucharist, unity is not represented by horizontal equality (all doing exactly the same thing) but by a vertical hierarchy (the presidency of the "single" presiding celebrant). That is Dom Lanne's thesis with regard to concelebration in the Eastern Churches, as can be seen from this short passage: "For the Orientals concelebration is essentially the sacramental manifestation of the Church's hierarchic unity."[34]

All this explains how a silent concelebration can be an excellent expression of unity. In fact, it brings out even more clearly the unique role of the president: the concelebrants recognize him as their representative and are united in his hierarchic function insofar as it is here a priestly function.

Finally, it is worth mentioning a distinction developed by the theologians. They distinguish between a sacramental and a ceremonial concelebration: in the former, all the priests pronounce the words of concelebration, while in the latter they stand silent. The distinction is an ingenious one that played a role in the development of the theology of concelebration prior to the Council. But, as Dom Botte points out, it is not supported by the tradition: "A purely ceremonial concelebration without any sacramental value is a myth from which we must free ourselves. It has no basis in the tradition."[35] The point is that in the early centuries, there is no trace of a ceremonial conception of the liturgy. What emerged at that period was solely the idea of the efficacy and truth of liturgical action; this was coupled with the idea of the efficacy of God's word, and there can be nothing less ceremonial than God's word.

A. Conclusion

The starting point for the liturgical reform was a view of eucharistic celebration that gave privileged status to the private Mass. The reform moved from there to concelebration, an essentially communal rite. Now, if reform is to be tackled in a realistic way, its promoters must know how much novelty they can introduce. They must try to restore what was done in the past but in the final analysis they must also settle for a rite that is sufficiently close to the mentality and theology of the contemporaries whom they hope to involve in the reform. Otherwise the reform will not be accepted and therefore will not occur.

The rite of concelebration most familiar is the rite which included the common recitation of the Canon. A reform that meant to be realistic had no choice but to opt for this rite as a bridgehead. It is possible that the slow rediscovery of tradition will lead the Church to a rediscovery of silent concelebration. That will take time, since the needed theological maturation must be slow if it is to be authentic.

In all this we are simply making our position that voiced by A. Franquesa, Secretary of the commission that prepared the present rite of concelebration, in 1965.[36]

Chapter Two

The Preface

I. MEANING

The origin of the term "preface" is obscure, and its meaning is not immediately evident.

According to J. A. Jungmann, the division of the eucharistic prayer into preface and Canon was unknown in the Roman liturgy before the Carolingian period. Not only did Canon refer to the entire eucharistic prayer, but it is also very probably that preface referred to the entire prayer. There is evidence of this in the Gregorian Sacramentary where the term "preface" is also applied to the *Hanc igitur* ("We therefore beg you to accept") and to the blessings which precede the final doxology.[1]

In Suetonius' usage, *praefatio* was the prayer that accompanied a sacrifice; there was, therefore (again according to Jungmann), no break in continuity when Christians took over the word for the Eucharist. The *prae-* in *praefatio* "designates an action that is performed *in the presence* of someone, and not one that precedes another in point of time."[2] A preface would thus be the solemn prayer uttered in the presence of the congregation[3] and would be synonymous with anaphora or Canon.

Like Dom B. Capelle, C. Mohrmann accepts this explanation but regards it as a point of departure for her research, which we shall summarize here. In the classical world, the verb *praefari* signified a "preliminary sacrifice" or also, in Suetonius, a *carmen* in the general sense of a "formula of solemn prayer."[4] In Livy, the *prae-* refers to priority in time ("preliminary formula" or "preliminary prayer"),[5] a point which Mohrmann strongly emphasizes then to turn to a passage in the *Metamorphoses* of Apuleius in which *praefari* means "to say a prayer," but without any implication of priority: *prae-* here is synonymous with *pro-*.[6] After studying the meaning that *praefatio* has in rhetoric, Mohrmann gives examples of *praefari* meaning *proclamare*, in which there is no suggestion of priority: "A derived noun occurs in Symmachus, *Rel. ad princ.* 10, 5: *meo praefatu*, 'by my proclamation.' This development reminds us of Apuleius' use in which *praefari* had the meaning of 'to say a prayer.' "[7]

After concluding that the use of *praefatio* in the classical world is of no great help,[8] Mohrmann examines Christian texts. The difference in the conclusions she reaches as compared with Jungmann is evidently due to the evolutionary method she adopts in historical linguistics.

The meaning of *praefatio* varies in Christian usage; it does not become a technical term in the Gallican liturgy before the seventh century or in the Roman before the eighth.

In the Gallican liturgy, preface bears the names *contestatio* (confession) or *immolatio* (sacrifice), while in the Mozarabic liturgy it is called *illatio* (offering), which would be an accurate translation of anaphora.

In the Gallican liturgy, *praefatio* appears with a different meaning. It designates the admonition that precedes and introduces the celebration. This admonition is not a simple bit of direction or instruction, but a proper, solemn invitatory. It is somewhat analogous to the opening section of the *Exultet* in the Roman liturgy which serves as an urgent exhortation and effective invitation to the faithful to cultivate suitable sentiments of Easter joy; this section is then followed by the blessing or praise of the Easter candle.

This use of *praefatio* is in continuity with that found in Cyprian, the first Christian writer to use it in the context of the eucharistic liturgy. "And then, before the [eucharistic] prayer the priest says the preface, by which he prepares the souls of the faithful, telling them, 'Lift up your hearts.' "[9] The same use is found in Sulpicius Severus, where a mute child is cured by St. Martin through an application of previously exorcized oil: "And then he blesses a little oil with the 'preface of exorcism' (*exorcismi praefatione*). In exorcisms of objects, we frequently find deprecative formulas which use performative utterances that are directives, in the true and proper sense, given to the objects in question,[10] though they are meant, of course, as prayers. In the fifth century, Fastidius gives the name *praefatio* to the acclamation *Sancta sanctis* ("Holy things to the holy!"), which tells the faithful that it is to the holy that the holy gifts are distributed in communion.[11]

An analogous use of *praefatio* occurs in the Roman liturgy in *Ordo Romanus* XI, which dates from the seventh century or even the second half of the sixth. That liturgy transmits the text of the creed to the catechumens. The admonitory exhortation that precedes the creed is called *praefatio symboli*.[12] Similarly, with the Our Father, the lengthy exhortation that presents this prayer to the catechumens and explains it to them verse by verse is called *praefatio orationis dominicae*.[13] The word *praefatio* does not occur frequently in the Roman sacramentaries. The reason may be that the word becomes a technical term in the Roman liturgy only after the eighth century.[14] In the Verona or Leonine Sacramentary, even the prayers do not have titles, whereas in the Gelasian, the titles *Secreta* and *Post communionem* already appear. *Praefationes* appears at the head of the *Vere dignum* in the Gregorian Sacramentary,[15] but its usage does not make it a solidly established technical term.

It is not easy to reach sure conclusions from this evidence; for this reason, Mohrmann abstains from drawing any. However, it is possible to attempt some. Surely, it has become clear that *praefatio* means "prayer or solemn proclamation during public worship." E. Dekkers properly calls attention that *praefatio* never refers to just any prayer or to a prayer of lesser importance.

"The reference might be to the great eucharistic prayer or to the prayer of ordinations, an exorcism, or a blessing. We have a *praefatio uvae* [preface of the grapes], a *praefatio exorcismi* [preface of exorcism], a *praefatio palmarum* [preface of the palms], and *praefationes ordinandi subdiaconi, ad clericum faciendum, ad virginem benedicendam* [prefaces for ordaining a subdeacon, making a man a cleric, blessing a virgin], a *praefatio lectoris* [preface for a reader], a *praefatio calicis consecrandae* [preface for consecrating a chalice], etc."[16]

Dekkers emphasizes that in every case *praefatio* refers to a prayer which we would call the "form" of a sacrament. He then points out a special link between the words "prophecy" and "preface." The texts he adduces are convincing, but we think it possible to carry the argument further and thereby seek to explain the prevailingly eucharistic use of the word "preface" in the Roman liturgy. The conclusion reached will not be incontestable, but the line of thought deserves nonetheless to be followed up.

The first text to be cited (we are indebted to Dekkers for it) is from a passage in which Augustine uses the Latin *praefator* for "prophet."[17] Isidore accepts the explanation of *propheta* as *praefator* and proposes it in words almost identical with those of Augustine.[18] Dekkers also cites Tertullian, an author who, as we shall see, deserves special attention. Tertullian, explaining the proclamation of the faith, speaks in this context of prophets; to account for the connection he says: " 'Preachers' are called 'prophets' because their function is to 'announce' (*Quos diximis praedicatores prophetae de officii praefandi vocantur*)."[19] From these passages it follows that *praefator* means "propheta" and *praefari* means "prophesy, announce."

If *praefari* is the activity exercised by a *praefator* or *propheta* and gives this personage his name, it follows that *praefatio* (a *nomen actionis* from *praefari*) is equivalent to prophecy. Dekkers reaches the same conclusion and goes on to ask whether in fact the Greek term *propheteia* was ever translated by "its literal Latin equivalent *praefatio*." He knows of no instance.[20]

Further data for pursuing this line of thought are lacking, so we cannot continue it. There are, however, two other interesting lines that deserve investigation. Our argument will, therefore, comprise three convergent lines of thought, the first of which is the one just examined, namely, the etymology of *praefari*. While we lack texts showing a direct link between "prophecy" and "preface," we shall inquire whether there may not be a direct connection between "prophet" and "preface." We shall hypothesize that there is indeed a connection between the activity of the prophet and the liturgical text we know as the preface (rather than the word preface as such).

The question of whether such a connection exists is answered in the *Didache*. Chapter 10 supplies a thanksgiving that is part of the liturgical tradition of the very early Church. We shall not go into the dispute over the eucharistic character of the passage, but shall be content with the minimalist interpretation that sees it as a thanksgiving for the eucharistic celebration and the equivalent of a modern preface.[21] At the end of the thanksgiving, there is this remark: "Allow the prophets to give thanks (*eucharistein*) as much as they wish."[22]

Thus, the person who proclaims this "eucharist" is a "prophet" whose action consists in "giving thanks." His action is *eucharistein*, the prayer itself is called *eucharistia*,[23] and he who pronounces it is a *propheta*. There is, then, an action in which a prophet produces a very special announcement or prophecy, namely, a thanksgiving. Thus, we have *eucharistein* which has *eucharistia* as its *nomen actionis* and which is an activity of a prophet. So, too, we have *praefari* which has *praefatio* as its *nomen actionis;* "prophet" would then be derived from the activity or function (*officium*) of *praefari*. Moreover, in liturgical Latin, the substantive *eucharistia* survived but the verb equivalent to *eucharistein* was lost; so, too, in liturgical use, the substantive *praefatio* survived but *praefari* was lost.

We conclude, therefore, that the search for a connection between "prophet" and the text of the preface has been successful: a connection did exist. In the early Church, we also see, however, the rapid disappearance of prophetism and the suspect reputation that the latter left behind.[24] Especially in worship did prophetism cease to have a place; thus, in the *Apostolic Constitutions,* the sentence from the *Didache* is changed to read: "Allow your presbyters also to give thanks (*eucharistein*)."[25] The thanksgiving formerly proclaimed by prophets is now proclaimed by presbyters. In addition, the texts have ceased to be improvised and are becoming fixed; there is a clear tendency to use unchanging formularies.

The first of our arguments was studied by Dekkers, and it yielded the connection *propheteia-praefari,* with special reference to Tertullian. Tertullian is, of course, far removed from the *Didache,* and we cannot but ask ourselves whether his testimony can really be coupled with that of the *Didache* and what connection between them justifies the association. The connection is the teaching of both on the eucharistic celebrant, for Tertullian is one of the few witnesses to a Eucharist at which the president is not a presbyter. In the *Didache,* the celebrant is a prophet; in Tertullian, he is simply a layman[26] who is regarded, on several grounds, as the equal of a presbyter.

On one point we find an extraordinary agreement between Tertullian and the *Didache:* both use the word "priest" of the nonpresbyter who celebrates the liturgy. The *Didache* calls the prophets "your high priests,"[27] and it says of bishops and deacons that they have the same "ministry" as the prophets[28] and are to be honored like the prophets.[29] Tertullian, for his part, asks emphatically: "Is it not true that we laypersons are also priests?" And again: "If, then, you possess priestly competence (*ius sacerdotis*) when necessary, you must also follow the priest's rule of life (*disciplina*)."[30]

In this passage, Tertullian means by *sacerdos* the eucharistic celebrant, since the force of his ad hominem argument depends precisely on this point. He says: "Where the ecclesiastical organization has not been established, you may celebrate the Eucharist and baptize (*et offers et tinguis*), and you are a priest in your own right; in fact (*scilicet*) where three are present, the Church is there, even if the three be laypersons."[31] Further, he says that a priest who has remarried is deprived of his *agere sacerdotem,*[32] that is, his power to celebrate the Eucharist.

It is clear that *sacerdos* in this passage refers to a liturgical role and designates the one who presides at the sacrament. There is thus a positive convergence in the passages cited from the *Didache* and Tertullian, even if this does not adequately ground a strictly philological argument proving that the word *praefatio* derives from the *praefari* of the prophet. It is possible, nonetheless, to construct a positive argument for the possibility that *praefatio* and the role of the prophet in the *Didache* are linked. We have successfully done this.

Praefatio, then, was the name given to a liturgical text solemnly proclaimed—not every liturgical text, but those that have special prominence in the celebration. Of all the texts to which the word was originally applied, the thanksgiving part of the Mass came to stand alone and, beginning with the Gregorian Sacramentary, almost exclusively appropriated the name for itself until it finally became a technical term for the first part of the Roman Canon.

A final observation, even if inadequate by itself, concerns the link between the constantly varying Roman preface and the creative freedom exercised in the liturgy of the prophets. The *praefatio* of the eucharistic liturgy is never a fixed text but always a varying one[33] and thus stands apart from the rest of the Canon, which is unchanging. If we look at the situation from this point of view, it is logical to say that the preface is quite distinct from the Roman Canon[34] as the proclamation of a variable text is distinct from the proclamation of a set text.

It is clear that we can only offer working hypotheses since the data needed for a definitive answer are lacking. Although we have not succeeded in demonstrating the origin of the word "preface," our argument does show its semantic range, which links it to the activity of the "prophet." Confirmation of this explanation is provided by the parallelism between *praefatio-praefari* and *praedicatio-praedicare* in referring to the eucharistic prayer.[35]

II. THEOLOGICAL VALUE

In the Roman liturgy, the whole of the "eucharist" or thanksgiving proper to the Canon is concentrated in the preface. Thanksgiving (*eucharistia*) is a characteristically Christian activity, and Paul the apostle even treats it as a way of life.[36] The opening words of the Roman preface have a clearly Pauline flavor: "It is truly right and just, proper and helpful toward salvation, that we always and everywhere give thanks to you, O Lord, holy Father, almighty and eternal God, through Christ our Lord." And here is a Pauline passage whose message the preface seems intent on actualizing: "always and for everything giving thanks in the name of our Lord Jesus Christ to God the Father."[37]

In the preface, the community offers God its own ardent thanksgiving[38]; it also lists and describes the reasons for this thanksgiving. The preface is composed of three parts, which need to be studied separately. We shall study the first two, since the third and concluding part is simply the introduction to the Sanctus and enumerates the angelic hosts. This final part has no connection with our subject, but will not be simply ignored, however, and will be discussed in the chapter on the fourth anaphora.

A. Opening Sentence

The original Latin preface begins with an expression of intention: to give thanks to the Father. It serves to give the action an aura of formality and solemnity. The act of thanksgiving is shown thereby to be based on reflection and deliberation; it is an act that is consciously done and involves the person.

Thanksgiving is defined as "right and just" (*dignum et iustum*), two words which Dom Botte regards as synonymous.[39] They are followed by a second pair: *aequum et salutare*.[40]

Salutare can be translated as "helpful toward salvation" or even "source of salvation"; as we shall see later,[41] it refers to the salvific value of thanksgiving. *Aequum* (proper) conveys the idea of "our duty"; "duty" is a suitable rendition of the Latin *aequitas*, which is a virtue analogous to justice[42] and closely related to *pietas*, the attribute of a person who "honors his commitments,"[43] especially to the gods.

It is immediately clear that these words have a juridical character, which should not astonish us. Every people has its culture, which cannot but influence the language it uses for prayer. When Rome accepted the gospel, the whole style and genius of Roman culture, including its juridical conception of religion, affected the way in which the Roman Church prayed. Both in private and public worship, the same character left its dominant mark. That mark was not moral, much less sentimental or mystical; it was juridical.[44] Just as civil law regulated relations among individual citizens, so divine law regulated relations between citizens and the divine powers. Divine law prescribed everything to be done to secure the *pax deorum* (peace of the gods), that is, an attitude on the part of the gods that was free of anger at humankind. The *pax deorum* controlled the entire religious thinking of Romans.[45] Roman religious vocabulary was, therefore, inevitably rich in juridical terms.

When introduced into the preface, these juridical terms signify that the thanksgiving being offered is a complete and perfect worship and that human beings are thereby carrying out their duty toward God. All that they owe to God they actually give him when they thank him.

From this point of view, it can be said that thanksgiving implies an offering. This oblative movement implicit in thanksgiving was to have its greatest development precisely in the Roman liturgy.

B. Main Body

The central part of the preface is its nucleus and most extensive part. Its literary genre is narrative, and it enunciates the reasons for giving thanks. Here again the text is dependent on Paul, who says that as the divine gift—salvation and grace—multiplies, it increases our thanksgiving.[46]

We do not give thanks on our own initiative, rather we are urged to it by our experience of having found favor with God in Christ. For this reason, it can be said that we are not the authors of our thanksgiving; it is God who produces it in us. The praise that rises to our lips is itself a gift, just as the faith in our hearts is a gift.[47] Paul, again, links the two concepts: "By believing from the heart you are made righteous; by confessing (*homologeitai*) with your lips you are saved."[48]

From the theological standpoint, it is possible to assign thanksgiving, praise, and "confession" to the same sphere.[49] From the standpoint of literary genre, however, it is not so simple.

Because the prefaces are now so numerous, we cannot analyze the thanksgiving offered in each.[50] Each gives thanks for some particular aspect or point in the history of the salvation which God has wrought for us. Each phase of the liturgical year becomes, in turn, the theme of the thanksgiving, which may include a description of human conversion and salvation or may emphasize the mystery being celebrated. Moreover, if the liturgical feast is not concerned directly with Christ but is a feast of, for example, the saints (among whom Mary, Mother of God, has first place), the preface that elucidates this particular aspect of the mystery of salvation is always theocentric in its focus.

The prefaces, although many in number (a phenomenon peculiar to the Roman liturgy), are in addition less successful from a literary point of view. But they have one thing in common: they are always concerned with the gift God has given to us, namely, his grace and the salvation he has wrought.

The prefaces commemorate and describe that gift; we respond to that gift with praise. God and his gift are praised in a single interior movement, since the gift reveals and manifests the giver. To praise giver and gift is to declare them pleasing and acceptable. To accept the gift is to remain obligated. That is the logic of gifts.

M. Mauss has left us a magisterial study of the law at work in gifts.[51] The anthropological and cultural datum, which he calls the "system of gifts," provides the framework to interpret the thanksgiving in the Christian anaphora and therefore in the Roman preface. In cultural ethnology, the system is known as "potlatch."[52] We are not, of course, attempting to reduce the eucharistic celebration to a primitive potlatch. The latter can, however, help us understand the eucharistic action, which may be regarded as the highest and indeed transcendent form of this phenomenon.

Potlatch means, in substance, an encounter between persons through the medium of a gift which serves precisely to establish the relationship. We are not speaking, therefore, of just any relationship, but of one governed by particular laws that are inherent in the very nature of the gift. "The exchange of presents did not serve the same purpose as trade or barter in more developed societies. The purpose that it did serve was a moral one."[53]

Ethnological studies have yielded three key elements in potlatch. First, gifts cannot be refused but must be accepted.[54] Refusals do not leave the intended recipients in the neutral state in which they were before; rather, they now stand in a negative relation to the giver, for whom a refusal is "the equivalent of a declaration of war; it is a refusal of friendship and intercourse."[55] A refusal creates a negative relation between recipient and giver. A gift is not neutral but creates or breaks a relationship.

If a gift is to establish a relationship, it "must" be given.[56] This is the second element in potlatch and the very heart of the system of giftgiving; the gift is offered because the system exists, but the offering is not simply a prerequisite in order that potlatch may come about. Rather, the gift is a requirement of relations among human beings: without gifts these relations degenerate and coexistence becomes impossible. When, on the other hand, a gift is accepted, the recipient acquires a spiritual tie that creates a special situation. Every gift brings with it an urgent invitation to offer a gift in return;

the tie or bond that has been created demands that there be an exchange of gifts.

We are already in the presence of the third element in the system of giftgiving: a gift received must be adequately recompensed by a gift given in return. "The obligation to repay is the essence of potlatch. . . . The obligation of worthy return is imperative,"[57] because a failure to give a gift in return puts the recipient in a position of inferiority[58] and of dependence on the giver,[59] whereas restitution in the form of a gift in return puts him on the same level as the giver. In fact, once he makes a gift in return, the recipient now becomes a giver.[60]

The entire persons of both giver and recipient are involved in potlatch; all endeavor, or should endeavor, to act as total beings, not as persons divided.[61] Potlatch is one of those phenomena that may be called "total": it is simultaneously religious, mythological, and shamanistic[62]; in some potlatches, one must give all one possesses and keep nothing back.[63]

There is a further point in Mauss' fine analysis: some tribes have but a single word to signify both gift and gift-in-return, both giving and receiving.[64]

It is with this last point that we may begin to apply the data discovered by Mauss to the Eucharist. Since the beginning of Christian history (chap. 9 and 10 of the *Didache,* for example), the word "eucharist" has referred to two things: on the one hand, the bread and wine, and on the other, the eucharistic prayer. The bread and wine are God's gift, given to human beings by Christ at his last meal; Christ himself is God's gift to human beings. The eucharistic prayer, on the other hand, rises from human beings to God. It is our gift in exchange, our response to God's gift. In the anaphoras of the Alexandrian liturgy, this gift of ours is the object of the verb "to offer"; moreover, in Greek liturgies the very name of this gift shows it to be subject to the logic of offering: an "anaphora" is something that rises aloft and is carried up to God.

One and the same word, "eucharist," designates two operations that are opposite in direction: one descending, the other ascending. The two are not identical but they call for one another and belong to the same order of things: the system of gifts.[65] The gift given in return is not something different, not a different reality, since it is nothing else but the spirit of the gift initially received.[66]

It is the aspect of reply or response in the eucharistic prayer that most clearly shows our Eucharist to belong to this "system of gifts" or the primitive potlatch. Here are two completely probative texts from anaphoras in the Syriac tradition. In the anaphora, we narrate and relive what God has done for human beings, with the gift of salvation coming as the crown upon the gift of creation. In the presence of this gift, human beings are unable to give any gift in exchange: "We your servants . . . bless you, Lord, because you have shown us your favor for which no repayment can be made."[67] When the gift thus exceeds the ability of the recipient to give an adequate gift in return, the only way of responding is with gratitude, that is, thanksgiving and praise: "And for all your favor to us, which we cannot repay, we offer you glory and honor in your holy Church before your altar of propitiation."[68] The same concept occurs in the Mozarabic liturgy: "It is right and just, truly our duty, and a source of salvation that we should praise and bless you, provided that—since nothing human beings give one another is worthy of your dignity and holiness—you would, in your ineffable devotion to your creatures, enable us to render (*referre*) you due praise and thanks."[69]

Given the impossibility of a true exchange of gifts, human beings can offer only their thanks. This is the sole gift that can be given to the giver who is God. By our praise and thanksgiving, we confess the greatness of his work and his gift. In the Eucharist, we reach the high point of the order of gifts, and we even pass beyond that order, since our gratitude, the gift we offer to God in exchange, does not represent an exchange in the true and proper sense. In fact, gratitude is simply the way of receiving and accepting a gift. We even pass beyond the order of giving, because here there is no return of an authentic gift on our part (such a return is simply impossible for us, since all we have has been received). Yet we do not leave behind the logic of the "system of gifts" since our response or "return," namely our thanksgiving, is defined as "truly right and just, and our duty."[70]

In this passage to the Eucharist, the "system of gifts" loses its content, since no true exchange of gifts is possible with God,[71] but the form of the system is retained because gratitude, which is our way of accepting God's gift, becomes a hymn of praise and thanksgiving that rises to God and is formally offered to him. A Mozarabic text expresses this well: "It is right and just, God our Father, that we should always offer you a hymn and present you with a song of praise."[72]

Let us conclude that this excursion into cultural anthropology has not been fruitless for our understanding of the thanksgiving that is celebrated in the preface. The present-day Missal contains a preface which expounds the theology of thanksgiving in such a way that the congregation is enabled to live this relationship with God in an increasingly perfect way. It is a preface that contains the very theory behind all prefaces: "You have no need of our praise, yet our desire to thank you is itself your gift. Our prayer of thanksgiving adds nothing to your greatness, but makes us grow in your grace."[73]

III. TEXT OF THE SANCTUS

The preface leads to the Sanctus as its logical conclusion. Here the celebration of God's praises becomes a contemplation of the praise which the angelic hosts, ordered in their might like an army, sing to the Father whom they see face to face.

This statement applies without qualification to the relation between preface and Sanctus in the present liturgy. It did not always apply, however, since the Sanctus was introduced into the Roman liturgy only at a relatively recent date.

The Canon as we know it has the singing of the Sanctus at the end of the preface and before the *Te igitur* ("Therefore, most merciful Father"). We do not know, however, whether the Sanctus was or was not part of the liturgy in the time of Ambrose. It was certainly not in the Anaphora of Hippolytus (ca. 220), and, while the Letter of Clement to the Corinthians attests that the Sanctus was used in the liturgy of the second century, the liturgy in question was not necessarily the Eucharist.[74]

In this matter, we shall follow P.-M. Gy, O.P., in his lucid exposition of the problem of the insertion of the Sanctus into the Roman Canon.[75] At the end of the fourth century or sometime during the first thirty years of the fifth, a pseudo-Ambrosian pamphlet, *The Holy Spirit*, stated that the Sanctus was in use in all the Churches of the East and in some Churches of the West.[76] And, in fact, we have evidence of its use at that time in Jerusalem,[77] Antioch,[78] and Egypt,[79] but no mention of it in Ambrose or Jerome or Augustine.[80] Father Gy tells us that L. Chavoutier has collected all the attestations of the Sanctus in the West and that comparison shows them all to be later than the pamphlet on the Holy Spirit.

Since, on the other hand, we have two prefaces with a Sanctus that are attributed to St. Leo the Great (440–61) and since there is still no evidence of the Sanctus as late as 430,[81] we may conclude that it was introduced not long before the pontificate of St. Leo. The preface had previously ended with "Through Christ our Lord."

Once the Sanctus was introduced, this final phrase was altered and probably became: "Through whom the angels praise your majesty (*per quem maiestatem tuam laudant angeli*)," the word "majesty" (*maiestas*) being taken from the old Latin versions of Scripture where it occurred as the translation of the Greek *doxa* (*gloria*, glory).[82]

Father Gy carefully analyzes that the Roman Sanctus could not have derived from the Egyptian liturgy, since in the latter the list of angelic choirs is preceded by a word-for-word citation of Ephesians 1:21, whereas the citation is completely absent from the Roman text. On the other hand, since the Roman text of the Sanctus is the same as that in the Anaphoras of Basil, John Chrysostom, and James, we can conclude that it came from Jerusalem and Antioch. In St. Leo, the Sanctus sometimes takes on a trinitarian meaning, perhaps under the influence of the Anaphora of Chrysostom.[83]

For an example of a preface without a Sanctus, we refer you to the "Mass of the Dead" in the *Supplementum Anianense*.[84] When a simple *per* occurs as the ending of prefaces in the sacramentaries, the word may, in theory, mark the beginning of a conclusion such as A. Mai found in an Arian fragment: "Through Jesus Christ, our Lord and God, through whom we beg and entreat."[85]

This brief notice on the entrance of the Sanctus into the eucharistic prayer shows that at the beginning of the fifth century the Roman Canon was still open to important developments. As a matter of fact, the Sanctus brought into the Canon the idea that by joining the angels in their song we participate in the heavenly liturgy. We do not know, however, the reasons that motivated the opening of the liturgy to this Eastern usage. At a later time, when Pope Gregory introduced his liturgical innovations, he would have to defend, explain, and justify what he did.[86] Nothing similar occurred when the Sanctus was introduced at this earlier period; there were no protests, no debates. The introduction of the Sanctus went unnoticed and left no trace in the patristic writings of the day. The situation in Pope Gregory's day had become quite different, and the difference was due to a change of attitude with regard to the fixity or immutability of the liturgy. In the fifth century, people still thought of the text of the Canon as susceptible to variation and development.

Chapter Three

The Roman Canon

I. TRANSLATIONS OF THE ROMAN CANON

LITERAL TRANSLATION

Therefore, most merciful Father, we humbly beg and entreat you through Jesus Christ your Son, our Lord, to accept and bless these gifts, these offerings, these holy and spotless sacrifices which we offer you first for your holy catholic Church, that you may grant her peace and protection, unity and direction throughout the world, together with your servant N., our Holy Father, and N., our bishop, and all faithful guardians of the catholic and apostolic faith.

Remember, Lord, your servants N. and N., and all here present, whose faith and devotion are known to you: for whom we offer, or who themselves offer, to you this sacrifice of praise, in their own behalf and in behalf of all who are theirs, for the redemption of their souls, for the hope of their salvation and protection from harm, and who now offer their promises to you, the eternal, living, and true God.

ICEL TRANSLATION

We come to you, Father, with praise and thanksgiving, through Jesus Christ your Son. Through him we ask you to accept and bless these gifts we offer you in sacrifice. We offer them for your holy catholic Church, watch over it, Lord, and guide it; grant it peace and unity throughout the world. We offer them for N. our Pope, for N. our bishop, and for all who hold and teach the catholic faith that comes to us from the apostles.

Remember, Lord, your people, especially those for whom we now pray, N. and N. Remember all of us gathered here before you. You know how firmly we believe in you and dedicate ourselves to you. We offer you this sacrifice of praise for ourselves and those who are dear to us. We pray to you, our living and true God, for our well-being and redemption.

In the unity of holy fellowship, and venerating the memory, first of all, of the glorious and ever-virgin Mary, Mother of our God and Lord, Jesus Christ, then blessed Joseph, spouse of that same virgin, your blessed apostles and martyrs Peter and Paul, Andrew, [James, John, Thomas, James, Philip, Bartholomew, Matthew, Simon, and Thaddeus; Linus, Cletus, Clement, Sixtus, Cornelius, Cyprian, Lawrence, Chrysogonus, John and Paul, Cosmas and Damian;] and all of your saints, through whose merits and prayers grant that we may be ever strengthened by the help of your protection. [Through the same Christ our Lord. Amen.]

We therefore beg you to accept, O Lord, this offering of our worship and that of your whole household. Regulate the days of our lives so that they may be spent in your peace; spare us from eternal damnation and help us to be numbered among those whom you have chosen. [Through Christ our Lord. Amen.]

We pray you, O God, be pleased to make this offering wholly blessed, to consecrate and approve it, making it reasonable and acceptable, so that it may become for us the body and blood of your most beloved Son, our Lord Jesus Christ.

Who, on the day before he suffered death, took bread into

In union with the whole Church we honor Mary, the ever-virgin mother of Jesus Christ our Lord and God. We honor Joseph, her husband, the apostles and martyrs Peter and Paul, Andrew, [James, John, Thomas, James, Philip, Bartholomew, Matthew, Simon and Jude; we honor Linus, Cletus, Clement, Sixtus, Cornelius, Cyprian, Lawrence, Chrysogonus, John and Paul, Cosmas and Damian;] and all the saints. May their merits and prayers gain us your constant help and protection. [Through Christ our Lord. Amen.]

Father, accept this offering from your whole family. Grant us your peace in this life, save us from final damnation, and count us among those you have chosen. [Through Christ our Lord. Amen.]

Bless and approve our offering; make it acceptable to you, an offering in spirit and in truth. Let it become for us the body and blood of Jesus Christ, your only Son, our Lord. [Through Christ our Lord. Amen.]

The day before he suffered he took bread in his sacred hands his holy and venerable hands, and lifting up his eyes to heaven, to you, O God, his almighty Father, and giving thanks to you, he said the blessing, broke it, and gave it to his disciples, saying: "Take this, all of you, and eat of it: for this is my body, which will be given up for you."

In like manner, after they had eaten, taking this noble cup into his holy and venerable hands, and again giving thanks to you, he said the blessing, and gave it to his disciples, saying: "Take this, all of you, and drink of it: for this is the cup of my blood of the new and everlasting covenant, which shall be shed for you and for the many for the forgiveness of sins. Do this in memory of me."

The mystery of faith! — Lord, we proclaim your death and we confess your resurrection, until you come.

Therefore, O Lord, we your servants and with us your holy people, calling to mind the blessed passion of this same Christ, your Son, our Lord, and also his resurrection from the dead and his glorious ascension into heaven, offer to your supreme majesty, of the gifts you have bestowed on us, a pure, holy, and spotless sacrifice, the holy bread of everlasting life and the cup of eternal salvation.

Be pleased to look upon these offerings with a gracious and

and looking up to heaven, to you, his almighty Father, he gave you thanks and praise. He broke the bread, gave it to his disciples, and said: "Take this, all of you, and eat it: this is my body which will be given up for you."

When supper was ended, he took the cup. Again he gave you thanks and praise, gave the cup to his disciples, and said: "Take this, all of you, and drink from it: this is the cup of my blood, the blood of the new and everlasting covenant. It will be shed for you and for all so that sins may be forgiven. Do this in memory of me."

Let us proclaim the mystery of faith: Christ has died, Christ is risen, Christ will come again.

Father, we celebrate the memory of Christ, your Son. We, your people and your ministers, recall his passion, his resurrection from the dead, and his ascension into glory; and from the many gifts you have given us we offer to you, God of glory and majesty, this holy and perfect sacrifice: the bread of life and the cup of eternal salvation.

Look with favor on these offerings and accept them as once

kindly countenance, and accept them as it pleased you to accept the offerings of your just servant Abel, and the sacrifice of our father Abraham, and that which your great priest Melchizedek offered to you, a holy sacrifice, a spotless offering.

Humbly we implore you, almighty God, bid these offerings be carried by the hands of your holy angel to your altar on high, before your divine majesty, so that those of us who by sharing in the sacrifice at this altar shall receive the sacred body and blood of your Son, may be filled with every grace and heavenly blessing. [Through the same Christ our Lord. Amen.]

Remember also, O Lord, your servants N. and N., who have gone before us with the sign of faith, and rest in the sleep of peace. To them, O Lord, and to all who rest in Christ, we entreat you to grant a place of comfort, light, and peace. [Through Christ our Lord. Amen.]

To us also, your sinful servants, who trust in your boundless mercy, graciously grant fellowship and a place with your holy apostles and martyrs, with John, Stephen, Matthias, Barnabas, [Ignatius, Alexander, Marcellinus, Peter, Felicity, Perpetua, Agatha, Lucy, Agnes, Cecilia, Anastasia,] and all your saints. Into their company, we

you accepted the gifts of your servant Abel, the sacrifice of Abraham, our father in faith, and the bread and wine offered by your priest Melchisedech.

Almighty God, we pray that your angel may take this sacrifice to your altar in heaven. Then, as we receive from this altar the sacred body and blood of your Son, let us be filled with every grace and blessing. [Through Christ our Lord. Amen.]

Remember, Lord, those who have died and have gone before us marked with the sign of faith, especially those for whom we now pray, N. and N. May these, and all who sleep in Christ, find in your presence light, happiness, and peace. [Through Christ our Lord. Amen.]

For ourselves, too, we ask some share in the fellowship of your apostles and martyrs, with John the Baptist, Stephen, Matthias, Barnabas, [Ignatius, Alexander, Marcellinus, Peter, Felicity, Perpetua, Agatha, Lucy, Agnes, Cecilia, Anastasia,] and all the saints. Though we are sinners, we trust in your mercy and love. Do not consider what

beg you, admit us, not weighing our unworthiness but freely granting us forgiveness.

Through Christ our Lord, through whom, O Lord, you constantly create, sanctify, enliven, and bestow upon us all these good gifts.

Through him and with him and in him all honor and glory is yours, almighty God and Father, in the unity of the Holy Spirit, for ever and ever. Amen.

we truly deserve, but grant us your forgiveness.

Through Christ our Lord.

Through him you give us all these gifts. You fill them with life and goodness, you bless them and make them holy. Through him, with him, in him, in the unity of the Holy Spirit, all glory and honor is yours, almighty Father, for ever and ever. Amen.

II. INTRODUCTION

A. The Problem

When we begin to speak of the Roman Canon, we feel a need to praise this venerable document of our tradition. And, indeed, it is deserving of respect both as a constant factor in the history of the Roman Church and because of its unchanging identity. The text as we have it today acquired its form between the end of the fourth century and the seventh century, and has not been changed significantly since the days of Pope Gregory the Great (d. 604).[1]

It is also deserving of veneration because of its widespread use. It was introduced into England in the seventh century, into Frankish territory in the eighth, into Spain in the eleventh, and finally into the Celtic countries in the ninth to the twelfth.[2] It is venerable because it was for so long the only eucharistic prayer of the Roman Church; until quite recently, no one thought that there might be an alternative to the Roman Canon.

It is venerable because of the impression its archaic and unusual language has made. It is full of words and phrases that are hard to understand and therefore evoke rather than communicate, suggest rather than say outright. It awakens a sense of the ineffable and undefinable or, in other words, a sense of mystery—but, be it noted, of mystery not in the biblical and patristic sense of the word, but in the sense of being mystifying and obscure.

Once this sense of mystery is roused, the rationalizing unconscious forms the attitude, or, more accurately, the psychological mechanism which we call the "sense of the sacred." In fact, all the characteristics listed as making the Roman Canon venerable can be summed up in its sacredness. Moreover, since immutability and untouchableness are two factors that constitute the sacredness, it can be said that Canon law and Roman practice gave this sacredness a theological status.

Contemporary author, A. Piolanti, provides an interesting example of the frame of mind we are describing. In his discussion of the Eucharist, he raises the question of the origin of the Canon of the Mass and asks whether it did not, even as a literary document, originate in Christ himself. He answers, of course, in the negative: "It cannot be said that the Canon in its entirety originated in Christ."[3] But the very notion, even though denied, that the entire Roman Canon might have come from Christ shows how venerable and sacred the incomparable text of the Canon is.

This same attitude was given authoritative expression by the Council of Trent:

"Holy things must be treated in a holy way and this sacrifice is the most holy of all things. And so, that this sacrifice might be worthily and reverently offered and received, the Catholic Church many centuries ago instituted the sacred Canon. It is so free from all error that it contains nothing which does not savour strongly of holiness and piety and nothing which does not raise to God the minds of those who offer. For it is made up of the words of our Lord Himself, of apostolic traditions, and of devout instructions of the holy pontiffs."[4]

If we keep this background in mind, it is easy to understand the amazement many felt when liturgists began to talk of reforming the Roman Canon. The need of reform had, of course, a basis in fact: it was difficult to make effective pastoral use of the Canon, chiefly because its structure had resulted from the juxtaposition of previously unconnected fragments and consequently there was no clear conception guiding the development of the text. This peculiar characteristic becomes immediately evident when we compare the Canon with the Antiochene anaphoras that eventually became the models for the present reform.

Nonetheless, the Roman Canon does have a precise logic of its own. However, this logic becomes visible only through study and analysis of the text and cannot be brought out in liturgical proclamation.

The Canon is made up of fifteen prayers, each complete in itself. These are set one alongside another like tiles in a mosaic, but it is not easy to see the resulting complete picture. What, then, is the thrust and what are the characteristics of the Roman Canon when looked upon as a unified text made up of its component parts? But, there is a prior question: Is the Roman Canon in fact a unified text, or is it simply a loose association of smaller euchological units? And what criterion will decide this point?

These are legitimate questions, but even after all the historical and philological discussions, no clear and certain answers can be given. A text thus characterized by fragmentation and discontinuity is evidently of questionable pastoral value. It is difficult to follow any text that is being proclaimed or read aloud; it is more so for a text that raises problems. In liturgical proclamation, the Canon does not reveal why it has the specific elements that it has, and why it has these rather than others. In fact, it is difficult—though not impossible—to answer these questions at all. It is clear, then, that such a text does not fulfill the function it should: to be a vehicle of and stimulus to participation in the Eucharist.[5]

For these reasons, scholars proposed to emend the Canon. Such proposals, however, carry risks; for example, the risk of changes that reflect the theological taste of the moment rather than a sense of tradition. What would we think today if the medieval theologians had changed the Canon to make it fit in with their theological principles? Fortunately, however, "the medieval theologians looked upon the Canon as a self-norming sacred text and carefully abstained from introducing their own ideas into it. They accepted it as a datum of tradition."[6] Proposals for emending the Canon have not shown the same modesty. According to B. Botte, they have been arbitrary and have disfigured the text without improving it.[7]

C. Vagaggini provided a good list of the merits and defects of the Roman Canon; his discussion was marked by respect and by calm balance.[8] Yet even today—and this applied both to Vagaggini and to emending proposals—everything depended on the author's theology and taste. But this, we must emphasize, is an impression rather than an argued judgment. The problem was, of course, serious and difficult to solve, precisely because there were no sure historical criteria to which one might try to "emend" the Canon.

B. *Proposals for Reform*
C. Vagaggini reported on two proposed Canon reforms and concluded with his own proposal that the Roman text should be left

unaltered and that a new text should be written on a solid basis of tradition.

The first proposal was that of H. Küng which consisted for practical purposes in a sober effort to shorten the intercessions.[9] After the preface and Sanctus, Küng had the *Te igitur* ("Therefore, most merciful Father") with its petition for the acceptance and blessing of *haec sancta sacrificia illibata* ("these holy and spotless sacrifices"). The remainder of the *Te igitur* was omitted, along with the Memento of the living and the *Communicantes* ("In the unity of holy fellowship") as well as the *Hanc igitur* ("We therefore beg you"), since the prayer for the acceptance of the gifts had already been made. The text thus passed directly to the *Quam oblationem* ("We pray you, O God"). The Canon was left unchanged from this point to the *Supplices te rogamus* ("Humbly we implore you") inclusive. The two prayers for the deceased and for the ministers of the Mass were then omitted, and the Canon ended with the doxology. Küng's plan thus represented an attempt to reorder the Canon by omitting duplications and later additions.

K. Amon's plan was much more radical.[10] It cut out everything between the end of the Sanctus and the beginning of the account of institution. The transition from the Sanctus to the account of institution was made with a short sentence from the *Missale Gothicum:* "Truly holy, truly blessed is our Lord Jesus Christ who dwells in heaven and manifests himself on earth."[11] The account of institution was followed by the unchanged anamnesis and prayer of offering, to which was added the *Communicantes*, slightly modified by the addition of the insert proper to Pentecost.

All this was followed by a prayer for the acceptance of the sacrifice; depending on the liturgical day, this prayer was either the *Te igitur* (for weekdays), the *Quam oblationem* (for Sundays), or the *Hanc igitur* (for special liturgies, such as weddings, baptisms, liturgies for the deceased). After this variable prayer came the *Supplices*, which was offered for those receiving communion and was focused on praise of God (as was the epiclesis in the Anaphora of Hippolytus). If special blessings were to be given, the prayer *Per quem haec omnia* ("It is ever through him") would be used. The whole ended with the doxology.

Furthermore, in order to give the text greater unity, both Küng and Amon omitted the Christological endings (with their Amens[12]) of the various prayers of the Canon.

Let us end with a brief evaluation. Küng's plan simply shortened the text, while Amon's was a complete revision. Amon retained and used the various parts of the Canon, but in different locations; he drew his inspiration from the structure of the Antiochene anaphora. Could the result of such a revision still be called the "Roman Canon"? We think not. At best it might be called a special "development" of the Roman Canon. Clearly, it was no easy matter to reform the Canon,[13] which could not continue to be itself when its most typical traits were eliminated.

Any important change would have transformed the old text into an entirely new one. Once this was realized, it seemed better to compose new texts that could be used as alternatives to the Roman Canon while leaving the latter its age-old identity.

C. Proposals Offered by the Consilium

The plans offered by Küng and Amon are background for the similar work undertaken by the Consilium. This group was not deaf to the appeals being made or indifferent to the proposals being offered in this area of the Church's life; rather it attempted to apply Paul's criterion: "Test everything and approve what is good."

The Consilium drew three plans for altering the Canon. The first, Schema A, kept the text as it now stands but emended it slightly in accordance with the principles of historical and philological criticism. The second, Schema B, retained the structure of the Canon but revised the text in one area: the lists of the saints. The third, Schema C, altered the structure by reorganizing the intercessions.[14]

When the Consilium's plans were set before Pope Paul VI, he replied: "Leave the present Canon unchanged; compose or find two or three anaphoras to be used at special times."[15] As a result, we have new anaphoras in addition to the Roman Canon, which retains its form.

D. Short Historical Overture

Earlier we said that it is difficult to pass judgment on the Canon inasmuch we do not know either its origin or the earlier documents upon which it depended. We do know from Gregory the Great that the Canon was composed by a *scholasticus*[16] after the Roman liturgy had shifted from Greek to Latin, sometime between the third century and the pontificate of Pope Damasus (366–384).[17]

It is important to note that this was also the period of transition from the age of improvization to the age of fixed formularies. In fact, we know some expressions in the Roman Canon that were in place by the end of the fourth century. Ambrosiaster is witness to a phrase (*summus sacerdos tuus Melchisedech*, "your high priest Melchisedech") in the *Supra quae* ("Be pleased to look"), which he tries to correct in accordance with his understanding of the Greek text.[18] He obviously supposes a Greek original, otherwise his argument would prove nothing.

Further testimony comes from the *Liber pontificalis* which tells us that Leo the Great (440–461) added the words *sanctum sacrificium, immaculatam hostiam* ("a holy sacrifice and a spotless victim") which immediately follow the reference to Melchisedech in the *Supra quae*.[19] Finally, it is very likely that the *Communicantes* and the *Nobis quoque* ("To us also"—which supposes the *Memento etiam*, "Remember also, O Lord"), each with a rudimentary litany of the saints, go back to the period before Leo the Great, that is, before 440.[20]

E. Ambrose

The most complete patristic witness to our Canon is in St. Ambrose's little book, *The Sacraments*.[21] The citation dates from about 390 and is not perfectly identical with the Roman Canon; on the other hand, the text is the same with minor variations which are characteristic of a "living" text that is altered somewhat with use.[22] C. Callewaert points out that the differences between the two texts are primarily stylistic. The alterations are due, he suggests, to Pope Gelasius (492–496)[23]; this explains why the Canon has the title *Canon dominicus papae gilasii* (Canon of Pope Gelasius for the Lord's Supper) in the Stowe Missal.[24]

G. Morin offers the likely hypothesis that Ambrose brought the Roman Canon to Milan, moved by his desire to follow Roman custom in all things.[25] This would mean that the *De sacramentis* gives us the Roman Canon in use before the time of Ambrose, and therefore the Canon in an early, developing form, prior to the redaction of the Roman liturgical books which later transmit the same text in a subsequent stage. In fact, when Ambrose cites the words of the Canon, he does not act as if the text was a new one or recently composed; he treats it rather as the customary, well-established text that is authoritative and can be used in his catechetical instructions. We may also note that in his catechesis, Ambrose explains the words of the Canon by means of synonyms which he also derives from tradition.[26] This implies that the test of the Canon was not in a fluid state but was already fixed and regarded as normative: a text that enjoyed reputation and prestige.

All this means that the text in question goes back two generations before Ambrose, since that is the period required for something to be regarded as traditional. In conclusion, therefore, the text of the Canon was already fixed in the first half of the fourth century.

A. Te igitur *("Therefore, most merciful Father")*
The preface and the Sanctus have been discussed earlier. We shall, therefore turn directly to the rest of the Canon.

After the Sanctus, which terminates the logical movement of the preface, the Roman Canon has the *Te igitur*,[27] a prayer which asks for acceptance of the sacrifice and also includes a petition for the Church. These two parts are linked: the second depends on the first inasmuch as the *commendatio*[28] of the sacrifice leads to prayer for those who are its beneficiaries.

God is addressed as *clementissime Pater* ("most merciful Father"), a title which, according to M. Righetti[29] and J. A. Jungmann,[30] is equivalent to the "holy Father" in the opening sentence of the preface. The adjective *clementissimus* ("most merciful") is "an imperial title abundantly attested in the inscriptions."[31] Here it describes the attitude of God, the supreme Lord (*despota* in Greek), toward the weakness and lowliness of his subjects. The attitude of the latter in turn is expressed in *supplices* ("humbly": "we humbly beg and entreat . . .").

Christians ask the Father "to accept and bless these gifts, these offerings, these holy and spotless sacrifices."[32] The three terms ("gifts, offerings, sacrifices") are today regarded as practically synonymous. The original sense, however, is not clear. J. Brinktrine, for example, links the three words to the three *oblata* which *Ordo Romanus* I[33] puts in the hands of the concelebrants,[34] but this interpretation seems forced. Far more attractive is the interpretation given by E. Peterson who sees an exact correspondence between the three Latin terms and the Anaphora of St. Mark, which speaks "of those who offer you sacrifices (*thysias*), offerings (*prosphoras*), and gifts (*eucharisteria*)."[35] The sequence of terms in the Anaphora of Mark is the reverse of what it is in the Roman Canon, but this is not a difficulty. The *dona* ("gifts") would be the offerings for the deceased, the *munera* ("offerings") would be the offerings for the living, and the *sacrificia* ("sacrifices") would be the offerings used directly in the sacrifice.[36]

The sacrifices are called *illibata*, that is, undiminished, unimpaired. The word is not cultic in origin and has nothing to do with libations, a pagan sacrificial rite. It indicates simply that the sacrifices are integral, intact, complete, and in the "good condition" they must be in if they are to be offered to God.[37]

The theme of approval or acceptance of sacrifices is well documented in scripture, beginning with the sacrifice of Abel: "Abel brought of the firstlings of his flock and of their fat portions. And the Lord had regard for Abel and his offering, but for Cain and his offering he had no regard."[38] This text links offerer and offering, and shows how God's acceptance embraces both. There can be no approval of a sacrifice without a simultaneous approval of its offerer. In the sacrificial act as seen by God, offerer and offering are a single reality.

The attacks of the prophets on Israel's cult fit into this picture.[39] Actually, the prophets were not attacking the cult as such, but rather cultic celebrations in which offering and offerer were disjoined, and the integrity or spotlessness of the offering was not matched by an integrity or spotlessness in the offerer.

It is in this perspective that the theological idea of a divine acceptance of sacrifice is to be explained and is helpful. The notion of God "accepting sacrifice" is not a naive anthropomorphism; it is rather an assertion that human beings come before God as what they are and that outward worship or the value of the offerings cannot be substitutes for a right interior attitude. Sacrifice is symbolic of human beings, not a substitute for them; the "spotlessness" of the act of worship or the offering cannot replace the "spotlessness" of the offerer but rather calls for it and makes it necessary.[40]

A prayer that God would accept a sacrifice evidently supposes that he is free to accept or reject. Cultic sacrifice does not put him at the mercy of human beings.

The Old Testament shows a horror of magic because magic means that God is in the power of human beings: certain practices enable them to impose their will on him and thus place them on his level; as a result, he is rendered subject to the human will and becomes helpless, unable to withdraw. According to the Old Testament, however, God is the supreme Lord, and cultic practices do not function as magic. Such a conception of cult would formally contradict the Old Testament concept of God. In the Old Testament, therefore, cult must always respect the freedom, autonomy, and supreme lordship of God.

When offerers pray for acceptance, they are acknowledging that their outward worship is not magical and does not have power to produce its effects automatically. A prayer for acceptance is a solemn proclamation that God is supremely free and remains transcendent even in regard to a cult which he himself has prescribed and which the offerers carry out exactly as ordered.

In all this, we are far removed from present-day theology which is concerned primarily with the real presence of God in cult. A theology of acceptance is concerned rather with the cultic presence of human beings before God. It is for God to decide whether to accept or reject those who come before him in worship.

When offerers ask God to accept their cultic sacrifice, they are saying that they submit to his judgment not only their act of outward worship but their whole lives as well. Far from claiming to impose their wills on him, they submit everything to his judgment, which they acknowledge to be just and true.

Since the New Testament complements the Old, it is inconceivable that the Christian idea of God should be less developed, less accurate, than the idea human beings had of him in the period of the Law and the prophets. And, in fact, the theology of worship that springs from the New Testament is also highly sensitive to the divine transcendence and freedom. Consequently, the prayer for acceptance of the sacrifice that we find in the Christian anaphora is to be interpreted not as a naive anthropomorphism but as an an affirmation of the supreme greatness of God.

In the Roman Canon, God is asked "to bless these offerings."[41] He is asked, therefore, to manifest his acceptance. No offering is in itself worthy of God. By blessing it, he will make it worthy of himself, and the acceptance will then be complete.

The prayer for acceptance leads into an intercession for the Church: "(sacrifices) which we offer you first for your holy Catholic Church, that you may grant her peace and protection, unity and direction throughout the world." Scholars usually find parallels for this text in the earliest prayers of the faithful.[42] There is, in fact, a similarity in literary expression, but a more nuanced approach to the subject is needed.

We may ask: Does this petition spring from the very nature of the anaphora or does it enter the anaphora from outside, that is, from the prayer of the faithful? If we examine the very early anaphoras, it is clear that the intercession for the Church is there from the beginning.[43] The anaphoras have always had an intercession for the Church; it is one of the oldest and most constant components. We thus ignore our basic data if we maintain that the intercessions in the anaphoras were taken over from the prayer of the faithful.

It is true, of course, that from as far back as we have documents which transmit texts for the prayer of the faithful, we can see the latter influencing the anaphora. That is to say that the themes of the prayer of the faithful are taken over in the intercessions of the anaphora, and that the latter at times expand to an exorbitant degree, becoming real duplicates of the prayer of the faithful. To that extent, there is a dependence that is attested with certainty. On the other hand, if we focus on the basic elements in the intercession for the Church in the early anaphoras, we must think it a priori probable that the text of the prayer of the faithful had its origin in the anaphora, and not vice versa.

After this needed clarification, let us return to the point in the Canon at which the celebrant prays to God for the Church; he speaks of the Church as "your holy catholic Church" and displays a moving and profound trust in God. The Church is called "catholic," but not in the modern equivalent to "Roman," nor in the etymological sense of "universal." From the third century on, "catholic" in this context does not mean "universal" but designates only the Great Church and what concerns it, in contrast to the sects; the term thus carries a doctrinal connotation of orthodoxy.[44]

God is asked to give his Church peace, protect it, unify it, and govern it. According to E. Lanne, the primitive text of the Canon had only one verb, *pacificare* (grant peace to), at this point. The other verbs, he thinks, were added only to spell out the implications of "granting peace": God is to unify, protect, and govern. This interpretation is quite justified inasmuch as *pacificare,* whether in the Roman Canon or in the Anaphora of Mark, referred to peace in the biblical sense, that is, the sum total of all divine blessings, including those of the messianic age. The peace in question is above all the peace flowing from salvation in Christ.[45] Admittedly, in the text as we now have it, "peace" no longer conveys its full biblical meaning, since *pacificare* is now only one in a series of complementary verbs. The meaning which the original one verb has lost is now distributed over the entire series of four verbs. The series explains the original *pacificare* and conveys the biblical meaning of "peace" as a synthesis of messianic blessings. It is this that the Canon asks for the Church.

B. Et omnibus orthodoxis (*"And all faithful guardians"*)
"And all faithful guardians of the catholic and apostolic faith." At first sight, the Latin text (*"et omnibus orthodoxis, atque catholicae et apostolicae fidei cultoribus"*) seems to be referring to all the baptized in whom the orthodox faith is embodied (we might then translate:

"and all orthodox believers and fosterers of the catholic and apostolic faith"). That is, in fact, how the earliest commentators (Florus of Lyons, Remigius of Auxerre, Sicard of Cremona, Innocent III, and William Durandus of Mende) interpreted it.[46]

Dom Capelle points out, however, that the only acceptable interpretation is based on a comparison with the texts in parallel liturgies. Such comparison makes it clear that these "fosterers of the orthodox faith" are "the bishops who form a single body with the pope of Rome."[47] It is therefore the entire episcopal body for which intercession is being made here. The prayer thus asks that the Father would grant peace and the fullness of his blessings to the entire Church and therewith to the pope of Rome and to the episcopal college that forms one body with him.

The passage can not be legitimately accused of verticalism, that is, of being interested primarily in the ecclesiastical hierarchy at the expense of due consideration of the faithful. The intent is quite different. The perspective of the prayer can be readily grasped from the words *catholicae et apostolicae cultoribus*. According to B. Botte, this phrase complements the preceding *orthodoxis*.[48] The bishops are *cultores* in the sense that they "apply themselves to" or "have care of"[49] the catholic and apostolic faith. In a prayer for the peace and unity of the Church, it is quite natural to be mindful of those who work for that very goal.

One of the institutional tasks of bishops is the preservation and protection of right faith; this explains the emphasis on "orthodoxy" at this point in the Roman Canon. If the bishops protect and take care of right faith, there will be a oneness in faith, and this will necessarily lead in turn to the unity of the Church itself. This ecclesial unity is a very ancient theme in the intercessions of the anaphora; it may even be said without qualification to be the oldest of all the intercessory themes. Since the unity of the Church is thus the central concern and since the hierarchy is the agent of this unity, it becomes a duty to pray for the hierarchy.

In antiquity, the title "pope" was synonymous with "bishop"; only in the sixth century did Christians reserve the title to the bishop of Rome.[50] Thus, when the Canon in its earliest form prayed for "our pope," it was praying simply for "our bishop" in each locality. Once the word "pope" came to refer exclusively to the bishop of Rome, it became necessary to alter the text of the Canon to keep the required commemoration of the local bishop. At this point, the words *et antistite nostro N.* ("for our bishop N.") were added to *papa nostro* ("for our Pope").[51] This fidelity to the local scene is reflected in the postconciliar rules which order or, as the case may be, permit the commemoration in the Canon not only of the diocesan bishop but also of all those who labor with him in the government of the Church.[52]

C. Memento, Domine ("Remember, O Lord")

The opening words of *Memento, Domine* have a ring of antiquity about them; they have typically been the first words of the intercessions for the Church.[53] The commemoration of the living faithful calls to mind the famous question of the diptychs, which were such a focus of disputes in the East. The inclusion of a name in the diptychs (two-leaved folders containing the list of names) was a public and official recognition of that person's orthodoxy and solidarity with the communion of the Church. The inclusion was, as indicated, an official act. Traces of it are still found in the contemporary Russian Church, where the inclusion of the patriarch's name is a proclamation of the Church's autocephalous status.[54]

The persons for whom prayer is offered are believers whose faith is well known to God. They are called "servants" (*famuli*), a title which in the final analysis connotes a "family" to which a person belongs not as son or daughter nor, on the other hand, as a slave, but as a faithful servant who is loved by the master.[55]

Who, concretely, are the ones who offer this "sacrifice of praise"? They are, first and foremost, the individuals whose names are recited so that we will know who they are. A passage from St. Jerome[56] tells us that this mention of names was a recent custom introduced around the time of his stay in Palestine and unknown to him shortly before when he was living in Rome. His words also make it clear that this part of the Canon is not a general "commemoration of the living" but a specific "commemoration of the offerers."

It is insofar as they are offerers that commemoration is made of the named servants of God, but also of all those around the altar, that is, all the participants in the liturgy. Two interesting identifications are made: to participate means to offer, and the object offered is the sacrifice of praise. The theological definition of the Eucharist as "sacrifice of praise" is profoundly biblical.[57] The participants are who they are, and the phrase "offer this sacrifice of praise" is completed and explained by another Roman phrase: *tibique reddunt vota sua* ("and who now offer their promises to you").[58] M. Righetti points out that this expression is "typical of the language found in pagan inscriptions."[59]

The purposes of the offering are, first, "the redemption of their souls" (*pro redemptione animarum suarum*). The similarity between this phrase and the one used by Jerome makes us think of deliverance from the penalties due for sin or even of deliverance from sin itself through penance for sins committed daily. A second purpose is "the hope of salvation," a phrase that reminds us of 1 Thessalonians 5:8 or, better, Romans 8:24: "In this hope we were saved." The idea of salvation is completed by that of "protection from harm" (*incolumitas*), which brings out the definitive character of the salvation.[60]

We must not be deceived by the words: "For whom we offer, or who themselves offer." They appear in the first half of the ninth century,[61] and the word "or" (*vel*) is rubrical, that is, it points to an alternative: either the offerers are themselves present, or they are absent, in which case the celebrant offers the sacrifice of praise in their stead. The idea that one can profit by the eucharistic celebration without being present and simply by having the celebrating priest express one's intention, is a sign that we are already in a period of decadence for eucharistic theology.

The Old Gelasian Sacramentary, on the occasion of the catechumenal scrutinies, introduces at this point the recitation of the names of the men and women who have accepted the role of godfathers and godmothers for the children being readied for baptism.[62]

A final remark on this prayer of the Canon: it can be said that despite additions made to it, there is a close continuity between it and the *Te igitur* inasmuch as the theme of offering is central to both. In the *Te igitur*, the focus is on the offerers; the result is the ensuing *Memento*. Therefore, as A. Nocent rightly points out, there is no basis for thinking that the intercessions of the Roman Canon underwent undue displacement and thus interfered with the proper development of the prayer.[63]

D. Communicantes (*"In the unity of holy fellowship"*)
According to J. A. Jungmann the *Communicantes* of the Canon resembles in a notable way the Antiochene liturgy of St. James and the Byzantine Anaphora of St. Basil. He concludes from this that it must have been introduced into the Canon at a time when the practice of reading the diptychs was in full flower in the East.[64]

The prayer introduces the theme of the communion of saints into the celebration. The Eucharist celebrates not only communion with God but the communion of the faithful among themselves: a mutual communion based upon and created by their communion with God. It therefore becomes necessary to mention and commemorate the faithful who already experience the glory of the Father and, among them, especially those who were the founders of the local Church or gave special witness to its faith.

It is worth noting that in the words *communicantes* and *memoriam venerantes*, we have two parallel participles (a literal translation brings this out: "sharing in the one holy fellowship" and "venerating the memory"). The coordination shows that venerating the memory of the saints and being in communion with them are activities that imply one another. "Popular religiosity," as it is called, might find a useful corrective here.

Twenty-four saints are named in two groups of twelve: twelve apostles and twelve martyrs. The list is preceded by a commemoration of Mary, Mother of God, who has a place apart and separate from the other names. Her name is followed now by that of St. Joseph, introduced by Pope John XXIII.[65]

In its revision of the Canon, the Consilium thought it opportune to shorten this list of saints, lest it be a hindrance to the vernacular proclamation of the text; only three names, Peter, Paul, and Andrew, have been kept. The others, however, have not been suppressed, and it is always permissible to proclaim the full text of the Canon, provided that pastoral considerations do not suggest following the shortened version.

Finally, even after the postconciliar reform, it remains possible to adapt the *Communicantes* to certain special celebrations[66] by means of a short embolism, or insertion, that brings out the significance of the feast day. Here again we shall limit the discussion, saying only that while it is legitimate to look for this adaptation to the special character of the liturgical day, the propriety of attaching the embolism to the *Communicantes* rather than to some other prayer of the Canon is not clear. But, we do not want to place undue emphasis on this criticism, since the postconciliar reform simply retains preconciliar usage here.[67] That usage can stimulate reflection on ways to introduce similar embolisms in the new eucharistic prayers, provided, of course, that they are suitable and in harmony with the basic theme of the entire anaphora.

E. Hanc igitur (*"We therefore beg you to accept"*)

The *Hanc igitur*, like others, raises many questions. Let us agree with J. A. Jungmann that it is difficult to see why the prayer was introduced at all, since the prayer for acceptance of the sacrifice has already been made and in a rather full way.[68] Jungmann goes on to ask what is specific to this prayer. He finds it in the *commendatio* or recommendation of those for whom the offering is being made.[69]

In any case, the prayer's purpose is to enunciate special intentions. It consists of a framework (the prayer in its ordinary form) and some short embolisms for certain occasions. When the latter are used, the prayer acquires a precise and specific meaning and ceases to appear simply as a generic repetition of the *Te igitur*. The embolisms make it closely resemble the Memento of the living, without however turning it into a duplicate of the latter, since here the embolisms bring out the very purpose of the Eucharist by indicating why and for whom it is being celebrated.

According to the *Liber pontificalis*, Pope Gregory I added the words: "Regulate the days of our lives so that they may be spent in your peace, etc."[70] This would mean that previously the *Hanc igitur* had consisted simply of the opening words (borrowed perhaps from the *Te igitur*) and a reference to the offerers: "our worship and that of your whole household," which closely resemble the corresponding words in the *Unde et memores*.[71] This modest beginning was followed by the embolism with its description of the particular intentions of that celebration. The remainder was contributed by Pope Gregory I,[72] who probably took as his model earlier prayers, such as the *Hanc igitur* of the Mass *in natale episcoporum*, where everything is in the first person singular: "I therefore beg you to accept this oblation which I, your servant and priest, offer to you. . . . Regulate my days with your most merciful governance."[73]

In all probability, the *Hanc igitur* served only to recommend particular intentions and was not yet a fixed part of the Canon; it was used only when it became necessary to announce special intentions. This interpretation is suggested by the fact that the prayer is inserted into the Mass formularies of the Verona Sacramentary, Mass by Mass, and not at the point where we may suppose it had its place in the Canon. Since not all the Masses have a *Hanc igitur*, we may think it was used only in special circumstances.

Whatever be the historical interpretation (an interpretation that remains unsatisfactory due to the paucity of sources), the fact remains that the prayer is meant for special intentions. That is all that can be said about it. If we want to give it a necessary function in present-day celebrations, we can only suggest using it to list the names of those to whose intentions the Mass is being applied. This "application" of the Mass is not to be confused with the remembrance and commemoration of various persons living and dead or with the various intentions being prayed for.

But, even if such a use of the *Hanc igitur* were historically justified, we would still have to ask whether it is in harmony with the spirit and logic of contemporary liturgical reform. If the answer is a decided no, then any suggestion along these lines must be dropped; the historical argument carries no weight, since liturgical reform is never an archeological recovery of the past.

This relatively unimportant question of the *Hanc igitur* helps us see the pastoral difficulties in the continued use of the Roman Canon. We assume, of course, that in our celebrations we want a degree of pastoral truth that is in accord with the historical truth of the prayers.

F. An Epiclesis in the Canon?

In the contemporary reform of the Roman eucharistic prayer, it was decided to have an epiclesis before the account of institution. The epiclesis (invocation) asks for the intervention of the Holy Spirit so that the bread and wine may be sanctified.

The decision applied to the new eucharistic prayers, but, once it was implemented, it could not but raise the question of an epiclesis in the venerable Roman Canon. As a result, the prayer *Quam oblationem* ("We pray you, O God") is commonly regarded as the first epiclesis in the Roman Canon, especially by those who force somewhat the interpretation of the words "to make this offering wholly blessed" so as to read into them a clear allusion to the Spirit.[74] There is no doubt, of course, that such an interpretation is legitimate from the standpoint of the Bible[75]; it remains to be seen whether it is part of the text and thought of the Canon.

The prayer underwent lengthy development and did not always have its present form. Two important witnesses to its previous form have long been known: Ambrose[76] and a *Post pridie* ("after the account of institution") prayer of the Mozarabic liturgy.[77] These texts show that the redactions in Ambrose and in the Mozarabic (more accurately, Old Spanish) liturgy are earlier than that of the Roman Canon; that of Ambrose seems to be the earlier of the two.[78]

The historical problem is relegated to a note; our chief interest here is in the text's evolution. Both the Ambrosian and the Mozarabic redactions show an important variation from the present text. In its present form, the prayer asks that "it [the offering] may become for us the Body and Blood," whereas the older prayers ask

68

that it may become what is expressed in three predicates (Ambrose: "approved, spiritual, acceptable"; Mozarabic liturgy: "blessed, approved, and spiritual"), since it is already the *figura* (Ambrose) or the *imago et similitudo* (Mozarabic liturgy) of the body and blood of our Lord.

As we know, *figura, imago,* and *similitudo* are classical terms for sacramentality in the very early Church and are thus the equivalents of our *sacramentum*.[79] But, if it is right to note the equivalence, it is also right to note the difference. That earlier terminology, now unfortunately forgotten, had its place within a specific sacramental theology: a theology of "mimesis" and "imitation," also known as a theology of "analogy." Let us explain.

According to that earlier theology, the sacramental character of the action being performed depends on the fact that what we do now is a copy,[80] image, and likeness of what Jesus did in the upper room and of what he commanded his disciples to do in his memory. Since he commanded us to repeat that final meal which he had just celebrated with his disciples, it follows that what we do in obedience to his command is a likeness, image, and figure of what he himself had done, that is, of the Last Supper.

This theology is older than our present theology of transubstantiation; it is even older than the patristic theology of the anamnesis of the Lord's death and resurrection. The theology of transubstantiation bypasses both middle terms, that is, "Last Supper" and "death and resurrection." The theology of anamnesis bypasses only "Last Supper" and highlights "death and resurrection." The theology of figure and image, on the other hand, takes the Lord's final meal as the starting point for everything else, and bypasses nothing, since it gives full emphasis to both middle terms: "Last Supper" and "death and resurrection."

We shall show in chap. 9 how the ontological content of the Last Supper is the death and resurrection of the Lord. Here we take that assertion as proved. If such is the content of the Last Supper, our Mass must be identical with the Supper, for otherwise it cannot possess the content of the Supper. If our Mass "is," ontologically, the Lord's Supper, its ontological content will be the same as that of the Supper, namely, the death and resurrection of the Lord. On the other hand, if the Mass is simply an external representational imitation of the Supper and is not ontologically the meal which the Lord celebrated in the upper room, how can it have the same ontological content as the latter?

We can see now why the theology of imitation is important. In speaking of it, we are not simply indulging in nostalgic evocation of an abandoned, archaic theology. Rather, it provides a necessary datum for understanding our Eucharist. The sacramental celebration of the Eucharist is a carrying out of the Lord's manifested will; because we do what he did, the sacrament exists. From this standpoint, the sacrament falls into the category of "following." This identity between Mass and Supper is not to be confused with the sacramentality of the Supper in relation to the cross. The two relations are of a different kind, even if both are ontological. Both the Mass-Supper relation and the Supper-cross (and consequent Mass-cross) relation belong to the ontological order and must be expressed accordingly.

The difficulty we have in describing this process is because we have only one theological category, that of sacramentality, which is also expressed in the term "real presence." When applied to one kind of relation, this theological category proves no longer capable of being aptly applied to the other; as a result, the Mass-Supper relation is reduced to a secondary position.

Both the Ambrose and the Mozarabic texts represent the older kind of thinking: they state that the bread and wine are already a *figura* (or sacrament) of the body and blood of Christ since we are celebrating his Supper in obedience to his command. This is the basic datum. At this point in the celebration, the texts then ask the Father that, precisely because of this sacramental presence, the offering may be accepted and spiritual.

The *Quam oblationem* of Ambrose is not, any more than the corresponding Spanish prayer, a consecratory epiclesis in the modern understanding of this term. If we are doing what Jesus told us to do, our bread and wine are the sacrament, the "figure" and "image" of the body and blood of Christ, that is, they are his body and blood. These older prayers do not ask for the consecration, but rather suppose it to have already come about by reason of the mimesis of the Last Supper, if we may be permitted thus to project our modern terminology into those sources.[81] The request in the *Quam oblationem* is not for the consecration of the gifts but for their acceptance; it is concerned with the same *commendatio sacrificii*[82] that has already been made but that is repeated here under a different title. The new element is the motivation. The *Quam oblationem* of those older sources asks the Father to accept our offering because it is already the sacrament of the body and blood of Christ; there is no concern with how and why the bread and wine have become the sacrament that they now are. Everything is left implicit—yet clear—in the con-

70

cept of *imago et figura*. Because the bread and wine have become the body and blood of Christ, the Father is asked to bless, ratify, and accept them.

The text in Ambrose and the Old Spanish liturgy is extremely logical and consistent. Once the theology of the *imago and similitudo* had disappeared, however, and once the Roman liturgy changed the text to its present form, it became much less logical and consistent. The approach of Ambrose and the Mozarabic liturgy was dropped, and the prayer was made to include a formal request for consecration. The earlier clause: "because it is the body and blood of our Lord Jesus Christ," now became: "so that it may become for us the body and blood of your most beloved Son, our Lord Jesus Christ."

The substitution, however, is not as harsh as a simple comparison of the two texts would suggest. An important nuance of the new text must be noted: the prayer does not ask directly for the transformation of the bread and wine into the Lord's body and blood. Rather, what is directly and formally requested is that the offering may be blessed, accepted (rather than "consecrated": *adscriptam*, not *consecratam*), approved, made reasonable and acceptable. That is the petition. It is by hearing and granting it that the Father transforms the offerings into the body and blood of his Son.

Summing up on the genesis of our present text, we would say that in theological evolution a real inversion occurred. In the older text, the Father was asked to bless, ratify, and accept because the bread and wine are the sacrament of the Lord's body and blood. In the later text—our text—he is asked to bless, ratify, and accept in order that the bread and wine may become the sacrament of Christ's body and blood.

This digression was necessary to make clear how the epicletic-consecratory prayer of the Roman Canon came into existence. After Ambrose and his remarks on the words of consecration,[83] the older text became meaningless and was replaced by the present *Quam oblationem*. According to the latter, the offering has to be "blessed, accepted, approved, and made reasonable and acceptable" to become (*ut fiat*) the Lord's body and blood.

To be completely accurate, not even the present-day *Quam oblationem* (i.e., the Latin prayer in the Canon) is a true and proper consecratory epiclesis. Moreover, as indicated, the text did not envisage such a purpose. In some translations, however, such as the Italian, the complexity of the Latin text disappears and the *Quam oblationem* becomes a prayer that parallels the first epiclesis in the new anaphoras produced by the liturgical reform of 1969.[84] The word *benedictam* is expanded into an epicletic phrase ("by the power of your blessing"),[85] whereas in the Latin text, it is simply one of five predicates that are all on the same level. If any of the five is given preeminence there, it is *rationabilem*.

The word *rationabilis* has a long history which we shall briefly summarize. The word was based on the Greek *logikos* and entered into the Christian vocabulary via the ancient translations of the Bible. Both in 1 Peter 2:2 and in Romans 12:1, it retains its Greek meaning: "spiritual." Dom Botte points out that this meaning was at least alien to Latin usage and that it therefore disappeared quickly.[86] The word itself, however, did not disappear. Its use continued in classical philosophy and jurisprudence, but with the meaning it has even today: "reasonable," "in conformity with reason."

What does *rationabilis* mean in the text of the Canon? In the *Quam oblationem* in Ambrose's *The Sacraments*, the word still has its biblical meaning and can readily be translated as "spiritual." But is our text of the Canon still to be read as that of Ambrose? It has in fact evolved, as we just saw, but the liturgy is extremely conservative and, once it has accepted a word's meaning, is loath to be rid of it simply because it is now outmoded, archaic, not understood in its original meaning. An example would be the use by the anaphoras of the Greek title *Pais* for Christ, even after Christology had abandoned it for good.

In his analysis, Dom Botte points out that in the present *Quam oblationem*, the word *rationabilem* is accompanied by *acceptabilemque* and that in the Canon the particle *-que* combines two and only two terms.[87] *Acceptabilis* is a typical sacrificial word and, since it is so closely associated with *rationabilis*, we are compelled to assign a sacrificial meaning to it as well. The conclusion is obvious: there is only one way of giving *rationabilis* a sacrificial meaning, and that is by translating it as "spiritual."[88] When we do, we have a rather clear allusion to Malachi 1:11, a classical text which links the divine acceptance of sacrifice to the theme of the spiritual sacrifice that is offered to God from one end of the earth to the other.[89]

G. Acceptance of the Sacrifice

One of the fundamental ideas and problems in the Old Testament theology of sacrifice is that the value and effectiveness of any sacrifice[90] depend on its being accepted by God. Behind this in turn is the idea that the acceptance of a gift entails a favorable attitude to the giver.[91]

The concept of the divine acceptance of sacrifice is closely bound up with the concept of "expiation" (*kipper*), even though acceptance and expiation are two quite distinct realities, as is suggested by the fact that while "acceptance" occurs almost forty times in the Priestly Document, it is used only once for a sin or guilt offering.[92] The notion of "acceptance" derives from the ancient expression "pleasing odor of sacrifice," which in the Gilgamesh epic has a literal, anthropomorphic meaning. In the Old Testament, the concept takes on a more spiritual meaning, the exact scope of which is not easy to determine.

The first point about the concept is that its meaning, though close to that of *kipper* ("propitiation, placation"), is not identical with it. The second point, brought out by R. J. Daly, is of interest: "sweet [= pleasing] odor" is not an objective quality inherent in the sacrifice and resulting from complete obedience to and perfect execution of the rules God set down for sacrifice. It indicates rather a quality in the sacrifice that God alone can perceive and judge.[93] He alone judges the acceptableness or nonacceptableness of a sacrifice. Acceptance is a sovereignly free act on his part, even though at the same time sacrifice is thought of as efficacious in the sense that it has an effect on him.[94] The theology of acceptance flows from these two opposed viewpoints, the opposition finding a rational solution in the statement in Genesis 4:4–7, which enunciates the criterion according to which God freely accepts sacrifice: "If you do well, will you not be accepted?"[95]

The explanation is simple: when a sacrifice is pleasing, the offerer is pleasing; but if the offerer is displeasing by reason of his wicked behavior, how can his sacrifice be pleasing? In other words, God cannot "accept" a sacrifice while ignoring the offerer's manner of life. What is lacking in the life of the offerer cannot be supplied by a sacrifice.

We have been speaking thus far of the theology of "acceptance" of sacrifice in the Old Testament. Let us turn now to the Canon of the Mass. We know that Christ was a fragrant offering that pleased God[96] and that consequently, since the Eucharist is a memorial of the sacrifice of Christ, it too must always be accepted by God. How could the memorial of Christ the Lord not be acceptable to God? And indeed, this memorial is, in itself, always acceptable. But it does not exist simply in itself or as such. It exists insofar as it is celebrated and it is inseparable from its celebrant. Consequently, the problem of acceptance arises in connection with the eucharistic sacrifice no less and no differently than it did for the theologians of the Bible in connection with the sacrifices of the Old Testament.

The persistent emphasis on this theme in the Canon shows how concerned the Roman liturgy is, like the men and women of today, with continuity and coherence between cult and life.[97] The theological theme of the acceptability of sacrifice should also make us more sensitive to the criticisms of nonbelievers and nonpracticioners who are scandalized when Christians do not carry over into their lives what they proclaim and celebrate in the eucharistic sacrifice. The discrepancy between liturgy and life is as much a cause of scandal to others as it is the reason why God does not "accept" our sacrifices.[98]

H. Anamnesis

Before the reform of 1969, the anamnesis in the Roman tradition used only three points of reference in specifying the mystery celebrated in the Eucharist: "the blessed passion, the resurrection from the dead, and the glorious ascension into heaven." Now, however, two of the three new anaphoras in the Missal of Paul VI contain an eschatological reference as well; that is, they mention the final coming of Christ.

The Roman Canon has rightly been left as it was. It continues to have its three classical referents[99] which, it may be said, sum up the kerygma that those who participate in the Eucharist of the Roman Church are to apply in their lives. The anamnesis is, in its own way, a profession of faith, and so explicit a one that it has at times been assimilated to the creed and therefore been amplified. Such is the case, for example, in the Greek Anaphora of James.[100]

We are not implying that the reformed Roman liturgy should accept and approve that kind of development (which perhaps exemplifies liturgical involution rather than liturgical evolution). We mention it simply as a reminder that participation in the Eucharist requires a formed faith which, in the Roman Church, finds expression in an explicit profession of faith in the blessed passion, resurrection from the dead, and glorious ascension of Christ, God's Son and our Lord. These are the three principal elements in the kerygma that has shaped the Roman eucharistic tradition. (We call your attention, in a note, that the theme of the nativity has had little influence in either the West or the East.[101])

Every eucharistic anamnesis begins with a conjunction indicating a conclusion; in the Roman Canon and in the Second Eucharistic Prayer, it is *unde* (wherefore), in the Third and Fourth Eucharistic Prayers, *igitur* (therefore). The words can be translated in various ways; the importance is the theology of the anamnesis.

The anamnesis begins with a "wherefore" or "therefore" to show that what is said and done in it depends on a preceding statement, namely, "Do this in memory of me." If the anamnesis is a conclusion or at least a consecutive proposition,[102] we should respect its dependent character and keep it closely connected with its dependent statement: the commandment of Christ that established the Church's celebration. We are not consoled at seeing translations which alter[103] a liturgical tradition that has always been followed in all the Churches (even those separated from Rome by communion) and in all the principal translations into the vernaculars.

It is easy to define the purpose of this part of the Canon, but less easy to shed light on its historical origin. In the anamnesis, the Church tells us the nature of the celebration in progress. It tells us that the rite is being celebrated in obedience to the Lord's word. It also gives an interesting interpretation of that word, since while Christ said: "in memory of me," the Church says: "in memory of the passion, resurrection, and ascension." In other words, it renders more explicit the "me" of the Lord's command: "in memory of me who have suffered, risen, and ascended into heaven."

In his mandate, then, the Lord bids us commemorate his person, and the Church obeys by commemorating his history. There is, however, no opposition between the two; the Church commemorates the Lord's history because it is in the events of this history that he manifested all the aspects and dimensions of his being and became an object of faith for other human beings. In consequence, we can proclaim our faith and message only by describing the key events which showed him to be Son of God and our Lord and savior.

In the anamnesis, the Church tells God what it is doing, why it does it, and what the object is of its commemorative action. And in telling him all this, the Church itself becomes conscious of it. The anamnesis is the moment in which the Mass defines itself,[104] and it does so through the text of the celebration. It follows that any correct theology must find here the elements for a proper approach to the problem.[105]

This text also tells us who is the agent of the celebration: "We, your servants and your holy people." The ministers and the holy people form a single "we," a single celebrating subject: "We," the Church. This consciousness of unity, so clear at the liturgical level, is not as clear and not as much respected in the extraliturgical life of the Church, where the distinction between clergy and laity turns into a real tension and sometimes an opposition. In the Roman Canon, which is a model for ecclesiology, the distinction is mentioned but simultaneously overcome in this splendid "we," which points to a single subject of the celebration in all its parts: commemorating, offering, petitioning, remembering, thanking, and giving honor and glory. Not one action of the anaphora is assigned strictly to the celebrating "priest"; the entire celebration has a single active subject: "we."

Theologians teach, indeed, that the priest alone consecrates the bread and wine of the Mass.[106] But, without going into this, we must point out that the consecratory action is not mentioned in the Canon as peculiar to the priest. His special role is not excluded but neither is it mentioned. We repeat: all the verbs for actions accomplished during the anaphora have but one subject: the "we" that is the entire Church. The Church as a whole is seen as the celebrating assembly. "Assembly" does not mean "laity" as opposed to "clergy" (or, more accurately, presiding priest), since even the president is a member of the assembly; he is such by a double title: as a baptized person who must, like every other believer, participate actively and fruitfully in the liturgy, and as a *sacerdos* (priest) who exercises presidency. Without his presidential activity, we would not have an assembly at all; he is, therefore, not simply one member among others, but an essential member whom the very nature of the assembly requires. If, then, the president is necessary for the assembly to exist, how can there by any opposition between him and it? If the assembly is always hierarchically structured, how can we set it over against the hierarchy? The name "Church" rightfully belongs to the hierarchically structured assembly[107]; how, then, can we oppose Church and hierarchy?

We can legitimately say, therefore, that the entire Church celebrates the liturgical action. This statement is not a novelty but a doctrine taught from the beginning. The innovation, the doctrine that is alien to the Church's tradition, is the doctrine that the presiding priest alone is celebrant of the eucharistic mystery.[108] We are denying a qualitative difference between the ministerial priesthood with its presidential role and the priesthood common to all of the baptized; to preside and to be presided over are not the same thing. Moreover, since the Church is the place where the Holy Spirit flourishes,[109] presidency of the assembly comes only through a gift of the Spirit, a gift directly connected with the laying on of hands.

76

The adjectives describing the mystery of Christ in the anamnesis deserve special attention. This is especially true of *beata* (blessed) that is applied to the passion. This description certainly does not harmonize with the spirituality of the *Devotio moderna*,[110] which still plays too large a part in devotional life and which the Canon urges us to transcend.

The offering of the gifts is closely connected with the movement of anamnesis. In the Latin text, "offer" (*offerimus*) is the main verb; its active subject is the "we" who "call to mind."[111] It is not said that the "we" who celebrate perform an action of remembrance; the remembering is not an action which is accomplished and done with, but a state of being.

The text strongly emphasizes that what is offered is not really ours in the sense that we are its source. If anything can be called "ours," it is only because God has put it into our hands. A short passage in Irenaeus comes very close to this idea of the Canon: "We offer him what is his. . . . We do not make offering to him as to someone in need, but rather in order to thank him by means of his own gifts and to sanctify creation."[112]

This same idea was deeply rooted in the Hebrew religious consciousness and passed from there into the Christian liturgies, which use the familiar formula of the Roman Canon, or some comparable formula: "We . . . offer to your supreme majesty, of the gifts you have bestowed on us. . . ."[113]

The source of these words is well known because it is scriptural: "But who am I, and what is my people, that we should be able thus to offer willingly? For all things come from thee, and of thy own have we given thee."[114] This text places our ability to offer in its proper light. We cannot offer God anything that is not already completely in his power; human beings are well aware of this, and yet, as though compelled by some inevitable law of religious psychology, they continually try to express themselves to him in gifts. Gratitude is the only thing we can really offer and is our spontaneous response to his free gift of salvation. That response goes by the Greek name *eucharistia* and finds its highest celebrative expression in the eucharistic meal which the Lord has left us as the summation and supreme embodiment of our relationship with the Father in Christ. It is neither by mistake nor by equivocation that the bread and wine are said to be "eucharistified" and thereby to become "the Eucharist." It is here that we understand why they are the objects of the verb "offer."

The Church offers the holy gifts to God's "supreme majesty." We tend to ask whether the title "majesty" was due to the influence of the imperial court and is therefore alien to our religious outlook. Dom Botte has asked the same question and reached a negative answer.[115] Limiting himself to the New Testament and the Psalms, he finds *maiestas* occurring fifteen times; in thirteen instances, it translates the Greek *doxa* (Latin: *gloria*), understood not at the praise which God receives from his creatures, but as the greatness he possesses in himself. The ultimate referent is the Hebrew *kabod*, which the early Latin Bibles translated as *claritas, gloria,* or *honor,* and the early European versions as *maiestas*.[116] The modern rediscovery of the scriptures and especially the extensive use of the lectionary in liturgical celebrations have familiarized the ordinary Christian with the use of certain biblical words, even if these are somewhat difficult. "Glory" is one of these: it means the divine greatness that is revealed to human beings and acknowledged and celebrated by them.

"Glory," rather than the literal but less meaningful "majesty," is perhaps the word that might best be used in translating the Latin *maiestati*. The Latin underscores the divine transcendence to the point of turning it into an impersonal force and grandeur that can only with difficulty be addressed as "Father." We suggest "splendor of your glory" as a translation of *praeclara maiestas tua*. (ICEL: "we offer to you, God of glory and majesty, this holy and perfect sacrifice: the bread of life and the cup of eternal salvation.")

The gift offered is described as "a perfect, holy, and unblemished victim." If the sacrifice is to be accepted by God, it must meet certain standards which God has established; the first requirement is that it be according to the will of God. The ritual purity demanded of sacrifices under the old law is typologically verified in the "victim" used in the eucharistic sacrifice, namely, the sacramental bread and wine. The purity of this victim transcends mere ritual execution, as is clear from the short passage cited earlier from Irenaeus. According to a modern editor, Irenaeus "views the Eucharist from the standpoint of antignostic polemics and, more specifically, in function of the gnostic thesis which rejects matter as evil and doomed to destruction."[117]

But the three attributes of the victim—perfect, holy, and unblemished[118]—are not fully intelligible if we consider them simply as referring to the victim or gift offered. We must bear in mind that in the Old Testament such attributes applied not only to the victim but to the sacrifice itself, that is, the sacrificial act, as well. Victim and sacrifice are, moreover, always to a certain extent equivalent or interchangeable in the Old Testament.

In like manner, the text of the Canon will become clearer if we take the three attributes as referring to the *hostia* or "victim" in the two senses of the term: "victim" as meaning "sacrifice" and "victim" as meaning the bread and wine when seen in light of the special theological concern manifested in the above cited passage from Irenaeus. In other words, the three attributes apply not only to the sacrificial act but to the material of sacrifice as well.

But is "victim" a suitable translation? It seems not. This "victim," after all, is immediately described as "the sacred bread of everlasting life and the chalice of eternal salvation." In everyday speech, even for a person with some education, it is difficult to understand how bread and chalice are a "victim" or of what they are a victim. It would be preferable, therefore, to translate *hostia* as "sacrifice" or even "worship and sacrifice,"[119] or something similar.

This passage of the Canon embodies an almost unrecognizable development of the ancient theology of sacrifice as seen in the prophecy of Malachi 1:11. The text has undergone an evolution in which its original tenor has practically been lost, although it is still visible when set alongside parallel texts. Once again, these textual difficulties make the Roman Canon a difficult prayer; when used in the eucharistic liturgy, they do not yield an immediate understanding of the mystery being celebrated.

You may be perplexed by our discussion of the word *hostia*. After all, when you read or hear the term "victim" applied to the bread and wine, your thoughts move in a different direction: you think of the bread and wine as consecrated and therefore as the body and blood of the Lord. "Victim" certainly applies to the dead Lord on the cross; therefore the problems we have raised are pointless.

True—but not entirely true, for this spontaneous interpretation requires a notable forcing of the text. In the latter, the victim is immediately identified as the sacred bread and the chalice of salvation, that is, the sacrament in its entirety and not simply the content of the sacrament. We can, of course, always say that Christ is the victim who brings salvation; we cannot, however, say that the sacrament of his body and blood is a sacrificed victim.

I. Prayer for Acceptance
The anamnesis is followed by a new prayer for acceptance of the sacrifice: God is asked to look upon our offering[120] with graciousness

and kindness. In the Old Testament, such a petition is a request for the acceptance of the sacrifice,[121] and, in fact, the Canon immediately introduces, as a motive for God's graciousness, a comparison with three Old Testament sacrifices that he found especially pleasing: the sacrifices of Abel, Abraham, and Melchizedek.

The sacrifices of these three serve as exemplars; they are the classical instances of sacrifice acceptable to God, and therefore models of what our sacrifice should be. But here the reference is to the personages as such and not to the particular rites or sacrificial customs which they may have practiced. Abel is described as "just" by Jesus himself (Mt 23:35). Abraham is the father of all believers.[122] Melchizedek is evidence of the universality of God's saving plan which embraces even those not of the Hebrew nation.[123] The three names thus reinforce the idea that divine acceptance of sacrifice does not depend on the logic of the rite but on the quality of the offerer. It is as exemplary offerers that the three are presented to us. But in these three names, there is something more, something deeper.

Although the Bible begins with the story of the creation, the story of salvation proper begins with Abraham.[124] "Abraham" even becomes a term descriptive of God, for God is the "God of Abraham, of Isaac, and of Jacob." The sacrifice offered by Abraham marks the beginning of the history of salvation as a history of sacrifice. His sacrifice was commemorated during the great Easter vigil, and Isaac was seen as an image of Christ.

This brings us, of course, into the world of typology. The sacrifice of Abraham is a prophecy of the sacrifice of Christ. Abel is an image of the sacrificed Christ, who was just beyond all other human beings and was put to death because of his justice. In the Letter to the Hebrews, Melchizedek illustrates the insufficiency of the ancient sacrifices and the perfection of the new sacrifice of Christ.[125] Melchizedek's sacrifice shows that the ancient sacrifices, even when acceptable to God, derived their value from the fact that they prefigured and prophesied the sacrifice of Christ.[126]

One inference is clear: If our sacrifice is acceptable to God, as were the sacrifices of Abel, Abraham, and Melchizedek, it is always because of its relation to the sacrifice of Christ. Henceforth, "acceptance" by the Father is inseparable from our being "in Christ."[127]

This first prayer of acceptance, the *Supra quae* ("Be pleased to look"), ends with words added by Pope Leo I.[128] They describe the sacrifice of Melchizedek, emphasizing its relation to the Eucharist[129]: "a holy sacrifice and a spotless victim."[130]

The *Supra quae* is followed by the *Supplices* ("Humbly we implore you"), which serves as its logical continuation. In fact, in the Canon cited by Ambrose,[131] there is no distinction between the two prayers; moreover, the mention of the three Old Testament sacrifices is connected there with the angelic mediation which is now part of the *Supplices*.

The *Supplices* is undeniably a difficult prayer. A first difficulty is that at different stages in the text's evolution the singular and the plural are used of the angelic ministry. Ambrose has the plural "your angels." Our Canon, on the contrary, has the singular "your holy angel," which, in view of the antiquity of the theme, could very well refer to Christ or the Holy Spirit. (As you may know, Judeo-Christian theology used angelology to express the mystery of the Trinity.[132])

Such a Christological or trinitarian explanation of "your holy angel" initially attracted Dom Botte, but there are serious considerations that finally persuaded him, and persuade us now, that such an explanation is not practicable.[133] Dom Botte offers three reasons for rejecting it: (1) the oldest text is in the *De sacramentis* which has the plural (*angelorum*) and therefore cannot refer to Christ or the Spirit. (2) The text in the *De sacramentis* is earlier than texts in the Egyptian liturgy, even where the two are parallel.[134] (3) Finally, it is fairly common in archaic texts to find the angels intervening in the eucharistic celebration.[135] We conclude with Dom Botte that the plural in Ambrose refers to real angels and not to Christ or the Spirit, although this whole question remains open to further discussion.

These angels or, in our text of the Canon, this angel exercises a mediatorial function in worship. What is the nature of this mediation? To begin with, there is no difficulty about angels exercising such a role, since in scripture God appears surrounded by countless angels (Dn 7) who are his army, his council, his court, and his household. "They intercede with God, especially Michael. They convey prayers from all the synagogues to God, and set them like crowns upon His head."[136]

The function of the angel in question is described in a slightly different but more enlightening way in the Mozarabic liturgy, where we find a prayer that is parallel to our *Supplices* but more archaic in form and closer to the *De sacramentis*.[137] The text brings out the cultic function of the angel, showing it to be like that described in the Apocalypse, where we read: "And another angel came and stood at the altar with a golden censer; and he was given much incense to mingle with the prayers of all the saints upon the golden altar before the throne; and the smoke of the incense rose with the prayers of the saints from the hand of the angel before God."[138]

Tobit 12:12 also bears witness to the mediatorial function of the angels in prayer to God.[139] Since the Psalms, too, liken prayer to sweet-smelling incense that rises to God,[140] it is not difficult to see how the angels, or an angel, acquired a function in the eucharistic sacrifice.

We ought also to keep in mind that persons possessing a profound sense of the divine transcendence find it difficult to think of direct contact with God; they prefer to have suitable mediators. The very concept of "angel" as mediator between God and human beings or even among human beings very nicely solves the problem.

"The essential function of the *mal'akim* (*angeli*) is to bridge a spatial distance and carry out a task, as is clear from passages that tell of the mission of God's messengers. . . . The *mal'akim* are closely linked to the one who commissions them; from him they receive full authority so that they can speak or act in his name; the one who sent them speaks and acts through them. For this reason the *mal'akim* are identified with him."[141]

It is difficult for human beings to face the fact that their every action is in the sight of God; they prefer to think that there is always an intermediary, who in this case is an angel. But such an outlook entails risks, and we find Jewish teachers already warning: "When a man is in danger or in need let him not invoke Michael or Gabriel but me alone, and I will hear him."[142]

It would be difficult to go further and specify in greater detail the mediation exercised by the angels in the eucharistic action. We would simply find ourselves repeating the idea of angelic mediation as a very strong way of emphasizing the divine transcendence.

The *Supplices* also supposes a clear awareness of a heavenly liturgy and that it is performed by the angels around an altar. Nor would the mere reading of the Apocalypse have given rise to a conviction so strong that it became an element in the anaphora. On the contrary, we are in the presence of a real current of thought (which is not easy to pin down historically) of which Irenaeus, among others, is a representative: "There is therefore an altar in heaven; it is to it that our prayers and offerings (*oblationes*) are directed."[143]

The purpose of the angelic intervention is to give our celebration the fruitfulness described in 1 Corinthians 10:18: Those who eat of the victims become participants in the altar. We participate in the heavenly altar because we eat the body and blood of the Son of

God. But that participation would not be possible if the angel or angels had not carried the victim from our altar to the heavenly altar.

In summary, our celebration is seen as a sharing in the angelic liturgy that goes on in heaven around the heavenly altar. A "theology of the Sanctus" is already at work in this prayer, even before the time when the Sanctus was introduced into the anaphora. This theology works with an idea of sacrifice and of eucharistic communion described with the aid of 1 Corinthians 10:18 (a principle valid for Jewish as well as pagan sacrifices) and not of 1 Corinthians 10:16–17, which contains a specifically Pauline view.

Let us raise the question, finally, of the relation between the Last Supper of Jesus and the heavenly liturgy. Jesus said: "Do this in memory of me." What is the relation between this command, its execution, and participation in the heavenly liturgy? If the liturgy of human beings is an imitation of and participation in the heavenly liturgy through the mediation of an angel, how can we say that the Last Supper plays the determining role? The heavenly liturgy or the Last Supper of the Lord Jesus: which of the two is the archetypal celebration that serves as model and point of reference for the Church's Eucharist?

The answer is obvious. We would not say, however, that the theology behind the *Supplices* is of no interest for the spiritual life. We believe that this particular theology of the Roman Canon can serve as a useful corrective to the absence of the eschatological theme in present-day Christianity.

Of particular interest are the final words of the *Supplices*, which ask for the fruits of communion: "that those of us who . . . receive . . . may be filled with every grace and heavenly blessing." "Grace and heavenly blessing" are almost certainly a translation of the biblical "peace." Nonetheless, the words as they stand give the impression that we are already in the period when participation in the Eucharist is seen as a means of obtaining one or other kind of grace according to need. But the archaic character of the text bids the scholar be prudent, and therefore we would say that that kind of thinking had not as yet entered into the Canon and was still a remote, though real, danger.[144]

J. Commemoration of the Dead

Two commemorations signal that the Canon is nearing its end. The first is of the dead, the second is of the ministers of the present liturgy.

The Memento or commemoration of the dead is, or at least appears to be, a late composition. It is absent from the Gelasian and Gregorian traditions. According to Dom Botte, Alcuin found it in the Irish tradition (see the Bobbio Missal, considered to be from the eighth century) and introduced it into the Canon.[145] The Memento of the dead was not originally part of the Canon because, again according to Botte, mention of the dead was not made in all Masses but only in those celebrated on their behalf at their burial or anniversary. As a result, the *Nobis quoque peccatoribus* ("To us also") followed directly upon the *Supplices*.[146] When the bishops and abbots of the Lyons province of Gaul met in council at Chalons-sur-Saône in 813, they decided that intercession should be made for the dead in all Masses without exception.[147]

The historical problem of the genesis of the Memento is too complicated to go into; it would require an excursion into comparative liturgy, and that is not possible in the present book. We refer you to the works of Righetti and Jungmann, although they must be read with caution, since they deal only with the current texts, and prescind from their origin and evolution. The reading they give of the Canon is primarily synchronic; only rarely do they make the diachronic perspective a hermeneutical criterion.

The "sign of faith" with which the dead have gone before us is baptism,[148] and the "sleep of peace" is the sleep of death which does not interrupt the communion of the dead with the Church. Even in the sleep of death, the deceased continue in communion with the Church, provided they enjoyed that communion when they died; they now "rest in Christ," and their state is one of "peace."[149] We pray that the Lord will give them "comfort, light, and peace."

K. Nobis quoque peccatoribus *("To us also")*
The second of the commemorations is an intercession for "us, your sinful servants." We immediately want to know who these sinners are for whom we are praying. Is the entire congregation being spoken of as sinful, or does *famuli* (servants) have a narrow sense, referring only to the presiding priest and concelebrants, along with the deacons and subordinate ministers?

The question is not the easiest to answer, but Jungmann has shed a great deal of light on the problem. In itself, *famulus* can refer to any baptized person; if that is the sense here, then "we sinners" are the entire congregation.

"But amongst all the designations for the congregation represented by the priest in prayer—we possess thousands of examples in the sacramentaries—this would be the only case of the kind. On the contrary, *peccator* had been used as a term of self-designation, especially as the self-designation of the clergy. . . . For centuries, it was the practice in clerical circles to add the word *peccator* to one's signature. Therefore here, too, the clergy must be meant by the *peccatores famuli*—the celebrating priest and his assistants."[150]

Jungmann adds that in this case *quoque* is to be understood not as "also" but as "and especially."[151]

What we have, then, is a prayer of intercession for the community's ministers, who feel the weight of their own sinfulness and therefore of their inadequacy and insufficiency for the function they must undertake. The expression of this awareness on the part of the ministers is not peculiar to the Roman Canon.[152] We need only turn, for example, to the Anaphora of the Apostles Addai and Mari in its Eastern Syrian or Chaldean recension, where an intercession for the celebrating priest is inserted in almost every prayer of the anaphora.[153] We do not want to lay too much stress on the similarity, however, since a comparison of this anaphora with its parallel, the Third Maronite Anaphora of St. Peter the Apostle,[154] shows that these intercessions for the priest are late additions (but not fully identifiable with the *apologiae*—"apologies," i.e., avowals of guilt and unworthiness—of the Roman liturgy).

A good parallel to this prayer of the Canon is found in the anaphora in the eighth book of the *Apostolic Constitutions:* "We pray to you for myself, the humble celebrant who presents the offering to you, for the whole college of priests, for the deacons, for all the clergy. Teach them wisdom, fill them with the Holy Spirit."[155]

Another passage that is even more relevant, as well as being closer to the Roman Canon from a literary standpoint, is from the Anaphora of St. Mark: "Be mindful also, Lord, of us sinners, your unworthy servants, and, being a good and kindly (*philanthropos*) God, wipe away our sins. Be mindful also, Lord, of me, a poor sinner and your unworthy servant."[156]

To this human sinfulness is opposed the great trust which these ministers have in the infinite mercy of God. This is a moving trait of our Canon and should be a source of helpful suggestions in our pastoral ministry of penance.

The ministers who are here acknowledging their own sinfulness offer a special plea: "Grant fellowship and a place with your holy apostles and martyrs." The language is classical and familiar; it can be found in the Passion of Polycarp[157] and in the ancient text of the Anaphora of St. Basil. The latter in particular closely resembles the *Nobis quoque:* "And may we find fellowship and an inheritance with all the saints who in ages past have been pleasing to you."[158] It is clear that if we were to add the names of various saints to this ancient Coptic text of the Anaphora of Basil, we would have something almost identical with our *Nobis quoque.*

The Roman Canon asks that the sinfulness of the ministers not prevent their communion[159] with the holy apostles and martyrs whose names are then given. Sin is of its nature an obstacle to salvation, redemption, or eternal life. But why this concern lest sin in the lives of the ministers prevents their having fellowship and a place with the Holy apostles and martyrs? There is certainly no implication that eternal life is reducible to communion with the saints and the elect; that would be too impoverished a notion to find in the Canon. For a tentative answer, we must look at another passage in the Anaphora of Basil; it bears a verbal resemblance to the passage cited a moment ago, but its meaning is more complex: "Since your only-begotten Son, Lord, bade us to have a share in remembering your saints (*tēs mnēmēs tōn hagiōn sou koinōnein; memoriae sanctorum communicare*), deign Lord, to remember also those who in ages past have been pleasing to you [there follows a list of various categories of saints]."[160]

If being mindful of the saints is indeed a precept of Christ, we can understand a theology that stimulates prayer in this direction. To comprehend Basil's reference to a command of the Lord, we turn to Romans 12:13 (JB): "If any of the saints are in need you must share with them (*koinōnein*)." This verse proves to be the source of the wording in Basil, provided we read the passage not as it stands in the received text but according to the Western text, which has "Share the memory of the saints" rather than "Share the needs of the saints."[161] It may be "that 'needs' replaced 'memory' when the thought of the temporal needs of the saints replaced the more than legitimate concern to draw inspiration from their memory."[162]

While allowance must be made for some obscurity, first, the Anaphora of Basil speaks of sharing and being in communion with the saints[163] as a command of the Lord, and, second, there is a verse in Paul which provides an objective scriptural basis for this asserted command, even if only in a corrupt but well-known reading.

If this explanation of the ancient Anaphora of Basil is correct, it can increase our understanding of the theology at work in the *Nobis quoque:* "Grant fellowship and a place. . . ."

I. Conclusion of the Canon

Two prayers conclude the Canon and both begin with "Through Christ." The first commemorates the goodness of God who is described as the one who creates all good things, sanctifies them, endows them with life, blesses them, and bestows them on us. The sentence sums up the generosity and magnaminity of God. Its theology is surely one that deserves careful consideration, especially today.

It is not immediately clear why the sentence is placed where it is. Commentators note that "in the earlier stage of the Roman Canon, and for that matter right on to the late Middle Ages and even after, a blessing of natural products was on occasion inserted in this spot."[164] Consequently, they argue, it is probably that the natural products blessed by God and given to human beings were remembered here with special attention before being distributed again. In this way, the religious significance of these fruits of nature was emphasized.

The Canon ends with the great final doxology (glorification) that sums up all the themes of the anaphora in a proclamation of the divine Name. Everything belongs to the Father. All honor and glory ascends to him in a Christocentric movement that is expressed by three prepositions: "Through, with, in." Our celebration, like our very life, derives all its value and meaning from its Christ-centeredness. The doxology makes this thought its own and broadens it to include all things.

This honor and glory ascend to him "in the unity of the Holy Spirit," not only because the only acceptable worship is that in Spirit and in truth, but also and above all because the unity of God enters into us through that same Spirit.

The holy Name, which the doxology proclaims over all of the faithful, is great throughout the entire world. Malachi 1:11 is fulfilled here. Here, too, the great blessing of God descends upon the *ekklēsia,* for the Church is the place where Yahweh has chosen to put his Name, that is, in the hearts and on the lips of the faithful who proclaim his glory. Truly, everyone who invokes[165] the Name of the Lord will be saved (Jl 3:5); "So shall they put my name upon the people of Israel, and I will bless them" (Nm 6:27). Such is the theology at work in the final doxology, which sums up the entire anaphora.

Chapter Four

The Second Eucharistic Prayer

I. TRANSLATIONS OF THE SECOND EUCHARISTIC PRAYER

LITERAL TRANSLATION

It is truly right and just, proper and helpful toward salvation that we give you thanks, holy Father, through your most beloved Son, Jesus Christ, your Word through whom you have created everything and whom you sent to us as savior and redeemer, made flesh by the Holy Spirit and born of the virgin. To carry out your will and win for you a holy people he stretched out his hands in suffering in order to destroy death and manifest the resurrection. And therefore with the angels and all the saints we proclaim your glory, saying with one voice: Holy. . . .

Lord, you are holy indeed, the fountain of all holiness. Therefore, we pray, sanctify these gifts with the dew of your Spirit, so that they may become for us the body and blood of our Lord Jesus Christ.

When he was about to be handed over to a voluntary

ICEL TRANSLATION

Father, it is our duty and our salvation, always and everywhere to give you thanks through your beloved Son, Jesus Christ. He is the Word through whom you made the universe, the Savior you sent to redeem us. By the power of the Holy Spirit he took flesh and was born of the Virgin Mary. For our sake he opened his arms on the cross; he put an end to death and revealed the resurrection. In this he fulfilled your will and won for you a holy people. And so we join the angels and the saints in proclaiming your glory as we say: Holy. . . .

Lord you are holy indeed, the fountain of all holiness. Let your Spirit come upon these gifts to make them holy, so that they may become for us the body and blood of our Lord, Jesus Christ.

Before he was given up to death, a death he freely ac-

death, he took bread and, giving thanks, broke it and gave it to his disciples, saying: "Take this, all of you, and eat of it: for this is my body, which will be given up for you."

In like manner, after they had eaten, taking the cup and again giving thanks, he gave it to his disciples, saying: "Take this, all of you, and drink of it: for this is the cup of my blood of the new and everlasting convenant, which shall be shed for you and for the many for the forgiveness of sins. Do this in memory of me."

The mystery of faith! — Lord, we proclaim your death and we confess your resurrection, until you come.

Mindful therefore of his death and resurrection, we offer you, Lord, the bread of life and the cup of salvation, thanking you for having judged us worthy to stand before you and serve you.

And we humbly pray that we who participate in the body and blood of Christ may be brought together in unity by the Holy Spirit. Remember, Lord, your Church that is spread throughout the world, and make it perfect in love together with N., our Pope, N., our bishop, and all the clergy.

cepted, he took bread and gave you thanks. He broke the bread, gave it to his disciples, and said: "Take this, all of you, and eat it: this is my body which will be given up for you."

When supper was ended, he took the cup. Again he gave you thanks and praise, gave the cup to his disciples, and said: "Take this, all of you, and drink from it: this is the cup of blood, the blood of the new and everlasting convenant. It will be shed for you and for all so that sins may be forgiven. Do this in memory of me."

Let us proclaim the mystery of faith: Christ has died, Christ is risen, Christ will come again.

In memory of his death and resurrection, we offer you, Father, this life-giving bread, this saving cup. We thank you for counting us worthy to stand in your presence and serve you. May all of us who share in the body and blood of Christ be brought together in unity by the Holy Spirit.

Lord, remember your Church throughout the world; make us grow in love, together with N. our Pope, N. our bishop, and all the clergy.

Be mindful also of our brothers and sisters who have fallen asleep in hope of the resurrection, and of all the dead who have died in your mercy, and admit them to the light of your presence. Have mercy on all of us, we pray, so that we may be worthy to share eternal life with the Blessed Virgin Mary, Mother of God, the blessed apostles and all the saints who have been pleasing to you through the ages, and that with them we may praise and glorify you through your Son, Jesus Christ.

Through him and with him and in him all honor and glory is yours, almighty God and Father, in the unity of the Holy Spirit, for ever and ever. Amen.

Remember our brothers and sisters who have gone to their rest in the hope of rising again; bring them and all the departed into the light of your presence. Have mercy on us all; make us worthy to share eternal life with Mary, the virgin Mother of God, with the apostles, and with all the saints who have done your will throughout the ages. May we praise you in union with them, and give you glory through your Son, Jesus Christ.

Through him, with him, in him, in the unity of the Holy Spirit, all glory and honor is yours, almighty Father, for ever and ever. Amen.

II. THE SOURCE

The Second Eucharistic Prayer in the Missal of Paul VI is not a new composition. Except for some differences, which we will discuss, it is identical with the anaphora in the *Apostolic Tradition*[1] that was composed around 215–220 and is attributed to Hippolytus.[2]

The Anaphora of Hippolytus is the earliest that has come down to us.[3] Indeed, it is so early that at the beginning of the present century, P. Cargin believed it to be apostolic in origin.[4] In any case, perhaps because of its attribution to the diocese of Rome, perhaps because of the archaic character of its contents, the Anaphora of Hippolytus enjoyed great renown; it entered the Ethiopian[5] and Syrian[6] liturgies; it influenced the whole family of Antiochene anaphoras via the Anaphora of Basil[7] and the anaphora in the eighth book of the *Apostolic Constitutions*.[8]

It is understandable that in view of this historical success, the commission (*Coetus* X) charged with the reform of the "rite of Mass" decided not to undertake an entirely new composition, but to use the Anaphora of Hippolytus with some slight changes.[9]

90

A. Changes in the Structure of the Anaphora

In the present reform of its eucharistic prayer, the Roman Church has opted for the pattern or structure of the Antiochene anaphora. The Sanctus and the intercessions are integral parts of that anaphora, whereas they are lacking in the Anaphora of Hippolytus. As a result, it became necessary to introduce both of these parts into the new text: the Sanctus at the end of the thanksgiving, and the intercessions between the epiclesis and the final doxology.

The insertion of the Sanctus was not simple, because, coming as it does at the end of the thanksgiving, the Sanctus breaks the text in two.[10] The need, then, was to compose a passage that would link the Sanctus and the account of institution. As far as possible, the two parts should not be simply set side by side, juxtaposed, without any real organic connection.

In the Western liturgies, the passage that links the Sanctus and the account of institution is a literary unit with characteristics that are for practical purposes fixed. Usually, the passage is very brief and begins with words that are taken from the Sanctus itself and that as it were repeat and confirm what has been said there. From these initial words, the passage derives its name, the *Vere sanctus.*

It is possible to begin the connecting passage in some other manner; nothing forbids a difference choice. Statistically, however, *vere sanctus* has been the preferred beginning. It has therefore been used in the Second and Third Eucharistic Prayers of the new Missal.[11] When a different beginning is used (as in the Latin of the Fourth Eucharistic Prayer and in various vernacular translations), the connecting passage is called by a more general but no less typical name: the *Post-Sanctus.*

In non-Roman Latin liturgies, the *Post-Sanctus* is often epicletic; that is, it includes an invocation of the Father, asking him to sanctify the bread and wine and transform them into the body and blood of Christ. An epicletic *Post-Sanctus* may also be found in the East, in the Alexandrian liturgy. Here the passage is very low-keyed, asking simply for the sanctification of the sacrifice; only in more recent texts does a specific petition for the sanctification of the bread and wine appear.[12] It was a realization of the form taken by the theme of sanctification in the scriptures that caused a pneumatogical development of the epicletic *Post-Sanctus.*[13] The new (second) Roman anaphora has behind it the evolution just indicated; therefore, it has an epicletic, pneumatological *Post-Sanctus.* The more appropriate theological name for this prayer is "the first epiclesis of the anaphora", "first" because there is a second which will come after the account of institution and the anamnesis.

In the present Roman liturgy, the first epiclesis asks for the sanctification of the bread and wine, while the second asks for the sanctification of those who receive communion. The first is, therefore, also called a "consecratory" epiclesis and the second a "sanctificatory" epiclesis or, more generally, a "communion" epiclesis. This terminology has become habitual, but closer examination of both Eastern and Western ancient texts shows that the distinction in its unnuanced form, which allows no room to digress, does not correspond to reality. It is a useful distinction for didactic purposes, but that does not mean that it sprang from an analysis of the texts in the liturgical tradition.

In fact, the epicleses of the eucharistic liturgy have never been that sharply divided into consecratory and sanctificatory types. The two have always been joined in endlessly nuanced ways that enrich the theology of the texts. Of the hundred or more anaphoras preserved for us by tradition, those in which the epiclesis can be clearly catalogued as consecratory or sanctificatory are truly exceptions. This is not to say that our new texts are not successful. The scholastic schematism that dictates the distinction has practically been forgotten, and a wise choice has been made of formulas from the tradition.

In summary, three structural changes have been made in the anaphora inherited from Hippolytus; the introduction of a Sanctus, the introduction of an epicletic and pneumatological *Post-Sanctus*, and the introduction of the intercessions. In other respects, the structure is still that of Hippolytus.

B. Changes in the Text of the Anaphora
We shall deal here with five areas:

1. THE THANKSGIVING
The text of our new eucharistic prayer is faithful to Hippolytus except for some terms and expressions that our present-day theological outlook would cause us to misinterpret.

A first example is the phrase "angel of your will," a Christological description of Judeo-Christian[14] origin that today says nothing to us even when translated as "messenger of your will." The phrase expresses the idea of the revealer, which, after being abused in the past, is today misunderstood as though it exempted Christians from the human labor of study and research.

Yet this kind of effortful quest is regarded today as a sign of our authentic humanity and a methodological criterion of true progress. According to the mind of our day, that which is not won by laborious research is not worth considering. Something that is not thus won but is the result of revelation is seen as belonging to the peculiar world of "mysticism" in which revelation is confused with dreams, enlightenment with fantasies about unauthentic realities. But, in fact, history, not dreams, is the place of both revelation and contemplation, since it is the historical cross and resurrection of Christ that reveals the fatherhood of God to the World.

"He manifested himself as your Son" is another expression that cannot be used today because it suggests that Jesus was not truly the Son of God but simply appeared to be such. The meaning in the Anaphora of Hippolytus is, of course, clear: Jesus manifested himself as what he is; if he showed himself as the Son, it was because he is the Son. To the modern way of thinking, on the other hand, "manifesting" and "showing" are often opposed to "being"; consequently, the language of Hippolytus becomes equivocal.

Other expressions have been eliminated because they are couched in a uncustomary language. For example: "You sent him from heaven into a virgin's womb; carried in the womb he became incarnate there."

Still other expressions have been removed in the Latin text of the new anaphora because their meaning is unclear. One is *terminum figere,* which may mean "to set a limit" to something or "to set down a rule" for doing something. The context in Hippolytus is not of much help in determining the meaning. Like the entire section of which it is a part, the phrase describes the saving "activity" of Jesus during his stay among the dead. This entire theme had to be eliminated; a present-day anaphora has no room for the great concern which the source shows in the salvation of the deceased and in explaining the redemption of the just who were dwelling in the world of the dead.

The beginning of the anaphora has also been changed, since the original short introduction of Hippolytus has been harmonized with the Roman tradition which has a lengthier opening sentence for its prefaces. We can, however, regret one change made at this point: the removal of the eschatological element in the description of Christ's coming. The text in Hippolytus reads: "Whom you sent us in the last days as savior and redeemer . . . (*Quem in ultimis temporibus misisti nobis salvatorem et redemptorem*)."[15] The mention of the last days is part of the ancient tradition found in "Easter Homilies" and gives the coming of Christ its eschatological connotation.

In our new anaphora, this eschatological dimension of the coming disappears. The only valid reason for eliminating it would have been that it did not harmonize with the rest of the anaphora. Yet, such a reference to the eschatological aspect of the incarnation would be quite in keeping with the remainder of the anaphora, since the latter strongly emphasizes the role of the Spirit, who is the eschatological factor beyond all others.

The classical biblical passage on the eschatological role of the Spirit is Ezekiel 36:26–28: "A new spirit I will put within you; and I will take out of your flesh the heart of stone and give you a heart of flesh. And I will put my spirit within you, and cause you to walk in my statutes and be careful to observe my ordinances. You shall dwell in the land which I gave to your fathers; and you shall be my people, and I will be your God." Three points are highlighted here: the gift of the Spirit for the renewal of human being, the covenant (expressed in the covenanting formula), and the gift of the land.

Strictly speaking, nothing is said here about God's coming. On the basis of this passage, which is fundamental to our entire eschatological perspective, it can be claimed, therefore, that in our new anaphora the eschatological element is adequately represented by the reference to the gift of the Spirit and that there is no need of assigning an eschatological dimension to the Lord's coming, that is, to the incarnation.

The Anaphora of Hippolytus evidently takes a different view and seems to draw its inspi.ation from elsewhere than Ezekiel, since it gives even the incarnation an eschatological significance. There is a passage in the intertestamental literature that will help us better understand Hippolytus. In this passage, an eschatological meaning is given both to the gift of the Spirit and to the coming of the Lord on earth:

"And I will create in them a holy spirit, and I will cleanse them so that they will not turn away from me again, from that day till eternity. . . . And I will be their father, and they shall be my children. And they all shall be called children of the living God . . . the weeks of jubilee till eternity, till I descend and dwell with them through all eternity."[16]

94

This passage obviously contains one element not found in Ezekiel, namely, the descent of God, his coming on earth to establish his kingdom. For the *Book of Jubilees*, the last days bring the descent of God who sets up his residence in the midst of human beings.[17] We are close here to the Johannine theme according to which God's "dwelling among us" is realized in the incarnation of Christ.

The author of our second anaphora has done well in giving greater space to the theme of the Spirit; in so doing, however, he could have allowed the coming of Christ to retain its eschatological connotation.

As we try to get an overall view of the relation between the Anaphora of Hippolytus and our new anaphora, it will be helpful to compare the two texts.

HIPPOLYTUS	ANAPHORA II
	It is truly right and just, proper and helpful toward salvation
We give you thanks, O God,	that we give you thanks, holy Father,
through your beloved Child, Jesus Christ,	through your most beloved Son,[18] Jesus Christ
whom you have sent us in the last days as savior, redeemer, and messenger of your will.	
He is your Word, inseparable from you,	your word
through whom you have created everything	through whom you have created everything[19] and whom you sent to us as savior and redeemer,
and whom, according to your will, you sent from heaven into a virgin's womb and whom, being carried in the womb, was made flesh and manifested himself as your Son,	

95

born of the Holy Spirit	made flesh by the Holy Spirit
and the virgin.[20]	and born of the virgin.
To carry out your will	To carry out your will
to free from suffering	and win for you a holy people
those who had believed in you.	he stretched out his hands in
and win for you a holy people	suffering
he stretched out his hands in	
suffering	
When he was about to	
surrender himself to vountary	
suffering[21]	
in order to destroy death,	in order to destroy death
and break the devil's chains,	
and tread hell underfoot,	
and enlighten the just,	
and set a limit,	
and manifest the resurrection,	and manifest the resurrection
he took bread. . . .	

The comparison makes it immediately clear that the new anaphora radically shortens the text of Hippolytus and retains only the essentials.

No other course was possible, since Hippolytus is synthesizing the theology of the "Easter Homilies" and using all the terminology and idioms peculiar to that literary genre. His words and phrases evoke a very rich paschal content completely strange to us. Once the function of evoking that broader and deeper content has lost its value, only the basic idea is left. Our modern text, therefore, eliminates everything not directly meaningful and retains only what is immediately intelligible.

Hippolytus introduced into the structure of the Eucharist the themes and phraseology distinctive of the literary genre known as "Easter Homilies," which reflected a new christianized Jewish Passover liturgy. In so doing, he "paschalized" the Eucharist. His anaphora represents a paschalization of the original, extremely simple prayer of thanksgiving.

Hippolytus thus produced something completely new, since he made every eucharistic celebration paschal, no matter what its temporal distance from Easter. In his anaphora, we have the elements of the paschal theology of his period, though they can only be appreciated with the aid of historians.

This, then, is why in the thanksgiving of his anaphora, there is a commemoration of the entire work of salvation.[22] But this work is interpreted in the light of second-century paschal theology, which was based on the Passover lamb. There is a clear reference to the passion of Christ, which fulfills the type represented by the lamb. In the perspective adopted here, the passion is heavily emphasized, much more so than the resurrection,[23] and as a result the death of the Lord is said to have wrought salvation.

In our own day, the emphasis is on the Passover of Christ as exodus, as passage into the promised land.

As a result of the shift, we do not read the preface of the second anaphora as a paschal preface. It retains some of the paschal traits of the Anaphora of Hippolytus, but they are so few that we do not even suspect the paschal theology they embody or, better, the paschal theology which the source embodied. On the other hand, the preface of the new anaphora does not reflect the paschal theology of our time. Because its contents are thus so attenuated, it is never used but is replaced by the various prefaces which the Roman Missal provides for the different seasons of the liturgical year.

The Passover of Christ as exodus or as passage from death to life, or as victory over death[24] is the basis of our modern theology of the resurrection; we evidently prefer this interpretation to one which his Passover is understood as his sacrifice and death. In the Anaphora of Hippolytus, it is this latter theology of the saving death of Christ that emerges clearly; in other words, the anaphora embodies the paschal theology of Hippolytus' age.[25]

The second anaphora of the Missal mutes this older paschal theology without, however, giving place and emphasis to our present-day paschal theology, which is a theology of the resurrection. It would have been interesting if the authors of the new anaphora had taken a different course: if, instead of simply correcting Hippolytus by eliminating outdated material, they had been inspired by Hippolytus to construct a text that would give thanks for the entire history of salvation as interpreted in the paschal mode. The text would then have profited by all the biblical research into this subject and have given expression to a truly present-day paschal theology, one that insists on the resurrection, but within a theology of the death of Christ. The new anaphora could have developed a felicitous synthesis of the theology of Christ's death and the theology of his resurrection, since his death and resurrection are not two independent realities but form a single "mystery" of salvation.[26]

The result would have been an anaphora that solemnly expressed the paschal dimension which every eucharistic celebration has, independent of the liturgical season. The second anaphora of the Roman Missal would have become renowned for its focus on the central mystery of the faith.

2. THE ACCOUNT OF INSTITUTION
This part of the new anaphora does not derive from the Anaphora of Hippolytus. The composers of the new eucharistic prayers have made the account of institution in all the anaphoras the same as that of the Roman Canon.

While the account of institution from the Canon has been substituted for that of Hippolytus, the anamnesis remains the same as in the source, where it has an extremely simple and archaic character: "Mindful therefore of his death and resurrection."[27]

3. THE OFFERING
As in Hippolytus, the new anaphora connects the anamnesis and the offering. *Memores* ("Mindful . . . , we") is the subject of *offerimus* (offer). There is thus a single statement that is both anamnesis and offering.

The bread and wine are described as the bread of life and the chalice of salvation, and it is as such that they are offered. Simple, unchanged bread and wine are never offered. They become, however, the sacrament, figure, and image of the body and blood of Christ, and that is the title under which they are "offered" in the celebration of the Eucharist. The bread and wine which Christ gave to his disciples at the Last Supper are the elements given to the Church so that it might celebrate its liturgy.

The Hebrew Passover originated in a nomad culture and was then enriched with new elements when Israel became a sedentary people. The contribution made by these two phrases in the social and religious evolution of Israel is quite evident in the Hebrew Passover. Nor does anyone doubt that the Passover was a food sacrifice containing two parts, an animal sacrifice and a vegetable sacrifice.

How does the Mass fit into this picture? Here we use bread and wine. Can we say that we have a food sacrifice and specifically a vegetable sacrifice? By no means! The bread and wine are never celebrated and offered as such; what is celebrated and offered is the bread and cup which Jesus left to his disciples at the Last Supper so that they might celebrate the same liturgy in memory of him. What he left to them and what we celebrate and offer is the sacrament of his body and blood.

We may, therefore, summarize that the present offering of the Church has no direct and immediate connection with the animal and vegetable sacrifices of the Old Testament or with the sacrifices of the nature religions, but only with the Last Supper. The Supper, in its turn, has a typological relation to the whole sacrificial cult of the Old Testament and to the sacrifices of the nature religions. At the same time, the Supper looks forward to or announces the cross of the Lord. By announcing the cross, the Supper contains it; in the subsequent celebration of the Eucharist, the bread and wine will be used always and only as part of the commemoration of the mystery of Christ.

The sacrifices of the Hebrews and of the nature religions have no place in the Christian system. When the Church offers bread and wine, it has to describe these in a particular way, since the offering is not two products of nature but the sacrament inherited from the Last Supper. If this were not so, there would be no point to the eucharistic discourses of Jesus on the true vine and the true bread which comes down from heaven and gives life.[28]

The second part of the new anaphora contains a second, very short, thanksgiving identical with that of Hippolytus except that the first *tibi* (to you) is omitted: "Giving thanks [to you] for counting us worthy to stand before you and serve you [tibi]." This brief thanksgiving refers to the action now going on.[29]

4. THE SECOND EPICLESIS

The epiclesis in the Anaphora of Hippolytus is obscure and difficult to interpret[30]; it could not be used as it stands. Two themes of the epiclesis are nonetheless utterly clear; the unity of those who receive the sacrament, and the cause of this unity, the Holy Spirit. These have been taken into the new text, which reads thus: "And we humbly pray that those who share in the body and blood may be gathered into unity by the Holy Spirit."[31]

The method adopted here was exemplary. First, the essential and sure content of Hippolytus' prayer was determined; a new text was then composed which fully conveys this essential content, while improving its stylistic expression.

5.THE DOXOLOGY

A radical substitution has been made at this point: the doxology of the Roman Canon replaces the archaic and very simple doxology of Hippolytus. The latter, however, contains an interesting point, inasmuch as it mentions the Church.[32] It might have been helpful to retain this peculiarity, for as a result of it the doxology of Hippolytus brings into a single focus the glorification of God, the work of the Spirit, and the assembly that celebrates the Lord's Supper.

The doxology is fixed and identical in all of the eucharistic prayers, thus ensuring the response of the faithful at the conclusion of the anaphora. Frankly, no other choice was possible at the beginning of the reform. Today, however, the level of celebrative competence of the various congregations seems to be higher than was thought, and it would be worth the effort to provide the Roman liturgy with other types of doxology.

IV. ANALYSIS OF THE TEXT

A. Jesus Christ, the Living Word

If Jesus is mediator of human salvation, he is also mediator of the thanksgiving human beings offer to the Father. But the archaic Christology expressed in the term *Puer* (child, servant) has been changed by the substitutions of *Filius* (Son), a more recent term, for *Puer*. There has been a theological development of the text, not simply a replacement of a word with a synonym.

The adjective *dilectus* (beloved [child]) has also yielded place to the phrase "[*Filius*] *dilectionis tuae*" (literally: "[Son] of your love"). "Beloved" comes from the liturgical tradition and, prior to that, from the theophany in Matthew 12:18 where there is the association of *Puer* and *dilectus meus* ("my beloved").[33] The Father is here manifesting Christ to the world and presenting him as his *Puer* (Greek: *Pais*, child, servant).

"Beloved" describes the close relationship between the Father and Jesus. Jesus is presented to humankind and accredited as messenger of God and executor of his will. Jesus is God's legate; he will anounce the Father's will and, like every true prophet, carry it out. That is the theology expressed in Matthew 12:18ff., and it is the theology of the Anaphora of Hippolytus.

The phrase "Son of your love" ("*Filius dilectionis tuae*") in the new anaphora is not taken from Matthew but from Paul, who writes in Colossians 1:13: "He [the Father] has delivered us from the dominion of darkness and transferred us to the kingdom of his beloved Son (*in regnum Filii dilectionis suae*), in whom we have redemption, the forgiveness of sins." "Son of his love" is in fact simply a hebraism for "beloved Son"[34] and thus fully equivalent to the "beloved Son" of Matthew 12:18. It is, therefore, not the mere change from

100

dilectus to *dilectionis* that shows the theological difference between Hippolytus and our new anaphora.

The significance of the verbal change is the different biblical source that explains that change. The two citations embody two different theologies. The theology in Hippolytus is that of the *Pais/ Puer* (child, servant), whereas in the new anaphora, the citation of Colossians 1:13 brings to bear the theology of the "*basileia* (kingdom) of the beloved Son" of God.

The kingdom of Christ is not the kingdom of God but the kingdom of reign which Christ has acquired through his resurrection. The risen and glorified Lord is to reign until all enemies have been placed beneath his feet. At the end, he will hand over his kingdom to the Father, and God will be all in all. The reign of Christ is, therefore, limited and is to prepare the way for the reign of God, an eschatological reign that will never end.[35]

The attribute "beloved," which describes the relation between Father and Son, also shows that the reign of the Son is not opposed to or ultimately different from the reign of God.

The theology of the *Paris/Puer* in the Anaphora of Hippolytus has become a theology of the glorious reign of Christ, and the change has been effected by a change of biblical citation. The theological change is very fitting, since the theme of the "kingdom of God" is typically eucharistic, being part of the discourses of Jesus at the Last Supper. "As my Father appointed a kingdom for me, so do I appoint for you that you may eat and drink at my table in my kingdom."[36]

The change was perhaps not made with full consciousness of the new anaphora on the part of the composers; in any case, it has been very profitable for the new Missal. We must always keep in mind that liturgical reform is never reducible to archeological fidelity.

At this point, the new anaphora leaves the kingdom theme, which is barely sketched out in Colossians 1:13, and goes in a new direction. The theme of the kingdom is nonetheless still in the background, since the new direction parallels the first, being inspired by Mark 9:7: "This is my beloved Son; listen to him." A subtle logic thus leads to the Christological title "your Word" (*Verbum tuum*), [37] which the Italian Missal improves by translating it as "your living Word."[38] The beloved Son is to be heeded because he is the very Word of God.

We can conclude that though the text is dependent from a literary standpoint on Colossians 1:13, it incorporates the theme of

Mark 9:7 and therefore of Matthew 17:5 as well. In the new text with its new meaning, the source—the Anaphora of Hippolytus—continues to be visible. The text is thus still dependent on Matthew 12:18.

B. Sent as Savior and Redeemer

After the statement that everything has been created through Christ[39] comes a description of the theology of redemption.

The word "send" (*Mittere*) is important. It says that the salvation which Jesus brings to believers is the salvation intended by the Father; it is inseparably salvation from the Father and salvation from Christ. The "economy" of the Father is identical with the "economy" of the Son; the Father and the Son have but a single will (*eusebeia*) toward human beings. This identity of wills is the very program of Jesus' life: "And he who sent me is with me; he has not left me alone, for I always do what is pleasing to him."[40]

This emphasis on the unity of the work of salvation leads us to think that neither the Father alone nor the Son alone is the Savior, but the two together are a single Savior: salvation is from the Father through the Son.[41] According to the Jewish faith nourished by the Old Testament, there is but one Savior and Redeemer, the Lord God of Israel; he himself and no other will save.[42] In the Anaphora of Hippolytus, the verb *mittere* tells us that the salvation Jesus brings is at every point salvation from God. Jesus is Savior and Redeemer, but not instead of God; the verb "send" ensures that God and Jesus are one in this work.[43]

All this has an explicit New Testament basis: "God sent the Son into the world, not to condemn the world, but that the world might be saved through him."[44] From a literary standpoint the text of Hippolytus calls to mind 1 John 4:14, in particular: "The Father has sent his Son as the Savior of the world."[45]

The words "Savior" and "Redeemer" express the same reality from different viewpoints. "Save" points to the preservation and restoration of the gift of life.[46] "Redeem" signifies a rescue from slavery and oppression. Just as the gospel is described as the word of salvation,[47] so Jesus, the living Word, is defined as Savior: in virtue of his resurrection, he has been established as head and Savior.[48] As a result, the Acts of the Apostles can tell of sick persons who have been cured by the power of the Name (of Jesus), since there is no other name by which human beings can be saved.[49]

After the resurrection and Pentecost, the message of the apostolic community centers on the salvation wrought by Jesus. In the early preaching, the theme of salvation is so important that according to Matthew and Luke Jesus exercises a saving role even from his infancy. Matthew tells us that the name "Jesus" means "The Lord saves,"[50] while according to Luke the proclamation to the shepherds contains the message that the child just born is the Savior.[51]

By his death and resurrection, Chirst has become for us "the source of eternal salvation"[52]; he is "our God and Savior."[53] He reveals himself as Savior by actions that tell us as much[54]; thus he saves the sick by curing them.[55] The essential thing is to believe in the Lord Jesus and proclaim faith in him, that is, to call upon his Name.[56] Salvation is the very purpose of the life of Jesus, for he came to save what was lost[57]; he came not to condemn the world but to save it.[58]

In both Hippolytus and Anaphora II, the titles "Savior" and "Redeemer" are placed on equal footing; Jesus is both Savior and Redeemcr. The words are to be interpreted, however, in light of the historical experience of Israel, so that each keeps its special nuance. When the Old Testament speaks of "redemption," it most often has the exodus in mind[59]; moreover, in Jewish experience, the exodus is inseparable from the convenant. "Redeem" and "redemption" emphasize being "rescued," and for Israel that meant being rescued from Egyptian slavery: that liberation was Israel's first and foremost redemption. As a result, a new word appeared to describe this people: because they have been redeemed and rescued from slavery and brought into God's marvelous light, they are a people whom God has "acquired": a people who have been "won," a people who are "God's own."[60] There is a third idea and term as well, that of "price paid": you have been bought at a great price.

Rescue from Egypt at the Exodus; a people whom God has made his own; price paid: these three ideas and terms point to the "paschal" or "Passover" dimension of the redemption theme and the resultant theology of convenant. The covenant gave birth to a chosen people and to the history and self-consciousness of Israel.[61] This explains why Passover was the principal feast of Israel and why every other saving event was linked to Passover.

The paschal character of the Anaphora of Hippolytus ensures that our interpretation of the words "Savior" and "Redeemer" is correct. The titles are applied to Christ because in him the salvation prefigured by the Old Testament events has become a reality.[62] But in this anaphora, "Redeemer" takes precedence over "Savior" and every other title. More accurately, according to Hippolytus, God saves by redeeming. Redemption expresses the manner of salvation. Redemption is the action that defines Yahweh for the people of Israel, and the same action is now assigned to Jesus, who thus shares the attributes of Yahweh.

According to Titus 2:13ff., Jesus is Savior because he sacrificed himself "to redeem us from all iniquity and to purify for himself a people of his own who are zealous for good deeds." This is a Passover or paschal theme applied to Christ: he has saved us by redeeming us through a new Passover which differs from that of the exodus from Egypt.

It is evident that in the Anaphora of Hippolytus as now found in the Missal of Paul VI, the Passover theme has disappeared. The two titles, "Savior" and "Redeemer," are now fully on a par and form a single confession of Christ. Any anaphora is a profession of faith and an announcement and proclamation of the divine Name[63]; what is proclaimed in this anaphora is that Jesus is the living Word, the Savior and Redeemer.

This eucharistic prayer is one of praise and admiration of God, rather than a self-centered thanksgiving concerned primarily with what human beings have obtained. It is a profession of faith in the marvelous God who manifests himself in history and allows himself to be contemplated as the God who is at every moment concerned for the salvation of human beings. To use the term found in the Greek anaphoras, he shows himself to be *philanthropos* (lover of human-kind).[64] A God who saves and who fills us with wonder: such is the God whose Name we proclaim,[65] as we call to mind the wonderful saving deeds he accomplished in an atmosphere of hostility and death. These wonderful deeds were historical manifestations of Yahweh, understood as concrete revelations of his saving power.[66]

C. Birth and Incarnation

Jesus is the enfleshing of God's love.[67] In the theology of the "Easter Homilies" of the second century, Easter expresses and commemorates the entire work of salvation, including the incarnation and birth of Christ.[68] This is in continuity with Johannine theology which regards not only the death and resurrection of Christ but also his incarnation as salvific. In fact, it seems that this theological perspective explains the absence of the account of eucharistic institution from John's Gospel.[69]

The Anaphora of Hippolytus, then, does not celebrate and announce solely the death and resurrection, with the brief mention of

Jesus' sending and birth serving only to fill out the picture and show that salvation had a historical context. On the contrary, the entire life of Jesus, including his conception and birth, is a saving event, and it is as such that Hippolytus presents it in reliance on the "Easter Homilies."

But everything is not, as it were, on the same level. There is a clear crescendo: salvation is complete with the death of Jesus, and the death is followed by the manifestation of his resurrection, even in the realm of the dead where the just received their enlightenment (a baptismal theme).

What of Anaphora II in the Missal? It has not set out to alter the Hippolytan perspective according to which the entire mystery of salvation is celebrated. But the text has been so shortened that the perspective becomes recognizable only if we compare it with its source. If we listen to the text in isolation, it is silent.

D. The Father's Will

We ask in the Lord's Prayer: "Thy will be done." The petition is characteristic and found throughout the scriptures, but the people of our day are not in a position to understand it properly. Today, the phrase "Thy will be done" signifies resignation to the divine will in the sense of resignation to the inevitable, to evil and all the misfortunes that occur in our lives. We do not say "Thy will be done" when we think of the great deeds of God, but only when we think of life's troubles. By the Bible, however, the "will" of God is his "good will": his will to save us. As such it is not simply identifiable with the divine plan; rather, the divine plan sums up the divine will. Nor is the divine will identifiable with the law of God; the law translates God's will into practical terms. The divine saving will transcends divine plan and divine law and is their source.

The divine saving will encounters and confronts the human will. God does not want his will to replace the human will; he wants only to render the human will "perfect" through conformity with his plan. To attain this end, he must triumph over human wickedness,[70] and it is precisely in the person of Christ that he succeeds in this endeavor.

Having discussed and overcome the difficulties with the theme of the divine will, let us turn to the second anaphora. Here Christ is formally presented as the one who fully accomplished the Father's will. In the Anaphora of Hippolytus, that will is focused on the passion of Christ.[71] That focus is not very evident in our modern

105

anaphora, but it is nonetheless present since it is explicit in the source and since the latter is summarized without being transformed or even adapted to modern theology.

E. To Win A People

In introducing the passion of Christ, the second anaphora wisely makes explicit the purpose of that suffering: "To win for you a holy people." If the winning of a holy people is a soteriolgical phenomenon, then the salvific character of Christ's passion will be clear.

The soteriological interpretation of Christ's passion is characteristic of the literary genre known as the "Easter Homilies." There each historical event is stated, and a description of the corresponding salvific result immediately follows.[72] In the passion, the fruit or result is the birth of a holy people. N. Füglister gives a fine explanation of what is meant:

"New Testament soteriology concerns itself primarily not with the salvation of individuals but with the Church, which comes into being as a result of the saving event and is continually established anew and actualized in the cultic representation of the saving event. Individuals achieve their salvation (which is secondary and subjective) by becoming members of the Church (which is primary and objectively precedes individuals in its existence). Christ's intention to build his Church is fulfilled in the saving event that is accomplished by and through him. In this event he has sealed the 'new covenant' with his blood (see Mk 14:26 par.), thus creating a new convenanted people and making it 'a chosen race,' 'God's own people,' 'a kingdom and priests to our God' (see 1 Pt 2:9; Rv 1:5; 5:9 [with Ex 19:6]; Ti 2:14). Thus was born the Church which the Lord 'obtained with his own blood' (Acts 20:28). A similar statement can be made about the saving event of the Old Testament Passover; there too the true and proper object of liberation is Israel in its totality."[73]

From this it follows that both the ecclesial character and the paschal character of salvation are formally expressed in one and the same phrase: "to win for you a holy people."[74]

"Holy" is an attribute signifying transcendence. God is the "Holy One" par excellence. A "holy People" is a people in communion with him because it has obeyed his command: "You shall be holy; for I, the Lord your God, am holy."[75] The holiness characteristic of the people of the last times is due to the fact that God walks among them: "I am . . . the Holy One in your midst."[76] This presence establishes the people as holy, and it has become a reality in Christ who "has pitched his tent among us."[77]

F. To Manifest the Resurrection

The presence of Christ among human beings finds it fullest expression in his death and resurrection.

According to Hippolytus, it is the death of Christ that saves, a point highlighted by describing the suffering as "voluntary." Here the resurrection is not brought in to complete the saving mystery—which for us contains two inseparable parts: the death and the resurrection. In Hippolytus, the resurrection has a different significance, as we shall explain.

Hippolytus describes the saving passion twice: first, the suffering of Jesus is on behalf of the living and has for its purpose the winning of a holy people; second, the focus is on the salvation of the dead, those dwelling in the lower world, the kingdom of shadows. When Jesus descends among the dead, he brings salvation even to those in the next world. The early Church regarded this descent as necessary and extremely important to preach the universality of salvation. In the lower world, Jesus enlightens the just[78] and manifests the resurrection; the just have been waiting for Christ, the firstborn from among the dead, to manifest the resurrection to them,[79] that is, to bestow the gift of life. When used with the theme of the salvation of the dead, "manifest" is synonymous with "bestow."

Such is the theology of the source of Anaphora II. In the latter, all this has been eliminated. How could the theme of the salvation of those who died before Christ's coming be presented so emphatically today? It is hard to understand the "descent among the dead" in the Creed; it would be even harder in the eucharistic prayer. As a result, our anaphora tells us (in the Italian translation) that the "proclamation"[80] of the resurrection (ICEL: "revealed the resurrection") is a fruit of the death on the cross. This is an idea full of hope for human beings of every age and condition.

"He stretched out his hands in suffering; by dying he destroyed death and proclaimed the resurrection." (ICEL: "For our sake he opened his arms on the cross; he put an end to death and revealed the resurrection.") The wording of the Latin text is justifiable but hard to situate in its context. At first reading, and without heed to the source, you may be puzzled by the Latin since you may not understand how the destruction of death and the proclamation of the resurrection can be the purpose of the cross. (As we have already indicated in the notes, we consider the choice of "proclaim" for *manifestare* to be a fine one. It notably improves a Latin text that has been constructed chiefly by shortening and summarizing the source.)

In fact, the modern text, in the translation given, respects the theological vision Hippolytus has of the redemptive death of Christ. Like is redeemed by like,[81] and consequently the death of Christ destroys death's sway over the world. Once death is destroyed, what follows? Human beings are now saved! Furthermore, the resurrection of Christ proclaims the resurrection of other human beings, but a resurrection won by the saving death.

The translation is, therefore, not simply a play on words, but conveys the profound truth which is contained in the theology of antiquity but which the new second anaphora touches only timidly, as though afraid of surprising or even astonishing its readers.

G. Sanctus

The singing of the Sanctus is an appropriate conclusion for the mystery of salvation contemplated in the preface. "Therefore, in union with the angels and all the saints, we proclaim your glory, saying with one voice: Holy. . . . " After contemplating the work of salvation and exalting the name of the Savior, the congregation is called to proclaim the thrice-holy divine Name. It is because of what the preface has said that the Church acknowledges and proclaims the holiness of God.

If the congregation understands and lives the connection between, on the one hand, the joyous, thankful description which the preface gives of salvation in Christ and, on the other, the singing of the Sanctus, then it will readily pass from preface to proclamation of God's holiness. Otherwise, it will not understand how and why it should celebrate that holiness. Such is the nature of liturgy: what precedes entails what follows, and if what precedes has not done its work, the action cannot proceed in a harmonious and orderly way.

Back to the Sanctus. Holiness is not just one divine attribute among others; rather, it signifies the very godliness of God. His name is "the Holy One."[82] When "holy" is predicated of God, it is an attribute indicating transcendence and signifies God as he is in himself. The divine includes all that God is and possesses in himself: riches, life, power, justice, mercy, fidelity.

If an anaphora is indeed a proclamation of the divine Name, then the singing of the glorious Sanctus is particularly relevant. In it, the holiness of God is proclaimed as the summation of all that is said and commemorated in the preface, where his great works have been recounted.[83]

H. Post-Sanctus

The second anaphora of the new Missal is known and remembered by the faithful as the prayer that begins, "Lord, you are holy indeed" (in the Latin text: "Father, you are holy indeed"). The words "holy indeed" link this passage with the Sanctus and reassert the divine attribute. The text goes on to say that God is "the fountain of all holiness," that is, that he sanctifies by communicating himself. The divine nature itself is the source of God's sanctifying activity; if sanctification by God is a process of self-communication on his part, it follows that sanctification and communion with God are one and the same.

"Therefore we ask you to sanctify these gifts with the dew of your Spirit that they may become for us the body and blood of our Lord Jesus Christ." A transitional "therefore" (*ergo*) leads to a petition that God would act in accordance with his nature and sanctify the gifts set before him.[84] Since the outpouring of the Spirit is the great characteristic of the last times, the sanctification of the holy gifts requested in the epiclesis is being expressed in the eschatological mode. When the gifts are thus sanctified, they become an eschatological reality, and our time becomes the day of the Lord.[85]

If we look for the source of the epiclesis in this second anaphora, we can go back to the Anaphora of James[86] and, to complete this, to some other texts of Western liturgies which we shall examine.

The Latin text speaks of *"Spiritus Sancti rore"* ("the dew of the Holy Spirit").[87] In Palestine, dew is greatly appreciated; it makes up for the rain that does not fall for half the year.[88] Lack of dew is a disaster and a curse. We can, therefore, infer that dew goes with water and shares both its positive and negative connotations.

Dew is an image for prosperity because it makes the soil fruitful[89]; Hosea tells us that God will be "dew to Israel,"[90] that is, a source of grace on which all growth and development will depend. Dew is also an image of reawakening life; in Deuteronomy 32:2, Moses prays: "May . . . my speech distil as the dew." Above all, however, because of its association with water, dew is an image of the efficacy of God's word: "As the rain and the snow come down from heaven, and return not thither but water the earth, making it bring forth and sprout, giving seed to the sower and bread to the eater, so shall my word be that goes forth from my mouth; it shall not return to me empty, but it shall accomplish that which I purpose, and prosper in the thing for which I sent it."[91]

This efficacious dew which the Father sends during the celebration of the eucharistic prayer is the Holy Spirit. It penetrates the sacred gifts and transforms them into the sacrament of the Lord's body and blood. The Italian translation omits the "dew" and instead has the Spirit being poured out upon the gifts (ICEL: "Let your Spirit come upon these gifts . . ."). "Outpouring" is a more erudite word, conveying an idea that is more complex and less direct than "dew." Moreoever, in omitting the word, the translation deprives itself of the evocative and poetic overtones which "dew" has inasmuch as it echoes the passages cited from Hosea and Isaiah.

A final point is the emphasis placed on "holiness" in Anaphora II; this is the only anaphora to mention the "saints" in the introduction to the Sanctus.[92]

I. Account of Institution

The epiclesis leads into the account of institution. At this point, the new anaphora introduces the idea of "voluntary suffering" of which Hippolytus had spoken in an earlier part of the text.

That the passion was "voluntary" or "freely accepted" is theologically relevant, for it brings out the fact that even though Jesus was taken prisoner and condemned, he was not at the mercy of his persecutors. He remained the protagonist and in control of events. He was condemned, but not defeated; he died, but the life in him triumphed in the resurrection. All this happened because he freely accepted his suffering.

The anaphora reports what occurred at the Last Supper. But it was precisely during the Supper that Jesus showed himself to be in control of events and to be entering deliberately into the dark tunnel of the passion, without deluding himself and without cultivating any hope that events might turn out differently. His clarity of mind at the Supper and his prediction of coming events are summed up in the word "voluntary."

The account of institution is not that of Hippolytus. From P. Jounel's report on the composition of the new eucharistic prayers, the account of institution in Hippolytus seemed overly brief; in addition, it lacked certain elements that are found in all the liturgies, for example, the reference to the new covenant and the forgiveness of sins. It was decided, therefore, to use the account of institution in the Roman Canon.

But why take the account from the Roman Canon and not, for example, from one of the four New Testament accounts? The question is legitimate, especially today when the Catholic world is rediscovering the scriptures. The answer is quite simple: no anaphora has ever used verbatim one of the four scriptural accounts.[93] In every case, the basic account has been filled out with elements from the other New Testament passages on the Lord's Supper. Since the account of institution proper to the Roman Church is the one in the Roman Canon, this fills in the elements lacking in the Anaphora of Hippolytus.

J. Anamnesis

"Mindful therefore of his death and resurrection, we offer you, Lord, the bread of life and the cup of salvation, thanking you for having judged us worthy to stand before you and serve you."

The anamnesis in the new anaphora simply repeats the corresponding passage in Hippolytus. As a result, it commemorates only the death and resurrection of Christ; the paschal mystery is given its most basic and essential expression. To carry out the command Christ gave us at the Last Supper is to commemorate his death and resurrection.

The prayer is extremely succinct, including in a single sentence the anamnesis, the offering, and the thanksgiving for the exercise of service.

A comparison of the Latin text with the Italian translation will help bring out the real character of the Latin. The Italian speaks of "celebrating the memorial," whereas the Latin says: "Mindful." (ICEL: "In memory of . . .") The "memorial" is part of the action being celebrated; "mindful" is an attribute of the persons who are performing the action of offering. In fact, the Latin does not express the action of commemorating, since "mindful" is not an action but, as we just said, an attribute of the offerers. In the Latin, what is celebrated is not a memorial but the offering of the bread of life and cup of salvation.

Does this mean that the Latin plays down the "theology of commemoration"? We think not, provided we have an accurate understanding of this theology. "Mindfulness" points to and defines the attitude of all who engage in the liturgical action; "mindful ones" can define the participants in the eucharistic celebration. We might, however, speak of them simply as "celebrants" and say the same thing, since the action being celebrated is commemorative and therefore its celebrants cannot but be "mindful."

At this point, we might say that the difference between the Latin and the Italian is not great, but it is a difference nonetheless. The Latin text takes its stand in the realm of being (being mindful), the Italian in the realm of doing (celebrating the memorial). When the element of mindfulness is objectified and defines the action, then the action takes first place. When the mindfulness is an attribute of the agents, they are given priority.

There is then a difference between the two texts, but this does not mean that one is better or worse, or that one approach is richer or better. In fact, there are good and equally strong reasons for taking either approach. It is simply a matter of choice.

Let us turn to the thanksgiving offered for being able to "serve." In the Latin text, the giving of thanks is expressed as a participle, *gratias agentes* (thanking), which is coordinated with the opening word, *memores* (mindful). Both are subordinated to the main verb, *offerimus* (we offer).

The reason for the thanksgiving is expressed in a phrase whose meaning is not immediately clear: *quia nos dignos habuisti adstare coram te et tibi ministrare* ("because you judged us worthy to stand before you and serve you"). First, the sense of *dignos habuisti* is not captured in the English "judged us worthy" (ICEL: "counting us worthy"); the sense is rather that "you made us worthy" and is a reference to divine election. In other words, God chose the participants in this concrete eucharistic assembly and made them capable of performing the action in question.

The action in question is *ministrare* (serve) which the Italian translation turns into "perform priestly service" (ICEL: "serve"). But, if we examine the Latin verb more closely, it contains surprises that do not come through in the Italian version.

The Italian text is based on the interpretation and translation which Dom Botte gives of Hippolytus in his critical edition.[94] Now the Anaphora of Hippolytus was intended for a Mass in which a new bishop is ordained and then celebrates the Eucharist; the thanksgiving would therefore be (according to Dom Botte) a thanksgiving of the bishop for his own pontifical role in the eucharistic celebration. In studying the meaning of the Latin verb *ministrare*, Dom Botte points out that while we do not have the original Greek of the *Apostolic Tradition* to shed light on the meaning of *ministrare*, we do have the Greek text of the eighth book of the *Apostolic Consti-*

tutions, which contains an anaphora based on that of Hippolytus, the so-called "Clementine Anaphora." The Greek word used by Hippolytus, therefore, and translated into Latin as *ministrare* would have been *hierateuein;* this is confirmed by the Ethiopic version of the *Apostolic Tradition* and by the *Testamentum Domini. Hierateuein* signifies the role and action of a *hiereus (sacerdos)* in the eucharistic celebration. Dom Botte concludes that *ministrare* is inadequate as a translation of *hierateuein*[95]; therefore, when reconstructing the original text, he translates the word in question as "serve (you) as priests."

In summary: according to Dom Botte, the words "thanking you . . . serve you" are a thanksgiving offered by the bishop for having been ordained a *sacerdos* and being able to exercise this priesthood in the eucharistic celebration.[96]

This interpretation is rejected by the English school as represented by A. Couratin. The latter says that in the time of Hippolytus, the distinction between *ordo* and *plebs* (= priests and laity) had not yet been developed[97] and that consequently *ministrare* could not be a reference to the priesthood of the bishop as distinct from the priesthood of the laity. It follows that the thanksgiving for standing before God and "serving" him is not peculiar to episcopal ordination but flows from the logic of every eucharistic celebration. Therefore, "those who stand before God and minister to him are here the whole Christian people, the true high-priestly race of Justin."[98]

Botte and Couratin are in agreement, then, that the thanksgiving has the action now going on for its object, that is, the celebration of the eucharistic sacrifice. They also agree in calling this action "priestly," since the underlying Greek word is *hierateuein.*[99] They disagree, however, in identifying the agent of this action that is defined as a *ministrare.*

In our view, the text of Hippolytus, independently of any dogmatic position, provides a sufficiently clear solution of the problem. We shall try to show that the *ecclesia* is the subject which God had made worthy of performing the priestly action of the eucharistic celebration.

The argument is simple. In one and the same sentence, the first person plural is involved twice: first, it is "we" as subject, that is, the "we" who give thanks; second, it is "us" as object (the "us" who have been made worthy). Unless there is some indication to the contrary—and there is none—the "we" and the "us" should be the same set of persons. The *nos* which is the object of *dignos habuisti* is, therefore, the same as the *nos* which is the subject of *memores, offerimus,* and *gratias agentes.*

Who, then, is the *nos*: the bishop or the *ecclesia*? If the *nos* is the bishop, it is a plural of dignity and really means *ego* ("I"). It is impossible, however, that the Anaphora of Hippolytus should be entirely under the sign of a truly plural *nos* in the opening thanksgiving and then shift, without giving any sign, to a camouflaged *ego*. Is, then, the *nos* of the opening thanksgiving truly a plural, that is, is it the congregation or is it the bishop alone? The answer is clear. In the words which the bishop speaks, it is the congregation that gives thanks; the *nos* is the congregation. But, if the congregation or *ecclesia* is the subject of the opening thanksgiving and of *offerimus* and *memores,* it is necessarily also the subject of *gratias agentes.*

In a recent article, published posthumously first in German and then in French, Dom Botte seems to share the view: "We can ask whether this [anaphora] is not a personal prayer of the newly consecrated bishop. Such an interpretation must be rejected."[100]

Our first conclusion, then, is that if the anaphora is not a private prayer of the bishop, the *nos* must be at every point a genuine plural. Our second conclusion follows from the first: the *nos* that is the subject and object of the various verbs can only be the *ecclesia.*

Dom Botte is in agreement and even provides a philological argument. He observes that in the prayer of episcopal ordination in Hippolytus,[101] the bishop's role is described by the verb *archihierateuein,*[102] whereas the anaphora uses the simple *hierateuein.* Since *hierateuein (ministrare)* is not the technical term used by the *Apostolic Tradition* for the specifically episcopal function, specific proofs are needed to overcome the contrary presumption and to maintain that in the anaphora this word signifies the presidential role of the bishop. We can conclude, then, that the *ministrare* of the anaphora cannot be identified with the specifically episcopal function; on the contrary, the two must be different.

Dom Botte also gives a theological argument: "Moreover, the action being performed is not peculiar to the bishop, but a collegial act of the entire priestly body."[103]

It is clear that the premises from which we are arguing are objectively the same as those of Dom Botte; yet, when the latter comes to the words "thanking you . . . serve you," he reaches a conclusion opposite to ours. There is no difference between us in the analysis of the text. If, then, his conclusion differs, it is because of some external circumstance to which he attributes great importance.

114

This circumstance is the occasion for which the anaphora was composed, namely, the consecration of a new bishop. This being so, the words which we are studying ("thanking you . . . serve you") must (in Dom Botte's judgment) represent the bishop's personal thanksgiving for the priestly role he is exercising in the eucharistic celebration. Dom Botte is so impressed by this external circumstance that he ignores the internal analysis and, despite what is indicated in the text itself, attends solely to the occasion for which the text was composed, a circumstance external to the text. In view of this circumstance and despite the inconsistency with his own analysis of the text, Dom Botte concludes: "The bishop gives thanks to God for having been judged worthy of celebrating the eucharistic sacrifice."[104]

The text of Anaphora II is identical here with that in the Anaphora of Hippolytus. The meaning determined for the *ministrare* in Hippolytus will, therefore, be that in the Missal. If the Anaphora of Hioppolytus is here giving thanks (as we have shown) for the priestly role which the *ecclesia* plays in the eucharistic celebration, then our new anaphora is likewise giving thanks for the priestly action of the congregation in the Eucharist.

There is a further argument to show that meaning of *ministrare* in the Missal. As we just saw, the disagreement in interpreting Hippolytus is about whether the meaning depends on the text itself or on a circumstance external to the text. In our new anaphora, this question does not arise, since the prayer has no connection with an ordination rite but can be used on any and every occasion. (In fact, the rites of ordination are not even in the Missal.)

We conclude, then, that in the second anaphora of the Missal, *ministrare* refers to the priestly action of the (hierarchically organized) *ecclesia* and not to the action of the bishop or priest who presides at the celebration.[105] If this conclusion is correct, we must abandon the Italian translation which follows Dom Botte in interpreting *ministrare* to mean "perform priestly service," i.e., to exercise a ministerial priesthood.

Let us turn to still another phrase in this short anamnesis: "to stand in your presence" (*"adstare coram te"*). The first thing to be noted is that the anaphora is celebrating not the presence of God or Christ in the Church's public worship but our presence to God. God is always present to human beings; in worship, they become present to him.

The words in question come, let us remember, from the Anaphora of Hippolytus. In that context, they are one more indication of the archaic character of this eucharistic prayer, since they reflect a paschal theology drawn from Judaism. What is being commemorated at this point in Hippolytus is not the real presence of the savior in the people's worship, but the real presence of the people, in their cult, to the saving deeds which the Lord accomplished once and for all in the past. The Jewish idea was that by means of the public worship they were now offering, posterity was really present to and really participating in those past events.[106]

Does it make sense to assign such an Old Testament meaning to this short phrase in Hippolytus? We answer that it does because, in addition to the paschal content of the Anaphora of Hippolytus, the literary form of the words in question comes from the Old Testament. We need only consult Deuteronomy 10:8: "At that time the Lord set apart the tribe of Levi to carry the ark of the covenant of the Lord, to stand before the Lord to minister to him. . . ."[107] The same thought occurs in 2 Chronicles 29:11, though the wording is not as close to that of Hippolytus: "My sons . . . the Lord has chosen you to stand in his presence, to minister to him, and to be his ministers and burn incense to him."[108] It is clear from these passages that Hippolytus does not show a strict verbal dependence on the Septuagint, but a literary and theological proximity is undeniable.

In fact, the anaphora and the two Old Testament passages agree on three points: (1) the divine election, (2) standing in the presence of God, and (3) the performance of a cultic action.

The divine election is to be seen, in the two Old Testament texts, in the choice of the tribe of Levi and, in the anaphora, in the choice of the *ecclesia*. The Church has already been defined in the first part of the anaphora as a holy people which was established as such by the redemptive passion of Christ. The paschal ecclesiology in the Anaphora of Hippolytus considers the worship of the Church, which was born of the pasch (passover)-passion of Christ, to be the typological actualization of the Old Testament cult.

It is less simple to establish the meaning of "before you ," inasmuch as in the Old Testament the phrase is often often a pleonastic expression simply emphasizing an idea already expressed. Thus, "to speak before the Lord" means simply to "speak to the Lord."[109] "To offer sacrifices of thanksgiving . . . and gifts before the Lord" means simply "to offer to the Lord" or "in honor of the Lord."[110] On other occasions, "before the Lord" means before the altar or the Ark or the place where the Lord dwells, all these being signs of his presence.

116

On the other hand, "eat and drink before the Lord" is the most archaic description of sacrificial cult,[111] the emphasis on communion with God. Communion with God is experienced in sacrificial worship, where human beings sit with God at table and are his companions there.

There are, in addition, texts which speak of the heavenly court as standing before the Lord,[112] a fact which may lend a degree of eschatological coloring to the words in our anaphora. This "standing before the Lord" is a characteristic behavior of the heavenly court; we need only think of the "angels of the Face" [i.e., the presence] in the apocryphal literature.

But, it will perhaps be more fruitful to abandon this last line of thought and to look to cultic action for the phrase's meaning. God takes the initiative in deciding to dwell in the midst of his people; the response he seeks in return is praise, hymns, glorification, and cultic worship.[113] The New Testament takes this theme and presents the coming of Jesus into the world as the climactic theophany; it even uses the Old Testament mode of expression: "He dwelt among us."[114] In Christ, the divine dwelling in the world becomes fully real; he is now the temple par excellence,[115] since the fullness of the godhead dwells in him.[116]

The property of being God's temple is communicated by Christ to his Church. Being the prolongation of Christ's body, the Church is the spiritual temple in which God dwells:

"The Church is the temple of God, built on Christ, the foundation and the cornerstone (1 Cor 3:10–17; 2 Cor 6:16ff; Eph 2:20ff); a shining temple where without distinction both Jews and pagans have access to the Father in the one identical Spirit (Eph 2:14–19). . . . Here is the definitive temple, which is not made by the hands of men; it is the Church, the body of Christ, the place of the encounter between God and man, the sign of the divine presence here below."[117]

If the Church is the true temple, we can apply to it the theology of the temple: "The temple is the place God has chosen in which to put his Name and to make his Name dwell; that is, it is the sacred place in which the godhead is honored. . . . It is the one place chosen out of all the tribal lands of Israel (Dt 12:14) where the people can recover their unity in worship of a single God."[118]

Finally, to the point: What does "stand before the Lord" mean in our anaphora? In light of all the data thus far, the primary meaning is "to be in communion with God." More specifically, it means to be in communion with God in the Church because God is present there as in a temple that is a prolongation of Christ's body. In this Church that is God's new temple, a new cult is offered to him which the anaphora describes as a *ministrare* (a "service"). In the final analysis, thanksgiving is offered to God through participation in the cultic assembly, and the assembly is described in terms of its action, which is *ministrare*. The entire *ecclesia* is in God's presence and in communion with him.

We have a further confirmation, if one be needed, that the Anaphora of Hippolytus is not a private prayer of a bishop who gives thanks for his own episcopal role. He is not alone in the presence of God, and "temple" cannot be predicated of him in any special way. Since thanksgiving is offered to God by a combined "being in God's presence" and "serving" him, those who are in God's presence are by that fact also the ones who celebrate the cult of the Lord's Supper.

In summary: in the anamnesis, the worshipers give thanks for being present in the assembly that is the temple in which God causes his Name to be remembered. This presence leads to cultic action, namely, the eucharistic sacrifice. The Church, therefore, gives thanks for having been made worthy to celebrate this eucharistic liturgy.

K. Epiclesis

The text of the epiclesis in Hippolytus is complex and obscure; our new Missal has legitimately eliminated everything that could cause difficulties. Two themes are very clear in the Hippolytan epiclesis: the descent of the Holy Spirit and the unity of the faithful. Everything else, however important, is a background for these two ideas. The editors of the Missal have, therefore, retained the two themes and dropped everything else. Their procedure will become clearer if we compare the two texts.

HIPPOLYTUS	ANAPHORA II
And we ask that you would send your Holy Spirit on the offering of your holy Church; bringing them together in unity,	And we humbly pray that

grant that all who participate in the holy (mysteries) may be filled	we who participate in the body and blood of Christ
	may be brought together in unity
with the Holy Spirit so as to be strengthened in their faith in the truth.	by the Holy Spirit.

In our new anaphora, the idea of unity is formally connected with the action of the Holy Spirit, while in Hippolytus, the theme of unity is left hanging and not fully integrated into its context. Furthermore, Hippolytus speaks of "the sacred (things or 'mysteries')," while our anaphora makes the thought more explicit by specifying "the body and blood of Christ."

This evolution of the Second Eucharistic Prayer in relation to its source in Hippolytus is fully consonant with the history of the Anaphora of Hippolytus. Thus, the "Clementine Liturgy" in Book VIII of the *Apostolic Constitutions* already introduces mention of the body and blood of Christ at this point and goes on to say: "in order that those who participate in it," etc.[119] Our new anaphora follows exactly the same line of development in relation to Hippolytus.

This evolution in texts dependent on Hippolytus is explained by the influence of 1 Corinthians 10:16ff. This Pauline text acquired a place in the epiclesis of Hippolytus and gave rise, in varying ways, to the epiclesis in the Coptic Anaphora of Basil,[120] in the Clementine anaphora, and in the Second Eucharistic Prayer of the Missal of Paul VI. Thus, the decision of the modern revisers to develop the text of Hippolytus in the direction of 1 Corinthians 10:16ff. was fully in harmony with the history of the Hippolytan anaphora.[121]

The Italian translation of the new epiclesis has introduced the theology of the Pauline text. That is, the translators were not content with simply reproducing the Latin text, which speaks of being "brought into unity," but explained the underlying Pauline thought.[122] The result was a fine prayer: "Through communion in the body and blood of Christ may the Holy Spirit unite us in one body."

Back now to our comparison of the new Latin epiclesis and the epiclesis in Hippolytus. As we said above, the explicit linking of unity with the action of the Holy Spirit is new. In 1 Corinthians, the theme of the one body and the theme of the quenching of thirst by the one Spirit are both of them eucharistic themes.[123] Consequently, the novel element in our present text is in complete harmony with both Paul and Hippolytus.

In Hippolytus, the unity that is asked has for its ultimate purpose the strengthening of our faith in the truth. In the new anaphora, the object of prayer is unity and nothing more. But this change is not an impoverishment. Rather, the theme of unity has been isolated to highlight a basic truth about the Eucharist, namely, that it is the sacrament of unity. Unity is prayed for; if it does not become a reality, then the sacrament and the sacramental action of the Spirit will have been frustrated.

In thus focusing on unity, the new anaphora goes back to the source used by Hippolytus himself: *Didache* 10.[124] The prayer in the latter passage asks for nothing but the eschatological unity that both in the Old Testament and in John is the sum total of messianic blessings and the climax of redemption. From that manner of praying, a conclusion emerges that is very important for the life of the Church as it seeks to get away from the individualistic spirituality produced by the *Devotio moderna*. The conclusion is that communicants bear the fruits of eucharistic communion only in a community that is growing in its unity. There is, thus, a criterion by which the fruit of the eucharistic celebration can be judged in a tangible, visible way: that criterion is unity.

If the Eucharist is the sacrament of unity,[125] its fruits influence the entire community. This is not to play down personal participation; it is simply to say that the individual benefits from the Eucharist as a member of the community and in function of the community's growth.[126] A community that does not grow in unity, or that grows only slowly and as it were gropingly (as with all human growth), is a community that does not derive good fruit from the eucharistic celebration, that is, from the action of the Holy Spirit, which consists in uniting all in the one body of Christ.[127] Such a community does not respond to the work of the Spirit and is therefore guilty of profaning the body of Christ.[128]

L. Intercessions

The intercessions and the epiclesis originate in the same way: both are a prayer for the Church. The difference is that the epiclesis is a prayer for the congregation taking part in the sacred action, while the intercessions are prayers for the Church scattered throughout the world.

The latter is the older of the two themes,[129] and it was Hippolytus who created the epiclesis by applying the theology expressed by the intercessions to the limited community of participants.[130] Having thus transformed the intercessions of his source into an epiclesis, Hippolytus had only an epiclesis in his anaphora, without any intercessions of the older kind. In the subsequent development of the eucharistic prayer, however, the intercessions were restored and placed after the epiclesis, at least in the Antiochene anaphora. As a result, anaphoras based on Hippolytus had not only an epiclesis but intercessions as well, which came later in the text.

Against this background, the composers of our new anaphora exercised historical understanding in dealing with the Anaphora of Hippolytus. The result is decidedly worthy of praise.

The epiclesis asks that the Spirit will bestow good fruits on those who receive the sacred gifts; the intercessions ask good fruits for the universal Church, which is described by listing the various ministries at work in it. A further difference between the two is that the epiclesis enunciates the theme of the Holy Spirit, while the intercessions do not. The intercessions are less specific, which is not a sign of vagueness but of their antiquity.

The Second Eucharistic Prayer restores the intercessions for the Church, and it takes them from the source of Hippolytus: *Didache* 10. The very language shows a literary dependence. Thus, *"perficere eam in caritate tua"* (*Didache* 10,5: "make it [the Church] perfect in your love") corresponds to *"ut eam in caritate perficias"* ("make it perfect in love").[131] The Church is described in Anaphora II as *"toto orbe diffusae"* ("spread throughout the world"); the words do not occur in the *Didache*, but the idea is expressed there. The phrase *"toto orbe"* is typical of the Latin liturgies. It occurs in the Roman Canon[132] and in other texts which we need not reproduce here since they have already been collected by L. Eizenhöfer.[133]

The theme of unity is not expressly present in our intercessions, but it is implicit as a supposition of the idea in "spread throughout the world." To say that the Church, and not simply the Churches, is spread throughout the world is necessarily to say that the Church is one.

The intercessions in Anaphora II are in three distinct sections. After the introductory prayer for the Church comes the first section, which is the intercession for the dead.[134] The second section is devoted to the living; the Church asks that they attain to happiness at the end. It is at this point that commemoration is made of Mary, the virgin Mother of God, of the holy apostles, and all the saints "who have pleased you through the ages" (an expression character-

121

istic of the East and found as early as the Coptic Anaphora of Basil).[135]

Finally, there is the remembrance and contemplation of the saints who are living in the vision of God and who contemplate the light of his face, his "glory." The face of God is Light, an idea conveyed by the biblical term "glory," which connotes phenomena associated with light.

In response, human beings proclaim the divine "glory" in the concluding doxology which is both a hymn and a proclamation of the holy Name of Father, Son, and Holy Spirit.

Chapter Five

The Third Eucharistic Prayer

I. INTRODUCTION

The Third Eucharistic Prayer lacks a preface and can be used with all the prefaces in the Missal; as a result, it becomes appropriate for all the phases of the liturgical year. For this reason, it is the eucharistic prayer that is most often used on feast days and on all Sundays of the year. If the second anaphora can be called the prayer for weekdays, the third can be called the prayer for festive days.

It is frequently said that this third prayer "adopts the development and certain of the most felicitous formulas of the Mozarabic and Gallican tradition."[1] It is not easy, however, to discern a connection between the third anaphora and the Gallican liturgy. Why then is this claim made?

A decision was made to compose a text (this third anaphora) that would draw its inspiration from Gallican texts.[2] This decision gave rise to the option that the third prayer is a Gallican or Mozarabic type, although no one asks whether the original intention was carried through in an actual project. A. Nocent is much more correct when he says that this third prayer "takes its inspiration from a 'composite' Oriental model, for on the one hand it has a broad basis of an Antiochene kind . . . while on the other it resembles an anaphora of the 'Alexandrian' type."[3]

It might be claimed that the structure of this Third Eucharistic Prayer relates it to the Gallican anaphoras, but the argument is weak. It is characteristic of the structure of Gallican and Mozarabic anaphoras that they are composed of various units or prayers which are complete in themselves and autonomous in relation to one another. Each of the parts making up an anaphora can be removed from that particular text and inserted into another. And, in fact, we frequently see one and the same unit of prayer appearing unchanged or, at most, with slight variations, in different anaphoras.[4]

It is not possible to perform such an operation on the Third Eucharistic Prayer. The only variable part is the preface, but this fact has no significance since the variable preface has always been characteristic of the Roman liturgy. For the rest, the third anaphora is a single block that does not allow for variable parts to be inserted or removed at will. That kind of structure is suggested rather by the anaphora for the Swiss Synod, which we shall be examining in a later chapter.

Having said this, we must admit there is an element in the third anaphora which argues for the position of L. Bouyer. The element is this: the divisions between the units making up the anaphora are in fact quite marked and noticeable. For example, there is a real quasi-doxology (obviously without an "Amen") between the end of the epiclesis and the beginning of the intercessions: ". . . may be filled with the Holy Spirit and become one body and one spirit in Christ." From the formal literary standpoint, this is not a doxology, but in the proclamation of the anaphora it takes on all the functions of a doxology. We must not forget that an anaphora is a verbal action and is therefore to be judged as a text to be recited rather than as a text to be read. But, this is all that can be said for the position taken by Bouyer when the text is analyzed from the viewpoint of structure.

H. Wegman discusses the problem of the Gallican relationship from the standpoint of content, and he reaches a negative conclusion. Despite the resemblance to some Gallican and Mozarabic texts, he says this anaphora is not dependent on that liturgical family. He proceeds by investigating two parts of the anaphora: the anamnesis and the epiclesis. As we shall see, he is examining the two prayers that have rather direct and evident parallels in the Mozarabic liturgy.[5] He is also able to show, however, that there are equally valid parallels in the Roman liturgy and that it is therefore not possible to speak of the prayers in the third anaphora as being specifically Gallican or Mozarabic in character.

Wegman's conclusion is also couched in positive terms: the model for this eucharistic prayer was the Roman Canon, which supplies us with the framework for interpreting the prayer.[6] This relationship would explain well the marked sacrificial emphasis in the third anaphora.

This conclusion agrees with T. Schnitzler on the third anaphora. After defining this eucharistic prayer as the Canon of openness to the world, Schnitzler adds: "But from a theological viewpoint it is perhaps more accurate to call this a 'sacrificial Canon,' for the idea of sacrifice and the word itself recur constantly in its paragraphs and lines; they are present in every individual part and give it its precise and essential meaning."[7] Wegman and Schnitzler are evidently in agreement, since the Roman Canon is pervaded by sacrificial themes.

In conclusion, we make our own the judgment of H. Wegman: it is inaccurate to say that this anaphora has been borrowed from Gallican and Mozarabic texts. Despite some evident parallels in the latter, the new anaphora is characteristically Roman.

II. THE AUTHOR OF THE TEXT

It cannot be said that Father Vagaggini was the author of the next text. On the other hand, it is indeed possible to say that much of it is attributed to him. In 1966, he published a plan for the reform of the Canon of the Mass, offering two anaphoras that are very close to the Third and Fourth Eucharistic Prayers. In addition, Vagaggini was a member of the ad hoc commission—the famous *Coetus X*—within which he acted as official expositor at the meeting in Nemi (near Ariccia, Italy) on March 12, 1967.[8] But there were certainly other positions taken on the text which Vagaggini presented at that meeting, since the definitive redaction of the third anaphora differs from those in his 1966 proposal[9] and those presented in his report of March 12, 1967. We shall conclude with another citation from Schnitzler:

"The entire commission that dealt with Holy Mass can be regarded as the author. . . . In laborious and irritating meetings held at Rome, Nemi, and Orselina and marked by fierce disputes and bitter disappointments, an effort was made to come to agreement on a schema which was then presented to the Holy Father. The one truly responsible for this liturgical prayer was Paul VI himself. When historians come to give it a name they will have no choice but to call it the 'Canon of Paul VI.' "[10]

We have to be satisfied with these few pieces of information as we wait and hope that those involved in the work of commission will publish their memoirs and diaries.

III. VERE SANCTUS ES, DOMINE ("LORD, YOU ARE HOLY INDEED")

LITERAL TRANSLATION	ICEL TRANSLATION
Lord, you are holy indeed, and your every creature rightly	Father, you are holy indeed, and all creation rightly gives

125

praises you, because through your Son, our Lord Jesus Christ, by the power of the Holy Spirit, you enliven and sanctify all things, and you do not cease to gather a people to yourself, so that from East to West a pure sacrifice may be offered to your Name.	you praise. All life, all holiness comes from you through your Son, Jesus Christ our Lord, by the working of the Holy Spirit. From age to age you gather a people to yourself, so that from east to west a perfect offering may be made to the glory of your name.

This first prayer links the Sanctus with the account of institution. The connection is not brief nor purely transitional. Instead, the prayer develops a precise theme; but, as pointed out by the official expositor on the eucharistic prayers in general,[11] this theme was not taken from the history of salvation, since that is reserved for the preface.

The Latin text is more coherent and linear in character than, for example, the Italian translation, which begins with an acclamatory exclamation[12] that is not matched by anything similar later on, since the remainder of the prayer simply tells of God's work without any expression of praise or gratitude. The Latin text, on the contrary, unifies the two elements of praise and narration, the opening praise being motivated by the narration that immediately follows. A careful reading of the Italian translation shows indeed that this sequence of ideas is also to be found therein, but what is clear to a reader is not equally clear to a listener. Even a very careful recitation of the Italian prayer does not show the connection, so clear in the Latin text, between the praise and the following narration.

After the opening praise of the "Lord," that is, the Father, the prayer contains four points.

1. The divine work is described in trinitarian terms. The Son is the mediator, while the Spirit makes his work effective. In reading these words, we should take 1 Corinthians 2:4[13] as the source and therefore the hermeneutical criterion for interpreting the phrase: "*Spiritus Sancti operante virtute*" ("by the power of the Holy Spirit" or, more literally, "the power of the Holy Spirit working [in him, the Son]"[14] (ICEL: "by the working of the Spirit").

2. Life and holiness are the divine gifts mentioned here. The perspective is cosmic: "*Vivificas et sanctificas universa*" ("You enliven and sanctify all things"). The idea is a splendid one, since it urges human beings to think of the entire universe as God's work that is

jubilant with life and holiness.[15] It is for this reason that every creature ("*omnis a te condita creatura*") praises the Father.

3. There is an ecclesial dimension: "You continue to gather a people to yourself." Two things are said of God here. He gathers a people, and he himself is the principle of the unity: he gathers a people to or around himself. For the Christological significance of the theme of unity, we refer you to our discussion of the epiclesis in the Fourth Eucharistic Prayer.

The Church is thus seen as a liturgical assembly in which God is present as the central personage and the principle of unity. He is in the midst of a people which he himself has gathered. We can easily foresee the purpose of this assembly: God acts and the people are called upon to interact with him. Thus, the very concept of cult or public worship is introduced, and we can hear in the background an echo of the Exodus and the themes of Passover.[16]

4. The final point made in this transition from the Sanctus to the epiclesis is a formal statement of the cultic theme. This has already been implicit, but now it is made explicit in a manner analogous to 1 Peter 2:5. The citation of Malachi 1:11 is typical in such a context. Eucharistic worship is prefigured in the passage from the prophet when it is explained typologically, as it has been by the entire tradition from *Didache* 14, 3 to the Council of Trent[17] and Vatican II.[18] In the New Testament, the process of the spiritualization of cult reaches its climax; in the New Testament, there is a concern to show that this culmination was inevitable because it was expressly foreseen and predicted by the prophets.

The passage in Malachi states that the worship of God will be universal, and at the same time describes its essential and constitutive nature. The Letter to the Hebrews in the New Testament explains this perfect worship: "Through him then let us continually offer up a sacrifice of praise to God, that is, the fruit of lips that acknowledge his name. Do not neglect to do good and to share what you have, for such sacrifices are pleasing to God."[19]

This complete spiritualization of cult is realized in the eucharistic celebration, since the anaphora, together with the preface and Sanctus just recited, is precisely such an "acknowledgment of his name" and an acknowledgment which is the fruit of our own lips. In the Fathers of the Church, the people described by Malachi as offering a "pure sacrifice" (*oblatio munda*) is the Church. The Latin text uses the term *oblatio munda* and thus cites the Vulgate translation of Malachi. To do so is to emphasize the offerers, in keeping with the logic of the "pleasing odor of sacrifice," discussed in Chapter Three in connection with the Roman Canon: God freely accepts the sacrifice, and the offerers of it are pleasing to him.

The Italian Missal translates *oblatio munda* as "perfect sacrifice" (ICEL: "a perfect offering") and thus shifts the emphasis to the sacrifice in its objective, ontological reality. Moreover, the Italian translation allows an equivocation, since on hearing "perfect sacrifice," we think spontaneously of the cross of Christ; only when we analyze the text, do we find that the emphasis is on the people. Malachi's "pure sacrifice" or "pure offering" is more meaningful here. In addition, the Italian "perfect sacrifice" does not convey much meaning and simply suggests the historical context in which it originated: the gradual spiritualization of the Old Testament cult.

IV. FIRST EPICLESIS

LITERAL TRANSLATION

Therefore we humbly pray you, Lord, to sanctify by that same Spirit these gifts which we have brought you to be consecrated, that they may become the body and blood of your Son, our Lord Jesus Christ, at whose command we celebrate these mysteries.

For on the night in which he was betrayed, he took the bread and, giving thanks to you, offered the blessing; he broke the bread and gave it to his disciples saying: "Take this, all of you, and eat of it: for this is my body, which will be given up for you." In like manner, after the supper, taking the cup and giving thanks to you he offered the blessing and gave the cup to his disciples, saying: "Take this, all of you, and drink of it: for this is the cup of my blood of the new and everlasting

ICEL TRANSLATION

And so, Father, we bring you these gifts. We ask you to make them holy by the power of your Spirit, that they may become the body and blood of your Son, our Lord Jesus Christ, at whose command we celebrate this eucharist.

On the night he was betrayed, he took bread and gave you thanks and praise. He broke the bread, gave it to his disciples, and said: "Take this, all of you, and eat it: this is my body which will be given up for you."

When supper was ended, he took the cup. Again he gave you thanks and praise, gave the cup to his disciples, and said: "Take this, all of you, and drink from it: this the the cup of my blood, the blood of the new and everlasting covenant. It will be

128

convenant, which shall be shed
for you and for the many for
the forgiveness of sins. Do this
in memory of me."

The mystery of faith! — We
proclaim your death, Lord, and
we profess your resurrection,
until you come.

shed for you and for all so that
sins may be forgiven. Do this in
memory of me."

Let us proclaim the mystery
of faith: Christ has died, Christ
is risen, Christ will come again.

Reading this prayer in Latin, we have the impression that it is
clearly intended as a parallel to the *Quam oblationem* ("We pray you,
O God") of the Roman Canon. The Italian translation, on the other
hand ("Now we humbly ask you: Send your Spirit to sanctify the
gifts we offer to you" [ICEL: "And so, Father, we bring you these
gifts. We ask you to make them holy by the power of your Spirit"])
makes the parallelism disappear. A first difference between the
Latin and the Italian is that the Latin asks God to sanctify the gifts
through the Holy Spirit,[20] while the Italian asks for the sending of
the Spirit. The Latin takes the theme in the *Quam oblationem* and relates it to the Spirit, whereas the Italian constructs an epiclesis
based on the coming of the Spirit.

A further difference is in the handling of the theme of offering.
The Latin has *detulimus* ("we have brought"); the Italian has "we offer" (ICEL: "bring") in the present tense. The Latin verb is in the
perfect tense and, therefore, indicates an action that has taken
place. Consequently, it cannot be translated as "we offer" because
the offering has not taken place; it will be made immediately after
the anamnesis.[21] The perfect tense is not applicable to the offering,
and the Latin *detulimus* must, therefore, refer to bringing the gifts
to the altar, an action that has indeed taken place.

We must not confuse the act of offering, which follows the
anamnesis, with the preparation of the gifts,[22] during which the
gifts are carried to the altar.

Our interpretation of the Latin text is confirmed by a comparable
prayer: the Verona Sacramentary has the expression *munera delata*
in a prayer over the gifts, where the only possible translation is
"gifts that have been brought" (past tense).[23]

It is hard to know what to make of the anticipated act of offering
which the Italian translation represents. Perhaps what is intended
is a historical present tense; or perhaps there is a reminiscence of
the Alexandrian liturgy of St. Mark or Serapion, though this is not
likely.

After the petition that the bread and wine may become the body and blood of Christ, mention is made of the command of institution: "at whose command we celebrate these mysteries" (ICEL: "at whose command we celebrate this eucharist"). The same is done in the fourth anaphora. This is a profound way of leading into the account of institution, namely, by expressing the theology of the account.

We celebrate these mysteries in consequence of and in obedience to Christ's command. His command has to do with the celebration of his Last Supper. It now introduces the account of that event, which motivates, confirms, and encourages the Church in its own celebration. The Church compares its action with the very story of the "Lord's Supper" by telling that story to the Father. The Apostle uses the same words in urging the faithful of Corinth to bear the fruit which the "Lord's Supper" should produce.

Like the Antiochene liturgies, the Third Eucharistic Prayer begins the account of institution in the Pauline manner. In the history of the liturgy, there have been three ways of beginning the account:

1. The Roman Canon, which uses the formula *Qui pridie* ("Who, on the day before . . .").

2. The Alexandrian, which uses the particle *hoti* ("Because he himself, the Lord . . .").

3. The Antiochene, which uses the Pauline introduction: "On the night on which he was betrayed . . ."

The last is the one chosen for the third anaphora. The choice is not simply a matter of detail or of literary style, rather it represents a theological choice, since the theology of the account of institution in 1 Corinthians is very precise and has a functional role in the celebration.

Unfortunately, the literature on this subject is limited; in fact, the only author we can cite is A. Rodenas.[24] The Pauline text describes the Lord's Supper which the Apostle gave the Corinthians as a norm and therefore as a means of remedying the serious distortions that had arisen in that community. Just before this passage in 1 Corinthians, Paul explains clearly the fault he finds with the Corinthians: their lack of unity.[25] His conclusion is in lapidary and typically Pauline form: the celebration lacks unity because it lacks conformity to the model which Christ gave us in the upper room; it lacks conformity to the will and intention which Christ manifested and to which he refers in his command: "Do this in memory of me." To use a word from a later time, we might say that what was lacking in the eucharistic meal at Corinth was "truth," the truth proper to the sacrament. Paul is, therefore, able to conclude: your supper is no longer the Lord's Supper.

The accusation is a serious one, and we can understand the embarassment of the commentators as they see the unavoidable inference they must draw from Paul's accusation and conclusion. In Corinth, unity was violated by disorders at table, but there is no denying that the unity of an assembly[26] can be violated in other ways. Whatever the manner of violation, if unity is broken, the Pauline accusation applies: you no longer eat the Lord's Supper.

When the Roman liturgical reformers chose the Pauline way of introducing the account of institution, did they also adopt the theology in light of which Paul understands the Supper? We think not. It is possible that the choice was motivated by a desire for variety and a desire to let it be seen that the Roman Church was not committed to a single way of beginning the account (namely, "On the day before he suffered").

On the other hand, if a Pauline formula is chosen to begin the account of institution, can we ignore the theology implicit in it? The question is rhetorical. If we choose a passage from Paul, the reason is not simply that it has been used in the Syrian tradition; sooner or later, we must accept the Pauline thinking that is embodied in the passage.

V. ANAMNESIS

LITERAL TRANSLATION	ICEL TRANSLATION
Mindful therefore, Lord, of the saving passion of your Son and of his wonderful resurrection and ascension into heaven, but also looking forward to his second coming, . . .	Father, calling to mind the death your Son endured for our salvation, his glorious resurrection and ascension into heaven, and ready to greet him when he comes again, . . .

The anamnesis gives expression to the self-consciousness of the celebrating Church, in the sense that the Church tells God what it understands to be the nature, meaning, and value of the rite it is celebrating, that is, of the sacramental action being performed. In telling all this to God, the Church gains a deeper understanding of it and ratifies it, since in listening to itself tell it to God it also tells it to itself.

In the Italian translation, there is no "therefore" connecting the anamnesis with the account and command of institution. As a result, the anamnesis is theologically separated from the command of institution that is its support. Since the anamnesis exists as a result of that command, it should be connected with it by a conclusive or consecutive conjunction which, in this Latin text, is *igitur*."[27]

The Italian translation also departs from the Latin in its theology of the eucharistic memorial. The Latin says simply: "Mindful therefore, O Lord . . . ,"[28] while the Italian has: "Celebrating the memorial of your Son who dies for our salvation . . ." (ICEL: "Father, calling to mind the death your Son endured for our salvation"). The difference is not small. In the Latin, which in this echoes the Roman Canon, it is persons who exercise mindfulness, while in the Italian, the element of remembering is shifted to the action and is objectified as "memorial." In the Latin, those who are mindful offer; in the Italian, a memorial is celebrated and an offering made. The Italian is thus a theological translation of the original, that is, what is translated is not the text itself but its theology or, more accurately, the theology which the translators think the text should contain.

We do not wish these remarks on the Italian translation to argue for a literal version that is materially faithful to the original. They are simply a reminder of the theological change that takes place in translation. Once again, there is no such thing as a pure translation; every translation is an interpretation influenced by the conceptions, ideas, and concerns which the translator has and which, without realization, make their presence felt in his work.

Another difference between the Italian and the original is in the object of the "remembering" or "memorial": in Italian, the object is simply the Son. The passion and resurrection no longer appear as saving "actions" but become attributes of Christ: "dead for our salvation,[29] gloriously risen and ascended to heaven" (ICEL: "endured for our salvation, his glorious resurrection and ascension into heaven"). In Latin, as pointed out in the previous note, it is the passion that saves, but the attribution does not mean a loss of the proper balance that should exist between the passion, on the one hand, and the resurrection and ascension, on the other. The resurrection, too, is accompanied by an important descriptive adjective: *mirabilis* (wonderful); this immediately calls to mind the "saving" works of God, which are known in Latin as the *mirabilia Dei* (wonderful works of God).

The Italian has "gloriously risen." If this meant that the resurrection is a manifestation of the "glory" of God, the translation would be an improvement on the original. But, if this were the intention,

132

the translator should have used the adjective "glorious" and not the adverb "gloriously," which is likely to suggest the display accompanying one more victory among many, rather than the manifestation of God's "glory" (*doxa*) in the crowning event of salvation.

The passage from the Latin to the Italian brings a theological impoverishment, since the balance between the passion, the resurrection, and the ascension has been removed and undue emphasis has been placed on the suffering Christ. In the original, the adjective *mirabilis* accompanies both the resurrection and the ascension, and the two are theologically one.[30] When this rather complex Italian sentence is read aloud, its structure isolates the resurrection from the ascension, and the latter is therefore left without its descriptive adjective. This is true, however, only of the oral text; from a literary standpoint, there is no difficulty, and the balance of the Latin is respected. Different translations produce different effects, depending on whether the version is conceived as simply a written one or whether it is intended for oral proclamation.

From this standpoint, Father Vagaggini is to be praised, since in his proposal for new Canons of the Mass, he focused his attention on the oral text and took full account of the Latin *cursus*.[31] We are well aware that in translations it is very difficult to do justice to the particular speech rhythms of each modern language; it must nonetheless be kept in mind that an anaphora is intended for recitation and that if it is not suitable for this use, it becomes an unsatisfactory anaphora.

Another point where the Latin original and the Italian translation differ is the eschatological reference. The words "*praestolantes alterum eius adventum*"[32] belong both logically and theologically with the preceding words, that is, with the passion, resurrection, and ascension, so that the paschal mystery is described fully, with all its parts. The Italian, however, says: "Celebrating the memorial of your Son, dead . . . risen and ascended . . . , we offer, as we await his coming" (ICEL: "Calling to mind the death of your Son . . . , his glorious resurrection and ascension . . . and ready to greet him when he comes again, we offer you").

This separation of the coming from the passion, death and resurrection, and its attachment to "we offer" are unfortunate. The sacrifice that is offered appears as something that fills the time of waiting rather than as what it is: the manner in which Christians experience the final coming in advance. They experience it by celebrating it in sacramental form, for in the liturgy, "celebrate" means "make present." Our expectation of the final coming finds expression in

133

the very celebration of the eucharistic sacrifice: as we celebrate the final coming, we experience it in advance. The Eucharist is the anticipation of the final coming and, therefore, it is the concrete form of our expectation of that coming.

VI. THE SACRIFICE

. . . we, giving thanks, offer to you this living and holy sacrifice.

. . . we offer you in thanksgiving this holy and living sacrifice.

In the preceding chapter at this point, the second anaphora, taken from the *Apostolic Tradition* of Hippolytus, had a brief statement of thanksgiving. The third anaphora follows the same course with a very brief expression of thanksgiving between the anamnesis and the prayer of offering: "We, giving thanks, offer to you this living and holy sacrifice."[33]

The Latin "giving thanks" (*gratias agentes*) can be understood in two ways:

a) The subjective situation or attitude of those offering the sacrifice is one of gratitude, so that those offering can be described as "giving thanks." In this case, "giving thanks" is part of the subject of the verb "offer"; it states a quality in the offerers, not in the sacrifice.

b) "Giving thanks" is a clause that explains *offerimus*; this means that it is of the nature of this "living and holy sacrifice" to be a "giving of thanks." In this case, "offer" and "thank" are identical. The offering of the living and holy sacrifice is a "eucharist," that is, an offering of thanks.

The Italian translation ("We offer you, Father, in thanksgiving this living and holy sacrifice" [ICEL: ". . . we offer you in thanksgiving this holy and living sacrifice"]) unfortunately does not adopt either of these alternatives. Instead it creates a third: the offering of the living and holy sacrifice is done "in thanksgiving," that is, it is the way of thanking the Father. The living and holy sacrifice becomes a means of expressing gratitude. Just as one thanks another by sending a bouquet of roses, so one thanks the Father by offering him the living and holy sacrifice. Is this the theology of sacrifice that the Italian intends to convey? We hope not; the translators could not really have intended the text to be thus understood.

The project of a new Canon which C. Vagaggini published in 1966 had the words: "*gratias agentes tibi hoc sacrificium incruentum.*" Translated this reads: "And, giving you thanks, we offer to you this bloodless sacrifice."[34] Had they wished, the Italian translators of Anaphora III could have used the translation at hand and prepared in fact by the author (or quasi-author) of the Latin text itself. That author, who was so concerned about the *cursus* of his Latin text, devoted no less attention and care to his Italian translation.

From the project for the Third Eucharistic Prayer (presented to the Commission on the Order of Mass on March 12, 1967),[35] at this point (anamnesis and epiclesis prayers) four alternative redactions were provided so that the Commission might have a choice. All four versions had a strong sacrificial emphasis in common: "We, giving thanks, offer to you this saving 'victim' (*hostiam salutarem*[36]) as a living and holy sacrifice." This text was then simplified: "saving victim" was omitted, and "this living and holy sacrifice" became the direct object of the offering. This change had already been made in the project of April 13, 1967,[37] only a month after the meeting in Nemi.

The first of the four proposals for the anamnesis had a significant addition at this point, since according to it what was being offered was not simply the saving victim as a living and holy sacrifice, but "with it, ourselves and all we have, for we are yours and all things are yours."[38] The words were evidently inspired by Vatican II: "Offering the immaculate victim, not only through the hands of the priest but also together with him, they [the faithful] should learn to offer themselves. Through Christ, the Mediator, they should be drawn day by day into ever more perfect union with God and each other, so that finally God may be all in all."[39] The Commission (*Coetus* X) decided to keep the addition, but there was no consensus as to where it should be placed. This was one reason why the official expositor offered four proposals for the anamnesis and epiclesis to the Commission.

The first proposal, as we have just seen, made the words in question part of the prayer of offering at the end of the anamnesis. The second shortened the text and changed its meaning somewhat, making it less close to the passage in Vatican II. This was the form that was finally taken into the definitive text of Anaphora III: "May he make us an everlasting gift to you."[40] At the point where the words just cited occur (in the epiclesis), the expositor's third proposal has the words: "May we learn to offer ourselves to you with Christ." The fourth proposal, once again, has: "Make us an everlasting gift to you," but introduces these words with others from the first proposal: "Because we are yours and all things are yours."[41]

After presenting the four proposals, the expositor (Fr. Vagaggini) recommended the adoption of the first because, as he saw it, the offering of the victim is still part of the "anamnesis" and is not yet the "recommendation of the sacrifice."[42] Consequently, the words in which the faithful offer themselves in association with the offering of the divine victim should be placed in the anamnesis and not in the following paragraph. The expositor also urged the inclusion of the words: "of the gifts you have bestowed on us" ("de tuis donis ac datis"),[43] which are so typical of the Roman Canon and a classical element in so many Eastern anaphoras.

In his commentary on his own project of a new Roman Canon (1966), Vagaggini shows the same concern he later voiced in his report to the reform commission. He begins his commentary on "de tuis donis ac datis" by saying that the phrase is biblical in origin (1 Cor 29:14), and he cites the Byzantine Anaphoras of Basil and Chrysostom, the Greek and Coptic Alexandrian Anaphoras of Basil, and the Greek Anaphora of Mark as preserved in the Coptic Anaphora of Cyril. He cites at length several passages in Irenaeus.[44] Later, in his report to the Commission on the third anaphora, he adds that in the first proposal the words about the offering of ourselves and all we have is a modern equivalent of the ancient "de tuis donis ac datis."

But, as we said, the second proposal was chosen. It is not easy to say whether the rejection of the first proposal meant a loss; we think not.

Another point was a subject of discussion: the phrase which in Anaphora III reads: "recognizing the *hostia* by whose sacrifice you willed to be reconciled." In the second and fourth proposals, these words read: "recognizing the victim by whose intercession you willed to be reconciled" (ICEL: "and see the Victim whose death has reconciled us to yourself"). The expositor had especially harsh words for this phrase; in hindsight the facts justified him. He says that "recognize the victim" will not do, since the term "victim" is not found in the best liturgical tradition and puts too much stress on the element of bloodshed, which in fact is absent from the Mass. There are, perhaps, not many who emphasize every single word of the celebration, but if one does, one will obviously be ill at ease with such a crude expression as "recognizing the victim by whose intercession you willed to be reconciled."

Father Vagaggini was right to stress this point; the Commission accepted his objection and substituted *hostia* for *victima*. It then made the whole phrase more balanced by changing "by whose intercession" to "by whose sacrifice[45] you willed to be reconciled."

The sacrificial meaning—or even its blood aspect—was not changed, however, but at least the Commission avoided the word "victim" which would be unsuitable for the further reason that it no longer has the cultic meaning it once had. Nowadays, a "victim" is one who has suffered injustice or whose lot is a wretched one; it has lost all its original cultic flavor. In Latin, *victima* has rightly been replaced by *hostia*; translators are thereby alerted to choose a word suitable to the special character of the action being celebrated, for if this is a "sacrifice," it is certainly not a blood sacrifice. "Victim" does not capture the cultic character of the eucharistic meal, which is free of the repulsive elements conveyed by that word. As we said, the Commission recognized the justice of all this and replaced *victima* with *hostia*.

In making this necessary criticism, we are quite aware of the difficulty which even the word *hostia* poses for a translator. Perhaps a circumlocution is the answer. Let us turn back once more to Fr. Vagaggini. In 1966 in his project for a Canon, he used the language which he rejected a year later in his exposition of the proposed new anaphora. In his own project, he had written: "*Agnoscens victimam cuius intercessione voluisti placari.*" The literal translation reads: "Recognizing the victim by whose intercession you willed to be reconciled." But he himself translated it as: "Recognize him who, in your mercy, reconciled us to you."[46] This version avoids all problems and yet respects the meaning of the Latin original.

VII. SOURCES OF THE TEXT

Father Vagaggini's report to the Commission at Nemi is often a summary of the critical documentation published in 1966 in connection with his own proposal for a new Canon.

The words: "We, giving thanks, offer to you this living and holy sacrifice," are from the Anaphora of Theodore of Mospuestia,[47] as Vagaggini indicates.[48] This source is especially important because it also contains the concept of "accepted by God," which is only implicit in the Latin text of Anaphora III. But the history of the entire passage we have been discussing ("We offer to you . . . reconciled") reaches much further back than Theodore, since the words and ideas are to be found, for practical purposes, in the Letter to the Romans: "I appeal to you therefore, brethren, by the mercies of God, to present your bodies as a living sacrifice, holy and acceptable to God, which is your spiritual worship."[49]

It is very important to regard this passage in Paul as the source of the offering prayer in our third anaphora. It is important because Paul is not speaking of a rite or a special act of offering that has for its objects our bodies, that is, ourselves. He is speaking rather of an attitude that is to permeate our lives, an attitude that is coextensive with and equivalent to our "being in Christ." The worship in question is not an act but a radical attitude of heart that is one of the fundamental options open to human beings. Indeed, everywhere in the New Testament, worship (cult) is viewed in this nonritual manner: true worship of God consists in a radical and totally pervasive holiness of the person.

That kind of cult, which is identical with the very lives of Christians insofar as they are lives of faith, becomes thematic in the third anaphora and provides terminology and concepts for formulating the sacrificial theme. The cult or worship which takes form in the living of human life thus becomes a sacramental action in the eucharistic anaphora.

In his report at Nemi, Vagaggini, as we saw, emphasized the problem with the word "victim," since the Eucharist is not in any sense a blood rite. His point was well taken. On the other hand, the Mozarabic liturgy has a theology which completely identifies the sacrament with the reality of which it is the sacrament,[50] that is, the cross of Christ. In such a theology, it is impossible not to use the terminology of blood sacrifices even for the Mass. Here is the text from this liturgy which Vagaggini himself says[51] is the source for his own proposed Latin text with its *victima* ("*agnoscens victimam cuius voluisti intercessione placari*"):

"This is the victim (*hostia*) which hung on the wood; this is the flesh which rose from the tomb. What our priest [Christ] offered in actual fact, we offer in sweet-tasting bread and wine. Acknowledge, we pray you, almightly God, the victim (*victimam*) through whose intercession you were reconciled, and receive as your adopted children those whose Father you have become by grace.[52]

In this text and the further text cited in note 52, what finds expression is not so much the celebration and remembrance of the

138

Lord's saving actions as the celebration of the sacrifice of the "Christ who suffered" (*Christus passus*) and, having risen, still lives in heaven and can therefore be immolated "once again."

The word "immolated" (*immolatus*) in these texts of the Mozarabic liturgy refers to blood sacrifice, since its object is the *Christus passus* who shed his blood. The unavoidable conclusion is that a blood victim is offered once again in the Mass, exactly as on the cross; only the manner of offering is "unbloody." In a theology in which the Mass is conceived as the offering of the divine victim, the vocabulary of blood sacrifices will inevitably be used. Working within the framework of such a theology, the Council of Trent specifies that only the manner of offering (*ratio offerendi*[53]) differs; in all other respects, there is a complete identity with the sacrifice of the cross.

In light of this, we can conclude that the real difficulty is less with a word that has implications of "blood sacrifice" than with the theological system behind it, a system based on the "repetition" of Chirst's sacrifice. The association between the word "victim" and a theology of repetition of Christ's sacrifice is clear in Gregory the Great:

"We ought to immolate daily sacrifices (*hostias*) of his flesh and blood. For this victim (*victima*) alone saves the soul from eternal death, inasmuch as in the sacrament the Only-begotten renews (*reparat*) for us his very death. Although as one risen from the dead he can no longer die and death has no more power over him, and although he lives an immortal and incorruptible life, he is nonetheless immolated for us again in this mystery of the holy sacrifice."[54]

In this passage, the concept of sacrifice has been completely separated from the commemoration, the Last Supper, and the mandate in obedience to which the Mass is celebrated. This entire section of Gregory's *Dialogues* is permeated by a "victim" theology, for he is bent on showing the efficacy of the sacrifice in regard to the sins of the living and the dead.

Anaphora III retains the concept of "immolation." Does this mean that it also accepts a theology of sacrificial repetition, of the "once again"? Not necessarily. Since the anaphora introduces the account of institution by referring to Christ's command that we remember him, the theology of anamnesis or commemoration has gained the upper hand over a theology of repetition.

In such an anamnetic theology (theology of commemoration or remembrance), the sacrificial character of the Eucharist depends on its relation to the Last Supper and, via the Last Supper, to the cross and resurrection. The Eucharist is a "relative" rather than an "absolute" sacrifice.[55]

Professor H. Wegman has examined the problem of the Mozarabic origin of the passage we are discussing and has concluded that that origin is not certain: the Mozarabic *Post-pridie* prayer which Vagaggini cites and which we have translated above is not the only parallel that can be adduced for the relevant section in Anaphora III. Wegman cites the following prayer from the Verona Sacramentary: "Accept, Lord, the sacrifice by whose immolation you willed to be reconciled. . . ."[56] But that is not the only text that might be cited. Here is a secret prayer from the Missal of Pius V (1570): "Lord, graciously accept the sacrifice (*hostias*) by which you willed that you be reconciled, and that we be restored by your powerful mercy."[57] And here is another prayer in the Verona Sacramentary: "God, our teacher, make known your gifts, and through this sacrifice (*hostias*) by which you willed to be reconciled, mercifully sanctify those who immolate them."[58]

Wegman rightly concludes that the expression "*hostiam cuius voluisti immolatione placari*" in Anaphora III is not typically Mozarabic, since it is also well attested in the Roman liturgy. We would add that the Roman tradition took precedence over the Mozarabic at the moment when, as a result of Vagaggini's report at Nemi, the *victima* of the initial redaction was replaced by the *hostia* of the definitive redaction. The text with *hostia* is in fact Roman; the text with *victima* seems closer to the Mozarabic tradition.

The verb *agnoscere* also deserves special attention.[59] "We do not ask God to take cognizance of our memorial, but to recognize in our offering the memorial of his Son's death. We pray him to assure us that our celebration is truly a commemoration of Jesus. The death and resurrection of Jesus are thus at the heart of the Eucharist."[60]

VIII. EPICLESIS

LITERAL TRANSLATION	ICEL TRANSLATION
Look, we pray, on the offering of your Church and, recognizing the "victim" by whose immolation you willed to be reconciled [or: the sacrificial offering	Look with favor on your Church's offering, and see the Victim whose death has reconciled us to yourself. Grant that we, who are nourished by his

140

by which you willed to be reconciled], grant that we who are nourished by the body and blood of your Son, being filled with his Holy Spirit, may be one body and one spirit in Christ.

body and blood, may be filled with his Holy Spirit, and become one body, one spirit in Christ.

In this anaphora, the epiclesis for the communicants is joined with the prayer for the acceptance of the sacrifice. The theme of acceptance occupies the first part of the prayer, down to and inclusive of the plea that God would "recognize" our celebration for what it is: a commemoration of redemption.

Those present at the Eucharist realize that this memorial is the holy supper of the Lord. They, therefore, turn to the Father, presenting themselves to him as persons who have been invited to a banquet, as men and women who will eat the same bread and drink from the same cup that Jesus gave to his disciples at the Last Supper, namely, his own body and blood.

The verb "feed upon," "be nourished" (*reficimur*) signifies both the physical activity of eating and drinking and the personal activity of the disciples who live and are nourished by something that is part of the master's own life. Communion is an action of the whole person, and it is "following."

To feed upon Jesus and be nourished by him means to absorb his every word and gesture so that the believer's heart is radically changed and "one begins to consider, judge, and arrange his life according to the holiness and love of God, made manifest in his Son in the last days and given to us in abundance."[61] There is no question simply of "eating" the body of Christ. To feed upon or be nourished means to attain to *metanoia*. Otherwise there would be no "communion" but only a swallowing.

The epiclesis asks that this complete and intense communion with Christ may bring us the fullness of the Spirit. This prayer, by itself, shows that the Eucharist is the crowning sacrament of Christian initiation and the greatest of all the sacraments. In making this claim, we do not lose sight of the Eucharist as a sharing in the death of the risen Jesus, since "when Jesus dies and 'gives up His Spirit of God' he 'hands [it] on' to the Church" (Jn 29:30).[62] In this verse of John, it is by his glorious death that he delivers the Spirit. John makes it more explicit elsewhere that it is his glorification which gives the Spirit[63] and thus inaugurates the time of the

141

Church.[64] This Spirit is the Spirit of Jesus[65] and preserves among the disciples the same union that existed among the immediate followers of Jesus: "The company of those who believed were of one heart and soul" (Acts 4:32).

It is *metanoia*, therefore, that is being asked in this epiclesis which ends with a theology of unity ("one body, one spirit") taken from the Anaphora of Basil.[66] We sum up with H. Wegman: "Thanks to the Spirit of God, participation in the Lord's Supper brings true communion" (Eph 4:4).[67]

The theme of unity in our anaphora comes by a complex development from the eucharist in the *Didache*.[68] Moreover, from the *Didache* on, the eucharistic theme of unity has been linked to the theology of Paul: "Because there is one bread we who are many are one body, for we all partake of the one bread" (1 Cor 10:17). But the Anaphora of Basil, followed by our Anaphora III, relocates this Pauline eucharistic theology in a pneumatological framework by linking it with a citation: "one body and one Spirit" (Eph 4:4).

The epiclesis thus ends in contemplation of the unity among those who are "in Christ." This unity is, as it were, a pathway built by the Spirit who is given to us in his fullness. He is the reality by which we are nourished when we feed upon the body and blood of Christ, since "the Lord is the Spirit" (2 Cor 3:17).

IX. INTERCESSIONS

LITERAL TRANSLATION	ICEL TRANSLATION
May he make us an everlasting gift to you, so that we may obtain an inheritance with your elect, especially with the most blessed Virgin Mary, Mother of God, with your blessed apostles and glorious martyrs, (with St. N. [saint of the day or patronal saint],) and with all the saints by whose intercession with you we hope to be always aided.	May he make us an everlasting gift to you and enable us to share in the inheritance of your saints, with Mary, the virgin Mother of God; with the apostles, the martyrs, (Saint N.—the saint of the day or the patron saint) and all your saints, on whose constant intercession we rely for help.
We pray, Lord, that this sacrifice by which we are reconciled will bring peace and salvation to the entire world. Deign to	Lord, may this sacrifice, which has made our peace with you, advance the peace and salvation of all the world.

strengthen in faith and love your Church that is a pilgrim on earth, together with your servant N., our Pope, and N., our bishop, with all the bishops and the clergy and the entire people you have won.

Hear favorably the prayers of this family which you willed should stand before you. Loving Father, be merciful and unite to yourself all your children, wherever they be scattered.

Receive graciously into your kingdom our dead brothers and sisters and all those who were pleasing to you when they passed from this world. We hope that there we may together be filled forever with your glory, through Christ our Lord, through whom you bestow all good gifts upon the world.

Through him and with him and in him all honor and glory is yours, almighty God and Father, in the unity of the Holy Spirit, for ever and ever. Amen.

Strengthen in faith and love your pilgrim Church on earth; your servant, Pope N., our bishop N., and all the bishops, with the clergy and the entire people your Son has gained for you. Father, hear the prayers of the family you have gathered here before you. In mercy and love unite all your children wherever they may be.

Welcome into your kingdom our departed brothers and sisters, and all who have left this world in your friendship. We hope to enjoy for ever the vision of your glory, through Christ our Lord, from whom all good things come.

Through him, with him, in him, in the unity of the Holy Spirit, all glory and honor is yours, almighty Father, for ever and ever. Amen.

The intercessions are in two parts, beginning with a commemoration of the Church in heaven and then turning to a commemoration of the entire Church that is "a pilgrim on earth."

The whole is introduced in a way that resembles the Eastern liturgies, where the theme of offering is briefly repeated at the beginning of the intercessions.[69] At the same time, however, the third anaphora represents a radical change by comparison with those liturgies. The gift to God, to which reference is made, is not the eucharistic sacrifice which is now going on. It is the Christian life, conceived as sacrificial worship offered to the Father. The life which the faithful lead in Christ is an act of worship in the true and proper sense; it is a true liturgy, even if nonritual.

The term "spiritual worship"[70] is not a metaphor emphasizing the importance of a Christian life. The novelty of Christianity is precisely that the essence of its worship is not ritual performance but relation to Christ. Wherever the human person and Christ are linked in the Spirit, there is worship and liturgy in the proper sense of the terms. If the "following" and "imitation" of Christ are an exercise of worship,[71] it follows that in Christian life there is no longer any distinction between sacred and profane.[72] Everything is unified for those who live in Christ.

This is the situation referred to at the beginning of the intercessions. The whole of life, not simply the eucharistic celebration, is the worship that is acceptable to God. The intercessions, therefore, begin by asking the Father that he would enable us thus to worship him and to be an "everlasting gift" or sacrifice to him.

Christians become this "everlasting gift" by being transformed into "one body and one spirit," and it is this in the eucharistic celebration which changes the faithful into images of Christ by uniting them. The unity bears fruit in our Christian lives, in our deepest and most authentic values, so that our existence becomes a living worship: from Eucharist to life, from "doing" worship to "being" worship. It is evident that when we speak of life as worship, we are revising the classical distinction between "practicing" and "non-practicing" Christians and giving it a theologically more nuanced theological form.

This process is a necessary and essential condition if human beings are to "obtain an inheritance" or, as the Italian translation has it, "obtain the promised kingdom" (ICEL: "share in the inheritance of your saints"). The substitution of "promised kingdom" for "inheritance" recalls another passage from the Last Supper. Toward the end of the celebration, Jesus says: "You are those who have continued with me in my trials; as my Father appointed (*dietheto*) a kingdom for me, so do I appoint (*diatithemai*) for you" (Lk 22:29).

The same theme reappears in chap. 10 of the *Didache*, but applied to the Church: it is for the Church that the Father has prepared a kingdom.[73] This makes it understandable that the prayer for entrance into the promised kingdom should, in the Anaphora of Basil (which is based on the *Didache*), follow upon the petition that the communicants may become "one body and one spirit." The same theme appears, but in a more developed form, in the early anaphora in Book VII of the *Apostolic Constitutions*, which is based on the *Didache*. Here the prayer has developed from a prayer for the Church into a prayer for those who have shared in the Eucharist.

144

Nonetheless, the point is still made that the kingdom has been prepared for the Church: "Gather all of us in your kingdom which you have prepared for it [the Church] (*hetoimasas autē*)."[74]

Entrance into the promised kingdom requires a holy life, a life which is worship of the Father in Christ and in the Spirit. This means concretely a life marked by the fullness of a love that bears fruit in unity: "One body and one spirit."

We noted, several paragraphs back, that the Latin and the Italian differ slightly here, and the Latin is not as rich. The Latin says simply: "that we may obtain an inheritance with your elect,"[75] whereas the Italian specifies the "inheritance" as the kingdom of God. The Latin text at this point is the same as that published by Vagaggini in 1966, but his Italian translation already suggested that the theme of the kingdom should be expressly stated.[76]

At this point in Anaphora III, there is a list of saints, headed by the Virgin Mary, Mother of God. Then comes mention of the apostles and martyrs and room for mentioning the name of some particular saint. The prayer ends with a general invocation of all the saints "by whose intercession with you we hope to be always aided" (ICEL: "on whose constant intercession we rely for help").[77] The singling out of the apostles and martyrs places the text in continuity with the Latin tradition; the older Eastern anaphoras, on the other hand, still place the saints in the broader category of the deceased for whom the eucharistic celebration is useful and helpful. As a result, prayers are being offered not only for the dead but also "for" the saints and especially "for our most holy, spotless, and glorious Queen, Mary ever Virgin, Mother of God, who is blessed above all human beings."[78]

As the eucharistic prayer draws to its conclusion, the Church broadens the horizon of its prayer to embrace the whole of human history, and prays for the peace and salvation of the entire world. It asks that the eucharistic prayer may bring this peace and salvation to the world. This prayer of the Church can perhaps provide a favorable impulse to the work of "political theology," for which the writings of J. B. Metz have won a place as a fully accredited theological discipline.

If the faithful have become "one body and one spirit" as a result of the Eucharist, it is evident that they will bear witness to this unity and become agents of it for the benefit of the world. The Eucharist is here described as a "sacrifice (*hostia*) of reconciliation,"[79] and it is perhaps for this reason that the intercession for the entire world is introduced here. It cannot be denied that the purpose of the sacrament of the death and resurrection of Christ is for the reconciliation of the entire world. Did Christ not say: "For you and for the many, for the forgiveness of sins". And again: "I am the living bread which came down from heaven; if any one eats this bread, he will live for ever; and the bread which I shall give for the life of the world is my flesh."[80]

The anaphora asks that the Church as a whole may be strengthened in faith and love. The petition is derived from the Anaphora of Hippolytus, which prays that the communicants might be "strengthened in their faith in the truth,"[81] or from the Anaphora of Serapion, which prays, in more general terms, for the strengthening of the Church.[82] The addition of "love" to "faith" is from the eucharist in the *Didache*, which says: "Lord, remember your Church . . . make it perfect in your love."[83] Hippolytus at this point rejoins his source, the *Didache*, thus producing an elegant variation on the Pauline theme of "the truth in love": "Speaking [or: doing] the truth in love, we are to grow up in every way into him who is the head, into Christ, from whom the whole body . . . makes bodily growth and upbuilds itself in love."[84]

In a eucharistic ecclesiology,[85] this passage from Paul provides, as it were, a plan of life for the entire Church, and is the best commentary on the prayer in the Eucharist that the Church may be strengthened in faith and love. The Church's relation to Christ its head cannot fail to build it up in love by constantly nourishing its faith.

The Church is called "a pilgrim on earth," a phrase that correctly describes the relation between the Church and the world. Like every individual Christian, the Church as a whole takes Paul's caution to heart: "Here we have no lasting city, but we seek the city which is to come."[86] For this reason, the certainty that the Church does not belong to this world but is present therein only as a "pilgrim" has become a firm point of reference in the postconciliar renewal of ecclesiology. The theme is given programmatic development in chap. 7 of the conciliar Constitution on the Church, where the Church that is a pilgrim on earth is distinguished from the Church that has entered the final state of eschatological salvation. "Pilgrim" emphasizes the element of incompleteness and therefore the possiblity (and reality) of sin. "The people of God is a wandering people on the way and in a state of incompleteness in spite of its firm grip on the *hypostasis*, the characteristic failing being *apostenai*" (Heb 3:12).[87]

Consequently, in the anaphora, the Church is not depicted as self-complacent because the eschatological tension inherent in the state of pilgrimage makes it to be "not of this world." It is not depicted as sure of itself because sin is of this world while it itself is not of this world but is intent rather on ultimate realities. The word "pilgrim" tells us indeed that the Church must focus its gaze on the kingdom of God, but it also reminds us that the Church is affected by everything that affects the world and that therefore sin is always at the door. In calling itself a pilgrim, the Church reminds God of the weak and fragile nature it shares with all pilgrims, and it implicitly asks him to protect and deliver it from evil. Thus, the eucharist in the *Didache* prays: "Deliver it [the Church] from all evil," before asking that the Church may be made perfect in love and be given the eschatological gift of unity in the kingdom of God.[88]

After praying for the earthly Church as a whole and recalling its pilgrim nature, the anaphora continues its intercession for the living by listing the various roles found in the Church. The Italian translation (ICEL as well) treats the Church as made up of the pope, the bishops, and so on, and asks for each group what it asks for the Church as a whole: to be strengthened in faith and love. Those specifically mentioned are the pope, the episcopal college, all the clergy, and the people whom redemption has brought into being.

The Latin differs slightly; it does not explicitly ask the same grace for each category it has asked for the Church as a whole. It is satisfied to pray simply for the Church "together with" the pope, the bishops, and so on. Each of the two choices—the Latin and Italian—has its interest, and there are good arguments for each. In our view, they are equivalent.

It has become customary, on reaching this point in the anaphora, to regret that a different outlook was not operative when the list of roles and ministries was being decided. Specifically, why did the list not begin with the people of God and end with the hierarchy and the pope?

The objection is based on a misconception. The anaphora cannot be said to depend on a pre-Vatican II ecclesiology, for when the intercession speaks of the "people of God," the reference is not to the laity as distinct from and contrasted with the hierarchy. "People of God" means the Church as a whole; this is clear from the description "the people you have won" or redeemed (ICEL: "the entire people your Son has gained for you"). The hierarchy is part of this redeemed people, and it is a hierarchy precisely because it is within, and not opposed to, the people of God.

For this reason, the intention in this intercession is not to pray

147

for the laity after having prayed for the hierarchy. The prayer is structured rather as an inclusion; that is, it begins and it ends with a petition for the Church. It is, therefore, rich in content for the student, but difficult to hear when proclaimed. The entire prayer could have been written more clearly.[89]

After the intercession for the Church, there is an intercession for the congregation that is celebrating. The congregation is called a "family," a felicitous term since it immediately indicates the kind of relations that ought to exist among the members of the congregation. Everyone has experience of being in a family, and knows the climate and circumstances that should prevail in it if it is to be worthy of the name.

Of this family, it is said that God himself has willed it to stand before him. The family is thus seen as a "Church," since a Church is by definition the holy "assembly of God." The Italian anaphora is therefore correct when it translates *"quam tibi adstare voluisti"* as "which you have called into your presence" (ICEL: "the family you have gathered here before you"), since "this Church of Christ is really present in all legitimately organized local groups of the faithful, which, in so far as they are united to their pastors, are also quite appropriately called Churches in the New Testament. For these are, in fact, in their own localities, the new people called by God, in the power of the Holy Spirit. . . ."[90]

It is for this extraordinary assembly that the prayer for unity is offered, but with nuances that make it different from the parallel prayer in the epiclesis. In the epiclesis of Anaphora II, the prayer for unity is for the Church that is "spread throughout the world." Here it is for "all your children, wherever they be scattered"; the words are from John 11:52, which speaks of Jesus dying to "gather into one the children of God who are scattered abroad" (ICEL: ". . . wherever they may be"). The thematic progress from epiclesis to intercession resides in the word "scattered," which evokes the reality of sin. Since the "merciful" Father is being asked to unite to himself all his "scattered" children, the sense must be that these children are "distant" from him. The intercession is therefore for those who are separated from God and not in communion with him. At the same time, the love God has for all human beings is solemnly affirmed because those "far" from him are also called his "children."

This universalist perspective in which a loving God is seen at work throughout the world is continued in the intercession for the dead. The prayer does not only ask that the dead "brothers and sisters," that is, Christians, be gathered into the kingdom of God. It intercedes for "all those who were pleasing to you" (ICEL: "and all who have left this world in your friendship"); these, as distinct from the "brothers and sisters," are non-Christians who have lived "justly." God acts in the world to establish his reign of justice, and he acts there on a scale that transcends the limits of the Church.[91]

Before the final doxology, the anaphora tells God once more of the expectation that fills the hearts of the faithful. Here the congregation asks for itself the grace of continuing, even in the kingdom of heaven, to be united as it is today. The Church is unable to imagine eternal blessedness except as a heavenly projection of its present reality as a liturgical assembly. Such an approach is not new, however, since, as P. Prigent has shown, the Apocalypse follows the same pattern.[92]

With this vision of heaven the faithful conclude their prayer of thanksgiving and thereby show that the definition of the liturgy as a place of contemplation is not mistaken. The experience of thanksgiving leads to the vision and desire of eternal blessedness. Therefore, after having proclaimed once more that every blessing comes to the world through Christ, Anaphora III ends with the usual Roman doxology.

The intense religious experience of thanksgiving leaves human beings incapable of further discourse. Once again, therefore, everything that has been said and done is summed up and recapitulated in the proclamation of the holy Name of Father and Son and Holy Spirit, whose glory rests upon the congregation.

X. APPENDIX TO CHAPTER FIVE

The following is a translation of the Latin anaphora presented, together with an introductory explanation and a brief commentary, to Commission X of Consilium by the official expositor, Cipriano Vagaggini, O.S.B., at a meeting in Nemi on March 12, 1967.

EUCHARISTIC PRAYER III

I

It is truly right. . . . Sanctus. . . . Hosannah in the highest.

II

1 Lord, you are holy indeed,
2 and your every creature rightly praises you,

3 because through your Son, our Lord Jesus Christ,
4 by the inpouring of the Holy Spirit,
5 you enliven and sanctify all things
6 and do not cease to gather to yourself a people
7 who from East to West
8 offer a pure sacrifice to your Name.

III

9 Therefore we humbly pray you, Lord,
10 to sanctify by that same Spirit
11 these gifts which we have brought to you to be consecrated,
12 that they may become the body and blood
13 of your Son, our Lord Jesus Christ,
14 at whose command we celebrate these mysteries.

IV

15 For, when he was about to be betrayed to death,
16 he took bread and, giving thanks to you, offered the blessing;
17 He broke the bread and gave it to his disciples saying:
18 "All of you, take and eat of this,
19 for this is my body which shall be given up for you."
20 In like manner, after the supper,
21 taking the cup and giving thanks to you he offered the blessing
22 and gave the cup to his disciples, saying:
23 "All of you, take and drink of this,
24 for this is the cup of the new covenant in my blood,
25 which shall be shed for you and for the many
26 for the forgiveness of sins.
27 Do this in memory of me."

(Acclamation of the congregation)

First Proposal

V

28 Mindful therefore, Lord,
29 of the saving passion of your Son
30 and of his wonderful resurrection and ascension into heaven,
31 but also looking forward to his second coming,
32 we, giving thanks, offer to you this saving victim

33   as a living and holy sacrifice
34   and, with it, ourselves and all we have,
35   for we are yours and all things are yours.

VI

36   We pray, eternal Lord,
37   that you will look with kindness on your Church's offering;
38   and grant that we who are nourished by the body and blood
       of your Son
39   may be filled with his Holy Spirit
40   and become one body and one spirit in him,
41   so that we may obtain an inheritance with your elect.

Second Proposal

V

28   Mindful therefore, Lord,
29   of the saving passion of your Son
30   and of his wonderful resurrection and ascension into heaven,
31   but also looking forward to his second coming,
32   we, giving thanks, offer to you this saving victim
33   as a living and holy sacrifice.

VI

34   Recognize, we pray, the victim by whose intercession you
       willed to be reconciled
35   and look with kindness on your Church's offering,
36   so that we who are nourished by the body and blood of your
       Son
37   may be filled with his Holy Spirit
38   and become one body and one spirit in him.
39   May he thus make of us an everlasting gift to you
40   so that we may obtain an inheritance with your elect.

Third Proposal

V

28   Mindful therefore, Lord,
29   of the saving passion of your Son
30   and of his wonderful resurrection and ascension into heaven,

31 but also looking forward to his second coming,
32 we, giving thanks, offer to you this saving victim
33 as a living and holy sacrifice.

VI

34 Look with kindness on your Church's offering
35 and grant that we who are nourished by the body and blood
        of your Son
36 may be filled with his Holy Spirit.
37 May we, we pray, become one body and one spirit in him
38 and may we learn to offer ourselves to you with Christ,
39 so that we may obtain an inheritance with your elect.

Fourth Proposal

V

28 Mindful therefore, Lord,
29 of the saving passion of your Son
30 and of his wonderful resurrection and ascension into heaven,
31 but also looking forward to his second coming,
32 we, giving thanks, offer to you this saving victim
33 as a living and holy sacrifice.

VI

34 Recognize, we pray, the victim by whose intercession you
        willed to be reconciled,
35 and look with kindness on your Church's offering,
36 so that we who are nourished by the body and blood of your
        Son
37 may be filled with his Holy Spirit
38 and become one body and one spirit in him.
39 Because we are yours and all things are yours,
40 make us an everlasting gift to you, along with Christ,
41 so that we may obtain an inheritance with your elect,

VII

42 especially with the most blessed Virgin Mary, Mother of God,
43 with your blessed apostles and glorious martyrs,
44 (with St. N.) and all the saints,

45   by whose merits and intercession with you we hope to be always aided.

VIII

46   Remember, Lord, your Church that is a pilgrim on earth, away from you,

47   for which we offer you this sacrifice of reconciliation.

48   In your love deign to ratify it,

49   with your servant N., our Pope, and N., our bishop,

50   with the entire order of bishops,

51   and with the holy people you have won for yourself.

52   We beseech you, hear with favor

53   the prayers of this family which you willed should stand before you,

54   and, merciful Father, compassionately unite

55   all whom you have created.

56   In your kindness admit into your kingdom

57   the faithful who have fallen asleep in Christ;

58   there, together with them, we hope to enjoy your glory for ever.

IX

59   Through Christ, our Lord,

60   through whom you bestow all good gifts upon the world:

61   through him, with him, and in him

62   all honor and glory is yours,

63   almighty God and Father,

64   in the unity of the Holy Spirit,

65   for ever and ever. Amen

Chapter Six

The Fourth Eucharistic Prayer

LITERAL TRANSLATION

It is truly right, holy Father, that we should thank you, truly just that we should glorify you, for you are the one God, living and true, existing before the ages and abiding for ever, dwelling in inaccessible light. You who alone are good and the source of life have made all things that you might fill your creatures with your blessings and give joy to many of them with the brilliance of your light.

Therefore do the countless throngs of angels stand before you day and night to serve you; as they look upon the glory of your face, they extol you unceasingly. With them we too—and through us every creature under heaven—joyously confess your name, singing: Holy. . . .

We acclaim you, Father, because you are great and have performed all your works in wisdom and love. You made human beings in your image and entrusted the entire world to their care, so that, serving you alone, their Creator, they might rule over all creatures. And

ICEL TRANSLATION

Father in heaven, it is right that we should give you thanks and glory: you are the one God, living and true. Through all eternity you live in unapproachable light. Source of life and goodness, you have created all things, to fill your creatures with every blessing and lead all men to the joyful vision of your light. Countless hosts of angels stand before you to do your will; they look upon your splendor and praise you, night and day. United with them, and in the name of every creature under heaven, we too praise your glory as we say: Holy. . . .

Father, we acknowledge your greatness: all your actions show your wisdom and love. You formed man in your own likeness and set him over the whole world to serve you, his creator, and to rule over all creatures. Even when he disobeyed you and lost your friendship you did

when through disobedience
they had lost your friendship,
you did not abandon them to
the power of death. In your
mercy you came to the aid of all
of them, so that they might seek
and find you. You offered many
covenants to human beings and
taught them through the prophets to hope for salvation.

Holy Father, you so loved the
world that when the fullness of
time had come you sent your
Only-begotten to us as Savior.
Having taken flesh by the Holy
Spirit and having been born of
the Virgin Mary, he shared our
condition in every respect save
sin; he preached salvation to the
poor, liberation to captives, joy
to the sorrowful of heart. That
he might carry out your plan,
he handed himself over to death
and, rising from the dead, destroyed death and restored life.

And in order that we might
live no longer for ourselves but
for him who died and rose for
us, he sent from you, Father, as
the first fruits for believers, the
Holy Spirit who would finish
his work in the world and bring
all holiness to completion.

Therefore, Lord, we ask that
this same Holy Spirit would
deign to sanctify these gifts, so
that they may become the body
and blood of our Lord Jesus
Christ and we may celebrate
this great mystery which he left
us as an everlasting covenant.

For when the hour had come

not abandon him to the power
of death, but helped all men to
seek and find you. Again and
again you offered a covenant to
man, and through the prophets
taught him to hope for salvation. Father, you so loved the
world that in the fullness of
time you sent your only Son to
be our Savior. He was conceived
through the power of the Holy
Spirit, and born of the Virgin
Mary, a man like us in all things
but sin. To the poor he proclaimed the good news of salvation, to prisoners, freedom, and
to those in sorrow, joy. In fulfillment of your will he gave himself up to death; but by rising
from the dead, he destroyed
death and restored life. And
that we might live no longer for
ourselves but for him, he sent
the Holy Spirit from you, Father, as his first gift to those
who believe, to complete his
work on earth and bring us the
fullness of grace.

Father, may this Holy Spirit
sanctify these offerings. Let
them become the body and
blood of Jesus Christ our Lord
as we celebrate the great mystery which he left us as an everlasting covenant.

He always loved those who

for him to be glorified by you, holy Father, having loved his own who were in the world, he loved them to the end; and as they were eating, he took bread, spoke the blessing, and broke the bread; he gave it to his disciples, saying: "Take this, all of you, and eat of it; for this is my body which will be given up for you." In like manner, taking a cup filled with the fruit of the vine, he offered thanksgiving and gave the cup to his disciples, saying: "Take this, all of you, and drink of it; for this is the cup of my blood of the new and everlasting covenant, which shall be shed for you and for the many for the forgiveness of sins. Do this in memory of me."

The mystery of faith! — We proclaim your death, Lord, and we confess your resurrection, until you come.

Therefore, Lord, celebrating now the memorial of our redemption, we recall the death of Christ and his descent among the dead, we profess his resurrection and ascension to your right hand, and, looking forward to his coming in glory, we offer to you his body and blood as a sacrifice that is acceptable to you and a source of salvation for the entire world.

Look, Lord, upon the sacrifice which you have prepared for your Church, and in your

were his own in the world. When the time came for him to be glorified by you, his heavenly Father, he showed the depth of his love.

While they were at supper, he took bread, said the blessing, broke the bread, and gave it to his disciples, saying: "Take this, all of you, and eat it: this is my body which will be given up for you."

In the same way, he took the cup, filled with wine. He gave you thanks, and giving the cup to his disciples, said: "Take this, all of you, and drink from it: this is the cup of my blood, the blood of the new and everlasting covenant. It will be shed for you and for all so that sins may be forgiven. Do this in memory of me."

Let us proclaim the mystery of faith: Christ has died, Christ is risen, Christ will come again.

Father, we now celebrate this memorial of our redemption. We recall Christ's death, his descent among the dead, his resurrection, and his ascension to your right hand; and, looking forward to his coming in glory, we offer you his body and blood, the acceptable sacrifice which brings salvation to the whole world.

Lord, look upon this sacrifice which you have given to your Church; and by your Holy kindess grant to all who share in this one bread and cup that, being gathered into one body by the Holy Spirit, they may become in Christ a living sacrifice for the praise of your glory.

Now therefore, Lord, be mindful of all for whom we offer you this sacrifice: first of all, your servant N., our Pope, N., our bishop, and the whole body of bishops, and all the clergy, those who make the offering, those who are present, and your entire people, as well as all who seek you with a sincere heart. Be mindful also of those who have died in the peace of your Christ, and of all the dead, whose faith is known to you alone.

Merciful Father, grant to all of us, your children, that we may obtain an inheritance in heaven with the Blessed Virgin Mary, Mother of God, with your apostles and saints in your kingdom where, with all creatures, now freed from the corruption of sin and death, we may glorify you through Christ our Lord, through whom you bestow all good gifts upon the world.

Through him and with him and in him. . . .

Spirit, gather all who share this one bread and one cup into the one body of Christ, a living sacrifice of praise.

Lord, remember those for whom we offer this sacrifice, especially N. our Pope, N. our bishop, and bishops and clergy everywhere. Remember those who take part in this offering, those here present and all your people, and all who seek you with a sincere heart. Remember those who have died in the peace of Christ and all the dead whose faith is known to you alone. Father, in your mercy grant also to us, your children, to enter into our heavenly inheritance in the company of the Virgin Mary, the Mother of God, and your apostles and saints. Then, in your kingdom, freed from the corruption of sin and death, we shall sing your glory with every creature through Christ our Lord, through whom you give us everything that is good.

Through him, with him, in him, in the unity of the Holy Spirit, all glory and honor is yours, almighty Father, for ever and ever. Amen.

The Fourth Eucharistic Prayer is the most theological of all the eucharistic prayers, and we shall, therefore, discuss its contents at greater length. First let us examine its structure.

I. STRUCTURE OF THE ANAPHORA

The anaphora is composed of the following:

Opening dialogue

Celebration of praise of God

Introduction to the Sanctus

Sanctus

Anamnesis of salvation

First epiclesis

Account of institution

Anamnesis in the narrow sense

Offering

Second epiclesis

Intercessions

Doxology

M. Arranz justifiably likens the structure of this prayer to the Syro-Antiochene anaphoras,[1] except, of course, for the first epiclesis, which comes from the Alexandrian liturgy.[2] After the opening dialogue, the prayer praises God for his greatness, that is, for himself.[3] Next comes the Sanctus and after it a lengthy thanksgiving for the history of salvation, beginning with creation: The first epiclesis asks that the Spirit would transform the bread and wine into the body and blood of the Lord. This petition leads into the account of institution. The account is followed by the anamnesis in the narrow sense, which leads, via the prayer of offering, into the second epiclesis. After the intercessions, the trinitarian doxology from the Roman Canon closes this anaphora as it does all the others of the Roman rite.

This structure is also found in the second and third anaphoras, as well as in the anaphoras of reconciliation. The only difference in the fourth anaphora is that the Sanctus is followed by a survey of the history of salvation.

II. ANAPHORA AS A PROFESSION OF FAITH

We take for granted the relation, already discussed, between the Christian anaphora and the Jewish prayer of blessing.[4]

158

This Fourth Eucharistic Prayer begins with a proclamation of the name of God, who is here called "holy Father," a title that occurs four times.[5]

In keeping with the Latin tradition, the preface begins by asserting the salutary value of thanksgiving: "It is truly right and just, proper and helpful toward salvation, that we always and everywhere give thanks to you, O Lord, holy Father" (classical beginning of prefaces). This saving value is easily explicable by the fact that the only proper response to the *eu-aggelion* (gospel) is the *eucharistia*, since what we have received so far transcends what our human nature might have expected from its creator.[6] This idea is well expressed in the Anaphora of the Apostles Addai and Mari where thanks is offered "for the great grace which you have given us and for which we can make no return."[7] The only possible response to a blessing that cannot be repaid is a profound gratitude that finds expression in the action of thanksgiving.

Properly speaking, then, the response of the Eucharist is not a repayment that cancels a debt and puts giver and recipient on the same level; that is impossible in the case of God and his creatures. Consequently, this thanksgiving needs to be repeated constantly, or "always and everywhere,"[8] precisely because of the relation that has been established in Christ between God and human beings. That relation creates an irreversible bond which is properly called a "covenant" and is to be identified with the grace and gift that elicit faith on the part of human beings. Christians, therefore, like Abraham, are justified by the faith[9] that lies behind thanksgiving and finds expression in it.

But, if faith is embodied in thanksgiving, then this thanksgiving is a profession of faith and therefore a place where justification occurs. And, in fact, the very structure of the anaphora shows that it is such a profession of faith. E. Lanne was the first to make this point,[10] but others have developed it after him.[11] The "confession of faith" in the first and strictest sense is the profession or symbol (creed) that is pronounced during the rite of baptism.[12] But, if we compare baptismal professions of faith with the anaphora as found in, for example, the *Apostolic Tradition* of Hippolytus, we find an interesting parallel between the two both in content and in trinitarian structure and Christological development. Both the Anaphora of Hippolytus and the baptismal confession of faith expand the Christological part until it becomes the dominant part of the text.

In time, the anaphora has evolved while preserving the substance of the earliest Christian kerygma as expressed in the confession of faith.[13] A. Hamann draws an interesting comparison between the anaphora in Book VIII of the *Apostolic Constitutions* and the baptismal catechesis in Book VII, 39, 25, and concludes to a positive parallelism.[14] Baptism and the Eucharist are sacraments of the same faith and the same mystery.[15] The "proclamation of the Lord's death" (Paul's reinterpretation of the Lord's anamnetic command) is to be understood as a profession of faith in which we confess the death of Christ as a mystery of salvation.[16]

We conclude that the word *salutare* ("helpful to salvation," "source of salvation") in the Roman preface is an accurate self-definition of the anaphora as a profession of the faith[17] that justifies.[18]

III. "HOLY FATHER"

The idea of God's holiness comes from the Old Testament; there, however, holiness is not simply one attribute among others,[19] but constitutes the very essence of the godhead: it makes God to be God. His holiness is his uncreated transcendence that manifests itself to human beings in his "glory."

John 17:11 (together with *Didache* 10, 2) is the source of the anaphoral term "holy Father." We shall therefore interpret it in the light of Johannine theology which, on this point, is practically identical with the theology of the eucharistic prayers in the *Didache*.[20]

In John 17:11, Jesus in prayer calls the Father "holy" because, it seems, he wants the Father to manifest his holiness by keeping the disciples in his name as in a sacred place. The Father's holy name is, as it were, a temple wherein Jesus would have believers kept.[21] The point is not simply that they should be kept safe from the contamination of the world, but that they should be sanctified in the proper sense of the word. The name "Father," which has been revealed to believers to be used in prayer, serves them as a temple or sacred enclosure in which they can live as true sons and daughters united with their Father.[22] To be "kept in the Father's Name" or to be "sanctified in truth"[23] means to be preserved in a filial life and in communion with the Father by means of communion with Christ.[24] If we compare John 17:3 ("this is eternal life, that they know thee") with John 17:26 ("I made known to them thy name, and I will make it known"), we discern a thematic parallelism[25] which allows us to say that the revelation of God's fatherhood and the consequent knowledge and acceptance of it are a saving event and redemption itself.

It is this revelation and acceptance that are expressed in the invocation "holy Father." If, then, revelation and redemption are identical in Johannine theology,[26] it follows that the Johannine invocation "holy Father" in the fourth anaphora is a proclamation of the filial status of believers, as a place of sanctification, and therefore as an expression and proclamation of the salvific and redemptive value of the Christ-mediated revelation of the divine name.

The invocation is thus a proclamation of the event of salvation and indeed a factor or moment in the very process of salvation,[27] since it causes believers to be in the filial state revealed in Christ. It thereby causes them to experience redemption. The very invocation "holy Father" is thus a mystery of salvation. In proclaiming this Johannine theme, the profession of faith that is the fourth anaphora is in accord with the other texts of the Missal in which "giving thanks" is explicitly called "helpful to salvation" or the "source of salvation."

The invocation "holy Father," which runs through the exposition of the *mirabilia Dei*, keeps us from understanding this narration as simply a list of historical facts. It turns the account into a proclamation and prophecy of salvation and, at the same time, of acceptance of salvation in faith, inasmuch as the invocation has epicletic overtones.[28]

IV. CELEBRATION OF GOD

The celebration or praise of God begins with contemplation of three attributes: "one,"[29] "living,"[30] and "true."[31] These sum up the knowledge of God that compels us to give thanks.[32] Then, after asserting the eternity of God,[33] the prayer describes God's kingdom as infinite light. The description paraphrases a Pauline doxology[34] and, at the same time, brings in a Johannine theme: that God is light and in him there is no darkness.[35] This theme might profitably have been developed in the Christological part by presenting Christ as light and as revelation of the divine glory, but the composers of the anaphora did not take the opportunity. This is rather surprising when we think of the importance of light in liturgical signs.[36]

The celebration of God turns finally to his goodness[37] as the origin of creation, which in turn has life for its purpose.[38] Creation is not an end in itself[39]; God's purpose in what he does is to pour out his love upon all creatures.[40] This is the basis for saying, in the final sentence of this section, before the Sanctus: "we too—and through us every creature under heaven—joyously acclaim your name." That final sentence sums up the doxological vocation of all created beings. Creation is not simply a collection of things; it is a cosmos and contains an order and harmony that are living and evolving.[41] All of creation celebrates the greatness of God via human beings, who are the synthesis, interpreters, and priests of that created world; only through them can the cosmos fulfill its vocation of praising God.

Creation is ordered to human beings who recapitulate it and are its masters. The same is true in creation's return to God; that is, its return is mediated by human beings and is accomplished in and with them.[42] The whole of creation sings the glory of God through human beings, who interpret its cry. In this theology of nature, therefore, human beings understand themselves to be in solidarity with all creation and to be part of the created world: the most illustrious part, indeed, but not separated from the rest. They mediate the goodness of created nature to God by becoming its voice in the process of sanctification in Christ.[43] Humankind redeemed by Christ supplies the created world with a voice and once again becomes part of the order which it had disturbed by sin and which has been restored through redemption. Human beings have the historical task of becoming one with nature and the cosmos so as to be its voice in a continual hymn of praise to God.[44]

This part of the fourth anaphora is a sound corrective for a practical dualism that has never been completely overcome in the lives of Christians. The thinking manifested in the text originates in the catechetical sermons of Cyril of Jerusalem who lays such a great emphasis on the beauty and goodness of creation. According to Tarby, this theology of Cyril finds expression in the Anaphora of James,[45] while the latter in turn is probably the immediate source of our modern text.[46]

V. SANCTUS

According to P.-M. Gy, the Antiochene rite is the immediate source of the Sanctus in the Roman Canon.[47] The first reference to the Sanctus in the West is in Peter Chrysologus, who gives it a Christological interpretation.[48] As noted earlier in the chapter on the preface, a Roman text without a Sanctus has been found among the Arian fragments edited by Mai[49] and in other passages which Gy cites from the ancient sacramentaries.[50]

The Roman Canon lacked the Sanctus before the end of the fourth century and imported it from the East in the first third of the fifth. Pope Leo I sometimes gave the Sanctus a trinitarian interpretation under the influence of dogmatic discussions and perhaps of contact with the Anaphora of John Chrysostom.[51] That, at least, is Father Gy's conclusion.[52]

In our fourth anaphora, the Sanctus, like the rest of the prayer, is addressed to the Father.[53] It is also one of the most successful forms of participation by the faithful, expecially when sung. But, perhaps, our impression derives solely from outward appearances, since the congregation is often removed from the theology of this part of the anaphora.

The theology is readily seen in the text itself. Ingrained habit, however, keeps Christians from appreciating the value of the individual words and phrases, so that the exhortation of the Constitution on the Liturgy[54] has gone unheeded.

The list of angelic orders[55] has disappeared from the new anaphora, perhaps because people are so unreceptive toward angelology or, more simply, because philosophers have rejected any cosmological role for the angels. We should bear in mind, however, that historically the angels played an integral part in the work of sanctification which is expressed in the Alexandrian Sanctus. For that theology, one may go to the trinitarian doctrine of Origen.

The introduction to the Sanctus says that throngs of angels serve[56] God, that is, worship him, standing in his sight, contemplating the glory of his face,[57] and singing his praises. Praise of God flows from knowledge of his name and contemplation of his face.[58] "With them we too": therefore our praise, which has just been voiced at the beginning of the anaphora and continues now in the Sanctus, likewise springs from knowledge of God's name and contemplation of his face. Though our experience of God differs from that of the angels, since we see dimly as in a mirror,[59] the effect should nonetheless be the same: "With them we too. . ."

The Sanctus thus expresses the union of the liturgy of heaven[60] with the earthly liturgy being celebrated by our community. We on earth take the angels and saints as models for our liturgical praise and glorification of God; as a result, the anaphora takes on an eschatological dimension.[61]

This is a theme on which those engaged in pastoral ministry ought to place a heavy emphasis. If they do not, the only pastoral value the Sanctus will have is as a song which interrupts the monologue of the president as he offers thanksgiving. But, then we would be denying the history of this text, both in its origin and in its development. The Sanctus is made up of several texts from scripture: "Holy, holy, holy Lord God of hosts. Heaven and earth are full of your glory.[62] Blessed is he who comes[63] in the name of the Lord. Hosanna in the highest."[64] The purpose of the prayer is to proclaim the name of God as the Holy One, that is, to proclaim the very essence of God. It is said in obedience to Matthew 6:9, as Tertullian pointed out long ago.[65] Moreover, since it acknowledges and proclaims the godhood of God, it achieves the very purpose of human life and realizes in the highest degree the relation that should exist between human beings and God. That is how we are to understand the function of the Sanctus in the Alexandrian anaphoras.[66]

In the Sanctus as cited in Revelation 4:8,[67] the divine name is given in amplified form: "Who was and is and is to come."[68] The last part: "(he) who is to come," was a basic Christological title in the early Church and underscored the eschatological aspect of the Lord's coming. In this light, it is easy to see that the Christological theme in the final part of the Sanctus ("Blessed is he who comes in the name of the Lord") has a necessary connection with the proclamation of the divine name in the first part. The Sanctus, thus, consists of a first part which is theological (directed to *ho Theos*, "God," i.e., the Father), and a second which is Christological; the two parts are not separated or simply juxtaposed, but form a single whole.

When seen in its totality, then, the Sanctus is a contemplation of the divine glory as manifested in Christ. The manifestation occurs both in his coming in the flesh and in his final coming. He is the incomparably complete epiphany of God. That is why he is "blessed" or praised.

VI. ANAMNETIC NARRATIVE OF THE HISTORY OF SALVATION

A. Humankind and Created Nature

"Thank" and "glorify" were the verbs that introduced the celebration of God. "Acclaim" or "confess" = "praise"[69] is the verb that controls the narrative of saving events which runs from the Sanctus to the account of institution.[70]

The object of praise is the greatness of God[71] which manifests itself in his doing everything in wisdom and love.[72] The logic of wisdom and love guides the creative activity of God, which therefore cannot fail to be perfect. The perfection is described concretely by speaking of human beings, who are defined as God's images. Because they are his images, dominion over the universe is entrusted to them,[73] and they become his representatives in the world.[74] But, human beings are not autonomous in their activity as caretakers of the universe; this activity is a service of God the creator and a form

164

of worship of him. Consequently, when human beings rule creation, they render to God their own special obedience and service.[75]

This theology of earthly realities is very positive and constructive. It also echoes the documents of Vatican II; for example: "Man . . . was commanded to conquer the earth with all it contains and to rule the world in justice and holiness . . . so that through the dominion of all things by man the name of God would be majestic in all the earth" (Pastoral Constitution *Gaudium et spes* on the Church in the Modern World 34; Flannery 933–934).

B. *The Human Being, Image of God*

The Anaphora of Basil and the original text of the Anaphora of James as reconstructed by Tarby do not have this theme; its subsequent addition represents a harmonization with the story of creation in Genesis 1:16.[76] Nonetheless, the idea of the image is certainly part of the oldest content of the Anaphora of James, since redemption is described as a restoration of the image.[77] Conversely, the fourth anaphora does not describe redemption as a restoration of the image, but the perspective is, nonetheless, the same as in James. In fact, the concept of restoration flows necessarily from the theology of creation we have been describing. All this means that there is a surprising theological agreement between Anaphora IV and the Anaphora of James.

Placed as they are at the summit of creation[78] as its living recapitulations and its priests, human beings are the masters of the universe,[79] but they in turn belong to God. This perspective on human beings receives its definitive formulation in the statement that the human person is the image of God. That statement is more than an obscure passage in the Bible; it is a formal theological anthropology. If human beings are the images of God, their relation to God is neither merely external nor an afterthought, but is part of their inmost nature and an ontological constituent of their being.

That is why the Eastern tradition can speak of the human person as a participation in the divine nature.[80] Human beings are in their totality shaped and formed in the image of God,[81] and the primordial expression of this likeness is the dignity of the free and responsible human person in whose depths is inscribed the call to communion with God:[82] human beings were created to become "gods." They were unable, however, to remain faithful to their nature and their vocation, but sinned and thereby lost their friendship with God.[83] Moreover, since their nature is in the image of God, they could not rebel against God without at the same time rebelling against themselves in a form of attempted suicide. The real drama of the original fall is to be seen in that in denying their vocation, human beings denied their nature as well.

In defining sin, the Fathers of the Church vacillated between calling it a "loss of the image" and a "loss only of the likeness, with the image remaining intact." Whatever the description adopted, they were sure that human beings had not in fact completely lost their original relation to God: the image in them is simply dimmed and tarnished. This means that they can no longer share the divine life by their own powers; but the image of God is still impressed upon them as a demand for a communion with God that has now become impossible, as a summons and a restlessness that can never be satisfied. In the state of sin, their createdness in the image of God weighs upon them[84] as an anguish over their situation, for sin is a contradiction within the person that emphasizes, even if only obscurely and unconsciously, the vocation of human beings to be something completely different from what they now are.

The fourth anaphora adopts this anthropology, but leaves it simply implicit or, more accurately, takes it for granted. It would have been better if the composers had brought it fully into the open and had defined the redemptive work of Christ as a "restoration of the image."[85] Then the conclusion, that in restoring human beings to God Christ restores them to themselves, would have been very clear and pastorally fruitful.

Even though through disobedience[86] human beings had lost the friendship of God, God did not abandon them,[87] that is, did not contemptuously turn his gaze from them. Instead, he sought them out[88] everyone of them,[89] so that the expectations of these creatures who are unconsciously searching for the wholly Other, might not be disappointed.[90]

At work throughout the entire course of revelation is God's concern[91] that human beings should rediscover the true way and the life they had lost.[92] Hence the divine care for creatures, which is expressed in our fourth anaphora: "You . . . taught them through the prophets to hope for salvation."[93]

During the Exile, the prophets kept Israel's hope alive, and by proclaiming God's word made up for the lack of a temple. God's guidance of the people took form in the Law and the prophets,[94] and then reached its fullest expression in Jesus. The text of the anaphora omits mention of the Law here, since the word has such a different meaning for us today. On the other hand, the Old Testament dispensation is adequately summed up in the activity of the prophets. The history of salvation can be defined as a continual offering of covenants to human beings: we need only think of Adam, Noah, Abraham, Issac, Jacob, and David.[95] All these covenants were preparations for the definitive covenant,[96] which in the person of Christ is offered to all human beings.[97]

God's steadfastness in offering covenants is witness and proof of his fidelity to humankind.[98] In the face of such fidelity, we have no choice but to say: "O Lord, thou art my God; I will exalt thee, I will praise thy name" (Is 25:1). Without this experience of the divine fidelity, it is not possible to know God (Hos 2:22, 25). Since the eucharistic prayer expresses knowledge of God in the form of joyous praise, it is evident that we shall find his fidelity expressed therein, even though it is not easy to read history as the manifestation of God's fidelity. The fidelity of God is both to himself and to human beings; but, he is faithful to human beings because he is faithful to himself. We, therefore, pray later on, in the intercessions: "Be mindful . . . of all who seek you with a sincere heart."[99]

The anaphora is filled with an atmosphere of joy in God, which is the atmosphere proper to the eucharistic celebration as a whole. In order that all of the faithful may be always in this atmosphere, the celebration must transmit the deep sense of peace, serenity, hope, and joy that links and permeates all parts of the anaphora.

C. Salvation in Christ

The description of the work of salvation that Jesus accomplished begins with citations of John 3:16 and Galatians 4:4.[100] The terms "Only-begotten" and "Savior" define Jesus in relation to God and in relation to his fellow human beings. He is said first to have taken flesh by the Holy Spirit[101] and to have been born of Mary. His humanity is then strongly emphasized by an effective citation from Hebrews 4:15,[102] and finally mention is made of the three messianic signs to which he himself refers in Luke.[103]

This Christological section of the anamnetic narrative ends with the paschal mystery, which is the fulfillment of what is often called the divine "plan of redemption." The Latin text does not speak of redemption, but simply of *dispensatio* (Greek: *oikonomia*; "economy"). The word "redemption" has been so abused in religious language that it can hardly be used in translating the Latin *dispensatio*. We must admit that it is not easy to find a current word capable of

167

expressing the theological range of the scriptural word "economy,"[104] though this was a favorite of the ancient anaphoras.[105] "Plan" is inadequate, but must suffice.

In a formulation quite successful from a literary standpoint, the death and resurrection of Christ are now introduced as connected with ours and as providing the instrument, so to speak, by which the Lord destroyed our death and restored our life.[106] This connection is classical in the theology of baptism (see Rom 6:4, 11) and also has its proper place in the Eucharist, which is the act that completes Christian initiation. The theological pattern we express is identical with that of Romans 6 on baptism, where the explanation of redemption is followed by an explanation of how Christians should live as followers of Christ.

The next paragraph begins with a citation of 2 Corinthians 5:15, which tells us that radical evangelicalism and a complete fidelity to Christ (to the point where "we . . . live no longer for ourselves") is possible only by the gift of the Spirit. Living no longer for ourselves but for Jesus who died and rose can be called a true program of life. It is, however, a program that sheds new light primarily on the ascetical side of Christianity, since the structure of the sentence puts the emphasis on the negative ("live no longer") and leaves somewhat muted the positive aspect, namely, living for Christ.

One might ask whether this is a felicitous way of approaching the subject. On the other hand, it must be pointed out that Basil cites this passage four times in his ascetical works and always in a eucharistic context, that is, in order to describe the consequences of eating the body and drinking the blood of Christ.[107] The most interesting of the four citations comes at the end of the *Moralia*, where Basil is answering the question: What is it that is specifically Christian? After a lengthy discussion, his answer is summed up in three points: the eating and drinking of the body and blood of the Lord is specifically Christian, those who eat and drink are constantly mindful of the great deeds of God, and those who are thus constantly mindful live no longer for themselves but for the Lord.[108] We can say, therefore, that the eucharistic use of 2 Corinthians 5:15 in the fourth anaphora is not a clumsy improvisation but an echo of patristic teaching.

The citation marks the passage from Christology to pneumatology; the bridge from the one to the other is the necessity of the Spirit for a Christian life understood as following Christ. The theology of the paschal mystery is being inflected in a pneumatological direction.

168

D. The Holy Spirit

The anaphora states that Jesus sends the Spirit from the Father. There is a clear reference to John 16:8 and Luke 24:49, but we can also see an allusion to John 19:30 with its "spiritual" interpretation of the Lord's death.[109] The unconditional necessity of the work of the Spirit if human beings are to be Christian can be easily shown but by a single verse of Paul: "All who are led by the Spirit of God are sons of God."[110] The Spirit plays a part in the work of salvation: he brings that work to completion by effecting every sanctification.[111]

According to John,[112] the Spirit is to interiorize God's word in us so that we will truly understand and accurately remember Jesus.[113] Moreover, the Spirit actualizes God's word and thereby makes Jesus present in the community; the Spirit is, therefore, the "first fruits,"[114] that is, the first of all the gifts given to believers, and his coming is ensured and guaranteed as the fruit of every prayer (Lk 11:13).[115] Since the Spirit is the first fruits or the first gift to believers, every other gift is given to them as a fruit of the Spirit.

In thus moving on from Christology to pneumatology, the narrative/confession of salvation gives a unitary and global vision of the entire economy.

E. Prayer for the Spirit

The designation of the Spirit as sanctifier immediately gives rise to a prayer that he may be sent upon the sacred gifts to sanctify (= consecrate) them.

We discussed the theology implied in the invocation "holy Father." We must now add that what was implicit is now explicitly thematized in the first epiclesis. That is why we spoke of the repetition of the title "holy Father" throughout the anaphora as being important.[116] It is in this light that the shift in divine names which occurs here is to be explained.

In the prayer leading up to the epiclesis (in the preceding paragraph), "Father" is used without the adjective "holy," but his holiness is clear from the fact that he is asked to send the Holy Spirit. Now, in the epiclesis itself, "Father" is replaced by "Lord" in connection with the prayer that the Holy Spirit would deign to sanctify the bread and wine. "Lord" is a title that expresses God's role in the revelation of his reign, for in his kingdom his lordship achieves its complete manifestation. If the reign of God embraces human beings by the coming of Christ, and if human beings come to Christ and are in communion with him by the bread and wine which he has left as a sign of the new covenant, then the accomplishment of the eucharistic mystery is truly an epiphany or manifestation of the kingdom, and in that context "Lord" is the appropriate divine title. "The Lord reigns"—and he does so by sending his Spirit.

F. Doctrine on the Trinity and Prayer

To understand the theology of the fourth anaphora, we must bear in mind that the underlying trinitarian doctrine is of the Eastern type,[117] which can be summed up in the scheme: *"to* the Father *through* the Son *in* the Spirit." In this formula, which cannot be accused of subordinationism, the principle of unity among the divine persons is the Father, who is the sole originator of processions: the one source of all processions is the source of unity within God. This dynamic interpretation of the divine unity is as ontologically valid as that of the Western interpretation. Western trinitarian thought uses the scheme; *"to* the Father and *to* the Son and *to* the Holy Spirit." When this simple scheme is misunderstood, it can give rise, in the practice of prayer, to a naive practical tritheism that is indeed unconscious and inculpable but nonetheless dangerous.

The advantage of the approach to the Trinity that is taken in the fourth anaphora and in liturgical texts generally is that the prayer in it and prayer based on it will always involve a relation at once with the Father and with the Son and with the Spirit. The anaphora should, therefore, be thought of as a place where the faithful can be formed in prayer; the individual's private prayer will then conform with liturgical prayer, and a perilous dualism will be avoided. We should not forget that orthopraxis is as important as orthodoxy for the Church; in fact, orthodoxy, fully understood, always implies an orthopraxis, for the word "orthodoxy" means "right glorification" as well as "right opinion."

VII. EPICLESIS

In the epiclesis (= invocation), God is formally asked to send the Spirit that he may transform[118] the bread and wine into the body and blood of the Lord—a theme lacking in the Roman Canon.[119] The epiclesis should not be called "invocation of the Spirit," since the prayer is addressed not to the Spirit but to the Father, and it is the Father who sanctifies through the Spirit.

In the anaphoras of the Missal, the Eastern epiclesis has been divided into two parts: one (before the account of institution) asks for the consecration of the bread and wine, and the other (after the anamesis) asks for the sanctification of the faithful who receive com-

170

munion. This solution was adopted for theological and pastoral reasons and represents a return, justifiable or not, to the Alexandrian anaphoral structure. The latter probably provides the sole conscious liturgical basis for the theological decision made.[120] Further support for the choice is found in some epicletic *Post-Sanctus* prayers in the non-Roman Latin liturgies, which contain texts that are also theologically closer to the position taken in the Roman Missal.

Independently of the historical bases for the decision, we must recognize the value of the choice made, namely the positive ecumenical significance it has and the pastoral success it has met with. It will be the task of catechists to bring out the fact that the sanctification accomplished by the words of the Lord is effected by the power of the Holy Spirit. Just as the Spirit brought about the incarnation of the Word, so too he continues to act in our celebration. That theme is a traditional one, especially in the Fathers.[121]

At the same time, however, we must commend the warning given by C. Vagaggini, who points out that the liturgy and the scriptures are a unique and different kind of "incarnation" of the Word.[122] Preachers too often regard the action of the Spirit in the eucharistic epiclesis as simply identical with his action in the historical incarnation. But, when the parallel is pushed that far, the doctrine becomes heterodox. That extreme was actually reached in Scholastic theology,[123] which for a while, beginning with Berengarius, accepted as a logical consequence the Lutheran theology of impanation; here the parallelism between Eucharist and incarnation was complete. Catholic theologians had to clarify the limits of the parallelism before they could reply decisively to the doctrine of impanation. To see how unconsciously theologians can push the parallel to extremes, we need only consider the joy with which V. Palashkovsky interprets the theology of Irenaeus as a theology of impanation, even though he rejects the word itself because it is associated with Luther.[124]

Since the Lord became our redeemer once and for all at a point in history, there can be but a single hypostatic union. If there were another, even in the Eucharist, there would be a new Christ; the historical uniqueness of Christ would be lost and with it the unlimited redemptive power and perennial validity of his death and resurrection. At the Last Supper the Lord said: "This is my body," and not "This is another body of mine," that is, a new incarnation of the Word as bread.

To properly safeguard the sacramental vision of the Fathers, it helps to reread Tertullian: "When he said 'This is my body' he turned into his body the bread which he had taken and distributed to his disciples; that is, he made the bread a 'figure of my body'; but it would not have been a figure if the body had not been the true body."[125]

G. Martelet sums up the matter:

"Luther was therefore mistaken if he thought that he could justify consubstantiation [= impanation] by an analogy with the hypostatic union; and to adopt the same analogy, even in defense of transubstantiation, is to share his mistake. . . . The Eucharist does not entail any 'other' hypostatic union, but simply reveals the unplumbed depths of the one unique hypostatic union."[126]

The Eucharist, which is a sacrament and a memorial, in no way detracts from the uniqueness and all-sufficiency of the one event of salvation, but, on the contrary, most clearly points to and protects that uniqueness and all-sufficiency. The Eucharist is not a prolongation or continuation of the incarnation; it is the sacrament that commemorates the one incarnation-death-resurrection. The early Scholastic doctrine (based on Augustine) that spoke of the *triforme corpus Christi* (the threefold body of Christ)[127] was the real root of the theological problems that have beset the eucharistic sacrament from the time of the Ratramnus-Radbert-Berengarius controversy down to our own day. Only now that we understand the biblical concept of sacrament as memorial is it possible to come to grips with the sacramental problem that arose in the ninth century and was not resolved even at Trent.[128]

It is still a fact that in popular devotion the theology of the Eucharist as memorial encounters an insuperable obstacle in the form of an erroneous theology of the consecration, one that is unconsciously formulated and practically applied[129] after the manner of Paschasius Radbert.[130]

We have dwelt on this question to bring out the task catechists face in dealing with the consecration. It would be naive to think that the introduction of the epiclesis with its request for the consecration of the sacred gifts will resolve all the problems of Western eucharistic theology. The introduction of the pneumatological epiclesis leaves the problems untouched. For as Y. Congar points out: "the epiclesis does not come primarily or principally from sacramental theology but from the doctrine of the Trinity and therefore from the vision of the economy of salvation which that doctrine reflects."[131]

The text of the epiclesis in Anaphora IV is thoroughly classical and traditional. It asks for the transformation of the sacred gifts without committing itself to any theological theory for explaining the transformation. Such a noncommittal approach is normative for liturgical texts.[132]

VIII ACCOUNT OF INSTITUTION

A. Value and Significance

The account of institution in the Fourth Eucharistic Prayer is introduced by two citations from John that are neatly combined.[133] They interpret the passion of Jesus as his glorification and, at the same time, as his total surrender to the Father's plan of salvation.

Historical research is making it increasingly clear that the account of institution in its present form was not primitively a part of the anaphora; it became a part by a slow development that has not yet been fully brought to light. The theological importance of the account of institution is to be seen in its concluding mandate: "Do this in memory of me." The response to that mandate is voiced in the anamnesis, the full point of which emerges best in a text of the Ambrosian liturgy: "We do this, Lord, we conduct this celebration, in obedience to your command."[134]

Therefore, this part of the anaphora reflects our concerns that our celebration should correspond accurately to what the Lord established in the upper room at the Last Supper; at the same time, it expresses our certainty that this correspondence and conformity exists. To use a favorite term in patristic theology, the desire and intention in the account of institution is to bring out the *veritas* (truth) of the sacrament.

The account of institution in the fourth anaphora is immediately preceded by a phrase that brings out its theological motivation: "that . . . we may celebrate this great mystery which he has left us as an everlasting covenant."[135] These prefatory words and the anamnesis that follows upon the concluding mandate of Jesus form an "inclusion" that gives the account a precise meaning and purpose. Since the institution at the Last Supper is the origin of our Eucharist, the account of that institution will always be the model for our celebration. That is, it presents the pattern for any celebration that is to be valid (both ritually and theologically), and it enables us to correct any deviations or deformations that may occur.[136] If a eucharistic celebration does not match the content, purposes, and values intended by Christ's institution (and authentically presented in

173

the account), then the celebrants no longer "eat the supper of the Lord" (1 Cor 11:20).[137]

The first value Paul wants to see restored when he speaks of the Lord's Supper is unity in the eucharistic assembly. This is fully in accord with 1 Corinthians 10:15–17 where the sacramental character of the bread that is broken is directly related to unity.

This necessarily abbreviated reading of the two passages in Paul is enough to show that the Eucharist is a sacrament of unity, the point of reference being the unity around Christ and the focus on Christ that are so evident at the Last Supper. According to 1 Corinthians 11:20, if unity is lacking in our celebration, we can no longer claim that our eucharistic meal is the supper which the Lord celebrated and instituted.[138] It is natural, therefore, to question the validity of a Eucharist celebrated by a divided community, although, of course, we cannot project our recent valid-invalid distinction as such back into the text of Paul without being guilty of an anachronism.[139]

From what we have said, it must be concluded that the presence of the account of institution in every anaphora is of capital importance, both theologically and pastorally. It sets before us, and actuates, the "model" that controls, because it instituted, our celebration. Like everything which Christ did, this norm for our celebration is God-given. (We are using "norm" as a synonym for "code," as we explained earlier in Chap. One.) That is why the president retells the story of the institution to the Father and not to the congregation. When we repeat this normative and institutive account to the Father, we proclaim our obedience to that norm and offer our celebration to him as an act of fidelity in our following of Christ. Or, we offer it to him as Christ's work in us, since through our fidelity to his instituting will, Christ himself celebrates his supper in our communities today.

Only when we adopt this perspective is it possible to explain the consecration of the bread and wine in terms of the celebrating community (the basic liturgical sign!) as gathered into unity by the presidential action of the priest who acts "in the person of Christ" and "in the person of the Church."[140] This theological statement is in continuity with the statements of the Council of Trent: "Christ instituted a new Pasch, namely Himself to be offered by the Church through her priests."[141] The word "Church" is generally used today in the sense it has in Vatican II and in the documents produced by the liturgical reform.[142] It is, therefore, applied to the assembly, which "celebrates" in the full sense of this term. It is the celebrant, however, insofar as it is gathered into unity or is transformed into a single body, by the presidential action of the priest who recapitulates it and represents it in his own person. This unifying action is part of the eucharistic sign and, indeed, a constitutive part.

The Eucharist is a celebration of redemption which, according to the gospel of John, consists in the restoration of unity that Christ has brought about. When the ordained priest by means of his presidential function constructs the unity of the assembly and represents the latter in his person, he is acting "in the person of Christ"[143] and, as such, becomes a foundational part of the eucharistic sign. The Council of Trent clearly says as much when it speaks of the priest's role as the means by which the Church becomes a celebrant.

B. Text

The account of institution is a narrative text and is proclaimed as such; but, it also has a precise theological function which determined its inclusion and role in the anaphora. It is, perhaps, for this reason that none of the accounts of institution in the many anaphoras has simply reproduced one of the four biblical passages on the Last Supper.[144] The direction taken in the development of the anaphoral accounts has always been toward a greater amplification that gives greater prominence to the action of Christ.

The composition of our new eucharistic prayers brought changes in the text of the account of institution; these changes were extended even to the Roman Canon. The phrase *"quod pro vobis tradetur"* ("which will be given up for you")[145] was added to the words over the bread. The enigmatic phrase *"mysterium fidei"* was removed from the words over the chalice[146] and became the cue for an acclamation of the faithful.[147] This latter shift created a situation comparable to what we find in the Eastern anaphoras, which allow ample room for acclamations by the congregation.[148] The reference to the "holy and venerable hands" of Christ was dropped in the new anaphoras.

The basic New Testament text for the account of institution in the Roman rite has traditionally been Matthew 26:26ff. For the sake of parallelism, the demonstrative *enim* (for), which Matthew has only for the cup (26:28), was added to the words over the bread. The result was to accentuate the explanatory nature of the words over the bread and cup in relation to the preceding commands: "Take and eat," "Take and drink."

Keep in mind that the whole emphasis in the account falls on these two commands. Unfortunately—and we do not understand the reason—the Italian translation has simply dropped the explanatory "for" at both consecrations, (and so has ICEL). But even without "for," the words over the bread and cup continue to explain the commands to eat and to drink. Therefore, since "for" is lacking, the manner of proclaiming the text will have to give greater prominence to the command of Christ than is customarily done today. The literary structure of the text effectively allows the theological situation to show through clearly.

The account ends with the mandate of Christ: "Do this in memory of me." This prescribes two objectives for the disciples: they are to repeat the supper in which they have shared, and they are to be very clear in their minds that what is remembered is no longer the Hebrew Passover but Jesus himself as center and principal actor at the supper, just as he is the center and protagonist in all of their life with him. He is the host at the head of the table, who welcomes and serves[149] his companions, thus symbolizing his work for the salvation of the world. The disciples are to repeat the supper which Jesus has celebrated with them: a supper which is the conclusion and summary of the life of Jesus that has been given for them.

The supper thus understood is already a proclamation of the death of Jesus and an announcement of the response of the Father, who will not let his just one see corruption.[150] For this reason, Paul can give the mandate an amplified formulation that brings out its fullness of content: "For as often as you eat this bread and drink the cup, you proclaim the Lord's death until he comes."[151] *Katangellō*, the Greek verb for "proclaim" that is used here, is rich in meaning: the supper of the Lord is a proclamation, prophecy, parable, and symbol of the entire course of his life, including his second coming as his final and complete self-manifestation.

In saying that the supper is "the Lord's" and is symbolico-prophetic in nature,[152] we are saying that it already contains everything that it proclaims. Modern theology uses the word "sacrament" to express this point; therefore, we may say that the supper of the Lord is the sacrament of his death and resurrection until he comes.[153] We must keep in mind, however, that the basic datum and point of departure is the concept of "proclaiming." In other words, the efficacy of the sacrament must be explained in terms of the efficacy proper to God's word in Christ.

IX. ANAMNESIS

The disciples received and transmitted the mandate of repeating the Lord's supper as a commemorative celebration of his saving work. Consciousness that this repetition was in obedience to the mandate led to explication of the fact. The result was the part of the anaphora known as the anamnesis (in the narrow sense of the term): "Therefore, Lord, celebrating now the memorial of our redemption, we recall the death of Christ and his descent among the dead, we profess his resurrection and ascension to your right hand, and, looking forward to his coming in glory. . . ."

The conjunction *unde* (therefore) serves as a hinge connecting the mandate and the anamnesis, for the latter flows from the former as a strict consequence, both ritual and theological.[154]

From both the theological and the pastoral standpoints, the anamnesis is the key part of the celebration[155] and must always be seen in connection with the mandate. This is clear in the relevant decisions of the Apostolic See with regard to the anaphoras for Masses with children. In these anaphoras, the post-consecratory acclamation of the faithful is placed after the anamnesis "in order that the children may clearly understand the connection between the words of the Lord, *Do this in memory of me,* and the anamnesis by the priest celebrant."[156] The same perspective explains another change as well: the mandate is separated from the words over the chalice by a transitional sentence: "Then he said to them."[157] The separation makes the mandate stand out more clearly, since it ceases to be a simple appendix to the words over the chalice. These two changes create a new and very clear thematic unit within the structure of the anaphora, namely, the mandate-anamnesis, which now forms a single block.[158]

When we celebrate the Lord's Supper, we live out its mystery of redemption. The mystery of redemption is not repeated; what is repeated is the supper, and, in repeating it, we celebrate the memorial[159] of our redemption. The entire eucharistic meal, including the anaphora,[160] is recapitulated in the bread and wine, which are its constitutive element. The bread and wine are, therefore, the concrete embodiment and synthesis of the memorial; in other words, they are in an unqualified sense the memorial of the Lord's death and resurrection.

"Both ideas [anamnesis and oblation] contain an objective element as well as a subjective one. What we hold here in our hands is a memorial and an oblation. But memorial as well as oblation must be realized within ourselves as our own remembrance and our offering. Then, and only then, can a 'worship in spirit and truth' in the fullest sense arise to God from our hands."[161]

This fine summation by J. A. Jungmann makes it very clear that active, conscious, and fruitful participation is based directly on the sacramental event as such and on the structure of the anaphoral text itself. That participation is indispensable for the life of the Church in direct proportion as the celebration of the liturgy is indispensable; the liturgy, by its nature, calls for and demands active participation.

X. THE PASCHAL MYSTERY

The object commemorated in the anamnesis is the paschal mystery, which is described by listing the various events which historically constituted it. But, this analytical list is introduced by a synthetic definition of the mystery: "Celebrating now the memorial of our redemption." This summary brings out the unity in the events making up redemption and also makes it clear that the anamnesis is a profession of faith.[162]

A comparative analysis of the anamneses[163] in the various anaphoras reveals a scheme that unfolds in three steps: (1) a transitional element linking the anamnesis to the mandate, (2) a list of the mysteries of Christ,[164] and (3) an offering of the sacred gifts to the Father.[165] The first two steps are always directed to the offering which flows from them: the commemoration moves toward the offering and the offering proceeds from the commemoration. There is an ontological connection between the two: admiration, expressed in the anamnesis, is necessarily followed by imitation, expressed in our offering of ourselves just as Christ offered himself.

The offering makes it clear that the Eucharist is a sacrifice, but a sacrifice only inasmuch as it is a memorial of the one sacrifice that was accomplished once and for all on the cross.[166]

The theologians rightly speak of the sacrifice of the cross as an "absolute" sacrifice (a sacrifice in and of itself) and of the Eucharist as a "relative" sacrifice (a sacrifice only by reason of its relation to an absolute sacrifice). The Eucharist is a sacrifice insofar as it is the sacrament of the sacrifice of the cross.[167] The Eucharist is usually said not to have an autonomous sacrificial character of its own, but to derive its sacrificial character *solely* from its being a *sacrament of the cross*, which is an "absolute" sacrifice. The problem is somewhat more complex, and the wealth of meanings which the word "sacrifice" has in the New Testament and in the liturgical texts must be brought to play in dealing with the Eucharist as a "sacrifice." We simply mention the problem, however, and refer you to W. Rordorf for a good discussion of proper method.[168]

The bread and wine, now the sacrament of the body and blood of Christ, are offered to the Father. What is offered is the sacrament, not the historical events of the passion and resurrection, in which Christ was victim, sacrifice, altar, and priest: He was his own priest[169] and offered once and for all.[170] The problem here is pastoral as well as theological, as we showed in discussing the first epiclesis.

The fourth anaphora says: "We offer to you his body and blood as a sacrifice that is acceptable to you and a source of salvation for the whole world."[171] The text here differs from that found in Vagaggini's Project B, which reads: "We offer you, from the gifts you have given us, this bloodless sacrifice: the pure victim, the holy victim, this spotless victim for the life of the world."[172] Vagaggini's Latin echoes the Roman Canon and has a solid basis in anaphoral tradition.[173] The text in Anaphora IV is much less traditional, being almost excessive in its theological grandeur. The anaphoral tradition to which we refer is unanimous, even if there are some very rare and late exceptions that have inspired the composers of the fourth anaphora. Here is one example: "We offer to you . . . your flesh your blood."[174]

The text just cited is atypical in many ways, but only one interpretation is possible, whether of that text or of the fourth anaphora: what is offered to the Father are the antitypes, that is, the celebration, in sacramental form, of redemption.

Having said this, we will end with the observation that this part of the fourth anaphora could have been improved and brought into greater conformity with tradition simply by retaining Vagaggini's Project B or some comparable text.

XI. OFFERING

The object of the verb "offer" is both "body and blood" and "sacrifice," but the prayer is not satisfied simply to juxtapose these two objects. "Sacrifice" stands in apposition to "body and blood" and has the function of interpreting the latter and explaining just what the character of the "body and blood" of Christ is here. There is, thus, a complete identity between the sacrifice of Christ and his body and blood that have been given for us. "Sacrament of the body and blood of Christ" and "sacrament of the sacrifice of Christ" are one and the same.

The sacramental sign of Christ's sacrifice is identical with the sacramental sign of his body and blood, namely, the celebration of the Lord's Supper, which consists completely of bread and wine.[175]

We do not understand, therefore, the concern of those who claim that to emphasize the one is to draw attention away from the other. When we emphasize the real presence, we do not neglect the sacrifice, or vice versa. And, if we emphasize the memorial, we do not neglect the real presence, or vice versa.

J. A. Jungmann has a good description of what is meant by "offering":

"When the words of institution are spoken to God in an attitude of prayer and when the mystery that is now present is 'presented' to him, at that moment the 'sacrifice' of the Church is accomplished. It must be admitted, indeed, that *offerre* (and its noun *oblatio*) was not a sacrificial term in prechristian texts. Even in the liturgy the word was used initially with the generic meaning of 'bring,' 'present.' "[176]

For this reason, the word "offer" carries strong affective overtones, and the gesture of offering touches the human heart deeply. This enormously important concept of "offering" needs to be protected against possible deviations: we must remember that we cannot offer anything to God that does not already belong to him; we offer him only what we have first received from him.[177] A spirituality based on "offering" easily becomes prey to deviations,[178] since the idea plays such a large part in religious psychology and is connected with the sacraments as well.

The best protection is to bear always in mind that the liturgy locates "offering" within the process of remembering, where it serves to express the remembering and present it to God: "Mindful . . . we, giving thanks, offer to you this living and holy sacrifice."[179]

XII. EPICLESIS FOR UNITY

The prayer that the celebration may be fruitful is the oldest form of intercession. It gave rise to intercessions in the narrower and more proper sense of this term and then, as pneumatology developed, to the epiclesis with its twofold theme: sanctification of the communicants and consecration of the gifts.

The beginning of the epiclesis[180] serves as a link with the preceding prayer of offering. It develops further the theme of "the gifts you have given to us," which is applied, however, not to the bread and wine, but directly to the Lord Jesus himself.[181]

No one can come to Christ unless the Father draws him (Jn 6:44). Therefore, we ask the Father that our encounter with Christ may be salutary and redemptive for us through the action of the Spirit.[182]

If, however, we want a fuller understanding of our epiclesis as an appeal to the Father to send the Spirit, we must begin with the anamnesis, since it is the latter with its commemoration of the ascension that leads us into, and even generates, the epiclesis.[183] Why and how is this so? Death, resurrection, and ascension are interconnected and constitute the paschal mystery as a single saving act. The various phases of that one act is a list both of its historical stages and of the facets of theological meaning which each and every phase includes.

The Letter to the Hebrews shows that when the redemption wrought by Christ is expressed in Old Testament cultic terms, it has two stages: (1) the bloody self-offering on the altar of the cross; and (2) the entrance into the heavenly sanctuary by means of the resurrection and ascension.[184] Death, resurrection, and ascension thus constitute a single sacrificial act that has two phases, an earthly and a heavenly. In his ascension,[185] the Lord "has entered . . . into heaven itself, now to appear in the presence of God on our behalf."[186] There "he always lives to make intercession for them,"[187] and his sacrificial blood is "the sprinkled blood that speaks more graciously than the blood of Abel"[188] in interceding with God.

In the last verse, the reference is to the cup at the supper, which in the crucifixion is poured out for the sake of reconciliation and fellowship among all human beings. This shedding of blood took place once and for all and remains an everlastingly definitive accomplishment. As A. Tarby says: "the mention of the ascension in the anamnesis affirms the uniqueness and eternal irrevocableness of the sacrifice offered. To put it differently, mention of the ascension reminds us that Christ carries on his work of salvation in an endless intercession based on the cross." If we ask what the concrete content is of this prayer of Jesus that eternalizes his sacrifice, we must turn back to John 14:16–17: "I will pray to the Father, and he will give you another Counselor to be with you for ever, even the Spirit of truth."[189] The sacrifice of Christ, as an endless prayer offered at the Father's right hand, is completed when the Father gives the Spirit. Thus, the ascension leads to Pentecost as to its fulfillment.

181

In still other words: "the ascension of Christ is the epiclesis par excellence," because the Son prays to the Father and the result is Pentecost.[190] We have already referred to a law or pattern: "admiration is followed by imitation." In the anamnesis, we contemplated and thankfully proclaimed the mystery of the Lord's death-resurrection-ascension; that was a moment of admiration, which is already a form of communion. Now in the epiclesis, we turn to imitation. Here the Church associates and identifies itself with the Lord who, having ascended to heaven, constantly intercedes with the Father for the gift of the Spirit. So, too, the entire assembly, in and through and with Christ, asks that the Father would bestow the Spirit on those who share in the Lord's Supper. The epiclesis is thus a further and more intense communion with the Lord and is the first fruit of the following and imitation of Christ that is established by the anamnesis.[191] We conclude, therefore, that the epiclesis springs from the anamnesis and that we can speak of an "inherent movement from anamnesis to epiclesis, corresponding to the movement from the ascension to Pentecost."[192]

The epiclesis of Anaphora IV[193] does not explicitly ask for the descent of the Holy Spirit; rather, it supposes that this has already occurred, and thus it reinforces the connection between anamnesis and epiclesis. This approach to the epiclesis strongly emphasizes the identity between the fruit of the Spirit's action and the fruit of the body and blood of the Lord as made sacramentally visible in the one bread and the one cup.

The fruit in question is the unity of the Church which is to become one body in Christ. In the creeds, unity[194] is one of the characteristic notes or properties of the Church: if the Church is not "one," it does not exist at all. Everyone recalls Augustine's theology of unity, which is summed up in the well-known exclamation: "O sacrament of piety, O sign of unity, O bond of charity!"[195] which was cited by the Council of Trent.

The theme of the unity of the Church was part of the Eucharist at the beginning, especially in 1 Corinthians 10:16–22; 11:18ff. It is a much richer theme than appears at first sight. It is rare in the eucharistic epiclesis of the Eastern liturgies, despite the strong influence of Pauline pneumatology[196]; the reason is that the prayer for the Church is already present at the beginning of the intercessions.

There is a danger that the unity of which the epiclesis speaks may be understood as simply one virtue among many or may give rise only to vague, poetic aspirations. The *Didache* is the first document that connects the "breaking of bread" with the theme of unity; the link is then inherited by eucharistic texts that derive from the *Didache*. Whether or not the prayer for unity is associated with the gift of the Spirit, it is characteristic of all the anaphoras; this universal presence is explicable only if the unity in question is special (not one virtue among many) and precise (not a vague aspiration).

To specify this unity, we must go to the theology of John. It is directly applicable to the unity intended in the eucharistic epiclesis, for there is a clear connection between the eucharist in the *Didache* and the Johannine texts on unity. Scholars have already subjected these texts of John to careful examination,[197] and we can examine their conclusions. First, however, we must call to mind the continuity between the Old Testament and John.[198]

The germ of the entire "unity" theme is developed in the Book of Jeremiah.[199] According to the prophet, God promises to gather the scattered and rebuild a national community in a new Israel. The sins and faithlessness of the covenanted people had provoked his anger, and he had dispersed the Israelites. Sin begets dispersion, which is its sign, and is even sin itself as concretely experienced. But, God has always been faithful and remains forever faithful; therefore, he promises to gather the scattered and reconcile them to himself. Obviously, this cannot happen unless the root situation of sin is changed, for sin is precisely a transgression of covenant. Therefore, the gathering and unification of the dispersed will consist above all in their return to God who draws them in merciful love.[200] In a new covenant, he will be their God, and they will be his people.[201] He will be the pastor who keeps his flock in unity.[202]

Ezekiel penetrates more deeply: God will act for his name's sake,[203] and he promises to make his servant David the shepherd of Israel.[204] David prefigures Christ who in the thanksgiving in the *Didache* is called *Pais* (child/servant), just as is David.[205] The unity of which Ezekiel speaks will lead to knowledge of God, who is the sanctifier of all the nations.[206]

According to Second Isaiah, the work of unification is a manifestation of the divine glory. The people will be gathered from the four corners of the earth—a theme which via the *Didache* becomes part of many anaphoras, especially those of the Alexandrian type.[207] Isaiah 49 is the foundational document which assigns the role of unifier to the Servant of Yahweh, who will gather all the nations together and thereby bring them to salvation. We might say that the history of salvation is a history of unification. Like salvation itself, unity is the object of prayer and appeal in 2 Maccabees 1:24–29, which is the direct source of the words "you who alone are good" at the beginning of Anaphora IV.

As the history of salvation reaches its climax in Christ, so too does the history of unity: the Lord's death, resurrection, and ascension established a new covenant, a new unity for a new Israel; the Church must be one, holy, and catholic. Such is the Johannine synthesis of the theme of unity.[208] In this gospel, Jesus three times predicts his coming exaltation[209]; the future exaltation at the Father's right hand is anticipated on the cross, because from the cross Jesus will draw all human beings to himself. It is this dimension of kingly rule that justifies speaking of the cross according to John as "glorious."

All human beings will be drawn to Jesus on the cross and will form a unity. The cross has become the supreme value and the true image of God; it is, therefore, what the Law was for the Israelites in exile: the key factor in a universal cohesion and convergence.

The death of Jesus is a light and a standard that is raised as a gathering point for the nations,[210] because it is the supreme testimony to the fatherhood of God. Those who are drawn will (negatively) "not be lost" but (positively) "have life," which is identical with "being in unity."[211]

The Father rouses in human beings a faith in the Lord Jesus, who in turn bears witness to the Father and brings us to faith in God. It is this faith that makes us one in Christ, that is, gives us life in him. Jerusalem was to have become the center and place of universal unification because the glory of the Lord was to be revealed there. In like manner, Jesus says: "The hour has come for the Son of man to be glorified . . . and I, when I am lifted up from the earth, will draw all men to myself."[212] Jesus is, therefore, the new temple and the new Jerusalem that is the center of eschatological unity. The body of Jesus on the glorious cross replaces the Jewish cult offered in the old temple; it is this new worship[213] that saves human beings by uniting them with Christ and among themselves. That is why the evangelist regards the pronouncement of Caiphas as so meaningful and interprets it as an authentic prophecy since Caiphas was high priest for that year: "Jesus should die for the nation, and not for the nation only, but to gather into one the children of God who are scattered abroad."[214]

That verse is the main one for our argument. It says that unity is the fruit of Christ's death. But, we know from elsewhere that the fruit of Christ's death is salvation and redemption as the climactic moment of the entire plan of salvation. John 11:51–52 is saying, then, that unity is identical with redemption and that the theme of unity deals with the high point and completion of redemption and salvation.

In John and in the first part of Anaphora IV,[215] Jesus is presented as the revealer of the Father. It is this gift that makes us conscious of divine filiation as constitutive of the Christian's very being. The work of revelation, which allows the disciples to address God as "Father," is already a work of unification.[216] There is, therefore, a close relationship between the theme of the epiclesis and the opening part of the fourth anaphora, which proclaims the divine name as it is in itself and as it operates in the historical economy.

With the aid of Caiphas' prophecy,[217] John proclaims that by dying Jesus will draw all human beings to believe in him, with the result that they will be not only children of God, but children brought to their completion and fulfillment in unity. When salvation and redemption are fully manifested, they are nothing else than unity. The definition of salvation as the "fulfillment of unity" has, therefore, an eschatological dimension.

In this way, that is, via the idea of unity, the theme of salvation enters into the thanksgiving in the *Didache:* "Lord, remember your Church . . . make it perfect in your love[218] and gather it from the four winds, this sanctified Church, into your kingdom[219] which you have prepared for it."[220]

Let us sum up. The epiclesis of the Fourth Eucharistic Prayer focuses on the theme of unity; this theme is interpreted in the light of Johannine theology because of the connections between the latter, the *Didache*, and 1 Corinthians 10:16–22 (which is the source of our new text either directly or via the Byzantine Anaphora of Basil). The unity in question is above all that with the Father through faith in Christ (John 17); when human beings share in this unity, it becomes salvation and redemption.

As a result, "salvation" and "unity" are one and the same. The "vertical" unity referred to gives rise, in turn, to a "horizontal" unity of human beings among themselves,[221] so that they form a single body. When we pray in the epiclesis for unity, we are praying that salvation and redemption (in their supreme manifestation, which is unity) may come to all who participate in the Eucharist. In other words, we pray that for all who sit at his table, the Lord's glorious death may achieve its purpose, which is unity.[222]

The process thus described brings about the true worship Christ foretold to the Samaritan woman: the worship in Spirit and in truth[223] that is the characteristic new element in the New Testament by comparison with the Judaism that preceded it. In the epiclesis of Anaphora IV,[224] unity serves a further end[225]: the worship which is the very life of the baptized and which Paul finely describes as a "spiritual sacrifice."[226]

If the history of liturgy is to be a theological discipline, it must follow the method proper to theology; an inquiry into the biblical idea of worship therefore becomes obligatory. But,

"the New Testament nowhere says that Christians have a cultic sacrifice of their own. The sacrifice proper to them is a spiritual sacrifice, which is the eschatological sacrifice that had been predicted. Sacrifice thus understood transcends the narrowly cultic understanding of the term and extends to the entire existence of the baptized, to the extent that this is dynamized and taken over by the Spirit. There are several passages in Paul[227] that speak of the Christian's whole person and life as a 'sacrifical offering.' "[228]

In Paul,[229] we normally find cultic terminology applied to the Christian's daily life as a life lived in Christ. Anaphora IV draws upon this theology[230] of worship as coextensive with the life of the Christian, a life here seen as the purpose and fruit of the eucharistic celebration. The epiclesis ends with a vision of Christian life that is put not in ethical but in cultic terms: Christ's life in us[231] as a prolongation and fruit of the eucharistic memorial.

XIII. INTERCESSIONS

The intercessions of the anaphora immediately precede the final doxology in both the Antiochene-Byzantine and the Roman traditions.[232] Historically, the intercessions are one of the basic and best documented components of the eucharistic prayer as a literary genre, since they were part of its original structure. With time and especially with the development of pneumatology in the East, some themes in the intercessions were taken into the epiclesis, a recently established part of the anaphora that would thenceforth have a life and history of its own. Thus, the theme of ecclesial unity, which is constitutive of the modern Roman epicleses, became the fundamental theme in the overture to the intercessions in the Eastern anaphoras. It is there frequently connected with a repetition of the *offerimus* idea (*offerimus*, "we offer," is a technical term in the final part of the anamnesis), thus making it clear that the theology of the intercessions prolongs the anamnesis, which has expanded to include those who profit and benefit from the mystery of salvation that has been recalled in the original anamnesis.[233]

In the Fourth Eucharistic Prayer, the intercessions begin with the words "Now, therefore," which are indicative of liturgical efficacy. Then comes a list of various individuals or categories of individuals: "Lord, be mindful of all for whom[234] we offer you this sacrifice."[235]

The movement in the intercessions is from the general to the particular; mention of the "Lord" is inspired by the thought of eucharistic efficacy rather than by the recall of those who are present. The mention of persons, whether as a group or as individuals, shows that attention turns from the sacrifice itself to the sacrifice as it relates to its celebrants, participants, and beneficiaries,[236] if indeed we can make so sharp a distinction between these two aspects of the one sacrifice.

The list of beneficiaries begins with those associated with the "(hierarchical) Church" and then includes all of whom we are mindful. Thus, it specifies the pope and the local bishop, "the whole body of bishops,"[237] and "all the clergy, those who make the offering,[238] those who are present." The text suggests a list of roles in order of their decreasing hierarchical importance. At the end of the list comes "your entire people,"[239] but the perspective at this point is no longer that of hierarchical order, as though the "people" came in the last and lowest place. The list of hierarchical roles ends with "those who are present," and not with "the people," conceived as either at the top or at the bottom of that order. The perspective has simply changed. Keep in mind that the hierarchy, too, is part of the "people," since "people" is a synonym for "Church." This last-named equivalence is now completely assured, and we have no choice but to accept it.

The mention of "all who seek you with a sincere heart" is a truly inspired addition which echoes an earlier sentence spoken shortly after the Sanctus: "In your mercy you came to the aid of all of them, so that they might seek and find you." This phrase of the intercessions makes movingly present in our Eucharist all those who have not yet discovered the greatness of the Lord but are journeying toward him, even if without their knowledge.

We do well to be mindful here also of all the sincere nonpracticers who live lives of justice and faith in God but who cannot be among those present because the Church and the language and logic of the liturgy are meaningless to them. Is this for historical reasons? For cultural reasons? Perhaps all of these together. Yet, in fact, these voluntary absentees are not cut off from the eucharistic mystery. The celebrating assembly understands their alienation and makes them present by remembering them in heart and mentioning them in so many words. They are always present.

This part of the intercessions ("all who seek you with a sincere heart") has no parallel in the early anaphoric tradition. It does, however, have a solid biblical basis: "You will seek me and find me; when you seek me with all your heart, I will be found by you, says the Lord."[240] This passage is to be taken together with the Johannine discourse in which Jesus speaks of himself as drawing all human beings to himself from the cross.[241]

This phrase of the fourth anaphora evidently includes all the religious movements, contemporary and past, in which human beings have sought or are now seeking God. It commemorates all the cultures, all the social and ideological movements, that because of their sincerity have objectively meant salvation for human beings and have, therefore, been forms of service to God. The phrase may be regarded, in other words, as including of those anonymous Christians who, though never physically present, have nonetheless never been absent from the Eucharist, since God the Father is always mindful of them and we, his faithful imitators, likewise continually remember them.

The intercessions mention next "those who have died in the peace of your Christ,"[242] that is, the deceased who died possessing a living faith that ruled their hearts and made them members of a single body.[243] The prayer then turns again to the final theme in the commemoration of the living, as it speaks of "all the dead, whose faith is known[244] to you alone." For, in fact, no mortal can know who truly belongs to God. He alone knows who are authentically his own[245]; the Good Shepherd alone knows his sheep.[246]

The recurring "Be mindful" gives the text a certain liveliness and expressiveness. The repetition does not imply any danger that God may forget his children. When we say "Be mindful," "God as it were enters into himself and into his own heart (re-cordare!), where he draws from the wells of his mercy. As he gazes into his own depths, he experiences nothing but love. This 'remembering' by God is thus our salvation."[247]

The last part of the anaphora, just before the concluding doxology, is a prayer for "us," all who celebrate the praises of God and his Christ. The prayer is that we may share in the ultimate realities, those heavenly realities which we have nostalgically contemplated during the celebration. This final section develops themes introduced in the Sanctus. We ask for "an inheritance in heaven,"[248] "in your kingdom,"[249] together with the saints who in their day took part, as we do now, in the eucharistic assembly. And not only with the saints, for it is the whole of creation, all living things, and all human beings that will become and be a new heaven and a new earth after being freed from the corruption of sin and death.[250]

We find here the same theology that we saw at the beginning of this anaphora: the human person is priest for creation. Final salvation will bring the redemption of all that exists and the definitive epiphany of the kingdom; in the glory of the end-time, the aspiration of every creature will be satisfied as all together form a choir that sings for ever the praises of the Father.[251]

We have seen that the eucharistic action is a *call*, a convocation, to us from God, our *justification* through the anaphoric profession of faith, and a *contemplation of God's glory* in union with the angels and saints. In addition, the anaphora is an *anticipation* of the final coming, and we realize that we are given the privilege even now of *glorifying* the Lord in song as we await his final manifestation. If we keep all these facets of the Eucharist before us, we will read with new eyes this text of Paul: "Those whom he *called* he also *justified*; and those whom he justified he also *glorified*."[252]

At the end of the intercessions, we say: "that . . . we may glorify you[253] through Christ our Lord, through whom you bestow all good gifts upon the world."[254] The last words are a synthesis of the *Per quam haec omnia* prayer of the Roman Canon and highlight God's benevolence toward us. He is good and there is no evil in him; he gives us unceasingly every good gift. The divine will is always and exclusively a benevolent will; this is the ontological foundation of the Jewish blessing, which was the Israelite response to God's gifts and became the historical source of the Church's eucharistic prayer. The fourth anaphora thus concludes with a reference to the reason for its own existence; in so doing, it returns to the theme enunciated at the beginning of the text.

XIV. DOXOLOGY

This final section[255] sums up the anaphora; at the same time, it both harks back to the opening thanksgiving and praises God in advance for that which has been requested in the anaphora and which, as we know, he has already granted.

In some types of anaphora (for example, the Anaphoras of Hippolytus, of the Apostles Addai and Mari, of Mark, and of Cyril), the doxology is not an independent literary entity but is connected with what precedes by "in order that." The connective is enlightening, for it shows that the doxology serves the purpose of the anaphora itself.[256]

The very purpose of human existence is to live for the glory of God, because, as created entities, human beings are participants in that glory. Since the anaphora gives expression to the experience of human beings in Christ, it evidently cannot ignore this doxological purpose of human existence. Throughout the anaphora, there is a tension toward the doxology, in which, as it were, we experience the granting of what we have prayed for during the anaphora. In it, a door long desired opens; we are given a pledge and anticipation of the events and experiences of eternal life in the heavenly kingdom.

One of the finest of all doxologies is found in the Byzantine Anaphora of Basil: "And grant that with one voice and one heart we may glorify and praise your venerable and magnificent name."[257] This doxology is in the form of an epiclesis; it emphasizes the truth that only by a gift from God can our hearts today burst forth in songs of praise. This is perhaps the best way to express the theology of grace as lived out with full awareness in prayer.

The doxology, be it noted, is accompanied by the great elevation of the species. This elevation makes it emphatically clear that we have reached the high point and completion of the entire prayer, which is here expressed in trinitarian form. In the trinitarian doxology, the anaphora becomes a triumphal proclamation of the divine Name which, when invoked and proclaimed over us, becomes supreme blessing and perfect sanctification (Nm 6:24–27).

The holy Name of God is proclaimed in the text of the doxology, but it is also said there to have been manifested to human beings in Christ through the gift of the Spirit. For that reason, the "mysteries"[258] and "likeness"[259] of Christ's body and blood are raised over the people of God as a visible manifestation of the mercy and fidelity of the Father who willed to call us, by an unmerited gift, from darkness to light. May he be blessed for ever!

Chapter Seven

The Anaphoras of Reconciliation
and the Anaphora for the Swiss Synod

I. THE ANAPHORAS OF RECONCILIATION

A. Introduction

1. THE OCCASION

The Eucharistic Prayers for Masses of Reconciliation originate with a contingent event: the Holy Year of 1975. They were promulgated together with the three anaphoras for Masses with Children,[1] and were intended as an experiment[2] to be controlled by the episcopal conferences that had requested them. Holy Years have always had a penitential function (among others) and have always been associated with the sacrament of penance. The theme for Holy Year 1975 was "reconciliation," because the new Rite of Penance takes precisely this approach to the sacrament of penance, seeing it primarily as reconciliation with God and with the brethren, in the Church.

The eucharistic prayers in question faithfully reflect the theme of reconciliation, but that aspect of reconciliation with the brethren received most attention from the editors of the texts. The two anaphoras are similar; the language of the second differs slightly from that of the first, being lively, modern, and immediately intelligible. An anaphora is a prayer meant to be proclaimed; from this point of the view, the second anaphora is quite successful.

When a eucharistic prayer is proclaimed in an assembly, one can usually observe a lessening of attention and participation in the congregation; it is one of the times when there is less active participation. The second anaphora of reconciliation is a happy exception to this general rule, for a sensible quickening of attention and a new tension can be observed in the congregation as the words of this anaphora begin to touch the hearers and awaken their interest.

Initially, the Holy See intended that each episcopal conference should choose only one of the two anaphoras,[3] although the au- · thorities did not close the door to further requests; today, however, both of the anaphoras are used, though still on an experimental basis. The Congregation for the Sacraments and Divine Worship recently called the Church's attention once again to these two little-known prayers, and said:

"The theme 'Penance and Reconciliation' which is shared by the Jubilee Year of Redemption (1983–1984) and the coming Synod of Bishops (October, 1983) gives new relevance to the Eucharistic Prayers of Reconciliation which were redacted for Holy Year 1975. In his Apostolic Letter *Aperite portas redemptori* (January 6, 1983) in which he proclaimed the Jubilee Year of Redemption, Pope John Paul II granted permission to use both of these Eucharistic Prayers of Reconciliation. It seems opportune, therefore, to publish the Latin text which the Sacred Congregation for Divine Worship promulgated for a three-year period on November 1, 1974 and which has not been published heretofore."[4]

The Latin text of the anaphoras for Masses with Children is not a liturgical prayer; this explains the unusual criterion set down for the redaction of the prayers in the vernaculars.[5] The same does not apply to the anaphoras of reconciliation, since the Latin text of these prayers is fully liturgical. Nonetheless, when the decree of promulgation speaks of their translation into the vernaculars, it makes no distinction between them and the anaphoras for children, but says simply: "The translation of the text may be made with a degree of freedom in order that it correspond fully to the requirements and idiom of the respective language . . . in accordance with nos. 9–11 of the Introduction to the Eucharistic Prayers for Masses with Children."[6]

Given the wording of this decree, translators of the anaphoras of reconciliation may follow the same criteria of creativity which are provided for the anaphoras with children and which we shall examine in the next chapter.

2. THE INTRODUCTION TO THE TEXTS

The introductory remarks of the anaphoras of reconciliation are very brief, and we shall deal with them with equal brevity. After explaining how the texts originated in the intentions proper to the Holy Year, the Apostolic See says that these prayers "have been prepared to shed light on aspects of reconciliation, insofar as they may be the object of thanksgiving."[7]

The next introductory paragraph limits the use of the prayers. They are to be used during the Holy Year, in Masses that bring home (*inculcatur*) in a special way the intentions of the year. Once the year is past, they may be used in Masses which call attention to (*insinuatur*) the mystery of reconciliation. The two Latin verbs, *inculcare* and *insinuare*, that refer to the themes of the Mass, are not taken from the language of the liturgy; perhaps they express a desire for greater unity between catechesis and liturgical text. It is undeniable that the liturgy, and, therefore, the anaphora, has a catechetical function, but that function is an accessory one which flows from the principal function, namely, the symbolic (= sacramental) celebration of the mystery of redemption.

The Italian version of the Introduction differs slightly from the Latin when it says that each of these eucharistic prayers forms a single whole with its preface and that the latter, therefore, cannot be replaced by another preface. It follows that these anaphoras cannot be used if the rubrics prescribe a proper preface.[8] For further discussion of the Introduction, we refer you to an article of A. Cuva.[9]

B. First Anaphora of Reconciliation

It is truly right and just, Lord, holy Father, that we should give you thanks. Unceasingly you challenge us to a more abundant life and, since you are a good and merciful God, you continue to offer forgiveness and you urge sinners to commit themselves trustingly to your tender mercy alone. Nor have you turned away from us who have so often broken your covenants, but through Jesus, your Son and our Lord, you have united the human family to yourselves by a new bond so strong that it can never be broken. In giving your people now this time of grace and reconciliation, you grant them conversion to yourself, new life in Christ, and the power to serve all human beings by entrusting themselves more fully to the action of the Holy Spirit. Filled, therefore, with wonder and gratitude we join our song of praise to that of the countless heavenly hosts; we proclaim the power of your love and confess our joy in your salvation:

Holy . . . .

God, from the beginning of the world you have helped human beings to be holy as you are holy. Look, we pray, on your people gathered here, and pour out the power of your

Father, all-powerful and ever-living God, we do well always and everywhere to give you thanks and praise. You never cease to call us to a new and more abundant life. God of love and mercy, you are always ready to forgive; we are sinners, and you invite us to trust in your mercy. Time and time again we broke your covenant, but you did not abandon us. Instead, through your Son, Jesus our Lord, you bound yourself even more closely to the human family by a bond that can never be broken. Now is the time for your people to turn back to you and to be renewed in Christ your Son, a time of grace and reconciliation. You invite us to serve the family of mankind by opening our hearts to the fullness of your Holy Spirit. In wonder and gratitude, we join our voices with the choirs of heaven to proclaim the power of your love and to sing of our salvation in Christ: Holy . . . .

Father, from the beginning of time you have always done what is good for man so that we may be holy as you are holy.

Look with kindness on your people gathered here before

Spirit so that these gifts may become for us the body and blood of your beloved Son Jesus Christ, in whom we are your children.

When we had perished and were powerless to draw near to you, you loved us with a supreme love: for your Son, who alone is righteous, gave himself into our hands and did not shrink from being nailed to the wood of a cross. But before extending his arms between heaven and earth as the indestructible sign of your covenant, he desired to celebrate the Passover with his disciples.

While at supper he took bread; he thanked and blessed you; he broke the bread and gave it to his disciples, saying: "Take this, all of you, and eat of it: for this is my body, which will be given up for you."

In like manner, after they had eaten, knowing that he was about to reconcile all things in himself through the blood he would shed on the cross, he took the cup filled with the fruit of the vine, and again giving thanks he gave it to his friends, saying: "Take this, all of you, and drink of it: for this is the cup of my blood of the new and everlasting covenant, which shall be shed for you and for the many for the forgiveness of sins. Do this in memory of me."

you: send forth the power of your Spirit so that these gifts may become for us the body and blood of your beloved Son, Jesus the Christ, in whom we have become your sons and daughters.

When we were lost and could not find the way to you, you loved us more than ever: Jesus, your Son, innocent and without sin, gave himself into our hands and was nailed to a cross. Yet before he stretched out his arms between heaven and earth in the everlasting sign of your convenant, he desired to celebrate the Paschal feast in the company of his disciples.

While they were at supper, he took bread and gave you thanks and praise. He broke the bread, gave it to his disciples, and said: "Take this, all of you, and eat it: this is my body which will be given up for you."

At the end of the meal, knowing that he was to reconcile all things in himself by the blood of his cross, he took the cup, filled with wine. Again he gave you thanks, handed the cup to his friends, and said:
"Take this, all of you, and drink from it: this is the cup of my blood, the blood of the new and everlasting covenant. It will be shed for you and for all so that sins may be forgiven. Do this in memory of me."

The mystery of faith! —
Lord, we proclaim your death
and we confess your resurrection, until you come.

Calling to mind, therefore, Jesus Christ who is our Passover
and our most sure peace, and
celebrating his death and resurrection from the dead and looking forward to the blessed day
of his coming, we offer you, the
faithful and true God, the sacrifice which wins your favor for
all human beings. Look with
kindness, merciful Father, on
those whom you unite to yourself through participation in this
one sacrifice of Christ, that they
may be gathered by the power
of the Holy Spirit into a single
body that is freed of all division.
Keep us united with one another in a communion of mind
and heart with N., our Pope,
and N., our bishop. Help us to
pave the way together for the
coming of your kingdom until
the hour when we stand before
you as saints among the saints
in the heavenly dwellings, with
the Blessed Virgin Mary and the
apostles and with our deceased
brothers and sisters whom we
commend to your mercy. Then,
established in the new creation
that is freed at last from the
wounds of corruption, we shall
humbly sing the hymn of
thanksgiving of your Christ who
lives for ever.

Through him and with him
and in him all honor and glory

Let us proclaim the mystery
of faith: Christ has died, Christ
is risen, Christ will come again.

We do this in memory of Jesus Christ, our Passover and
our lasting peace. We celebrate
his death and resurrection and
look for the coming of that day
when he will return to give us
the fullness of joy. Therefore we
offer you, God ever faithful and
true, the sacrifice which restores
man to your friendship.

Father, look with love on
those you have called to share
in the one sacrifice of Christ. By
the power of your Holy Spirit
make them one body, healed of
all division.

Keep us all in communion of
mind and heart with N., our
pope, and N., our bishop. Help
us to work together for the coming of your kingdom, until at
last we stand in your presence
to share the life of the saints, in
the company of the Virgin Mary
and the apostles and of our departed brothers and sisters
whom we commend to your
mercy. Then, freed from every
shadow of death, we shall take
our place in the new creation
and give you thanks with
Christ, our risen Lord.

Through him, with him, in
him, in the unity of the Holy
Spirit, all glory and honor is
yours, almighty Father, for ever
and ever. Amen.

is yours, almighty God and Father, in the unity of the Holy
Spirit, for ever and ever. Amen.

1. THANKSGIVING AND SANCTUS
The thanksgiving begins with a sentence modeled on the opening
of the Fourth Eucharistic Prayer.[10] The text then recalls the attitude
of God who ceaselessly challenges (*provocas*) his children to an ever
fuller life.[11] It goes on to speak of how God, who is good and merciful,[12] continually offers forgiveness and urges sinners to trust in
his tender mercy alone. In this context, "sinners" is not a generic
term, a kind of rhetorical flourish applied to those who already acknowledge their sin and have already returned, or are returning, to
God. "Sinners" are those who cannot bring themselves to trust in
the God who was described a moment ago as "holy Father."

We are at the central point in this opening paragraph: sinners are
human beings who are disenchanted with God and no longer expect anything from him. What, then, can it mean to "trust in God"
in a post-Christian situation in which the very idea of God is regarded as meaningless?

In this prayer, sinners, who are far from God and have no reason
to approach him, are contrasted with God who, despite everything,
continues to challenge and urge human beings to an ever more intense life. The prayer evidently presupposes that sinners retain
their capacity to respond to the theme of life and that it is possible
for them to experience trust once again. The object of this trust is
said to be the *indulgentia* (kindness, tenderness, fondness) of God:
not God himself, but his tender kindness.

The term is not simply a matter of style, but it embodies an authentic theological approach to the problem. If God manifests himself and is known through his manifestation, a lack of faith may be
due to insufficient knowledge or to a defective perception of his
self-manifestation. This is the only way in which God can be
thought of as meaningless or as not relevant to us here and now. It
is even possible to admit intellectually the existence of God, while
failing to reach a corresponding value judgment. After all, many
people do believe that God exists, but they maintain that this existence has no relevance to them. And indeed, if in all their undertak-
ings and decisions, human beings are compelled to act as if God
did not exist, how is his existence to become relevant to them?

In the present anaphora, it is supposed that God is well aware of
the situation which we have just expounded. His response to it is

an unchanged concern for human beings. The biblical basis for this theology is found in the prophet Hosea, who responds to the disinterest of his wife Gomer with a persevering longing and activity. The reason for this is given in lapidary verses:

"My people are bent on turning away from me; so they are appointed to the yoke, and none shall remove it. How can I give you up, O Ephraim! How can I have you over, O Israel! How can I make you like Admah! How can I treat you like Zeboiim! My heart recoils within me, my compassion grows warm and tender. I will not execute my fierce anger, I will not again destroy Ephraim; for I am God and not man, the Holy One in your midst, and I will not come to destroy."[13]

The next part of the thanksgiving ("Nor have you turned away . . .") contains several elements which link it to the *Post-Sanctus* of Anaphora IV: (1) the reference to covenants, (2) the sin of human beings, and (3) the refusal of God to abandon them. There is, however, a slight difference between the two texts: when Anaphora IV speaks of covenants, the emphasis is on God's persistent offer of them,[14] whereas here the emphasis is on the repeated human violations of the covenants. In Anaphora IV, human beings lost God's friendship; here they break the covenants. But, both texts agree in saying that God has not distanced himself from human beings nor abandoned them.[15]

The reference to broken covenants leads to the Christological section of the thanksgiving. Christ's work is described as the forging of a new bond between the human family and God, a bond so strong that it can never again be broken. The text is astonishing in the dramatic sense it handles this crucial point. As good theologians, we would expect that the "bond" would be immediately defined for us—perhaps as the Spirit or as the new covenant. But, the text is silent and leaves the listeners to define the bond for themselves. Each individual must give the answer.

The text is not easy to proclaim, since it makes a statement whose precise meaning is not determined but is left as an open question. In any case, the bond is new and will last for ever (since it is unbreakable). These are two characteristic attributes of the covenant by which God in Christ has pledged himself to be "for" human beings and can never again draw back. The new covenant is seen as definitively committing God.

In a time when God is meaningless, the covenant cannot be presented as something that binds human beings to God. It is, there-

198

fore, presented as an act by which God embraces human beings for ever. In this perspective, we must say, with Heinz Schürmann, that the existence of Christ is an "existence for."[16]

A final point: although the human race and the human individual are the beneficiaries of the divine action, the anaphora prefers to speak of the "human family." The term is consistent with the theme that is being developed, for when we speak of the human race as a family, we are already saying that in dealing with God, the wars, divisions, and hatreds we find among human beings have no place; in its covenant with God, the human race is called to be a single family and to be at one and in harmony. But, if this is the demand and commitment that characterize the covenant, human beings can begin to see that a relationship with God is indeed meaningful, since solidarity among nations and peace among peoples is a most urgent need for modern society and for each individual.

The sentence just analyzed carries a depth of meaning which we have barely touched. The text itself is conscious of this density and strives to bring out some of the meaning by starting with the opposite pole, namely, human beings and the effects which God's action has on them. Disappointingly, however, the anaphora focuses on the rather narrow theme of the "favorable time," which is identified with the Holy Year: "In giving your people now this time of grace and reconciliation . . ."[17]

On the other hand, the "favorable time" is not trivialized. It is a time to open ourselves to the Holy Spirit, a time for conversion, a time for return to the house of Christ. When the time is thus profitably used, it produces a renewed commitment to the service of the brethren.

The thanksgiving ends here. It is followed by its logical consequence, the Sanctus: "Filled, therefore, with wonder and gratitude we join our song of praise to that of the countless heavenly hosts; we proclaim the power of your love and confess our joy in your salvation." In this introduction to the Sanctus, the angelic hymn is a "reception" of what has been said in the preface. The assembly that sings the Sanctus is one that has identified itself fully with the preceding thanksgiving and made it its own.

2. POST-SANCTUS

This very short passage serves as a transition to the account of institution. It is, nonetheless, also very stimulating.

To begin with, God is shown as a God of longing love: "From the beginning of the world you have helped human beings to be holy as you are holy."[18] The purpose of God's action is to put human beings in contact once more with their deepest nature as his "image and likeness"[19] and thereby to restore them to communion with himself. God's nature is "holiness"[20]; consequently his work of reforming human beings in his image coincides with his activity as sanctifier. Human holiness is a gift of God, and the anaphora will, therefore, not allow us to be discouraged when confronted with the God who offers us holiness.

The text then becomes an epiclesis as it asks God to look upon (respicere) his people gathered here[21] and to pour out the power of the Holy Spirit. The purpose of the sending of the Spirit is the transformation of the bread and wine into the body and blood of Christ. This first epiclesis speaks of the *potentia* (power) of the Spirit, while the second will use *virtus*, which is practically synonymous. The term "power" does not appear in the second Anaphora of Reconciliation; we must, therefore, conclude that the "power" of the Spirit does not have any special connection with the mystery of reconciliation.

The epiclesis concludes with a mention of "your beloved Son Jesus Christ," which becomes the occasion for a further narrative passage on the theme of Christ's work of salvation. From the standpoint of anaphoral structure, this passage is a novelty. The Christological section usually precedes the first epiclesis which is, as always, closely connected with the account of institution. It is not easy to find a reason for this structural inversion.[22] A pure hypothesis is that perhaps there is a deliberate effort to preclude a theology based on the structure of the four new Roman anaphoras, a structure that is the same in all four formularies.

3. CHRISTOLOGICAL EXPANSION

The passage opens with a description of the human situation. Human beings are incapable of dialogue with the Father and are, as it were, dead.[23] God takes remedial action by sending his Son. By not refusing the cross, the Son proves that he is righteous beyond all other human beings, even to the point of choosing not to assert his own righteousness.[24]

P. Béguerie and J. Evenou claim that this Christological passage serves to emphasize the connection between the Supper and the cross.[25] In fact, the two themes are juxtaposed, but no connection is developed. For a connection to be stated, the text would have to indicate what link exists between Supper and cross and thus to pro-

200

duce a passage resembling the anamnesis after Christ's command of repetition. Christ's gesture of extending his arms between heaven and earth as a sign of covenant is not particularly significant in this context, since it is linked to mention of the supper only as part of a temporal sequence: "Before extending his arms . . . , he desired to celebrate the Passover with his disciples."

There is a further argument against any real connection being stated here between Supper and cross. The theme of the cosmic cross asserts that the cross is the sign of an indestructible covenant. But, if the term "sign" were being used in the perspective of the Supper-cross connection, it would be predicated of the Eucharist and not of the cross.

We do not deny, of course, that the retrieval of this ancient theme is of interest. In Irenaeus' view, the cross is a mystery of salvation precisely because it is a cosmic cross on which Christ triumphs and by which human beings ascend to heaven. The idea of the cross as vehicle of ascension[26] complements the idea of the cross as vehicle of a unity that embraces all of creation. Today, however, these ideas are only fragments of a past poetry, although they are backed up by Genesis 13 in which the rainbow—a link between heaven and earth—is a sign of the covenant.

We agree with F. Brovelli that the eschatological passage in Luke 22:15–16 is the inspiration for the words: "He desired to celebrate the Passover with his disciples."[27] If this claim is valid, the relation between Eucharist and reconciliation is placed in an eschatological perspective. In such a perspective, the relation can be more easily developed in a synthetic way and with less dependence on contingent factors.

The account of institution is not remarkable except that in the introduction to the words over the chalice, the cross is said to effect the reconciliation of the world.[28] Jesus is presented as deliberately linking to the chalice the reconciliation wrought by the cross. The reconciliatory function of the Eucharist is further emphasized in that Jesus gives the cup to his "friends." The allusion is to John 13:1 and 15:15, as Brovelli rightly points out.[29]

More can be said, however, with regard to "friends." The context of the word here is reconciliation; the eucharistic prayer which we are examining was composed for the Holy Year and the celebration of the mystery of reconciliation. Therefore, we see a reference to sin, which the new Rite of Penance describes as "an offense against God which disrupts our friendship with him."[30] In the Eucharist, therefore, the chalice celebrates our friendship with God in Christ.

This connection between the Rite of Penance and the anaphora is not direct, but it is relevant in view of the connection between penance and Eucharist that is characteristic of the Eucharistic Prayer of Reconciliation.

4. ANAMNESIS AND OFFERING

The Latin text divides the anamnesis in two parts. The first is governed by the participle *memores* ("calling to mind," an imitation of the Roman Canon), which has for its object "Jesus Christ who is our Passover and our most sure peace." The memorial does not focus, therefore, on the actions of the death and resurrection, but on the person of Christ. The anamnesis thus reflects Christ's command of repetition: "Do this in memory of *me.*"

The second part is governed by the participle *celebrantes* (celebrating), which is paratactically coordinated with *memores*. The object of the "celebrating" is the death and resurrection; the statement thus reflects the theological description of the Supper. In Christ's command, the "this" is the Supper, but the Supper has a content: the death and resurrection. The Eucharist is, therefore, described as directly related to that content. The assertion of sacramentality is complete.

Yet a third participle is coodinated with these two: *praestolantes* (awaiting, looking forward to), which has for its object the final coming of the Lord. The same verb is used in Anaphora III of the Missal and serves as a characteristic expression of the eschatological element in the modern Roman anaphoras.

The eschatological element originates in the Eastern anaphoras, but there has been a significant change. The Anaphora of James connects the eschatological theme with fear of the last day when the Lord will come to judge; the same can be said of the two Anaphoras of Basil and the Anaphora of Mark. All these anaphoras speak of the coming as "striking terror" or "awe-inspiring." Our new anaphora of reconciliation takes a different view[31] and speaks of "the blessed day of his coming." The result continues the theme (found in the thanksgiving) of the hope that must be restored to human beings. Fear of the final judgment has no place here; even the *parousia* is a salvific act,[32] and that day can, therefore, only be a blessed day. We cannot but be impressed by the quiet serenity which this anaphora shows even at the most difficult points.

The description of Jesus as our Passover is from 1 Corinthians 5:7, a classical text in paschal theology. For Christians, Passover is not a day but a person: Christ. In thus alluding to paschal theology, the anaphora supposes that the Church has already reached maturity in regard to the pascal dimension of its faith. This is perhaps one of the points on which there is the greatest need of careful reflection and penetration.

The same can be said of the immediately following description of Christ as "our most sure peace."[33] The danger with this second description is that it may too easily lend itself to a purely devotional interpretation: peace as interior tranquillity and peace of heart, whereas "peace" here means the communion which binds together those who believe in Christ. This understanding of "peace" is the basis for the offering which concludes this part of the anaphora: "We offer you, the faithful and true God, the sacrifice which wins your favor for all human begins."[34]

5. EPICLESIS

The epiclesis of the anaphora echoes the Fourth Eucharistic Prayer. Not only is the same opening verb used (*respice*, look), but the focus of both is on the unity (a fruit of the Spirit) which is to reign among all those who share in the sacrifice.[35] Eucharistic communion produces unity through the gift of the Spirit. By bestowing the gift of the Spirit, the Eucharist functions as sacrament of unity.

Another influence, traceable back to Hippolytus via *The Testament of the Lord*, seems to be at work in this epiclesis. Hippolytus begins his statement of the purpose of the Spirit's coming with the words "bringing them together in unity" ("*in unum congregans*"),[36] a phrase not easy to interpret. *The Testament of the Lord* then alters Hippolytus to say "that all may be united to you" ("*ut tibi uniantur omnes*").[37] The reference is to union with God. There may be a connection between Hippolytus, as reformulated in *The Testament of the Lord*, and the Anaphora of Reconciliation, which formulates the theme of union with God as follows: "Look with kindness, Father, on those whom you unite to yourself through participation in this one sacrifice of Christ." Participation in the eucharistic supper brings unity with the Father. Through the power of the Spirit this unity is to extend horizontally as well, so that all "may be gathered . . . into a single body that is freed of all division."[38]

We might think that union with God through the sacrifice of Christ should produce something more than mere freedom from division and discord. The text is admittedly inadequate for expressing the biblical concept of unity, of which we spoke earlier in Chap. Six. On the other hand, the words do reflect reality and should be interpreted in that light. We need think only of the situation of the

Church, which is afflicted by divisions and discords. The "truth" of the prayer has been given precedence over the wealth of theology that might have been included in dealing with the theme of unity. The choice of the redactors was a correct one.

6. INTERCESSIONS

Faithful to its choice of truthfulness as a criterion, this anaphora bases the intercessions on the theme of unity, whose various aspects have just been examined. It asks that we be "united in a communion of mind and heart" with the pope and our bishop. This, again, is a realistic approach.

Let us end the discussion of the first Anaphora of Reconciliation by calling attention to two points of the intercessions that are new by comparison with other texts. The first is the idea that human beings become new creatures in their passage through death; their new state is one of assimilation to Christ who stands at the Father's right hand singing a perpetual hymn of thanksgiving. The anaphora itself is a hymn of thanksgiving which human beings offer to God even now. In this perspective, then, the anaphora provides a foretaste of the blessed state of heaven, which is conceived as an endless hymn of thanksgiving. Thus, the eschatological value of the anaphora is suggested here, at a point shortly before the final doxology.

The second point is contained in the prayer asking God to help us "pave the way" (paremus, prepare) for the coming of his kingdom. The text is quite reserved. It does not say that human beings "build" the kingdom, even with God's help. It simply asks for help to prepare the way for the coming of the kingdom. We can only be astonished at this highly nuanced theme which is not to be confused with human participation in the work of creation or with the commitment to the brethren that emerges in the preface.[39] The kingdom of God transcends all those things. Human beings do not build the kingdom or reign of God, if for no other reason than that this is an eschatological gift.

204

C. Second Anaphora of Reconciliation

Almighty God and Father, we thank and praise you through Jesus Christ our Lord for your work in the world. For though the human race is fragmented by dissension and discord, we know from experience that you alter minds and prepare them for reconciliation. Your Spirit moves hearts so that enemies speak to one another again, adversaries clasp hands, and nations seek fruitful encounter. By your power love of peace moves wills to settle quarrels, forgiveness overcomes hatred, and vengeance yields place to pardon. Therefore must we continually thank and praise you with the heavenly choirs that unceasingly cry out to your majesty:

Holy. . . .

Therefore we bless you, Ruler of all the powers, through Jesus Christ your Son, who came in your name. He is the word which saves humankind, the hand which you extend to sinners, the way by which you offer us your peace. God, Father of us all, when we were estranged from you, you brought us back through the Son whom you handed over to death in order that we might turn back to you and might love one an-

Father, all-powerful and ever-living God, we praise and thank you through Jesus Christ our Lord for your presence and action in the world. In the midst of conflict and division, we know it is you who turn our minds to thoughts of peace. Your Spirit changes our hearts: enemies begin to speak to one another, those who were estranged join hands in friendship, and nations seek the way of peace together. Your Spirit is at work when understanding puts an end to strife, when hatred is quenched by mercy, and vengeance gives way to forgiveness. For this we should never cease to thank and praise you. We join with all the choirs of heaven as they sing for ever to your glory: Holy. . . .

God of power and might, we praise you through your Son, Jesus Christ, who comes in your name. He is the Word that brings salvation. He is the hand you stretch out to sinners. He is the way that leads to your peace. God our Father, we had wandered far from you, but through your Son you have brought us back. You gave him up to death so that we might turn again to you and find our way to one another. Therefore

other. Therefore, celebrating the reconciliation acquired for us by Christ, we pray that you would sanctify these gifts with the dew of your Spirit as we carry out the command of your Son.

For when he was about to give his life to set us free, he took bread into his hands while reclining at table and offered you thanks and blessing; he broke the bread and gave it to his disciples, saying: "Take this, all of you, and eat of it: for this is my body, which will be given up for you."

On that same evening he likewise took a cup and, praising your mercy, gave it to his disciples, saying: "Take this, all of you, and drink of it: for this is the cup of my blood of the new and everlasting covenant, which shall be shed for you and for the many for the forgiveness of sins. Do this in memory of me."

The mystery of faith! — Lord, we proclaim your death and we confess your resurrection, until you come.

Lord our God, your Son has left us this pledge of his love for us. Mindful therefore of his death and resurrection, we offer you what you have given to us: the sacrifice of perfect reconciliation. Holy Father, we ask you to accept us together with your Son, and through this banquet to give us his Spirit who takes

we celebrate the reconciliation Christ has gained for us.

We ask you to sanctify these gifts by the power of your Spirit, as we now fulfill your Son's command.

While he was at supper on the night before he died for us, he took bread in his hands, and gave you thanks and praise. He broke the bread, gave it to his disciples, and said: "Take this, all of you, and eat it: this is my body which will be given up for you."

At the end of the meal he took the cup. Again he praised you for your goodness, gave the cup to his disciples, and said: "Take this, all of you, and drink from it: this is the cup of my blood, the blood of the new and everlasting covenant. It will be shed for you and for all so that sins may be forgiven. Do this in memory of me."

Let us proclaim the mystery of faith: Christ has died, Christ is risen, Christ will come again.

Lord our God, your Son has entrusted to us this pledge of his love. We celebrate the memory of his death and resurrection and bring you the gift you have given us, the sacrifice of reconciliation. Therefore, we ask you, Father, to accept us, together with your Son. Fill us with his Spirit through our sharaway whatever divides. May he preserve us in communion with N., our Pope, and N., our bishop, and all the bishops and your entire people. We pray you, make your Church be in the midst of humanity as a sign of unity and instrument of your peace. Just as you have gathered us here at the table of your Son in communion with the Blessed Virgin Mary, Mother of God, and all the saints, so too bring all human beings, of whatever rank and nation, to the banquet of abiding unity in the new world where peace in its fullness sheds its radiant light, through Christ our Lord.

Through him and with him and in him all honor and glory is yours, almighty God and Father, in the unity of the Holy Spirit, for ever and ever. Amen.

ing in this meal. May he take away all that divides us.

May this Spirit keep us always in communion with N., our pope, N., our bishop, with all the bishops and all your people. Father, make your Church throughout the world a sign of unity and an instrument of your peace.

You have gathered us here around the table of your Son, in fellowship with the Virgin Mary, Mother of God, and all the saints. In that new world where the fullness of your peace will be revealed, gather people of every race, language, and way of life to share in the one eternal banquet with Jesus Christ the Lord.

Through him, with him, in him, in the unity of the Holy Spirit, all glory and honor is yours, almighty Father, for ever and ever. Amen

1. PREFACE

The thanksgiving is concerned with God's work in the world. The very low-keyed and reserved opening sentence[40] is developed by describing the human race as living in a world "fragmented by dissension and discord." Even in that situation, human beings experience the efficacious action of God.

Precisely because the world as fragmented by discord is not an object of "information" but of common and daily experience, "information" does not suffice to produce the present thanksgiving: "experience" of God's action in favor of human beings is required: "We know from experience."[41] The object of this experimental knowledge is that God sways souls so that they are ready for reconciliation. He is at work in the human heart, which scripture describes as straying and rebellious, wicked, uncircumcised, and full of duplicity.[42] He accomplishes his purposes by means of the interior situation. Once he has done this, human beings must themselves seek the road to reconciliation.

The anaphora clearly distinguishes these two levels of action. God does not take the place of human beings nor does he exempt them either from seeking him or from commitment within history where they have a responsibility which they may not evade. Psalm 115:16 provides a very clear basis for this theology: "The heavens are the Lord's heavens, but the earth he has given to the sons of men."

To this gift, human beings must respond; the world is their kingdom and they are responsible for it. The solution to the problem of evil is found in that God reclaims the hearts of human beings so that they can be reconciled with him. In the theology of covenant, it is the Spirit who renews hearts and dwells in them where he acts as a new law.[43] And, the anaphora introduces the Spirit at this point, thus giving the preface a trinitarian cast. Three examples are given of the Spirit's action: (1) enemies renew dialogue,[44] (2) adversaries clasp hands, and (3) nations seek encounter.

Such is the activity of the Spirit in the work of reconciliation that marks the beginning of the mystery of covenant. The final part of the preface that leads into the Sanctus comments on the effects which the Spirit's activity produces. The power[45] of God works unwearyingly so that love of peace will bring the settling of quarrels, forgiveness will conquer hatred, and pardon will replace vengeance. This is a vision of an ideal that accurately describes the reign of God on earth.

We regard as excessive the criticism that the perspective here is utopian.[46] The vision, after all, conveys the theology of Isaiah in modern dress, for according to Isaiah in the messianic age, God will judge between the nations and decide for many peoples. Then "they shall beat their swords into plowshares, and their spears into pruning hooks; nation shall not lift up sword against nation, neither shall they learn war any more."[47]

This description is not a chronicle of events. It is a prophecy of the transcendently different final state toward which the world is journeying. But, that does not make it any less real or any less an object of experience and thanksgiving. The Spirit's work in human hearts can already be recognized; the final state has already begun.

The Sanctus, which proclaims the Lordship of God over heaven and earth, is followed by a proclamation of the work of Christ.

2. CHRISTOLOGICAL SECTION

Though still unswervingly addressed to the Father, the hymn of thanksgiving and praise now focuses on the work of Christ. Here again the language is always lively, direct, and incisive.

Jesus is described in several ways which immediately establish him as redeemer. The passage starts with his mission: "He came in your name." The sentence stops here, without any further addition, though we might have expected the thought to be completed by a statement of the purpose of the coming. By stopping where it does, the text focuses on the relation between Father and Son and postpones any statement of why Christ came. The choice is very effective stylistically.

Next, three titles are given to Jesus: "He is the word which saves humankind, the hand which you extend to sinners, the way by which you offer us your peace."[48] The three are meant to describe the person of Jesus in itself rather than to give a complete list of his actions; however, all three titles have to do with "communication."[49] And, in fact, the Logos made flesh is essentially "for human beings." It is, therefore, possible to say that this anaphora avoids a ontological description of Jesus in favor of one that reflects the "economy" of redemption.

The primary action of Jesus is related to human history, which is described as a history of estrangement from God; the action in question is his sacrifice. There is a clear echo here of John 11:51f. The death of Christ is regarded as a source for human beings of conversion to God and love for one another. The text does not say, however, why or how this death is a source of conversion. Luke's theology of the death of Christ[50] might have supplied the needed thematic complement to this description of the redemptive death.

After the proclamation of Christ's redemptive work comes the first epiclesis. Its introduction is noteworthy: "Therefore, celebrating the reconciliation acquired for us by Christ." This echoes the phrase "this sacrifice by which we are reconciled" in the Third Eucharistic Prayer of the Missal (it occurs in the intercessions).

The second anaphora of the Missal supplies the phrase "dew of the Spirit." In using the image of dew, the text goes back to the theme of water which, in the Old Testament, can either bring blessing or be an instrument of God's anger. In the present context, of course, water can only have a positive meaning, since the preface has spoken of the Spirit's work and his changing of hearts in the same terms in which the biblical passage that is in the background here speaks of water.[51]

3. ANAMNESIS AND OFFERING

"Lord our God, your Son has left us this pledge of his love for us."[52] Such a beginning for the anamnesis is unusual. One might suggest the Anaphora of Addai and Mari as a source or parallel,[53] but the resemblance is probably accidental, although the anamnesis is built in accordance with a carefully studied plan. In fact, both anaphoras of reconciliation have two-phase anamneses.

The first anaphora distinguishes between the remembrance of Christ and the celebration of his death and resurrection. The second begins the anamnesis with a reference to our reception of the Eucharist from the Last Supper. That is, the pledge which Jesus left us at the Last Supper is our present eucharistic action itself that is now being celebrated.

This theological approach can be connected with the account of institution in the Roman Canon. There it is said that after they had eaten, Jesus "took this (*hunc*) noble cup." The meaning is that the cup which now stands on the Church's altar is the very cup which Jesus held in his hands at the Last Supper. The actions described in the account of institution are in the past. Thus, the identity of Mass and Supper is not due to a new presence of Christ (in the minister) so that his past gestures are performed *once again* today. No, the identity of Mass and Supper is asserted by saying that our cup is the cup which Jesus used, that is, consecrated, at the Last Supper, and not some other cup. Analogously, our eucharistic bread is the very bread which Jesus consecrated at the Last Supper.

All this is reminiscent of the eucharistic theology of Antoine Chavasse, which we shall expound in Chap. Nine and which we are here endeavoring to complete by asserting the real and ontological identity of our present-day celebration with the supper that Christ celebrated in the upper room. In celebrating its Eucharist, the Church receives the pledge of love that was the Last Supper. That is the first point being made in the anamnesis. The second is that this reception is accomplished without any specifically new elements: "Mindful therefore of his death and resurrection, we offer you what you have given to us: the sacrifice of perfect reconciliation."

The Italian translation combines the two moments or phases of the anamnesis into a higher synthesis that brings out fully the theology of the Supper-cross relationship: "Accepting this pledge of love which your Son has left us, we celebrate the memorial of his death and resurrection and offer to you this sacrifice of perfect reconciliation which you yourself have placed in our hands."

210

It is easy to discern the phrases in which this anaphora echoes the Third and Fourth Eucharistic Prayers of the Missal. The phrase "what you have given to us" echoes "the sacrifice which you have prepared for your Church"[54]; "sacrifice of perfect reconciliation" corresponds to "sacrifice by which we are reconciled" in the Third Eucharistic Prayer. In addition, the words "Holy Father . . . accept us together with your Son" are like "May he make us an everlasting gift to you."[55] However, the source of these words in the second anaphora of reconciliation is not to be found in the Third Eucharistic Prayer of the Missal but in the four alternative versions which Father Vagaggini prepared for the commission that was to produce a definitive text of the Third Eucharistic Prayer. The first alternative, abandoned then, has been used in the second anaphora of reconciliation.[56]

As in the epiclesis of the first anaphora of reconciliation, the Spirit is seen in relation to unity, inasmuch as he "takes away whatever divides." The comments made on the epiclesis in the first anaphora apply here as well.

4. INTERCESSIONS

The intercessions of this anaphora are quite restrained. After a prayer for the pope, the local bishop, the episcopal college, and the people, there is a prayer for the unity of the Church. As in the Roman Canon and in the Alexandrian and Antiochene anaphoras, the intercessions are the place of prayer for the unity of the universal Church,[57] whereas the epiclesis is the place of prayer for the unity of the celebrating community. Once the Church itself has received the gift of unity, it becomes a sign of this unity among human beings and therefore an instrument of God's peace in the world.

This statement is pregnant with consequences for the mission of the Church. A very clear distinction is usually made between the task of the Church in the world and the actual historical development of the Church, which has frequently been marred by episodes and elements that have nothing to do with the gospel and its proclamation. The distinction between these two levels or aspects allows a degree of serenity when we are confronted with the not always edifying history of the Church. But, this eucharistic prayer disturbs our serenity, for it asserts that the Church is a *sign* of unity for all human beings. It is obvious, however, that the Church can be a sign only in its historical visibility. Consequently, it must be one and free of internal division and discord. In other words, the mission of the Church here is connected with and conditioned by the Church's own commitment to the gospel. Insofar as the historical life of the Church is a sign, it cannot be regarded as an indifferent variable. The anaphora of reconciliation thus represents a commitment of the Church to conversion through a continuing reform that will speed it on its journey to unity.[58]

The intercessions end in a reprise of the anamnesis in which we praise the action of God who has called the congregation into unity by means of the eucharistic celebration. This is already a sign of the Church's unity. Now that we have experienced this limited unity, we can legitimately look forward to the fullness of unity in the end time. Our prayer, therefore, becomes at this point an eschatological contemplation on the theme of unity. We mentioned that these anaphoras of reconciliation are marked by realism. This conclusion of the intercessions displays such realism, for it says that complete and all-embracing unity is reserved for the time of the eschatological banquet when God will be all in all because the Son will have handed over the kingdom to him.[59] On the other hand, the Eucharist is the sacrament of the eschatological banquet; therefore, that final unity must begin now.

The anaphora of reconciliation ends with the theme of unity and of the resplendent peace that characterizes the reign of God. From a literary standpoint, the anaphora reaches a climax that leads into the doxology, the supreme moment of contemplation.

II. THE ANAPHORA FOR THE SWISS SYNOD

A. Variable Prefaces

1. GOD LEADS HIS CHURCH

It is truly just that we should thank you, holy Father, creator of the world and source of life. You do not leave us alone on the road, but live and work in our midst. With your mighty arm you led the people who wandered in the wilderness; today, you give the light and strength of your Spirit to your Church as it makes its pilgrim way in the world. Through Christ, your Son and our Lord, you guide us along the paths of time to the perfect joy of your kingdom. In thanksgiving for these incalculable gifts, we join the angels and saints in singing unceasingly a hymn to your glory: Holy. . . .

2. JESUS OUR WAY

It is truly just that we should thank you, great and merciful God, who created the world and now preserve it with immense love. As a Father you watch over all your creatures and unite in a single family the human beings whom you created for the glory of your name, redeemed by the cross of your Son, and signed with the seal of the Spirit. Christ, your living Word, is the way that leads us to you, the truth that sets us free, the life that fills us with joy. Through him we raise to you a hymn of thanksgiving for these gifts from your loving kindness, and with the assembly of the angels and saints we proclaim your praises: Holy. . . .

3. JESUS, MODEL OF LOVE

It is truly just that we should thank you, merciful Father, for you have given us your Son, Jesus Christ, as our brother and redeemer. In him you revealed to us your love for the lowly and the poor, the sick and the outcast. He never closed his heart to the needs and sufferings of his brethren. By his life and his words he told the world that you are a Father and that you care for all of your children. For these signs of your loving kindness we praise and bless you, and in union with the angels and saints we sing a hymn to your glory: Holy. . . .

4. THE CHURCH ON THE ROAD TO UNITY

It is truly just that we should thank you and raise to you, Lord and kind Father, a hymn of blessing and praise. Through the incarnation of your Son, who is the splendor of your eternal glory, you have gathered all nations into the unity of the Church. By the

power of your Spirit you continue to unite the peoples of the earth
into a single family, and you offer all human beings the blessed
hope of your kingdom. Thus the Church is a radiant sign of your fidelity to the covenant which you promised and then made a reality
in Jesus Christ, our Lord. For this mystery of salvation the heavens
praise you, the earth rejoices, and the Church sings your glory
with one heart and voice: Holy. . . .

B. Invariable Section
We glorify you, almighty Father, for you constantly sustain us on
our journey, especially in this hour in which Christ, your Son,
brings us together for the holy supper. As he did to the disciples at
Emmaus, he reveals the meaning of the scriptures to us and breaks
bread for us.

Almighty Father, send your Spirit, we pray you, on this bread
and this wine so that your Son may be present in our midst by his
body and his blood.

On the eve of his passion, while he was at table with them, he
took bread and gave thanks, broke it, gave it to his disciples, and
said: "Take this, all of you, and eat of it: for this is my body, which
will be given up for you."

In like manner, he took the cup of wine and gave thanks with a
prayer of blessing, gave it to his disciples, and said: "Take this, all
of you, and drink of it: for this is the cup of my blood of the new
and everlasting covenant, which shall be shed for you and for the
many for the forgiveness of sins. Do this in memory of me."

The mystery of faith! — Lord, we proclaim your death and we
confess your resurrection, until you come.

Celebrating the memorial of our reconciliation, we proclaim,
Father, your work of love. Through the passion and cross you
brought Christ your Son into the glory of the resurrection and
called him to your right hand as deathless king of the ages and lord
of the universe.

Holy Father, look upon this offering: it is Christ who gives himself, body and blood, and by his sacrifice opens for us the road that
leads to you. God, Father of mercies, grant us the Spirit of love,
the Spirit of your Son.

C. Variable Intercessions

1.
Strengthen in unity all whom you have called to your table, to-

214

gether with N., our Pope, N., our bishop, the priests and deacons, and the entire Christian people. May they radiate joy and trust to the world and journey in faith and hope.

2.
Strengthen your people with the body and blood of your Son, and renew us in his image. Bless N., our Pope, N., our bishop, and our people. May all members of the Church be able to read the signs of the times and commit themselves consistently to the service of the gospel. Make us open and available to the brethren whom we meet on our journey, so that we may share their griefs and anxieties, their joys and hopes, and advance together with them on the path of salvation.

3.
Strengthen your people with the bread of life and the chalice of salvation; make us perfect in faith and love, in communion with N., our Pope, and N., our bishop. Give us eyes to see the needs and sufferings of our brethren; fill us with the light of your word; help us give ourselves faithfully to the service of the poor and the suffering. May your Church be a living witness to truth and freedom, justice and peace, so that all human beings may open their hearts to the hope of a new world.

4.
Grant that the Church of N. may be renewed in the light of the gospel. Strengthen the bond of unity between laity and priests, priests and our bishop, N., bishops and our pope, N. In a world torn by discord may your Church be a resplendent prophetic sign of unity and peace.

D. Invariable Intercession for the Dead and Doxology
Remember also our brethren who have died in the peace of your Christ and all the deceased, whose faith is known to you alone. Allow them to enjoy the light of your face and the fullness of life through resurrection. Grant that at the end of this pilgrimage we too may reach the eternal dwellings where you wait for us. In communion with the Blessed Virgin Mary, with the apostles and martyrs, (St. N. [saint of the day or patronal saint],) and all the saints we offer you our praise in Christ, your Son and our Lord.

Through him and with him and in him all honor and glory is

yours, almighty God and Father, in the unity of the Holy Spirit, for ever and ever. Amen.

E. Origin
In the document on the eucharistic prayers published in 1973, the Congregation for Divine Worship said that for various reasons four eucharistic prayers were enough for the time being; it also said, however, that it was willing in special circumstances to allow a new text.[60] The Swiss Synod of 1972 was regarded as meeting this criterion. The new text, which was the work of an appointed commission, was finished toward the end of 1974 and was approved by the Congregation on August 8, 1974.[61] Switzerland is a trilingual country, and the text therefore has three originals: German, French, and Italian. The Latin version was never composed.

The new anaphora was subsequently adopted by Luxembourg on the occasion of its synod and by Austria on the occasion of the twelve-hundredth anniversary of the cathedral of Salzburg. The diocese of Strasbourg adopted it in 1975, and the whole of France in 1978, while on January 5, 1980, Italy was also authorized to use it.

F. Description
The text is made up of a fixed section and two variable sections for which four alternative texts are provided. The preface and the intercessions are variable; the rest of the text is invariable.

The decision to allow variation in the intercessions as well in the preface (the themes of which are picked up in the intercessions) is a novelty in the history of the anaphoras of the Roman Church; it appears here for the first time.

The themes of the four alternative texts are not completely different and distinct. Rather, the four texts contain variations on a theme, which can be summed up thus: "God leads his Church to unity in Christ, who is the way, the truth, and the life." The invariable central part of the eucharistic prayer focuses on this same theme; the four alternative texts, while remaining faithful to the theme, orchestrate it in different ways. There is, thus, a close unity between the invariable part and the variable parts, so much so that the variable parts prove to be but four different ways of formulating the one theme. For this reason, the prefaces cannot be replaced by others from the Roman Missal, since the thematic unity would then be lacking.

The titles given to the four variable formularies are (a) God leads his church, (b) Jesus our way, (c) Jesus, model of love, and (d) the Church on the road to unity.

G. Discussion

When the anaphora had been approved for the Italian Church, Abbot S. Marsili wrote an article of introduction and commentary.[62] The rather harsh article elicited a response from J. Baumgartner of Fribourg. This response, which appeared in *Rivista liturgica,* was introduced by a letter from Abbot G. Holzherr, president of the Swiss Liturgical Commission.[63]

Marsili's first criticism was concerned with the four themes just listed; he claimed that each of the four formularies contains the theme of one or more of the others, but in a rather incoherent way: "At times the theme proper to a formulary practically disappears or is fused with a theme from another formulary."[64] In response, Baumgartner said that this was deliberate, since the purpose was to create a unified text: "There is only one basic motif which, amid four variations, gives a precise imprint to the entire prayer."[65]

The two commentators were in basic agreement. Marsili had obviously been deceived by the different titles given to the four variable formularies. On the other hand, since there are different titles, we ought to expect different contents corresponding to the titles. Otherwise, it would be better to use a single title and to describe the four variations simply as different formularies.

The connection of the four formularies among themselves and with the invariable central section is established not so much by a theme inherent in the anaphora as by the circumstances of the redaction, namely, a Church's celebration of its synod. The basic theme is precisely the existence of the synod, and the eucharistic prayer expresses very well what the Eucharist, the memorial of the Lord, is in such circumstances. If we look for coherence in the theme "Jesus, model of love" or "Jesus our way," we will inevitably be disappointed. If, however, we ask how a Church in synod can pray with Jesus as model of love or with Jesus as our way, we will see that the anaphora is functional in its context.

The anaphora was fine, then, for the Swiss Church and its synod. The Italian Church, however, is not in a time of synod, and, therefore, there is a danger that the text will cease to be functional.

Marsili had a further point to make in regard to the doctrine on sacrifice that is expressed in this anaphora. We shall forgo this for the moment because it will come up again in the discussion of the text itself.

Despite his criticisms, Marsili acknowledged the literary value of this anaphora, which he describes as marked by "a properly simple style."[66] And, indeed, this is the great merit of this text. When proclaimed, it immediately awakens the attention and interest of the faithful. Its ideas are clear and deal with realities which the faithful recognize in themselves. They see themselves in the text that is being proclaimed; in this celebration, they are one in prayer with the other members of the congregation. The effect is notable and can be compared with the effect of the second anaphora of reconciliation, although in the latter, the emphasis on the eschatological theme can create difficulties.

The literary and linguistic aspect was indeed a prime concern of the compilers, so much so that Baumgartner theorizes that "its [the anaphora's] principal aim is to lead the participants to the highest possible degree of existential involvement."[67] Just before this remark, he had observed: "This is above all a prayer." It must be acknowledged that from this point of view, the anaphora for the Swiss Synod is fully successful; this is a matter of experience. But, for that very reason, some deficiencies in its content stand out all the more clearly.

H. Text

1. The Road or Journey
"You do not leave us alone on the road, but live and work in our midst. With your mighty arm you led the people who wandered in the wilderness; today, you give the light and strength of your Spirit to your Church as it makes its pilgrim way in the world."[68] The theme of the road, or journey, occurs both in the *Post-Sanctus*[69] and in Preface A, the first of the four variable texts. It also occurs, however, in Preface B: "Christ, your living Word, is the way that leads us to you."[70] In the invariable section of the anaphora, the "recommendation of the sacrifice" again refers to the road: "Christ . . . by his sacrifice opens for us the road that leads to you."[71] And, again in the invariable ending of the intercessions, just before the doxology: "Grant that at the end of this pilgrimage we too may reach the eternal dwellings where you wait for us."[72]

The theme also finds expression in Intercessions A, but in the form of an allusion,[73] while it is present more explicitly in Intercessions B.[74] On the other hand, it is completely absent from Intercessions C and D and from Prefaces C and D.

The presence of the theme in the invariable part of the anaphora leads us to think that it is fundamental to the whole eucharistic prayer and plays a constitutive part in it. It is in fact quite congenial to the modern mind which likes to think of life as a journey through time and history.

At the same time, the idea is also biblical. The text shows an awareness of this, and Preface A even begins with a picture of the Israelites wandering in the wilderness. The same passage refers to the actualization of this type in the new Israel, the Church. God led his people of old; now he accompanies the Church. The two testaments are thus in continuity. Just as the pilgrimage of Israel in the wilderness had an ultimate goal, so does the Church's pilgrimage: the Church is journeying toward the kingdom of God. There is a careful thematic succession being developed here: from Israel to the Church, from the Church to us who wander along the paths of time. Human beings are guided (as Israel was) on the paths of time and (like the Church) will reach the kingdom.

All of this is expressed in the framework of a thanksgiving, and, therefore, the kingdom of God is described as a place of perfect joy. Every human being longs for joy and seeks it; consequently, in expressing itself as it does, the anaphora relates to the existential experience every human being has of this fundamental need. The reign and kingdom of God fulfills every human need, as the logic of the exhortation in Matthew shows: "Seek first his kingdom and his righteousness, and all these things shall be yours as well."[75] That is why Preface A ends with the words: "In thanksgiving for these incalculable gifts. . . ."

The image of Israel in the wilderness is a suggestive one, since a wandering people is a people without a precise goal. Israel's experience resembles that of life itself in which we often spend our time looking for meaning in various trials and experiences. Given this situation, the statement at the beginning of Preface A is programmatic: God does not leave us alone on the journey. Evidence of this is his use of his "mighty arm," a metaphor for his efficacious interventions. He is, therefore, the one who constantly sustains us on our journey.[76]

In all this, the theme of salvation and redemption is fused with the theme of the way or journey, in keeping with the archetypal journey, the Old Testament Exodus, which also describes the basic experience of redemption.[77] Salvation takes the form of "journeying in faith and hope"[78] to the eternal dwellings where God waits for us.[79] The text depends at this point on the parable of the prodigal son,[80] which provides a good picture of the journey of human life. That life too takes the form of a "journeying in faith and hope,"[81] that is, in the two virtues which are the source of salvation: "A man is justified by faith," and "In this hope we are saved."[82]

On this journey of salvation, the faithful ask God to "make us open and available to the brethren whom we meet[83] on our journey."[84] The reference is to the following of Christ, that is, to a communion with him which leads to communion among human beings. This communion with Christ is not something we can elicit out of ourselves; it is a gift from God: "so that we may share their griefs and anxieties, their joys and hopes,[85] and advance together with them on the path of salvation." Salvation is never a state possessed in tranquillity; it is a journey on which we advance slowly as a result of help received.

As soon as we speak of salvation, we must also speak of the savior, who is Christ. He is introduced into the anaphora as having a central role in the theme of journeying, for he is the "way."[86] This title, along with "truth" and "life," is found in Preface B, where it follows upon another Christological title, "your living Word," which comes from Anaphora II of the Missal. In commenting on that anaphora, we pointed out the paschal significance of "living Word." As the Word, Jesus is the sure way to the Father, but he is so especially in his death and in the resurrection that completes his passage: "Christ . . . by his sacrifice opens for us the road that leads to you."[87] Precisely, because he both died and rose, he is the sure way, the Word that gives life.

In the gospel of John, "truth" and "life" are gifts which Christ gives us here and now.[88] "Way" can likewise be understood as something which Christ gives to his disciples, since he himself is the way. There is a valuable connection between the role of Jesus as living Word and his role as the man offered in sacrifice on the cross. As living Word, he is the way in the sense that he gives us the way. By his sacrifice, he "opens for us the road that leads to the Father." The Torah (Law) is no longer the way to the kingdom, for Jesus himself has taken the place of the Law that had been given so that we might be able to reach God. Seen in this light, the sacrifice of Christ is the typological fulfillment of the entire economy of the Law or Torah in the Old Testament.

This conception of the sacrifice of Christ is not obvious and requires a process of interpretation to bring it out and clarify its terms. To that extent, Marsili is right when he laments the inadequacies of the text from the standpoint of the sacrifice. On the other hand, we cannot but accept Baumgartner's response when he says that the theme of sacrifice is indeed present and not at all played down.[89]

We have dwelled on the theme of the road or journey because it is the one that occurs most frequently in the anaphora and because, as noted, it is the link connecting all the variable parts. This fact confirms the claim at the beginning that this anaphora has to be interpreted in light of the experience of synod.

One last point: the word "synod" means "a meeting of ways," in the sense of a road or journey that is shared. In patristic Greek, "synod" (*synodos*) can also mean "companion on a journey."[90] It is the path of the Church that becomes a common path or path of unity. It was right, therefore, that the basic theme of an anaphora composed for the Swiss Church in synod should be the theme of the road or journey.

2. UNITY

The theme of synod leads to the theme of unity. This finds expression in a short but important sentence in the invariable part of the anaphora: "You constantly sustain us on our journey, especially in this hour in which Christ, your Son, brings us together for the holy supper."

The means by which Christ sustains human beings on their journey is the eucharistic assembly. The latter is, therefore, seen as fulfillment of both the theme of synod and the theme of unity. For the assembly is the basic liturgical sign; but, if an assembly is not united, it is not an assembly. Unity is thus an attribute of the eucharistic sacrament.

Preface B contains a further reference to unity: "You unite in a single family the human beings whom you created for the glory of your name." The purpose of human life in Christ is the glorification of God's holy Name. An intermediate purpose that leads to this ultimate goal is the unification of human beings into a single family. This sequence (formation of family—glorification of God), which is the theme of the thanksgiving, occurs in Hippolytus as the theme of the epiclesis: unity—fullness of the Spirit—glorification of God.[91]

Another brief reference to unity is found in Intercessions A: "Strengthen in unity all whom you have called to your table." The statement, although couched in general terms, is clear enough to indicate that "unity" is synonymous with "love," since the sentence goes on to call for a deepening harmony between the various orders making up the Church.

It is formulary D, however, that places the greatest emphasis on the theme of unity, as we expect from its title. The Preface explicitly says that the peoples of the earth are to be united by the power of the Spirit; moreover, the end result of the unification is to be a family. We are close here to the anaphoras of reconciliation. But, there is a departure from the usual development of the theme, inasmuch as the Church is described as a sign of God's fidelity to the covenant. The theme that is thus enunciated in the Preface becomes an object of prayer in the Intercessions: "In a world torn by discord may your Church be a resplendent prophetic sign of unity and peace."

Marsili comments: "It can certainly be said that the 'unity of the Church' which has already been brought about by Christ is the start of and the way toward the unification of all peoples into 'a single family.' But the question remains: To what extent does the unity of all peoples have the Church as its common denominator?"[92] Marsili's words are prophetic. They certainly stimulate reflection on how Church reform can go forward and be "a way" to unity, so that the quoted words of the anaphora may be fulfilled.

3. DISCIPLES AT EMMAUS

"As he did to the disciples at Emmaus, he reveals the meaning of the scriptures to us and breaks bread for us."[93] This short passage brings together two themes: word and Eucharist. The conjunction implies that the Lukan story of the two disciples at Emmaus is a eucharistic story and, more specifically, that "the Eucharist is a permanent manifestation of the risen Jesus."[94]

Our one regret to the sentence of Emmaus is that the reference is overly succinct. It requires considerable knowledge of scripture to reach Durrwell's conclusion. Let us therefore discuss briefly the way in which the story in Luke 24 confirms such a theology.

The experience of the two disciples who set out from Jerusalem is a religious experience shared by many in the post-Christian era. These men are well acquainted with the life of Jesus and they summarize it appropriately in Luke 24:19–24. Their remembrance of Jesus as "a prophet mighty in deed and word before God and all the people" is nostalgic. They had great hopes in him, but his death put an end to these hopes, and now they experience only disappointment. In leaving Jerusalem, they leave the place where the death of Jesus has also killed their hope.[95]

This loss of hope is due above all "to a radical misunderstanding of the event of the cross"[96]; that is, the two disciples fail to understand the "necessity" of Christ's suffering and death (Lk 24:26). Luke, therefore, sets up a dialogue on scripture in which the suffering of Christ is justified by an appeal to the prophets. His death is to be understood not as the end of hope, but as the beginning of its fulfillment.

In addition, however, the entire narrative in this passage of Luke is compellingly directed toward the "recognition" of Jesus[97] that comes with his action of breaking bread at table. A correct understanding of the scriptures bears fruit during the celebration of the supper, for the supper brings both an assertion of the presence of the risen Jesus and a "confession of an invisible but real Lord."[98] "The place where bread is broken is also the place where we grasp the true interpretation of the scriptures."[99] The supper is the starting point for the disciples' return journey: they go back to Jerusalem, thus making it clear that the death of Jesus there is an unforeseen but authentic new point of departure.

The passage conveys essentially the Easter experience of two minor disciples.[100] Their experience is not that of the apostles and first disciples on Easter morning,[101] but that which is given to the Church through the sacraments. The experience has two phases or stages: in the first, Jesus lets himself be seen without being recognized; in the second, he lets himself be recognized without being seen, inasmuch as he vanishes from their sight. But, it is at this second stage that the disciples profess faith in the Jesus who is henceforth invisible.[102] They have now understood the cross: the death of Jesus receives its full meaning from his resurrection, and Jesus is confessed as the Lord who now lives.

Neither the recollections of the disciples that are described in vv. 19–24 nor the discussion of the Bible in vv. 25–27 enable the disciples to recognize Jesus. It is only at the breaking of the bread that they realize the presence of the risen Lord: "an invisible presence that is manifested through a sign."[103] "The recognition in v. 31 is accompanied by a complete reversal of the situation described earlier in vv. 15–16."[104] In other words, the recognition of Jesus coincides with a conversion of heart and the beginning of a new life.

The story of the disciples at Emmaus is thus "one important historical testimony, among others, to the essential connection be-

tween the supper and the Christian experience of resurrection."[105]
The "breaking of bread" is and will always be "the sign par excellence of the presence of the risen Jesus and the place where Christians can and should discover this presence, so that they will then be able to bear witness to the resurrection."[106]

In summary, the reference to the disciples at Emmaus is a most valuable novelty in the anaphora for the Swiss Synod. All present are invited to make their own the experience of the two disciples: an experience that passes from disappointment to faith in the risen Lord who is joyously proclaimed and witnessed as a result of the recognition that comes with the breaking of bread. The anaphora says, moreover, that Jesus "breaks bread *for us*." The invitation to the congregation to identify with the disciples at Emmaus is thus not merely a rhetorical flourish, but is based on the objective fact that our "breaking of bread" is identical with that described in Luke 24 and that the events described there belong to the very nature of the sacrament. Every Eucharist is, therefore, a manifestation of the risen Jesus who is invisibly present and a source for us of conversion and the power to bear witness.

In this passage, the sacrificial nature of the Eucharist is stated only indirectly. There is no denying, however, the connection of death, resurrection, and supper which Luke intends to assert and which is part of every celebration using this anaphora, since the reference to Emmaus is in the invariable part. In addition, the Emmaus theme fits in well with the basic theme of the road and the journey. The "journey" of the two disciples is initially a journey of shattered hopes; once the risen Jesus manifests himself in the eucharistic meal, it becomes a journey of faith. At this point, the synodal journey of the Swiss Church displays its full eucharistic significance.

Chapter Eight

The Eucharistic Prayers for Masses with Children

God our Father, who has brought us together, we stand before you to celebrate and praise you and to tell you how greatly we admire you. Praise be yours for the beauty of the world and for the joy with which you fill our hearts. Praise be yours for the light of day and for the word with which you enlighten our minds. Praise be yours for the earth and for the human beings who dwell on it and for the life which we know is your gift to us. You are truly good, for you love us and do wonderful deeds for us. Therefore we all join in singing to you:

Heaven and earth are full of your glory. Hosanna in the highest!

Father, you are always thinking of human beings and you refuse to be distant from them. You sent us your beloved Son to save us: he healed the sick and pardoned sinners; he made clear to all the love you have for them; he welcomed and blessed

God our Father, you have brought us here together so that we can give you thanks and praise for all the wonderful things you have done. We thank you for all that is beautiful in the world and for the happiness you have given us. We praise you for daylight and for your word which lights up our minds. We praise you for the earth, and all the people who live on it, and for our life which comes from you. We know that you are good. You love us and do great things for us. [So we all sing (say) together: Holy, holy, holy Lord, God of power and might, heaven and earth are full of your glory. Hosanna in the highest.]

Father, you are always thinking about your people; you never forget us. You sent us your Son Jesus, who gave his life for us and who came to save us. He cured sick people; he cared for those who were poor and wept with those who were

225

the little children. Therefore we gratefully proclaim:

Blessed is he who comes in the name of the Lord. Hosanna in the highest!

We are not alone in celebrating you, for your people glorify you throughout the world. In our prayer, therefore, we are united with the entire Church, with N., our Pope, and N., our bishop. In heaven meanwhile the Blessed Virgin Mary and the apostles and all the saints praise you unceasingly. With them and with the angels we worship you, as we say with one voice:

Holy, holy, holy Lord God of hosts. Hosanna in the highest!

Holy Father, in our desire to thank you we have brought bread and wine. Grant that they may become the body and blood of your beloved Son, Jesus Christ. Then we will be able to offer you what you have first given to us. For on the evening before he suffered, while eating with his apostles he took bread from the table. He offered you thanks and praise. He broke the bread and gave it to them, saying: "Take this, all of you, and eat of it: for this is my body,

sad. He forgave sinners and taught us to forgive each other. He loved everyone and showed us how to be kind. He took children in his arms and blessed them. [So we are glad to sing (say): Blessed is he who comes in the name of the Lord. Hosanna in the highest.]

God our Father, all over the world your people praise you. So now we pray with the whole Church: with N., our pope and N., our bishop. In heaven the blessed Virgin Mary, the apostles and all the saints always sing your praise. Now we join with them and with the angels to adore you as we sing (say): Holy, holy, holy Lord, God of power and might, heaven and earth are full of your glory. Hosanna in the highest. Blessed is he who comes in the name of the Lord. Hosanna in the highest.

God our Father, you are most holy and we want to show you that we are grateful.

We bring you bread and wine and ask you to send your Holy Spirit to make these gifts the body and blood of Jesus your Son. Then we can offer to you what you have given to us.

On the night before he died, Jesus was having supper with his apostles. He took bread from the table. He gave you thanks and praise. Then he broke the bread, gave it to his friends, and

226

which will be given up for you."

In like manner, when supper was ending, he took a cup filled with wine. He thanked you and gave it to his friends, saying: "Take this, all of you, and drink of it: for this is the cup of my blood of the new and everlasting covenant, which shall be shed for you and for the many for the forgiveness of sins."

Then he said to them: "Do this in memory of me."

What Jesus Christ told us to do we now do; and, proclaiming his death and resurrection, we offer you the bread of life and the cup of salvation. He leads us to you: receive us, we pray, together with him.

Christ died for us. Christ rose. We await you, Lord Jesus!

Father who loves us so greatly, allow us to draw near to your table and, united in the joy of the Holy Spirit, to receive the body and blood of your Son. Lord, you forget not even one of us; we pray you, therefore, for N. and N., whom we love, and for those who have departed from this world in peace. Remember all who suffered pain and sorrow, your Christian family that is scattered far and wide, and all human beings on earth. When we see what you accomplish through your Son

said: "Take this, all of you, and eat it: this is my body which will be given up for you."

When supper was ended, Jesus took the cup that was filled with wine. He thanked you, gave it to his friends, and said: "Take this, all of you, and drink from it: this is the cup of my blood, the blood of the new and everlasting covenant. It will be shed for you and for all so that sins may be forgiven. Then he said to them: do this in memory of me."

We do now what Jesus told us to do. We remember his death and his resurrection and we offer you, Father, the bread that gives us life, and the cup that saves us. Jesus brings us to you; welcome us as you welcome him. Let us proclaim our faith: Christ has died, Christ is risen, Christ will come again.

Father, because you love us, you invite us to come to your table. Fill us with the joy of the Holy Spirit as we receive the body and blood of your Son.

Lord, you never forget any of your children. We ask you to take care of those we love, especially of N. and N., and we pray for those who have died.

Remember everyone who is suffering from pain or sorrow. Remember Christians everywhere and all other people in the world.

We are filled with wonder

we are filled with wonder and again we praise you:

Through him and with him and in him all honor and glory is yours, almighty God and Father, in the unity of the Holy Spirit, for ever and ever. Amen.

and praise when we see what you do for us through Jesus your Son, and so we sing:

Through him, with him, in him, in the unity of the Holy Spirit, all glory and honor is yours, almighty Father, for ever and ever. Amen.

Loving Father, you give us the
joy of thanking and praising
you together with Jesus Christ:
  Glory to you who love us!

You loved us so much that
you created this vast and beautiful world for us:
  Glory to you who love us!

You love us so much that you
give us your Son Jesus so that
he may lead us to you:
  Glory to you who love us!

You love us so much that you
gather us together as children of
a single family:
  Glory to you who love us!
For such great gifts of love we
thank you with the angels and
saints who worship you in
song:
  Holy, holy, holy Lord God of
hosts. Heaven and earth are
filled with your glory. Hosanna
in the highest! Blessed is he
who comes in the name of the
Lord. Hosanna in the highest!
  Truly blessed be Jesus whom
you sent as friend of children
and the poor. He came to show
us how to love you and one another. He came to remove from
human hearts the evil that prevents friendship, and the hatred

God, our loving Father, we are
glad to give you thanks and
praise because you love us.
With Jesus we sing your praise:
Glory to God in the highest.
(or:) Hosanna in the highest.

Because you love us, you
gave us this great and beautiful
world. With Jesus we sing your
praise: Glory to God in the highest. (or:) Hosanna in the
highest.

Because you love us, you sent
Jesus your Son to bring us to
you and to gather us around him
as the children of one family.
With Jesus we sing your praise:
Glory to God in the highest.
(or:) Hosanna in the highest.

For such great love we thank
you with the angels and saints
as they praise you and sing
(say): Holy, holy, holy Lord,
God of power and might,
heaven and earth are full of
your glory. Hosanna in the highest. Blessed is he who comes in
the name of the Lord. Hosanna
in the highest.

Blessed be Jesus, whom you
sent to be the friend of children
and of the poor. He came to
show us how we can love you,
Father, by loving one another.
He came to take away sin,
which keeps us from being

229

that keeps us from being happy. He promised that his Holy Spirit would be with us always so that we might live your life.

Blessed is he who comes in the name of the Lord. Hosanna in the highest!

We ask you, God our Father, to send your Holy Spirit so that these gifts of bread and wine may become the body and blood of Jesus Christ, our Lord.

On the day before he suffered he showed your endless love. For while reclining at supper with his disciples, he took bread, gave thanks, broke it and gave it to them, saying: "Take this, all of you, and eat of it: for this is my body, which will be given up for you."

Jesus Christ, who was given up for us!

He likewise took the cup full of wine and prayed to you in thanksgiving; he gave the cup to them, saying: "Take this, all of you, and drink of it: for this is the cup of my blood of the new and everlasting covenant, which shall be shed for you and for the many for the forgiveness of sins. Do this in memory of me."

Jesus Christ, who was given up for us!

Then he said to them: "Do this in memory of me."

We do remember, therefore, loving Father, the death and resurrection of Jesus, Savior of the

friends, and hate, which makes us all unhappy. He promised to send the Holy Spirit, to be with us always so that we can live as your children. Blessed is he who comes in the name of the Lord. Hosanna in the highest.

God our Father, we now ask you to send your Holy Spirit to change these gifts of bread and wine into the body and blood of Jesus Christ, our Lord.

The night before he died, Jesus your Son showed us how much you love us. When he was at supper with his disciples, he took bread, and gave you thanks and praise. Then he broke the bread, gave it to his friends, and said: "Take this, all of you, and eat it: This is my body which will be given up for you." Jesus has given his life for us.

When supper was ended, Jesus took the cup that was filled with wine. He thanked you, gave it to his friends, and said: "Take this, all of you, and drink from it: this is the cup of my blood, the blood of the new and everlasting covenant. It will be shed for you and for all so that sins may be forgiven." Jesus has given his life for us. Then he said to them: "Do this in memory of me."

And so, loving Father, we remember that Jesus died and rose again to save the world. He

world, who gave himself into our hands to be the sacrifice that draws us to you.

Glory and praise to our God! (or:) We praise you, we bless you, we thank you!

Hear us, Lord God, and give your Spirit of love to all who share in this banquet, so that they may become more and more one in your Church, together with N., our Pope, N., our bishop, and the other bishops, and all who serve your people.

May they be one body for your glory!

Do not forget those whom we love, . . . , and those whom we do not love enough. Remember, too, those who have departed from this life in peace, . . . , and in your goodness accept them into your house.

May they be one body for your glory!

Gather us to yourself some day, we pray, together with the Blessed Virgin Mary, Mother of God and our mother, so that we may celebrate the everlasting day in your kingdom where all the friends of Jesus Christ, our Lord, will sing an endless song to you.

May they be one body for your glory!

Through him and with him and in him all honor and glory is yours, almighty God and Father, in the unity of the Holy Spirit, for ever and ever. Amen.

put himself in our hands to be the sacrifice we offer you. We praise you, we bless you, we thank you.

Lord our God listen to our prayer. Send the Holy Spirit to all of us who share in this meal. May this Spirit bring us closer together in the family of the Church, with N., our pope, N., our bishop, all other bishops and all who serve your people. We praise you, we bless you, we thank you.

Remember, Father, our families and friends (N.), and all those we do not love as we should. Remember those who have died (N.). Bring them home to you to be with you for ever. We praise you, we bless you, we thank you.

Gather us all together into your kingdom. There we shall be happy for ever with the Virgin Mary, Mother of God and our mother. There all the friends of Jesus the Lord will sing a song of joy. We praise you, we bless you, we thank you.

Through him, with him, in him, in the unity of the Holy Spirit, all glory and honor is yours, almighty Father, for ever and ever. Amen.

We thank you, God. *You created us to live for you while loving one another. It is by your
gift that we see and speak to
one another and that we can
share our good times and our
hardships.

[*Easter season: You are the
God of the living; you have
called us to life and you will
that we should enjoy eternal
happiness. You raised Jesus
Christ from the dead as the first
of us to rise and you gave him
new life. You have promised
the same to us: life without end,
without sorrow or suffering.]

For this, Father, we are glad
and we thank you together with
all who believe in you. With the
angels and saints we rejoice and
praise you, saying:
    Holy. . . .
You are truly holy, Lord, and
kind to all of us, and you show
your mercy to all human beings.
We thank you above all for your
Son, Jesus Christ. *In his goodness he came into the world, because human beings were desert-
ing you and were no longer of
one mind with one another. He
opened our eyes and ears so
that we might recognize one another as brothers and sisters,
and you as Father of us all.

[*Easter season: He brought us

We thank you, God our Fa-
ther. *You made us to live for
you and for each other. We can
see and speak to one another,
and become friends, and share
our joys and sorrows.

[*Easter season: You are the living God; you have called us to
share in your life, and to be
happy with you for ever. You
raised up Jesus, your Son, the
first among us to rise from the
dead, and gave him new life.
You have promised to give us
new life also, a life that will
never end, a life with no more
anxiety and suffering.]

And so, Father, we gladly
thank you with every one who
believes in you; with the saints
and the angels, we rejoice and
praise you, saying:
    Holy. . . .
Yes, Lord, you are holy; you
are kind to us and to all. For
this we thank you. We thank
you above all for your Son, Jesus Christ. *You sent him into
this world because people had
turned away from you and no
longer loved each other. He
opened our eyes and our hearts
to understand that we are brothers and sisters and that you are
Father of us all.

[*Easter season: He brought us

news of the life that is to be lived for ever in your presence and amid your splendors, and, going on before us, he showed us how to walk in love the way that leads to that life.]

Now Christ gathers us at one table and wishes us to do what he once did.

Father, in your goodness sanctify these gifts of bread and wine so that they may become for us the body and blood of your Son, Jesus Christ.

For on the evening before he suffered death for us, while reclining at table with his disciples for the last time, he took bread, gave thanks, broke it, and gave it to them, saying: "Take this, all of you, and eat of it: for this is my body, which will be given up for you."

He likewise took the cup filled with wine, gave thanks, and gave it to his disciples, saying: "Take this, all of you, and drink of it: for this is the cup of my blood of the new and everlasting covenant, which shall be shed for you and for the many for the forgiveness of sins."

Then he said to them: "Do this in memory of me."

Therefore, holy Father, we stand before you, remembering with joy what Jesus Christ did for our salvation. In this holy sacrifice which he entrusted to his Church we recall his death

the good news of life to be lived with you for ever in heaven. He showed us the way to that life, the way of love. He himself has gone that way before us.]

He now brings us together to one table and asks us to do what he did.

Father, we ask you to bless these gifts of bread and wine and make them holy. Change them for us into the body and blood of Jesus Christ, your Son.

On the night before he died for us, he had supper for the last time with his disciples. He took bread and gave you thanks. He broke the bread and gave it to his friends, saying: "Take this, all of you, and eat it: this is my body which will be given up for you."

In the same way he took a cup of wine. He gave you thanks and handed the cup to his disciples, saying: "Take this, all of you, and drink from it: this is the cup of my blood, the blood of the new and everlasting covenant. It will be shed for you and for all so that sins may be forgiven." Then he said to them: "Do this in memory of me."

God our Father, we remember with joy all that Jesus did to save us. In this holy sacrifice, which he gave as a gift to his Church, we remember his death and resurrection.

and resurrection. Holy Father in heaven, accept us, we pray, together with your beloved Son. He suffered death voluntarily for our sake, but you raised him up. Therefore we cry:

We praise you, God who are good, and we thank you!

He lives with you today, but he also dwells with us.

We praise you, God who are good, and we thank you!

At the end he will come in glory, and in his kingdom there will no longer be any who are afflicted, any who weep, any who mourn.

We praise you, God who are good, and we thank you!

Holy Father who have called us to this table that we might receive the body of Christ in the joy of the Holy Spirit, grant, we pray, that being strengthened by the power of this food we may please you more and more. Remember, Lord, N., our Pope, N., our bishop, and the other bishops.

*Help all disciples of Christ to win peace and to bring others the gifts of joy.

[*Easter season: Fill the hearts of the faithful with Easter joy, and let them bring this joy to all who sorrow.]

Grant all of us, together with the Blessed Virgin Mary and all the saints, to dwell some day in

Father in heaven, accept us together with your beloved Son. He willingly died for us, but you raised him to life again. We thank you and say: Glory to God in the highest. (Or some other suitable acclamation of praise.)

Jesus now lives with you in glory, but he is also here on earth, among us. We thank you and say: Glory to God in the highest. (Or some other suitable acclamation of praise.)

One day he will come in glory and in his kingdom there will be no more suffering, no more tears, no more sadness. We thank you and say: Glory to God in the highest. (Or some other suitable acclamation of praise.)

Father in heaven, you have called us to receive the body and blood of Christ at this table and to be filled with the joy of the Holy Spirit. Through this sacred meal give us strength to please you more and more.

Lord, our God, remember N., our pope, N., our bishop, and all other bishops. *Help all who follow Jesus to work for peace and to bring happiness to others.

[*Easter season: Fill all Christians with the gladness of Easter. Help us to bring this joy to all who are sorrowful.]

Bring us all at last together with Mary, the Mother of God, and all the saints, to live with

234

heaven with Christ and to be with him for ever in your presence.	you and to be one with Christ in heaven.
Through him and with him and in him all honor and glory is yours, almighty God and Father, in the unity of the Holy Spirit, for ever and ever. Amen.	Through him, with him, in him, in the unity of the Holy Spirit, all glory and honor is yours, almighty Father, for ever and ever. Amen.

I. INTRODUCTION

"At the first Synod of Bishops (1967) various bishops speaking on liturgical reform expressed the desire of their respective episcopal conferences for Masses specially adapted to children. In his reply to these petitions Cardinal Lercaro said: 'There is certainly no question of establishing a special rite. The need is rather to determine which elements are to be kept, shortened, or omitted, and to choose more appropriate texts.'[1]

"At its meeting of March 10, 1967, the first at which Cardinal Tabera presided, the Congregation for Divine Worship decided to send a letter to the presidents of the national liturgical commissions, asking their thoughts on the problem, the steps possibly being taken in their countries, any publications and proposals."[2]

This decision of the Congregation began a process that eventually led to the publication of a *Directory for Masses with Children* on November 1, 1973. This latter document shows that while the problem of eucharistic prayers for children was already felt, the Congregation was not prepared to offer a new solution[3]: "For the present, the four eucharistic prayers approved by the supreme authority for Masses with adults and introduced into liturgical use are to be employed until the Apostolic See makes other provision for Masses with children."[4]

On October 23, 1973, in a letter sent by the Secretariate of State, Paul VI ordered the Congregation for Divine Worship "to prepare two or three formularies for use throughout the Church."[5] The commission appointed for this purpose took some existing models as the basis of its work: for the best anaphora, a Belgian and Dutch text; for the second, a text prepared by the commission for liturgical texts in French; for the third, a text prepared by the Germans.[6] The new texts were written in French and German; then translated into English, Italian, and Spanish; finally, the texts were sent to 49 experts throughout the world. When this preliminary work had been done, three anaphoras for children and two of reconciliation were submitted for examination to the Congregation for the Doctrine of the Faith.

As part of its reply on May 10, 1974 the Congregation observed: "We suggest that the two new eucharistic prayers which may eventually be approved should, for various reasons, not become part of the Missal; for example: the interest in special eucharistic prayers for children may not last. These new types of prayer, then, are approved for the time required and for occasions on which they may prove useful."[7]

All difficulties were at last overcome, and the three new anaphoras for children, together with their *Introduction*, were promulgated on November 1, 1974 for use by the episcopal conferences that had requested them. The special character of these prayers, which we shall discuss in a moment, explains why the prayers were mimeographed, not printed, and why the booklet containing them was reserved for the use by the episcopal conferences requesting them.

II. THE PROBLEM

In the liturgical reform of Paul VI, the anaphoras for Masses with Children are a unique phenomenon. We would even call it anomalous, except that this has negative connotations.

1. In its composition of new liturgical texts and books, this reform took as one of its starting points the general principle that Latin is the official language of the liturgy.[8] Every liturgical book is therefore promulgated in Latin, with the intention that it then be translated into the various modern vernaculars by the respective episcopal conferences. We live in a world of translations, since the liturgy that is celebrated is a translation from Latin.

Vatican II's Constitution on the Sacred Liturgy speaks only once of translations; on the occasion, it remarks that translations, too, must be approved.[9] The principle that the Latin text is normative became programmatic[10] in the post-conciliar reform, and was respected even in cases where the original liturgical text was composed in a vernacular and then translated into Latin. In such cases, the Latin text became the "typical" (normative) text from which translations into the vernaculars were then to be made, as prescribed in the Instruction of September 26, 1964: "The basis of the translations is the Latin liturgical text."[11]

2. But, the limitations of a translated liturgy soon became clear, even in cases where the translators followed the principle of "adap-

tation" sanctioned by Vatican II,[12] and the resultant principles of legitimate diversity and a respect for the cultures of the various nations.[13] These principles are difficult to apply with a translated liturgy. The problem becomes especially pressing in countries whose culture is non-Latin. You may read about the adaptations in Thailand, Pakistan, Laos-Cambodia, India, China, Zambia, and the other countries listed in A. Bugnini's memoirs.[14] Here is a telling testimony:

"The missionaries were European. Vatican II opened the door to some extent, since the Mass was now translated into our own language. A different kind of liturgical ornament was adopted, depending on the climate and on the complexions of our peoples. Use was now made of our traditional rhythms in singing and praising God.

"At a further stage, however, we came to see that all this is superficial and that there is a substructure which no one has the courage to take into account in the liturgy: I mean our peoples' conception of the world and of relations between the world and God, our interweaving of symbols, the depths contained in our languages.

"We have faced the fact that it is not enough simply to translate; or, if you will, translation itself requires that bridges be built between two cultures."[15]

The principle of adaptation, then, has given rise to new rites, but these are still closely dependent on the modern Roman rite, in keeping with the norms of Vatican II's liturgical constitution.[16] At times, this dependence may seem excessive, especially when it has to do with the structure of the texts.

The problems that have surfaced in the "adapted" liturgies composed in recently evangelized countries surface once again in liturgies for children. Children are not miniature adults; they are different from adults. This acknowledged difference is behind the principles set down in the *Directory for Masses with Children* and in its complement, the Eucharistic Prayers for Masses with Children.[17]

III. ANAPHORAS FOR CHILDREN: A NEW DIRECTION

The Introduction[18] to these anaphoras speaks of the meaning and nature of the celebration and offers some suggestions for transposing the texts into the vernaculars:

"It is strongly recommended that this work of translation be given to a group of men and women with competences not only in the area of liturgy, but also of pedagogy, catechetics, language, and music."[19]

"The committee of translators should always remember that in this case the Latin text is not intended for liturgical use. Therefore, it is not to be merely translated. The Latin text does determine the purpose, substance, and general form of these prayers, and these elements should be the same in the translations into the various languages."[20]

The norm indicated in these passages can be described as the "law of creativity"; in asserting it, the present liturgical reform has taken a novel step, while at the same time returning to the earliest tradition of the Church. The reformers have chosen a middle between the two extremes of translation and free improvisation: it is that of free creation based on a model[21] which has been determined by the Apostolic See. Such a procedure ensures respect for the genius of the various cultures and, at the same time, the substantial unity of the Roman rite, since the various episcopal conferences are to take one and the same model as their reference point. At the present time, of course, we do not know whether the new norm will have further consequences, that is, whether the same method will be applied across the board in future phases of the liturgical reform. In any case, applying such a principle in the limited area of anaphoras for Masses with children is already a historically significant change of direction.

The statement that the Latin text is nonliturgical is extremely important.[22] Latin is an esoteric language learned through study and not from life (as one learns one's mother tongue). It is, therefore, obvious that no Latin text can effectively serve children in their celebration of the Eucharist.

The Introduction also observes that the principle of creativity comes into play even more in the case of languages that are far removed from Latin.[23] This means that the principle certainly applies also to languages closer to Latin, where translation would not be a problem. From this we conclude: the Introduction is in principle moving beyond the norm that texts are to be translated, and is not simply avoiding the factual problems which arise in the attempt to translate Latin into certain languages, especially those of the Far Eastern world. There is an explicit intention of renewing the entire project and program of liturgical reform by putting an end to the whole regime of "liturgy in translation" and moving instead toward direct composition in the vernaculars.

238

For confirmation of this interpretation, we refer to the original draft of the norms regarding the translation of the anaphoras for children:

"[These eucharistic prayers] are instead to be substantially rethought so that they may be cast in a form that ensures their more effective liturgical use in the various vernaculars. Lexical departures from the Latin text, which will be greater in non-Western languages, should create less difficulty than in the case of liturgical texts already published, since for the first time the Latin texts will never be used in liturgical celebrations."[24]

This passage will receive more nuanced expression in the final and official edition of the Introduction, but its content will be unchanged.

The eucharistic prayers for Masses with children thus introduce a new situation from the juridical standpoint. They begin a new genre of liturgical texts, since the Latin version is liturgical only in the sense that it inspires and guides the composition of vernacular texts which reflect the genius of the various languages. If the Latin texts are liturgical only in this very limited sense, it is clear that they can never be translated.

IV. MEANING OF "THE LATIN AS A MODEL"
In view of what is said in the Introduction, no. 11,[25] the Latin texts of these anaphoras can be described as models for new creations. But, if we look only at the norm set down, it is not easy to see what constitutes this "creativity based on a model."

1. This passage in the Introduction explicitly excludes from the "model" whatever is a matter of Latin literary style. As an example, the Introduction mentions the "hieratic and solemn"[26] style of the Latin and the so-called "cursus."

2. Mentioned as normative and binding are the "purpose," "substance," and "general form" of the Latin eucharistic prayers. In our opinion, "purpose" refers to the use made of the prayers: they are addressed to the Father and they serve to thank him and thereby eucharistify the bread and wine. As a result, the liturgical action in which they are used can properly be called "the Lord's Supper." "Substance" should then mean the contents of the texts, their basic themes; and "general form" should mean the sequence of the parts that make up the structure of the anaphora.

It must be acknowledged that these few points made in the Introduction do not greatly help composers to decide just how and in what respects the three model texts are normative. The only practical way to advance any further is to make a detailed analysis of the three texts. The Introduction itself seems to advise such a course, if we take no. 11 in conjunction with no. 4.[27] But, composition in the vernacular cannot then be reduced to more extensive use of synonyms or paraphrases that make the texts more explicit. Such an approach would only return us to the world of "liturgy in translation."

V. EXAMINATION OF THE THREE ANAPHORAS

A. Structure or General Form

The exceptions in these three anaphoras when they are compared with the *General Instruction of the Roman Missal*, no. 55, are indeed "very few," but they are nonetheless important and worthy of our attention.

1. The third anaphora does not have the intercessory commemoration of the dead; this commemoration may, however, be implicit in the commemoration of the saints.

2. The first and third anaphoras do not mention the Holy Spirit in the first (preconsecratory) epiclesis.[28] It follows that in these two eucharistic prayers, we no longer have the two epicleses so characteristic of the contemporary Roman rite; the "second" epiclesis becomes the sole epiclesis properly so called.[29] The elimination of the "first" epiclesis solves in a felicitous way the problem of having a single anaphora with two epicleses (one of which is there for reasons which appeal solely to theologians).

3. The anamnesis is customarily followed by the offering of the bread and wine and, sometimes, of the holy sacrifice as well. This offertorial theme is completely absent from the second anaphora, a phenomenon that puzzles anyone with a good knowledge of the Roman rite, since the latter always gives considerable space to the theme of *offerre*. The Italian edition of this anaphora supplies the missing element; as a result, it unfortunately "deliberately emphasizes not only the offering of sacrifice but also the element of *commercium* [exchange] in this offering: 'He offered himself into our hands, and we offer him to you. . . .' "[30] (ICEL: "He put himself into our hands to be the Sacrifice we offer you.")

In the third anaphora, the theme of offering is replaced by a prayer for the acceptance of the sacrifice: "Holy Father in heaven, accept (*suscipe*) us, we pray, together with your beloved Son." The active verb here is not *offerimus* (we offer), but *suscipe* (accept); since

240

no action of offering is expressed, we cannot speak of an offering and an offertory, and we therefore call this part of the text a "recommendation of the sacrifice" (*commendatio sacrificii*).

This "recommendation of the sacrifice" is distinguished, moreover, since the object of the prayer is the acceptance not of a ritual sacrifice but of "us."[31] The sentence marks a development in the theology of sacrifice. We have moved from the concept of sacrifice as made up of ritual actions and gestures to a concept of personal sacrifice. Sacrifice is not an act but the entire person with his or her history of "life in Christ" and thus with his or her fundamental and most profound options. The person in all its complexity has become "cultic"; the person has even become the supreme cultic reality: a sacrifice acceptable to God.[32] This is possible only in, with, and through Christ. That is why we ask to be accepted "together with your beloved Son."

The introduction of the recommendation theme, and the accompanying elimination of the offering of the bread and wine, is a notable gain for the theology and spirituality of the anaphora.[33]

It is possible to maintain that the first of the three prayers also shares this rethinking of the "offering." At the beginning of the so-called "first epiclesis," the celebrating priest says: "Holy Father, in our desire to thank you we have brought bread and wine." Then, after asking that the bread and wine be transformed, he adds: "Then we will be able to offer (*offerre*) to you what you have first given to us." And, in fact, immediately after the anamnesis, we do have, in this first anaphora, a prayer of offering.[34] This, however, is immediately followed by a "recommendation of the sacrifice" that marks the climax of this section.

The presence of the "recommendation" is reason for saying that this first anaphora, even though it contains an offering of the bread and wine, represents the same theological thinking as found in the second and third anaphoras, where the recommendation is stressed to the point of omitting the offering. In the first anaphora, the redeemer is described as the one who "brings us to you."[35] If, as is the case, this description fits better with the theme of "receive us" than with the theme of "we offer," then we must infer that what is normative in this particular model is precisely the theology expressed in "receive us," which may indeed be accompanied by "we offer," but need not be.

It is useful to cite a passage from Irenaeus that seems to lie behind the section cited from the first anaphora: "Thus the oblation (*oblatio*) which the Lord teaches is to be offered (*offerri*) throughout the world is said to be a pure sacrifice, acceptable to God. It is not that God needs our sacrifices; but those who offer are themselves glorified in what they offer, if their gift is accepted. The gift expresses honor and devotion to the King."[36] In the perspective expressed here, the act of giving the bread and wine to the Father is simply a continuation and a translation into a gesture the act of giving thanks—which we know to be the formal constituent of anaphoras.

4. Another novelty affecting the structure of the text is the insertion of numerous acclamations that are meant to involve the children more fully in the eucharistic prayer and make them share more intensely in the "mystery of faith." In the first anaphora, the thanksgiving contains three acclamations obtained by breaking down the Sanctus into its three component themes.[37] The result is a completely new anaphoric structure that cannot be compared with any other. At least in this instance, the Antiochene structure characteristic of the Roman anaphoras disappears.

5. Also of great interest in the first anaphora is the change in the anamnesis, which has two phases.[38] The first, from the non-Roman Western liturgies,[39] describes the celebration of the Eucharist as an act of obedience to the mandate of Christ. The second describes the celebration as a proclamation; this is characteristic of the anamnesis in the Alexandrian liturgies, although it is also well documented for the West.[40] The biblical basis for the second phase is 1 Corinthians 11:26.[41]

This passage in the first anaphora tells us that, with a theology of the Eucharist as memorial, two other theologies are legitimate: a theology of the Eucharist as proclamation of the Lord's death and resurrection, and a theology of the Mass as obedient imitation of what the Lord did at the Last Supper. This change in the anamnesis is extremely valuable for catechists explaining the liturgy, since it is not easy to present the Eucharist as a memorial.

6. In the first anaphora for children, the commemoration of the Mother of God, the saints, and the pope and local bishop is in a new location. Instead of coming in the second part of the anaphora among the intercessions that lead into the doxology, it occurs in the first part. In this anticipated intercession, moreover, prayer is offered not "through" the Blessed Virgin and the saints, but "with" them. The remote basis for the "with" as well as for the location is the *Communicantes* of the Roman Canon.

In the next text, the commemoration of the saints and the communion of the universal Church (which is ensured by pope and bishop) serve the "truthfulness" of the praise directed to the Father by a Church dispersed throughout the world. In addition to having a novel location, the passage is also novel in that the saints and the Church are drawn into the cosmic praise and heavenly liturgy which are characteristic of the introduction to the Sanctus. A change in structure has thus led to a change in content. The Church and the ecclesiastical hierarchy are described as forming a single assembly of praise, a doxological community. Such a liturgical ecclesiology is quite different from that of the "Church as perfect society" and immediately calls to mind the eucharistic ecclesiology of N. Afanassieff.[42]

In the second of the three anaphoras, the commemoration of the Mother of God is part of the eschatologically oriented conclusion of the anaphora. The theological framework, however, is the same as in the first anaphora, since in the end time "all the friends of Jesus, our Lord, will sing an endless song to you." The kingdom of God is seen as a place of unending praise. There is thus a close coordination between the liturgical ecclesiology previously mentioned and the theology of the kingdom conveyed in the present passage. It is, therefore, chiefly in the liturgy that the Church is the sacramental anticipation of the kingdom to which it is ordered.[43]

7. In all three anaphoras, the words "Then he said to them" are inserted between the end of the account of institution and the command of repetition.[44] The purpose of this innovation is to emphasize more fully the theology contained in the anamnesis; and, in fact, the separating of the command from the words over the chalice establishes a closer link between command and anamnesis.[45] It is permissible, therefore, to say that in these anaphoras for children, we see the emergence of a new structural part of the eucharistic anaphora, one that must be added to the traditional list given in no. 55 of the *General Instruction of the Roman Missal*; this new part is the "command—and—anamnesis," which follows immediately upon the "account of institution." The two sections are, of course, not completely and adequately distinct, since the commandment is evidently part of the account of institution. In view of the connection between anamnesis and commandment, it might be better to say simply that the anamnesis is an embolism in the account of institution.

If we ask again what are the normative elements in the model, we must surely include this link between command and anamnesis and the resultant emphasis on the anamnesis as an embolism that contains a description of the mystery being celebrated.

8. The third anaphora provides a good example of the emphasis on the anamnesis that we have been describing. In this eucharistic prayer, the anamnesis develops into a lengthy confession of Christological faith.[46] The prayer has three sections. The first commemorates "what Jesus Christ did for our salvation." The second makes more explicit both the work of salvation and the manner in which we commemorate it: it says that we recall his death and resurrection (= work of salvation) in the sacrifice which his Church is now celebrating (= manner of remembering). In the third section, the work of salvation, which has been mentioned and specified, is proclaimed and described in a broad confession of Christological faith interspersed with acclamations.[47]

Such a confession of faith, proclaiming Christ and taking the form of an embolism in the anamnesis, is another structural novelty. Historical instances of it are rare.[48] The imbalance between this section and the remainder of the anaphora suggests that the confession of faith is the pivot of the entire prayer. Certainly we are not dealing with a simple variant of the classical anamnesis. What is shown rather is the Eucharist as a confession of faith precisely because it is an anamnesis of the Lord.

Let us return to the question of how the model serves as exemplar. We would say that the episcopal conferences should not simply translate this part of the anaphora, but should rather ask themselves what is the best formula of Christocentric faith that has been lived, witnessed, and transmitted in their respective Churches. Unfortunately, "profession of faith" today simply means the creed; we have to go back to Irenaeus to see the importance of the profession of faith. There are about one hundred and fifty such confessions[49]: all different, all adapted to the concerns of the moment, yet all identical in their substance, in their undiminished orthodoxy, in their liveliness of expression, and in the unction that comes from the Holy Spirit. This past, almost forgotten wealth should reemerge and find a place in this section of the Third Eucharistic Prayer for children.

B. Contents of the Texts

In discussing the structure of the texts, we already referred to their contents. The distinction between structure and content is necessarily artificial.

It should be clear that if an anaphora is a profession of faith which is the object of thanksgiving, then this thanksgiving may not include anything and everything but only what is connected with the formulation of the faith. The thanksgiving will, therefore, take the form of either a narration of the events of salvation or a description of the fruits of salvation.[50] Here, more than anywhere, the principle holds: "No innovation that does not accord with tradition" ("*Nil innovetur nisi quod traditum est*").

1. THE DIVINE ATTRIBUTES

According to Origen, the Church decides what are the divine attributes, as well as everything having to do with relations between the divine persons; only a decision of the Church, which in practice means a synodal decision, can justify any alteration in this area.[51] Therefore, if we ask in what ways these model anaphoras are normative as far as content is concerned, we must answer that the trinitarian theology, and therefore the Christology as well, of the model is binding.

The trinitarian theology of the eucharistic prayers for children is very simple, consisting almost exclusively in a description and elucidation of the economy. The Son has been sent[52]; we encounter him, therefore, as the one who comes to save us.[53] In the first of the three eucharistic prayers, salvation is described as a journey: the Son leads us to the Father.[54] The image of descent and ascent, so typical of second-century paschal theology,[55] is operative here.

2. THE WORKS OF GOD

The Father is said to "do wonderful deeds for us"[56]; these deeds or works are then specified. In the first anaphora, the emphasis is on the works of creation, but each is coordinated with a divine gift which children experience within themselves: joy in the heart, word enlightening the mind, life cherished as a gift.

In the second anaphora, on the other hand, creation is hardly mentioned.[57] The work of God that is commemorated here is neither creation nor redemption, but the divine attitude behind both, namely, God's love for human beings. The theme of "You love us so much" is sounded three times as an introduction, respectively, to the work of creation, the sending of the Son into the world, and a description of the liturgical assembly as a family. These various divine initiatives are simply the concrete ways in which God manifests and embodies his love for human beings.[58] This entire section of the second anaphora ends with the singing of the Sanctus; this is introduced by the phrase "For such great gifts of love," which sums up the content of the first part of the anaphora. If a title had to be supplied for this whole passage, we would suggest "God's love."

The second, or Christological section of the second anaphora likewise highlights the theme of love, which is at the very heart of soteriology. Salvation consists in being able "to love you and one another."[59] In keeping with this emphasis, the title given to Christ is "friend of children and the poor." We can only conclude that this theme is normative for any attempt to compose a vernacular second anaphora for children.

The theme that determines the entire text of the third anaphora is God's plan for human beings. In the introduction to the Sanctus, it is specified as the formal object of thanksgiving.[60]

The divine plan is set forth in a very rich and carefully worked out way. Nonetheless, the idea of "unity" summarizes the whole, inasmuch as unity among human beings is the purpose of the economy of salvation.

Before the Sanctus, the point of the divine plan is expressed twice, and both times the text speaks of unity among human beings.[61] The second (*Post-Sanctus*) section of the text describes the path taken by Jesus for the salvation of human beings. Christ and his work are the main object of thanksgiving.[62] The reason for Christ's coming is that human beings had abandoned God and were living in discord. We cannot think of a description that is superior either in directness or in theological accuracy. This description of the human condition leads logically to a description of redemption as the restoration of our filial relationship with God, which in turn guarantees and gives rise to a new human brotherhood.[63]

The gathering of all around a single table is a vivid image of unification. The account of institution is, therefore, rightly preceded by a recall of Christ's command of repetition and a statement of what he intended by it: namely, to establish among us the same unity which he created among his disciples at the Last Supper: "Now Christ gathers us at one table and wishes us to do what he once did." In other words, the Eucharist of the Church ought to create the same unity around Christ that existed in the upper room.[64]

If, then, a title were required for this second eucharistic prayer, we would suggest "The Mystery of Unity," even though the theme of unity is absent from the second epiclesis. The epicleses of the three new anaphoras in the Missal all have the theme of unity, but the epicleses in the three anaphoras for children lack it. The reason for this change may be that the theme of unity is difficult for children and becomes more accessible if it is recast as the theme of love.

In the first anaphora for children, the movement of praise—from creation to Christology and then on to the Church—is such that no theme accounting for the entire text is immediately evident. To find such a theme, we must look at the three acclamations from the Sanctus that divide this first section of the anaphora into three distinct parts. Each acclamation is introduced by a short phrase that is especially significant in our quest of a unifying theme: "Therefore (*quapropter*) we all join in singing to you"; "Therefore (*ergo*) we gratefully proclaim"; "With them [the saints] and with the angels we worship you, as we say with one voice."

The word "therefore" in the first and second introductory phrases shows that the verse from the Sanctus is in each case the thematic climax of the section. The third introduction makes the same point without the "therefore," since it uses the theme of the heavenly liturgy to show that the cosmos, the Church, and eternal blessedness itself are, as it were, a single hymn that finds its flowering in the verse from the Sanctus.

We may conclude, therefore, that the (section of the) Sanctus is in each case a summary and synthesis of the contents of the preceding thanksgiving. Since the Sanctus itself is a proclamation of the name of God, the Holy One, it follows that the theme of the three thanksgivings which lead up to and into the three Sanctus verses is likewise a confession of the Name. The verbs that introduce the verses from the Sanctus are respectively "sing," "proclaim," and "worship." These three form a crescendo and thus indicate a significant intensification of the theme. If we take into consideration also the allusion to Malachi 1:11, we may say that if a title is wanted for this first anaphora, it should be "The Sacrifice of Praise" or, even better, "Adoration of the Holy Name."

The element of praise that characterizes this first anaphora emerges very strongly again in the last sentence before the doxology: "When we see what you accomplish through your Son we are filled with wonder and again we praise you." The meaning is that the review of God's works gives rise to wonder and, therefore, in the anaphora, to praise of the divine Name.[65] The sentence thus repeats what was said in the very opening sentence of the thanksgiving, before the great works of God were listed: "We stand before you to celebrate and praise you and to tell you how greatly we admire you."

In view of the course followed in ascertaining the theme of the text, we conclude that the division of the Sanctus into three verses serving as doxologies for the three sections of the thanksgiving is a normative element in the model; the division, in other words, determines the very structure of this part of the anaphora. Those whose task it is to transform the model into a text for celebration in the vernacular will have to preserve this structure; otherwise, the model will cease to be what it is.

VI. PROSPECTS (IN LIEU OF CONCLUSIONS)

In no. 11 of the Introduction to the anaphoras for Masses with children, the liturgical reform has entered a new phase. Liturgical texts now come into being directly in the living languages themselves, where account is taken of the need to adapt the liturgy and incarnate it in the cultures and diverse situations of the local Churches.

The problem to which this process is a response is the problem of inculturation. The liturgical reform was initially seen as having three phases or stages.[66] The anaphoras for children can only be interpreted as the first action of the third stage. In a historical perspective, however, the third stage cannot be regarded as the final and conclusive stage. This stage is that of adaptation and fidelity to local cultures. But, adaptation cannot be complete until it reaches the level of individual assemblies. In other words, "creativity based on a model" must be allowed not only to the episcopal conferences, but to each minister who presides over a liturgy. History tells us that such was the usual practice in the Great Church down to the fourth century.[67] If so, then a return to the practice of improvisation in the anaphora does not violate the fundamental principle of liturgical practice: "No innovation that does not accord with tradition" ("Nil innovetur nisi quod traditum est").

A historian can only suggest the theoretical possibility of a fourth stage, definable as the stage of "improvisation of liturgical texts" by each minister on the basis of predetermined models. The texts that serve as models will be established by the Church in light of its understanding of the data of tradition. But the historian's judgment that such a fourth stage of the reform must eventually come is not yet a judgment that this stage is now opportune. This last judgment falls outside the scope of historico-liturgical analysis; it is a pastoral judgment. And, when the Church makes decisions about liturgical reform, it makes them on the basis of pastoral opportuneness.

If then the fourth phase might well mean a significant qualitative

248

improvement in the celebration of the Eucharist, it would be the Church's duty to move in that direction. On the other hand, if the lack of preparation on the part of ministers would prevent such a result, it would be equally the Church's duty to proceed no further along this line. Historians studying the liturgy can only examine the available data and point out the possibilities which the data suggest.

Chapter Nine

Theology of the Anaphora:
Prayer of the Lord and Proclamation of the Passion

I. INTRODUCTION

In this chapter, we shall take up two problems that were mentioned but not discussed. The first has to do with the anaphora as "form" of the Eucharist, the second with the statement that the anaphora "proclaims the Lord's death."

We have said that the Last Supper was a "proclamation" or "announcement," of the Lord's death and that this describes the relation between supper and cross, that is, the sacramental dimension of the Last Supper. Let us refer again to the theory of "codes" described briefly in Chap. One. If the Last Supper is the code of the sign and if the Last Supper is also a sacrament of the cross, then since every mass has within it the presence of the code, every Mass will also be a sacrament of the cross. Every Eucharist of the Church stands, therefore, in a sacramental relation to the cross of Christ because it is a response of obedience to Christ's command regarding the Supper: "Do *this* in memory of me."

We shall study the relation between Supper and cross through an analysis of the four New Testament accounts of the Supper. Since we are dealing with the Last Supper as such, we shall study the account of institution as contained in the scriptures and not in the anaphoras. But, since every Eucharist of the Church is related to the Last Supper, the theology which we shall bring to light in this chapter will apply to all the anaphoras.

Among the books which Giovanni Cardinal Mercati[1] bequeathed to the library of the Reggio Emilia Seminary there is a reprint of an article on the words of consecration which Dom De Puniet had published.[2] De Puniet had cited the Cardinal in a note and for this reason had sent him a reprint.

Among the patristic texts studied by De Puniet is the well-known letter of Gregory the Great to Bishop John of Syracuse, saying that in the apostolic period the *oratio dominica* had provided the only words used in celebrating the Eucharist.[3] Now, what De Puniet was attempting to prove in his article was that ecclesiastical tradition has always attributed the power of consecration to the words over the bread and wine in the account of institution. It seems strange, then, that he should use the passage from Gregory in his argument, since the letter seems to say something quite contrary.

Cardinal Mercati noticed that the testimony in the letter seems not in accord with De Puniet's thesis, and he jotted the following comment in the margin: "If this be so, then in sixth and seventh century Rome Gregory the Great himself did not believe that the formula which Jesus established and which is in fact indispensable, consisted of the Lord's words: 'This is . . . ,' 'This is . . . !' "[4]

This episode is interesting in that it gives us a glimpse of what a complex problem we are raising. As a matter of fact, the Fathers do speak of the consecratory power of the *Oratio dominica*. By this term, however, they do not mean "the Lord's Prayer," as Gregory thought, but simply "the Lord's prayer," that is, the words he spoke at the Last Supper.

Further clarification is in order. At the Last Supper, Jesus did not limit himself to speaking the declarative words over the bread and wine, thereby telling his disciples that the bread and wine were now his body and blood. He also spoke a prayer of thanksgiving to the Father before he distributed the bread and wine to the disciples.

The treatise *De oratione dominica* of St. Cyprian is a commentary on the Our Father; nowadays, we would call it a spiritual commentary. But, after explaining the individual phrases of the Our Father, Cyprian goes on to speak of the nature of prayer as such. One example that he uses is the eucharistic prayer, which he calls simply *oratio*[5] and which serves him as a point of departure for catechesis, just as the Our Father had. At the beginning of his treatise (Chap. 2), Cyprian says that Christ gave us the proper form for prayer and taught us to pray. Moreover, the only true prayer is that which comes from the mouth of the Son who is truth. The only "spiritual" prayer is prayer taught by Christ who also bestows the Holy Spirit.

Tertullian, in his *De oratione*, likewise comments on the Lord's Prayer; frequently, however, the discussion becomes a discussion of prayer as such. The first principle given is that "God alone could have taught us how he wanted to be prayed to"; the author immediately adds that this prayer is the one "which the Son has taught us."[6] At this point, a legitimate question suggests itself: Does the eucharistic prayer likewise come from Christ and was it taught by him?

In this context, Gregory's statement about the consecratory power of the *oratio dominica* is especially interesting. He is bearing witness to an undeniable patristic tradition of which we, like him, do not know the precise content. The teachings of Cyprian and Tertullian certainly offer a true and proper theology of prayer as such, one that looks beyond the simple recitation of the Our Father. May we hypothesize that the expression "Lord's prayer" included without distinction both the Our Father and the prayer of thanksgiving at the Last Supper? This point requires further study.

The Our Father and the thanksgiving at the Supper both are "prayers of the Lord," and both serve as "models" for the prayer of his disciples. The Our Father is offered by Christ as concrete teaching on prayer in general: "When you pray, say: . . ." (Lk 11:2), while the thanksgiving at the Last Supper is norm and model for our prayer of thanksgiving. As a matter of fact, the command "Do this in memory of me" (Lk 22:19) applies to Jesus' prayer of thanksgiving as well as to the "words of institution." John Chrysostom saw this point clearly: "He gave thanks before giving [the bread and wine] to his disciples, so that we too might give thanks. He gave thanks and sang a hymn after having given it so that we might do the same."[7]

The earlier tradition attested by Gregory could hardly have confused the Our Father with the words: "This is my body/my blood." Such a confusion at a later time is more readily explainable, since of these two prayers which are equally from the Lord, one (the thanksgiving at the Last Supper) is for practical purposes unknown to us and has thus become irrelevant in our celebrations.

In other words, the Lord spoke two prayers: the Our Father and the thanksgiving at the Supper, but only one has come down to us verbatim: the Our Father. In this situation, it was natural that the prayer whose words were not transmitted should cease to be known as a "Lord's prayer" and that even the memory of its once having been thus known should disappear. The name "Lord's prayer" came to be applied exclusively to the Our Father.

II. SOME DATA FROM THE FATHERS

Our next task is to see whether the tradition attested by Gregory existed; that is, whether the Fathers applied the name "word *or* prayer of the Lord" to the thanksgiving at the Last Supper.

252

For evidence of such a tradition in which the "word of the Lord," understood as a "word of prayer," did have consecratory power, we need look only at two texts which closely resemble one another. The first is from Justin and the second from Irenaeus.

Justin writes:

"Just as Jesus Christ our Savior was made flesh through the word of God and took on flesh and blood for our salvation, so too (we have been taught) through the word of prayer that comes from him, the food over which the eucharist has been spoken becomes the flesh and blood of the incarnate Jesus, in order to nourish and transform our flesh and blood."[8]

G. Cuming recently made a careful examination of the phrase *di'euchēs logou* and concluded that the meaning is "a word that comes from Christ."[9] Now, if the Greek spoke simply of a "*logos* coming from him," I would agree with Cuming that the reference was to the words of institution. But, the Greek speaks of a *euchēs logos*, that is, a "word/discourse of prayer," and one thing certain is that the words of institution are not a prayer! Justin is attributing consecratory power to a prayer of Jesus; but, the evangelists in the story of the Last Supper know of but one prayer of Jesus: his prayer of thanksgiving or blessing.

The words, then, that eucharistify the bread and wine are the words of the prayer of thanksgiving which Jesus spoke at the Last Supper and which he himself handed on so that we like him might give thanks. Such a conclusion is fully in accord with the vocabulary of Justin. If the bread and wine become the body and blood of Jesus because they have been "eucharistified" (Justin: *eucharistē-thentes*),[10] it follows that the words of consecration take the form of a *eucharistia*, a prayer of thanksgiving. The *eucharistia* of Justin is the prayer of thanksgiving which we call the anaphora or eucharistic prayer.

Further evidence is to be found in the *Adversus haereses* of St. Irenaeus. In fact, we find three passages which we shall place in parallel columns.[11]

the	the	the
bread,	bread	grain of wheat
taken from the earth,		that fell into the earth
	that is prepared	
having received	receives	receiving
the invocation	the word	the word

of God	of God	of God
is no longer		
ordinary bread		
but	and becomes	becomes
the Eucharist,	the Eucharist,	the Eucharist,
constituted by		
two elements,		
an earthly and		
a heavenly		
		that is,
	the body of Christ	the body of Christ.

Each of these passages completes the others; together they give us the same doctrine that is found in Justin. Note that in the first passage Irenaeus speaks of the "invocation" (*epiclēsis*), while in the other two he speaks of the "word" (*logos*); Justin has the same two notions, but combines them into a single phrase: *euchēs logos* ("word of prayer"). The result in both authors is the same: the bread and wine become "eucharist," that is, the body and blood of Christ. Moreover, Irenaeus is familiar with and uses the term "eucharistify."[12]

One further point in Irenaeus needs explanation: the ending of the first passage with its two elements, an earthly and a heavenly. The earthly element is not difficult, since the bread is said to have been taken from the earth. The second and third texts help us to determine the heavenly element, for they say that the bread receives "the word of God." This word is certainly a heavenly element since it is from God and since "heavenly" is equivalent to "divine." Given the parallelism between the first passage and the other two, we can say that the "invocation of God" in the first passage is the heavenly element in question. But, a difficulty arises: It is easy to understand the word of God as "heavenly," but how can the invocation of God be "heavenly"? The difficulty vanishes if we interpret this invocation in light of the earlier passage in Justin, where "invocation" is represented by "word of prayer that comes from him" (i.e., from Jesus).

This interpretation is confirmed by Tertullian who describes as "heavenly" the teaching on prayer given by Jesus: "Can anything from the Lord Christ—such as this teaching on prayer—not be heavenly?"[13] This is indeed a confirmation and nothing more. But, the passage is especially interesting inasmuch as all the elements in it are to be found in the three passages from Irenaeus. We conclude, therefore, that the heavenly element is the prayer which comes from Christ, or God. The passages from Justin, Irenaeus, and Tertullian shed light on each other to such an extent that we may legitimately say the theme they express was traditional.

We conclude, then, that in Irenaeus, as in Justin, it is the "eucharistic" prayer or prayer of thanksgiving that consecrates, but also that in Irenaeus it is no longer called *eucharistia* but *epiclēsis* (invocation/prayer).[14] The thanksgiving is still the prayer of consecration, but it has changed its name.[15] Except for this change of name, the parallel with Justin is complete.

The term "epiclesis" was to have an unexpected use in the East as a name for the "prayer of consecration." However, it would no longer designate the prayer of thanksgiving in its entirety but only a part of this, namely, the "epiclesis" in the narrow sense, that is, the prayer to the Father for the sending of the Spirit. That is how Basil uses the term in his treatise on the Holy Spirit.[16]

We now have the elements required for describing the two opposing theories of the consecration that have historically divided East and West. Eastern theologians maintain that the consecration is due to the "epiclesis" or invocation, but they mean by this the prayer asking for the coming of the Spirit on the gifts. Western theologians maintain that the consecration is effected by the words which the Lord spoke during the Last Supper, but they mean by this not his prayer of thanksgiving but only the explanatory words: "This is my body," "This is my blood."

III. HISTORICAL PROBLEM

A. The Data

The opposition between the two theologies could not be clearer, despite the fact that "the Orthodox rightly tell us that the anaphora forms a whole, from which one element, the account of institution, for example, or the epiclesis, cannot be isolated and treated separately. No Orthodox would think of the consecration as taking place simply through the epiclesis."[17]

Unfortunately, this asserted unity of the eucharistic prayer goes unheeded in both the Orthodox and the Catholic worlds. Congar goes on to say in his next sentence: "It is, however, possible to ask [an Orthodox Christian] whether consecration would take place if the epiclesis were omitted." He is surely right in the answer which he implicitly expects to this question: an Eastern Christian faced with an anaphora lacking the epiclesis would say that no consecration takes place.

And, if a Catholic were confronted with an anaphora that lacks the account of institution? Congar gives the answer that would surely come: "This is, if not a dogma, at least a commonly accepted and official doctrine in the Catholic Church . . . [that] the consecration of the bread and wine is accomplished by the words of the account of institution."[18]

Clearly, the assertion of the unity of the anaphora does not eliminate the question of whether the consecration is effected by the epiclesis or by the Lord's explanatory words over the bread and wine. It is important, nonetheless, to inquire into the legitimacy of the view that attributes consecratory value to the entire anaphora; the answer has ecumenical implications.

B. Assessment

On this point, the Roman Church has accepted the precise teaching of Thomas Aquinas. Accordingly, the consecration is effected by the Lord's words, "This is my body. . . . This is the cup of my blood . . . ," and the transformation effected is instantaneous.

Let us look first at the second point: the consecration is instantaneous. It follows from this that the anaphora as a whole cannot be the sacramental "form" of the Eucharist, since if it were, the consecration would take place gradually. Aquinas' argument allows no evasion: the consecration is instantaneous because "the substance of the body and blood of Christ cannot vary quantitatively."[19] That is, the bread and wine cannot be more or less the substance of the body and blood of Christ: they either are that substance or they are not. Given the presuppositions, the argument is unassailable. This position of Aquinas is the classical one in theology textbooks and has become the norm that guides devotion and piety.

What of Aquinas' first point: the form of the Eucharist is the Lord's explanatory words over the bread and wine? His argument is that the form must express what is produced here and now,[20] as in the case of "I baptize you" or "I absolve you." But, "This is my body" is a different kind of statement, and therefore the theory does not apply. Aquinas explains away the difficulty by an appeal to the excellence of this sacrament.

If, however, we look more closely at Aquinas' theory, we find a major lacuna, since the words he settles on as consecratory do not express the effect of the sacramental action in relation to the bread and wine which lie on our altar here and now. Rather, they tell us what the bread was that he gave to his disciples during the Last Supper. As we have said before and shall say again when we come to the hypothesis of A. Chavasse, in the account of institution, we tell the Father what Jesus said when he gave the bread and wine to his disciples at the Last Supper.

This means that the explanatory words over the bread and wine do not enunciate and bring about the sacramental effect produced in the bread and wine on our altars here and now. The reason is simple: the words refer not to the bread and wine on our altars, but to the bread and wine Jesus took into his hands in the upper room two thousand years ago. But, how could Aquinas have been deceived to such an extent and so vociferously? For an answer, we need only look carefully at the way he argues. He takes the words "This is my body," etc., in themselves and without reference to their context, that is, that they are part of a larger whole, namely, the account of institution. The account is a piece of narrative that is part of the anaphora. If the anaphora is directed to the Father, so too is the account of institution, and nothing is said to the Father that expresses the sacramental effect which takes place on our altars. We shall offer a better explanation of this effect later.

Nowadays, the prevailing opinion, based on P. Cagin's study in comparative liturgy,[21] is that the entire anaphora is the form of the eucharist. Moreover, "there is nothing, it seems, to keep a Catholic from maintaining this hypothesis, which gives a better account of the liturgical rites and prayers than does the view of St. Thomas."[22]

This statement of S. Salaville is especially significant since it appears in an article wholly directed to proving the thesis traditional in Western theology. Today, however, the argument is different and based on history.

First of all, there is no doubt that an epiclesis with a consecratory function appeared quite late; as far as we know, the first pneumatological epiclesis is that of Hippolytus (beginning of third century), but this is not yet a consecratory epiclesis since it does not ask for the transformation of the bread and wine but only for the sanctification of the faithful. The first document with a consecratory pneumatological epiclesis is the Anaphora of Basil in its Coptic redaction,[23] which dates from the first half of the fourth century and is closely related to the Anaphora of Hippolytus. This Anaphora of Basil is the source of the other two Anaphoras of Basil (the Alexandrian and the Byzantine); the latter is the source of the Anaphora of James, which in turn lends its own epiclesis to the Egyptian family of anaphoras.

It is possible to maintain that a pneumatological epiclesis is absolutely necessary for the eucharistic consecration when its presence is not certain prior to the fourth century? Evidently it is not. The pneumatological epiclesis, however, does represent a splendid development of the theology of the anaphora; its presence is an accomplished fact and the development is irreversible. In it, the theology of the anaphora as sanctifying is made explicit, and the sanctifying action is attributed to the Holy Spirit. Now that such a development has taken place, it is impossible to go back to earlier anaphoric structures. Congar rightly points out that this development relates not so much to sacramental theology as to ecclesiology and the theology of the Trinity.[24]

What of the account of institution? The historical origin and development of the account of institution as part of the anaphora is too complex to give here. You need only know that historians are practically in agreement that the account of institution was not originally part of the anaphora, even though it appeared quite early (in the Anaphora of Hippolytus, it is a regular part of the structure.)[25]

We do not entirely accept this view. It is possible to maintain that the account of institution was indeed an original part of the eucharistic prayer even in its most archaic form; on the other hand, the account did not have the form it has today. It did not appear as an extended description of the Last Supper, but as a simple mention of what Jesus instituted and commanded his disciples to do in turn; in other words, the account lacked the explanatory words over the bread and wine.

A correct theology must provide explanations that agree with historical fact. How, then, are we to explain the archaic anaphoras that simply mention what the Lord instituted, and do not cite the explanatory words? Whatever theories historians may elaborate, there is no disputing that an entire Church—the Chaldean or East Syrian—has lived for centuries with an anaphora of that archaic type which does not contain an account of institution but simply refers to the institution; we mean the Chaldean Anaphora of the Apostles Addai and Mari. Furthermore, no one wants to or can deny the validity of the Eucharist that has been celebrated for centuries in the Chaldean Church. What arguments could possibly justify denying that the legitimate tradition of this Church is also a completely valid tradition?

We draw, then, the same conclusion for the account of institution as for the epiclesis: it was not an original part of the anaphora, but once it appeared, it brought out so well the singleness of Christ's work and the dependence of our Eucharist on the "once for all" of the Last Supper that it has become an irrevocable part of the eucharistic prayer. If the account of institution were still lacking in the anaphora, we would have to introduce it to bring out better the unity of the Mass and the Lord's meal in the upper room.

When confronted with these facts about the epiclesis and the account of institution, the Eastern and Western positions appear alike fragmentary and paradoxically naive; they represent two parallel developments that should reach out and complete one another in a single theology of the anaphora. They are naive precisely because they ignore the history and development of the anaphora. Moreover, the historical knowledge we now have is the fruit of study and research that has gone on for a hundred years and is still in progress; the journey is still far from over.

We remind you that this judgment on the anaphora is at every point a historical judgment. For this reason, we must keep in mind that the theological dispute between East and West is of relatively recent origin; the problem of the epiclesis "was not mentioned, apparently, at the time of the schism of 1054; nor was it at the reunion Council held at Lyons in 1274. It was only with the fourteenth century that any problem arose, Latin missionaries having discovered the then centuries-old usage of the 'Greeks.' "[26]

In addition, according to the carefully weighed opinion of J.-M. R. Tillard, the whole question becomes secondary when discussion of the Eucharist is solidly based on scripture and the Fathers.[27] How very different the situation was as late as the beginning of the present century when M. Jugie could end an article by saying: "I hope that some day the Orthodox will follow the lead of Cardinal Bessarion and accept the authority of their great teacher [John Chrysostom] who writes: "The priest says, "This is my body." His words effect the change in the sacred gifts.' "[28]

For our part, this thorny dispute could be settled simply by attributing consecratory power to the anaphora in its entirety. A necessary balance must indeed be maintained between its component parts (taking into account its gradual historical development), but this does not mean that what belongs to the whole may be attributed to a particular part. On the other hand, it can be admitted that every eucharistic prayer may have its culmination, its thematic and structural center in a particular part of the anaphora. Then we would acknowledge that the sanctificatory or consecratory focus of the anaphoral text has its culmination and focus in that same particular part. We would say, therefore, that in that particular part the sanctificatory or consecratory power which belongs to the anaphora as a whole is better and more formally "expressed."

We will never be able to say that the consecratory power of the Roman Canon is expressed in its epiclesis; on the contrary, it is expressed in the account of institution. On the other hand, we will never be able to say that the Alexandrian Anaphora of Gregory of Nazianzus gives climactic expression to its consecratory power in the account of institution; it expresses it rather in the epiclesis.[29]

C. A Caution

P.-M. Gy, O. P., has reservations about the theory that consecratory power belongs to the anaphora as a whole.[30] He acknowledges that this is usually said to be the view of the Fathers, but he would have us be on guard against such a generalization. He is correct. He says specifically that the generalization does not apply to the Roman Canon or Ambrose among the Fathers.

We must distinguish three stages in the development of this teaching about the anaphora as a whole being consecratory.

1. The first stage is the one illustrated earlier when we cited Justin and Irenaeus. They call the eucharistic prayer "eucharist," and say that the prayer "eucharistifies" the bread and wine. That is why today we still call the bread and wine "the Eucharist."

To the two Fathers mentioned, we can add Cyprian and Isidore of Seville. The latter attributes the consecration to the "mystical [=sacramental] prayer" (*prex mystica*).[31] But, Isidore is standing on the boundary between two eras: for him the word "Eucharist" designates solely the consecrated bread and wine and describes them as God's gift; "eucharist" means *bona gratia*[32] (valued favor or grace or gift), an explanation that would remain unchanged until the revival of biblical theology in our own time.

2. In Isidore, Ambrose, and John Chrysostom, we reach a turning point. Although Chrysostom is an important witness to the first stage, we place him here because he also marks the beginning of a new way of thinking on the subject. He still attributes the transformation of the holy gifts to the eucharistic prayer as a whole, but the role of the epiclesis and the determining role of the words over the bread and wine also begin to emerge.[33] Meanwhile, in a passage that parallels those of Chrysostom, Ambrose,[34] too, expresses with all desirable clarity the efficacy of the Lord's words at the sup-

per, although he still links these with the rest of the Canon: "By means of what words does the consecration then take place, and whose words are they? They are the words of the Lord Jesus. In fact, all the other words spoken previously (*in superioribus*) are the words of the priest."[35]

Despite the connection which Ambrose still asserts, the unity of the eucharistic prayer has been broken, since a distinction is now made between the words of the priest and the words of Christ. The Scholastic theologians will only bring out the implications of this position.

3. The final period runs from the beginning of Scholasticism to our own time. The Scholastics made extensive use of the passages in Ambrose. Peter Lombard (the supreme authority) cites in particular the text which we cited just above, but with the significant omission of the word "previously" (*in superioribus*).

For all this information, we rely completely on a study of P.-M.Gy to which we refer you for more particulars.[36] Gy says that Peter Lombard regarded the words of the Lord not as past words narrated by the priest, but as words spoken here and now by the priest in the person of Christ, without reference to the rest of the Canon. Soon after, Sicard of Cremona and then Peter the Cantor clearly stated that the words of Christ by themselves, when spoken with the intention of consecrating, are enough to effect transubstantiation.

The way was thus prepared for Thomas Aquinas who used the distinctions between *sacramentum tantum* (that which is entirely a sign), *res et sacramentum* (that which is reality [of the first sign] but also a sign in turn), and *res tantum* (that which is the ultimate reality signified and not in any way a sign) to divide the Canon into three parts.[37] Such a division of the Canon is without foundation and prescinds completely from the text and the literary structure of the prayer. In Thomas' view, a valid consecration depends solely on the (explanatory) words of the Lord, without reference to the rest of the Canon. Henceforth, the Canon was regarded simply as a framework lending solemnity to the words of consecration.

What is to be thought of a eucharistic theology that can exist only if the text of the celebration itself is ignored?

D. Conclusion

As a disproportionately privileged place was thus given to the account of institution, the eucharistic prayer lost its unity. Consecration was originally attributed to the prayer which the Lord spoke at the Last Supper and passed on to us that we might do likewise. This starting point of the development is attested in the earliest Fathers. Gradually, the idea of consecration by the Lord's words attracted into its specific orbit the explanatory words: "This is my body" and "This is the cup of my blood." Finally, these words alone came to occupy center stage.

No other development was really possible. Once we say that the consecration is effected by the Lord's words and once we ask what these words are, there can be only one answer, since the New Testament transmits, in this context, only one kind of words from the Lord: the explanatory words over the bread and wine. Meanwhile, however, despite his erroneous interpretation of history, Gregory the Great is an authentic witness to tradition, as are the other early Fathers cited above.

In addition, there is a liturgical witness to the passage from consecration by the Lord's words of thanksgiving to consecration by his explanatory words over the bread and wine. The witness is the way the account of institution is structured in the Anaphora of Serapion.[38] This structure is the same as that which underlies the "mystical Eucharist" in Book VII of the *Apostolic Constitutions*,[39] but with one important difference: in place of the prayer of thanksgiving over the bread, Serapion puts the explanatory words in the account of institution ("This is my body"); he then has the prayer for the unity of the Church (the prayer is substantially the same in the two documents). Finally, the prayer of thanksgiving over the cup is replaced by the explanatory words in the account of institution ("This is . . . my blood").

At the beginning of this chapter, we said we would be dealing with two problems. We have been considering the first: the anaphora as form of the Eucharist. It is clear now that this first problem is really two: the "form" of the Eucharist and the "moment" of consecration. But, though distinct, the two are so closely connected that it is impossible to deal with one without touching the other. As a result, we have passed from one to the other without confusing the data proper to each.

IV. THEORY OF ANTOINE CHAVASSE

The declared purpose of Chavasse's proposal[40] is to identify a common basis for two doctrines: that of the East which connects the consecration with the epiclesis, and that of the West which connects it with the Lord's explanatory words. As we shall see directly, the solution offered by the well-known liturgist goes far beyond his purpose and provides a solid basis for a global approach to the problem.[41] Let us follow his argument, which is in four stages.

1. "The first fact that draws our attention is that in all liturgies the part of the Canon which contains the words 'This is my body,' and so on, takes the literary form of a narrative. It tells what Christ did at the Supper."

2. "The literary form poses a problem that needs to be solved. To narrate what Christ did at the Supper is not, strictly speaking, to say what is happening here and now on the altar. From a literary standpoint the words to which the consecration of the bread and wine are attributed are part of a narrative of the Supper; it must be said (we are still looking at the literary form of the text) that they apply not to the bread and wine here present on the altar but to the bread and wine Christ held in his hands at the moment of the events of which the narrative speaks. How, then, can these words consecrate the bread and wine of our sacrifice today?"[42]

3. Chavasse continues: "In the narrative of the Supper which the priest tells at the altar, the pronoun 'this' refers, in its context, to what Jesus held in his hands. . . . There are two conceivable ways of making his words apply effectively to the bread and wine here present on the altar: either to add something to the text of the narrative or to make such an application in a purely interior way through a simple intention of consecrating the bread and wine here present."[43]

Chavasse concludes that the latter represents the way chosen by the Roman Church with its "doctrine that the minister must have the necessary intention." Congar, who revives Chavasse's thesis, also opts for a solution based on the minister's intention.[44] It is no accident that the two authors reach the same conclusion after carefully evaluating the theological positions of the medieval writers. To better assess the validity of this solution, we must follow Chavasse's theory to its end.

Chavasse says that the solution by way of intention is also adopted "by the Roman Canon, which supposes an interior intention of the minister, even though this intention is not given literary expression in the text."[45] This is the most debatable point in Chavasse's entire construction, and it is not admissible. Before we say that the Canon supposes an interior intention which is not verbally expressed, we must ask what does the Canon verbally express, and try to see whether this does not already solve, at least incipiently, the problem for which the theory of an unexpressed ministerial intention was developed.

The anamnesis of the Canon contains the statement that what we are doing in the Mass corresponds to what Christ instituted and ordered us to do. The account of institution ends with the command: "Do this in memory of me." The anamnesis responds by saying that what we are doing corresponds indeed to the command received: "Therefore . . . calling to mind the blessed passion. . . ." What is expressed here is not an "intention of doing" but a "description of what is being done and a certainty of being faithful to the institutive command."

Chavasse goes on to say that the texts of the Eastern liturgies show an awareness of the problem and give literary expression to this awareness by placing after the account of the Supper a prayer asking explicitly for the consecration; that prayer is the epiclesis. But, this new statement is again questionable, since from a historical standpoint there is no evidence that the epiclesis came into existence to give literary expression to the consecratory intention of the minister.

Chavasse's argument thus far reduces the two theologies of consecration to a single theology of ministerial intention, which may be purely interior or be given verbal expression. We have already offered our criticism of such a solution. But, the validity or invalidity of his analysis regarding intention is not important here, since his theory does not depend on that analysis. As we said earlier, his thinking on the matter under discussion is much broader in scope. It is the general conclusion that deserves to be retained; we could not, however, present this conclusion except in the context of his entire argument, and for this reason we have had to go through the stages of his study.

4. Chavasse's conclusion springs from the homily on the treason of Judas which John Chrysostom delivered on Holy Thursday: "As the words 'Increase and multiply and fill the earth' were said only once but gave our nature its abiding power to reproduce, so the words 'This is my body,' and so on, were spoken only once, yet they bring about the perfect sacrifice on every altar-table in the Churches from that moment on until the Savior's return."[46]

This passage makes it clear that there has been only one consecration in history: that accomplished by Jesus at the Last Supper. Congar comments: "There was (and there is), in fact, only *one* Eucharist—the one celebrated by Jesus himself the night he was betrayed. Our Eucharists are only Eucharists by the virtue and the making present of *that* Eucharist."[47]

This expresses in different words what we said at the end of Chap. One of the Last Supper as the "code" of our contemporary Eucharist: a code that is really present in and internal to every eucharistic celebration. Keeping to the language of semiology used there, we would say that that first and only consecration "created" the code.[48] In this hypothesis, there is no need of any other consecration; provided the code is correctly "used" (provided there is obedience to the code), the Lord's Supper, which took place once and for all, will be present on our altars. Proper use of the code is simply a matter of "doing the same," that is, of obedient imitation.

The consecration, then, took place only once; it took place once and for all at the Last Supper and is applied today to the Church's Eucharist. In Chavasse's view, this fact enables us to solve the problem posed by the narrative character of the words of institution; unfortunately, Chavasse introduces the question of an intention that is or is not verbally expressed.

We must acknowledge that if God's word was effective once and for all at creation, it can also be effective once and for all at the institution of the Eucharist during the Last Supper. Chavasse deserves recognition for so lucidly developing the suggestion in Chrysostom's homily and giving us an organic theory that can explain the relation of the eucharistic consecration to the Last Supper. The "once and for all" principle enunciated in the Letter to the Hebrews[49] is applied with splendid results. Such an approach has considerable ecumenical importance.

Chavasse and Congar both face the problem raised by the narrative character of the Supper story. Congar writes: "The real question is: how are we to know by what means and by what mediation the words of institution will be effectively applied, now, to the bread and wine of this particular celebration?"[50]

This, however, is a defective statement of the problem, for it presupposes what needs to be proved, namely, that a consecration occurs only when the words of institution are applied to the bread and wine. This would be difficult to prove, since the entire anaphora, including the account of institution, is addressed to the Father. Behind this part of Chavasse's presentation lurks a theory of consecration that is not sufficiently based on the liturgical texts.

We have given a partial response to this theory in speaking of the sanctifying function of the anaphora as a whole; such an approach to the consecration is quite different from a simple "application of the words of institution to the bread and wine." If we examine carefully the various anaphoras which tradition has preserved for us in all the liturgical families, we see that there is never any question of "applying the words of institution to the bread and wine." Not even the epiclesis can be interpreted as such an application, since this prayer simply asks for the sanctification and transformation of the bread and wine. We might indeed say that the epiclesis asks for the application of the Holy Spirit to the sacred gifts, but not for the application of the words of institution; such epicleses have never existed. Congar and Chavasse derive their position not from the text of the anaphoras, but from the theology manuals, where the whole eucharistic action was reduced to the consecration, which was regarded as independent and separable from the anaphora.

It is the anaphora that "eucharistifies" the bread and wine, even though it is entirely addressed to the Father and not to the sacred gifts. This fact cannot be readily integrated into the theological schemata of the manuals, which simply repeat Scholastic theology, but it is a constant in the tradition of the Church with its continuity from the most archaic liturgical documents down to our present-day texts.

Even the words of institution are part of the anaphora and are addressed to God, not to the bread and wine. It is in our dialogue with God, a dialogue that sanctifies us because he freely enters into it, that the bread and wine become a sacrament. There is no need of directing any words to the bread and wine so that these may be sanctified and become a communion in the body and blood of Christ. If such a need existed, there would have been no valid Eucharists down to the fourth century, when the epiclesis was introduced as a formal prayer for consecration, or even later, when the first Scholastics developed their theory of intention. But, it is obviously absurd to maintain that Eucharists celebrated before these developments were invalid.

Enough on the negative side. Let us turn to the positive: the theology of God's efficacious word supplies the answer to our problem.

V. THE SUPPER, SIGN OF THE CROSS
God's word is efficacious always and for all; therefore, it is not repeated but only commemorated; repetition would imply a lack of efficacy. This statement is the basis and point of departure for our discussion. God's word is creative, effecting what it signifies and

abiding for ever.[51] It does not return to him without having borne fruit.[52] It is not only an intelligible message addressed to human beings, but a dynamic force that acts infallibly.[53]

Relevant here are not only the Lord's words, but also his actions and gestures. We are attending to all three under the single rubric of his "word." It is a classical view, is it not, that a prophet can proclaim God's word in two ways: by saying it or by doing it?

A. Some Examples

Gestures, or actions, and words are two ways a prophet expresses himself; in his pronouncements, we find both the spoken word and the acted word.

"So, when Sargon captured Ashdod in 711, Isaiah walked around naked and barefoot to presage the discomfiture of those who were relying on Egypt (Is 20:1–6); Jeremiah smashed a jug, declaring: 'Yahweh Sabaoth says this: "I am going to break the people and this city just as one breaks a potter's jug, irreparably"' (Jer 19:10–11); and Ezekiel mimed departure into exile to announce the captivity of Israel (Ez 12:1–10).

"Now, in Israelite thought, predicting future events was definitive proof that Yahweh is indeed lord of history. He can foretell the future because he holds it in his hand."[54]

Seen against this background, tne prophetic character attaching to the gestures and words of Jesus are part of his revelation of himself as master of his own destiny: "Consequently, when Jesus predicted his sacrificial death, he declared himself lord of history. He did not undergo his passion: he took charge of it and transformed it into a voluntary offering."[55] Here we perceive what the Last Supper was: an announcement in the form of action, a gestural-verbal prophecy of his imminent death on the cross.

B. The Supper: A Parabolic Action Prophesying the Cross

X. Léon-Dufour correctly emphasizes that if we wish to examine the Last Supper in its relation to the cross, we must first determine and isolate the points to be considered. For "what is directly given to us is not an event but a text that reports and interprets it. Such is the presupposition of all historical knowledge: in our investigation of the past we have access to the facts only through reports of them."[56]

This being the case, we must study not only the explanatory

words over the bread and wine but the entire context provided by the supper. Consider, then, what B. Welte said at the German congress of dogmatic theology in 1959:

"The statement was made that 'Christ becomes food.' I would like to fill out . . . this valuable thought by making the subject of the sentence 'the death of Christ' instead of 'Christ.' If we say simply 'Christ' we have said nothing as yet about the significance of the Lord for faith and still less about the fact or event that founds this faith. . . . In that same sentence I would replace the predicate, 'food' with 'supper' or 'repast.' Food is food in the full and strict sense only insofar as it is (really or potentially) eaten. . . . It is from the eating of it that food acquires its meaning and nature as food. 'Meal,' then, that is, food (to be) eaten, is the idea that gives food its character of food.

"My suggested substitutions are also in keeping with the words of the consecration: 'Take and eat. . . . Drink.' The explanatory words, 'This is my body. . . . This is my blood,' should not be taken in isolation.

"In my opinion, the exhortation to eat and drink, which marks the beginning of the meal and turns it precisely into a meal, is no less constitutive on the sacramental level than are the explanatory words. . . .

"All this shows us that even in the biblical account the Eucharist is to be considered first as a meal and only then as food."[57]

The point being made here by Welte has to be taken as our point of departure in interpreting the text. Jesus ate his last meal with his disciples and at the end of it said: "Do this in memory of me." The command is to "do" something and it refers to the entire action that is the supper. It cannot be limited to the moment of consecration. The obedient carrying out of the command is not satisfied by the consecration alone: eating is no less essential a part of what is to be repeated, for the action that is the meal or supper is accomplished only in the eating of the bread and wine.

In the eyes of a devout Jew, a meal and the eating of it are a way of accepting, receiving, contemplating, and tasting the blessings of God that are mediated by the food. That is the thinking Jesus embodies at the supper. At his farewell meal, he gives his disciples the bread and cup; he is engaged here in

"the distribution of a nourishing food and a comforting drink. We

268

must reckon with the possibility that the distribution of a 'salvific gift' at a meal which was celebrated precisely as a farewell meal was meant to give a farewell gift, bestow the blessing of the imminent death, and thereby at the same time illumine the meaning of that death."[58]

Strictly speaking, Jesus is giving us a revelation not of his death but of the life that flows from his death,[59] since to eat and drink is to be nourished, and in the Bible to be nourished means that life is being preserved and renewed[60]: food gives life.

There is another important gesture to be emphasized: the giving of the same cup to all who are present. The usual custom was for each guest to drink from his own cup,[61] and it was exceptional for the presiding head of the family to send his own cup around so that each guest might drink from it. Such an action was a sign that a special relationship of communion and predilection existed between the host and those at table with him. Schürmann concludes that in giving the bread and cup to his disciples, Jesus intends to convey, or even simply to indicate, a special blessing. Léon-Dufour points out that in his act of giving, Jesus is showing that his own life is being communicated[62]: "In saying what he does over the bread and wine Jesus expresses the gift of his life even to the point of embracing death; he gives himself to those who are sharing in his supper."[63]

If the supper was a farewell meal and if the account of it belongs to the literary genre of the testamentary story, then these facts must serve us as norms in interpreting the actions and words of Jesus: "Testamentary literature sees the farewell meal as an act of communion with the testator and an important bond uniting the legatees."[64]

By giving the twofold gift of bread and wine, Jesus showed that salvation was coming through his own death[65]; the reign of God would come about not in spite of his death but because of it.[66] The reign of God belongs to the eschaton, and a farewell meal has the same eschatological connotation. A banquet is the classical image of God's kingdom, and the last supper is to be seen as the sacrament of the eschatological banquet in the kingdom of God.[67] For this reason, drinking the cup which Jesus gives to his disciples means sharing in eschatological salvation, in the eschatological covenant that is established by the now imminent death of Jesus.

All this makes it clear that taking part in the Lord's Supper is more than simply sharing a meal. Everything refers us to something beyond the supper, something that happens elsewhere, on Calvary. But, participation in the events of Calvary is possible only by means of the supper. Calvary is a personal event peculiar to Jesus himself: no one can share in the death of another person; death is a strictly personal and incommunicable event, in which human beings are alone with themselves. This incommunicability can be overcome only through gestures that belong to the order of symbolic communication; that is precisely what happens at the Last Supper. The words and actions of Jesus at the supper refer to the events of Calvary; what he does and says finds its fulfillment there. The supper is a bridge linking the disciples with Calvary; at and in the supper, they experience Calvary.

It is possible to say that Jesus dies (and rises) twice: at the supper and on Calvary, At the supper, he dies "verbally," in his words and actions. On Calvary, he dies physically, in flesh and blood. But is such a "verbal" death a real death? It is, since Jesus is the Word of God. His words are efficacious words, and what he proclaims takes place: it takes place at that very moment and by reason of the fact that he proclaims it. At the Last Supper, the disciples are not simply being given advance notice of the events that will take place on Calvary; these events are already actual and present in the supper, and the disciples are experiencing them.

H. Schürmann points out accurately that the supper is "a symbolic action anticipating his imminent death, an *ôt* rather in the manner of the Old Testament prophets. But here it is not really a case of prophesying the future; prophesied future is proferred as a gift. . . . The sign is in the gift, the gift is not the effect of the sign"[68]

X. Léon-Dufour takes the same approach: "Here he is symbolically anticipating his death and the increased life which that death will bring to his followers."[69] And again: "A word or symbolic gesture that in effect is not simply an announcement is already a reality that unfolds before our eyes, a reality that both is and is not the thing said or done. In these actions and words of the Supper Jesus 'expresses' and 'lives' his death."[70]

There is a difference, however, between what these authors are saying and the view we are presenting. We lay a greater emphasis on the difference between the action of Jesus and the actions of the Old Testament prophets. Old Testament prophecy only provides a framework to locate the action of Jesus; the efficacy of his action surpasses that of the prophetic *ôt*, since his action reflects that he is the very Word of God made flesh. Clearly, we are trying to be faithful to the line of thought opened up by John Chrysostom in his homily on the betrayal of Judas. It is God's word, the word of Jesus at the Supper, that establishes and ensures the relation between Supper and cross.

Schürmann, stresses only the point that the prophetic action of Jesus transcends that of the Old Testament prophets; therefore, he sees the actualization of the future by Jesus as a fulfillment of Old Testament typology.[71] This is, of course, undeniable; nonetheless, we depart somewhat from his point of view to see the situation from a different angle. For, if the Supper is a parable and gestural prophecy of the cross and if it is the efficacious word that proclaims the cross, then we must conclude that at the Supper Jesus accepts the cross: the present creates the future. The Supper interprets the cross precisely because it contains and produces the cross.

It is time to clarify an expression used a few paragraphs back: "Jesus dies twice," once in his words at the Supper and again in his body on Calvary. For, if we cannot use the word "again" with regard to the Mass, neither can we use it with the Supper. Clearly, then we speak of Jesus dying "twice" (i.e., once and "again") simply for didactic purposes, namely, to bring out the realism of the symbolism of the Supper in relation to the cross. This much is certain: no human being can die twice; the death rattle of the final agony did not rise from Jesus' throat at the Last Supper, nor did blood and water flow from his side. He died once and for all on Calvary, and there is no reason for trying to evade this categorical statement.

Consequently, having asserted the identity of Supper and cross, we must add that there is always a difference and a distance between a symbol and the event of which it is the symbol. It is, of course, the symbolic nature of the Supper that makes it possible for the disciples to be in communion with the saving death of Jesus. The symbol is thus a genuine means of access to an event which would otherwise be inaccessible. At the same time, however, the event is unique and unrepeatable. For the reason, then, that the symbol gives access to the inaccessible and is a repetition of the unrepeatable, we say that it is never identical with its content, that is, with the event to which it is related. Léon-Dufour is, therefore, quite right to say of symbolic action that it "is and is not" its symbolized content.[72] Similarly, R. Taft says he cannot see how it is possible to assert a complete identity between the sacrament and the event of which it is the sacrament.[73]

We shall, therefore, stop saying that Jesus dies twice; instead, we shall say that he "lives" or experiences his one death twice: in his words during the Last Supper and in his body on the cross. The event itself is never repeated, even in symbol.

If we understand A. Gerken correctly,[74] he is saying that the event of the Lord's death and resurrection does not have two modes of existence: a natural, historical mode, in which the death occurred once and for all, and a sacramental (= symbolic) mode that can be repeated in the course of history. This, he says, would really be a camouflaged duplication of the event. Rather, then, the event exists but once, unique and unrepeatable. Symbols provide access to that otherwise inaccessible event. People today, therefore, have access to the event in its natural mode of existence as it happened two thousand years ago.

Gerken's theory is based on the concept of "real symbol," which he finds in the Greek Fathers. The concept originated in Platonism, in which the doctrine of participation belongs to both ontology and gnoseology.[75] We are not competent to engage in a philosophical discussion of this point; we simply report Gerken's thought as a stimulus to deeper reflection on the subject.

The logic at work in Gerken's thought is also operative elsewhere today, inasmuch as writers speak increasingly of the Eucharist as the sacrament of the absence (as well as of the presence) of Jesus. "Since the eucharistic celebration is simply a mode of the special absence of Jesus, it has a role only during the Church's journey and tends therefore toward its own suppression by the full presence of Christ."[76]

As this citation makes clear, it is precisely the symbolic (sacramental) character of the eucharistic meal that introduces the eschatological dimension of the sacrament. For, in fact, the historical event of the death and resurrection of Christ calls for its completion by the *parousia*, the final coming of the risen Lord. Communion with the first event is necessarily "expectation" of the completion which the second will bring.

F. X. Durrwell has emphasized that the body present in the Eucharist is the glorified body of Christ, which in turn is the eschatological body resulting from resurrection.[77] This presence of the glorified body means the definitive presence of salvation in all its stages, and, therefore, of the second coming. The Church's Eucharist may thus be correctly defined as the sacrament which renders present the eschatological kingdom.

In discussing the sacramentality of the Supper, we have taken the relation of the Supper to the cross as our starting point, and we have been explaining in what this relation consists. We have also cited the interesting explanation given by Gerken; but, while this explanation has the advantage of embracing all the data presented, we have refrained from adopting it without reservation, since we think riper reflection is needed.

It is time to show that the texts of the Supper narrative speak to us of the cross.

Nowadays, no one accepts the allegorical explanation of the bread separated from the wine as being an image of the death of Christ; in that explanation, it was said that since the bread is the body of Christ and the cup contains his blood, the separated elements image forth his death. The theory will not stand up, because in the New Testament there is question not so much of the separation of the bread from the wine as of the distinction of two rites: the rite involving the bread is distinct from the rite involving the wine. From the outset, the two rites are separated by the course of the meal and are independent of one another. The meaning of the rite involving the bread must, therefore, be complete in itself, independent of the rite involving the cup. Only in the Matthew/Mark tradition are two rites set side by side so that they can take on a meaning that springs from the reciprocal relation thus established.

A. This Is My Body
These words explain the bread which Jesus gives to his disciples to be eaten. In biblical anthropology, "body" denotes the entire person and not simply the physical element, as it does in our modern languages. Semites used *basar* (flesh) to designate persons insofar as they can express and manifest themselves. Jesus, too, expressed himself by means of his body, and it was through his body that he related to other persons.[78] When, therefore, he gives the disciples his "body," he is bidding them to be nourished by the relationship which he has established with them. Just as devout Hebrews were nourished by the gifts of the earth which were signs of their election by God, so the disciples are to be nourished, as a group, by the relationship which Jesus has created with them through his personal presence among them.

"Body" also conveys a nuance of creaturely weakness; this enables us to glimpse the attitude of Jesus in his relations with others.

In addition, "body" in the Bible can mean "corpse." Consequently, "the range of meanings which the word has bids us interpret it along two lines: the person in relation to the universe, and the person who will die."[79] Finally, if we take into account the Pauline addition "which is for you"[80] and its Lukan variation "which is given for you,"[81] we must conclude that "Jesus is here speaking of his life that is given, even to the point of dying as a personal sacrifice."[82]

It is worth noting that throughout the biblical world, bread has a sacral significance that was connected with life: bread sustains life. For this reason, it became the locus of relation to God: whenever the devout Jew ate, he was to praise God for the gift received. In the same situation at the Last Supper, the center of attention is no longer the bread but the person of Jesus, who is the source of life in the special relationship which he has established with others, a relationship unto death. Life is the central theme, but life that comes through the death of Jesus.

"For you." In the Paul/Luke tradition the Greek for this phrase is *hyper hymōn.* The words have given rise to extensive discussion, inasmuch as the prevailing opinion used to be that *hyper* (for) referred to Old Testament sacrifices and specifically to the doctrine of vicarious satisfaction. Léon-Dufour goes into the matter carefully and concludes that only by doing violence to the text can *hyper* carry this meaning. Only in Philemon 13 (and perhaps in 1 Corinthians 15:29 and 2 Corinthians 5:14) does *hyper* mean "in place of," surely a weak philological support for the doctrine of vicarious satisfaction in the New Testament! We refer you to Léon-Dufour's discussion[83] and will be content to accept his conclusion. Accordingly *hyper hymon* means simply "to your advantage," and he paraphrases Christ's words: " 'I give myself as food so that you may live': that is the meaning of 'to your advantage,' since we eat in order to live."[84]

B. The Verb "Is"

Theologians discussed at length the verb "is" in the sentences: "This is my body," "This is the cup. . . ." Today, interest in the subject has greatly diminished, since from a literary standpoint these sentences are indistinguishable from "I am the true vine" (Jn 15:1), "I am the light of the world" (Jn 8:12), and other statements of the same type.

In any accounting, the copula "is" guarantees a relation between bread and body, cup and blood, such that what happens to the bread must be understood as happening to Jesus. Thus, when he gives the bread, he gives himself as food. According to Paul, because the bread is one, it is a source of unity.[85] But, it is Christ who creates unity among his disciples, and who even dies for the sake of this unity.[86] It is correct, therefore, to say that the work of Christ is carried on by the bread. If we read closely 1 Corinthians 11:23–27, we see Paul doing a careful job of editing as he eliminates all the actors except Jesus himself. The focus is wholly on him. By means of the verb "is" in the words of explanation, the centrality belonging to Jesus in 1 Corinthians 11:23–27 is ensured also in the celebration mentioned in 1 Corinthians 10:16ff. where the bread and wine are central.

Christ's body is "given for you."[87] The words are true only of Christ's body on the cross, and yet they are predicated of the bread that is given to be eaten. Conclusion: the bread being eaten acquires its "truth" only on the cross as described by John: the glorious cross on which the risen Lord triumphs.[88] The Johannine cross shines radiantly in the bread which Jesus gives to his disciples. A Jesus who does not sweat blood in a symbolic death now lives with his disciples and blesses the Father with all his heart in a great prayer of thanksgiving.

C. The Cup

In the Bible, the word "cup" has many metaphorical meanings. It can signify a person's destiny[89] or trials to be endured[90] or punishment to be suffered.[91] In addition, cups were used in worship and, therefore, they recall sacrificial rites.

Note that in almost all liturgies, the explanatory words read: "This is the cup of my blood," and not "This is my blood."[92] The cup is not just any container, but one for drinking. Wine for its part is a sign of the joy which God gives to human beings; at a solemn festal meal and especially at the Passover meal, wine was indispensable.

Paul gives the cup a technical name: "cup of blessing."[93] The reason is that this particular cup at a meal was accompanied by the great prayer of thanksgiving for the land, for food, for the covenant and the Law.[94] All these gifts are climaxed by the Spirit whom Jesus gives from the cross[95] and whom in his risen state he continues to give as the characteristic post-Easter gift.[96] On the cross, he seals the new covenant (Heb 9:18–20) which is distinguished precisely by the gift of the Spirit.[97] This covenant is concluded in his blood, blood which in fact is shed only on the cross.[98] The fact that the Asian tradition, to which the Syrian is heir, speaks of the cup as filled with the Holy Spirit confirms this relation between cup and cross.

"Cup of the covenant" is an expression based on Exodus 24:4–8, but with a significant alteration. In Exodus, it is the Lord, i.e., God, who concludes the covenant with Israel. At the Last Supper, it is Jesus who concludes it in his own blood. In this new covenant, then, there are no intermediaries, not even a form of cult that uses the sacrificial blood of a victim. Jesus is both the one who concludes the covenant and the way in which it is concluded. In Exodus, the Lord concludes the covenant; here the covenant is in "my blood." This "my" has a special connection with "Lord" and is, therefore, an indirect claim to resurrection. In the words over the cup, the cross takes undisputed first place, since the shedding of blood refers to the crucified Jesus. In the background, nonetheless, is the "my" that specifies the blood which is shed. Jesus concludes the covenant precisely because he dies, but a covenant with a dead person is an absurdity and foreign to every logic operative in Israel.

In addition, this covenant is "everlasting." Jesus must, therefore, live on even after the defeat of death if he is to be for ever a partner in the covenant and continue to play his part in it. The resurrection already appears on the horizon after his death.

D. Shed

The word "shed" can refer only to a bloody death, since the technical term used in Israelite cult was "sprinkle."[99] There is no room for "sprinkle" in the language of the Supper, since the disciples are being asked simply to drink his blood and not to sprinkle it on an altar. "Instead of purification acquired through expiatory sacrifices with their sprinkling of blood there is question only of a drink and therefore an intensification of life."[100]

E. For the Many

At their Passover, Israelites prayed for a blessing upon Israel, while calling down God's wrath on their enemies. Jesus acknowledges no frontiers or enmities. He embraces everyone. He thus becomes the focal point to which all others must relate themselves if they are to be blessed. Only the Lord can have such a status and position. This expression, too, is an indirect reference to the resurrection.

F. For the Forgiveness of Sins

Only Matthew has this phrase, which simply renders explicit the covenant theme. A covenant with God means communion with him who is by definition the Holy One. Israel, therefore, had to purify itself of its sins and walk in the paths of the Lord. When the people turned back to their sins, the covenant was broken; God then undertook to work anew for their conversion, which was to be sealed by a new agreement, a new covenant. The covenant in the blood of Jesus is new but it is also eternal. This means that sin has been eliminated from the world by his blood. But, who can forgive sins except God alone? The forgiveness of sins foretells the coming of God's reign.[101] All this is directly connected with the cup.

G. Blood and Life

The theme of blood or, more accurately, theme of blood that is shed is at the center of the explanatory words over the cup. In the Old Testament, blood is life; that is, it is the locus of life and the means by which life is transmitted. Because of this connection with life, it is considered sacred.[102] In addition, bloodshed and the idea of violent death are very closely connected: "To shed blood is to destroy the bearer of life and therefore life itself."[103] Evidently, then, Jesus could not have more clearly prophesied his cross than he does in the words over the cup.

In giving his disciples the cup of his blood that will be shed, Jesus is giving them his death that they may derive new life from it through the covenant. If blood is life and blood which is shed is death, he is giving them his life as origin and locus of a relationship with God who is the supreme source of life. Christ's life is the source of life for his disciples, but if that life is to reach them, the life of Jesus himself must pass through death. Blood, because it is life, belongs to God alone; he alone may dispose of it. Here we have Jesus disposing of it in an authoritative way; he is, then, aware that his death does not mean the failure and end of his plan to give life, but is rather the way in which this plan will come to its fulfillment.

Here again the structure of the proclamation puts death in the foreground, while at the same time keeping present in the background the theme of the life which Jesus possesses and which no one has power to wrest from him.[104] But, as often happens, it is the background that illumines and gives meaning to what is in the foreground.

If we attempted to translate the words over the cup into the language of today, we would have to say that Jesus gives his disciples not a cup of blood but the cup of a life devoted completely and unrestrictedly to them, even to the point of dying for them.

H. The Suffering Servant

There can be no denying that in the accounts of the Supper, with the exception of Luke's, Jesus applies to himself Isaiah's prophecy of the Suffering Servant. In the Bible, the title "Servant of God" is a title of honor, since it signifies a person called to collaborate in God's plan.

Jesus follows the prophets in asserting the priority of life over ritual.[105] If, then, we want to understand the meaning of the Supper as a sacrifice, we must go back to the prophecy of the Suffering Servant which Jesus fulfills throughout his life and in his death on the cross. He foretells his passion using word for word the language describing the personal sacrifice[106] of the Servant of Yahweh. His words at the Supper likewise bring before us the figure of the Suffering Servant. We said that the cup of blood/covenant is an allusion to the ritual sacrifice in Exodus 24:4–8, but that as the account of the Supper progresses the whole meaning shifts when the word "shed" is introduced. With this word, we leave behind the reference to Exodus and turn to Isaiah 52:13—53:12 where the theme, as at the Supper, is the exaltation of the Servant through his martyrdom.

"What the prophet is contemplating is no longer the blood of animal victims by which the commitment of the people was given ritual representation. He is contemplating rather the *lived* commitment of a human being, the servant who is faithful until death. As covenant of the people he accomplishes by the gift of his 'soul' that which the blood rite signified: communion with God."[107]

The personal sacrifice of the Servant of Yahweh has universal import, but it is also described with the help of cultic terminology: the Servant, despised and tortured, carries out in a new way the sacrifice of expiation.[108] "We must not let ourselves be deceived by the cultic language used here. The language has become metaphorical, using familiar categories in order to convey an ineffable reality: just as the sacrifice of expiation was regarded as having value for the whole of Israel, so the personal sacrifice of the Servant has a universal value."[109]

278

As Suffering Servant, Jesus is now the covenant in himself. There is no longer a rite of covenant making, for he is the covenant in his own person. In the New Testament dispensation, the person of Jesus replaces all rites: instead of saving rites, we have the Savior himself.

I. I Shall Not Eat/Drink Until. . . .
H. Schürmann correctly notes that all the sayings examined in the account of the supper show traces of post-Easter revision by the redactors of the texts, or can at least be suspected of having undergone such revision.

He then suggests that we concentrate on two sentences belonging to a very early tradition, one that is older than the revision of the accounts of institution. The sentences are: "I shall not eat it [the Passover] until it is fulfilled in the kingdom of God" (Lk 22:16); "I shall not drink again of the fruit of the vine until that day when I drink it new in the kingdom of God" (Mk 14:25). Schürmann continues: "According to this passage the *basileia* (kingdom) is coming despite the catastrophic death of Jesus; afterwards there will be a new banquet for him in the coming kingdom."[110]

The prospect both of Christ's death and of the ensuing kingdom of God (represented by Christ) is indeed present even in these texts which are regarded as above suspicion because of their antiquity and the intense eschatological tonality they give to the supper. Later developments all endeavored to reduce the eschatological character of the Eucharist. "This prophecy, uttered in the final hour, takes the form of an 'even though,' that is, it reveals an eschatological prospect despite defeat."[111] Though faced with disaster, Jesus continues to the very end to promise his disciples the gift of eschatological salvation; he does so specifically when giving his disciples the bread and cup of blessing, which are the signs of election and divine favor.

Even this earliest text, then, speaks of the supper of Jesus as related to his death and the ensuing eschatological banquet. If we were to look for a single text that sums up the aspect of the supper as proclamation of the death of the risen Lord, we would have to choose a sentence from Paul: "As often as you eat this bread and drink the cup, you proclaim the Lord's death until he comes" (1 Cor 11:26). The verb "proclaim" (*kataggellō*) is most fitting in a text whose purpose is to describe the sacramental relation between supper and cross.

VII. CONCLUSION

We have been able to show, even if only in a summary way, that the Lord's Supper is truly related to his death and, via his death, to his eschatological glorification as something perceptible in the background. The symbolic character of the verbal and gestural parable that is the supper compels us to say that the content of the supper is not the supper itself but the events of the cross, as described above.

The relationship is based concretely on the efficacy of the word of God as uttered by Jesus. Moreover, what is true of the supper as a whole is true of the bread and wine that are its constitutive elements and the elements in which the supper is concentrated as it were. Because the word of God is efficacious, the bread and wine are truly, really, and substantially the prophecy and parable, that is, the symbol and sacrament, of the events making up the glorious cross of Christ.

As a final thought, events do not exist in themselves but in the persons who accomplish them. We conclude from this that the bread and wine are the prophecy and parable, the symbol and sacrament, or mystery, of the body and blood of Christ.

All this has to do with the relation between the Last Supper and the cross; it still leaves the problem of the bread and wine on our altars today. It is here that we must recognize the value of Chavasse's theory.

If we faithfully obey the command "Do this in memory of me," the result will be a sacramental identity of our Eucharist with the Last Supper. If the bread and wine of today's eucharistic celebration are identical with the bread and wine which Jesus gave to his disciples at his final meal,[112] then because of that identity our bread and wine too will be the mystery of the body and blood of Jesus, no more and no less than were the bread and wine of the Last Supper. Briefly, our bread and wine too are the mystery of the body and blood of Jesus because our Eucharist is an imitation (mimesis) of the Last Supper, an anamnesis–parable–sacrament of the Lord's death and resurrection.

Abbreviations

AAS	*Acta Apostolicae Sedis.*
Alberigo	J. Alberigo, et al. *Conciliorum Oecumenticorum Decreta.* 3d ed. Bologna, 1973.
Andrieu, *OR*	M. Andrieu. *Les Ordines Romani du haut moyen âge.* (Spicilegium Sacrum Lovaniense 11, 23, 24, 28, 29) Louvain, 1931ff.
Andrieu, *PR*	M. Andrieu. *Le Pontifical Romain au moyen âge.* (Studi e Testi 86, 87, 88, 89) Vatican City, 1938–1941.
Botte	B. Botte. *La Tradition apostolique de saint Hippolyte. Essai de reconstition.* (LQF 39) Münster, 1963.
Botte-Mohrmann	B. Botte and C. Mohrmann. *L'Ordinaire de la Messe. Texte critique, traduction et études.* (Etudes liturgiques 2) Paris-Louvain, 1953.
CCL	Corpus Christianorum, Series Latina.
CSEL	Corpus Scriptorum Ecclesiasticorum Latinorum.
DACL	*Dictionnaire d'archéologie chrétienne et de liturgie.*
DB	*Dictionnaire de la Bible.*
DBS	*Dictionnaire de la Bible, Supplément.*
Deiss	L. Deiss. *Springtime of the Liturgy. Liturgical Texts of the First Four Centuries.* Translated by M. J. O'Connell. Collegeville, MN, 1979.
Did	*Didaskalia.*
DOL	*Documents on the Liturgy, 1963–1979. Conciliar, Papal, and Curial Texts.* Ed. by the International

	Commission on English in the Liturgy. Collegeville, MN, 1982.
DS	H. Denzinger and A. Schönmetzer, eds. *Enchiridion symbolorum*. 32d ed. Freiburg, 1963.
DTC	*Dictionnaire de théologie catholique.*
EEFL	E. Lodi. *Enchiridion euchologicum fontium liturgicorum*. Rome, 1979.
EL	*Ephemerides Liturgicae.*
ETL	*Ephemerides Theologicae Lovanienses.*
Férotin	M. Férotin, ed. *Le Liber Mozarabicus Sacramentorum*. (Monumenta Ecclesiae Liturgica 6) Paris, 1912.
Flannery	A. Flannery, ed. *Vatican Council II. The Conciliar and Postconciliar Documents*. Collegeville, MN, 1975.
Funk	F. X. Funk, ed. *Didascalia et Constitutiones Apostolorum*. 2 vols. Paderborn, 1905.
Gel	(Old) Gelasian Sacramentary, Ms. Bibl. Vat., Reginen. Lat. 316, edited by L. K. Mohlberg, et al. *Liber sacramentorum romanae aecclesiae ordinis anni circuli. (Sacramentarium Gelasianum)* (REDMF 4) Rome, 1960.
GIRM	*General Instruction of the Roman Missal*, in *DOL* 1376–1731
Gr	Gregorian Sacramentary, edited by J. Deshusses, *Le sacramentaire grégorien. Ses principales formes d'après les plus anciens manuscripts*. (Spicilegium Friburgense 16) Fribourg, 1971, 2d ed., 1979.
Greg	*Gregorianum.*
Hänggi-Paul	A. Hänggi and I. Pahl. *Prex Eucharistica. Textus e variis liturgiis antiquioribus selecti*. (Spicilegium Friburgense 12) Fribourg, 1968.
HJ	*Historisches Jahrbuch.*

JB	Jerusalem Bible.
JBL	*Journal of Biblical Literature.*
JEH	*Journal of Ecclesiastical History.*
Irén	*Irénikon.*
Jungmann	J. A. Jungmann. *The Mass of the Roman Rite: Its Origins and Development (Missarum Sollemnia).* 2 vols. Translated by F. A. Brunner. New York, 1951–1955.
Léon-Dufour	X. Léon-Dufour. *Dictionary of Biblical Theology.* 2d ed. Translated by J. Cahill, E. M. Stewart, et al. New York, 1973.
LMD	*La Maison-Dieu.*
LQF	Liturgiegeschichtliche Quellen und Forschungen.
LXX	The Septuagint.
Neuner-Dupuis	J. Neuner and J. Dupuis. *The Christian Faith in the Doctrinal Documents of the Catholic Church.* Rev. ed. Staten Island, NY, 1982.
NRT	*Nouvelle revue théologique.*
NTS	*New Testament Studies.*
OCP	*Orientalia Christiana Periodica.*
OR	*Ordo Romanus.*
PG	Patrologia Graeca.
PL	Patrologia Latina.
PO	Patrologia Orientalis.
QL	*Questions liturgiques.*
RBén	*Revue bénédictine*
RBib	*Revue biblique.*
REDMF	Rerum ecclesiasticarum documenta, Series maior: Fontes.
Renaudot	E. Renaudot. *Liturgiarum orientalium collectio.*

	Paris, 1716; 2d, more accurate ed., Frankfurt, 1847.
RHE	*Revue d'histoire ecclésiastique.*
Righetti	M. Righetti. *Manuale di storia liturgica* III. *La Messa.* 3d ed. Milan, 1966.
RivLit	*Rivista liturgica.*
RSR	*Recherches de science religieuse.*
RTAM	*Revue de théologie ancienne et médiévale.*
RTL	*Revue théologique de Louvain.*
SC	Sources chrétiennes.
SE	*Sacris erudiri.*
TDNT	*Theological Dictionary of the New Testament.*
TZ	*Theologische Zeitschrift.*
Ver	The sacramentary formerly called the "Leonine"; ms. in Verona, Bibl. Capit., LXXXV [80]; edited by L. K. Mohlberg, et al. *Sacramentarium Veronense.* (REDMF 1) Rome, 1955–56; 3d, improved ed., 1978.
Vg	The Vulgate.
VSC	Vatican Council II. Constitution *Sacrosanctum Concilium* on the Sacred Liturgy.
Wor	*Worship.*

Notes

INTRODUCTION

1. L. Bouyer, *Eucharist. The Theology and Spirituality of the Eucharistic Prayer*, trans. C. U. Quinn (Notre Dame, IN, 1968).

2. B. Botte, et al., *Anaphores nouvelles* (Assemblées du Seigneur, 2ᵉ sér., 2; Paris, 1968).

3. T. Schnitzler, *Die drei neuen eucharistischen Hochgebete und die neuen Präfationen in Verkündigung und Betrachtung* (Freiburg, 1968).

4. *VSC* 23 (Latin in Alberigo, 26; English in Flannery, 10).

5. H.-I. Marrou, *The Meaning of History*, trans. R. J. Olsen (Baltimore, 1966), 33. Even though history is written with the aid of documents, it is also inseparable from the historian, and the historian in turn lives in his own present time. The problems he seeks to solve in the past may be the very one that preoccupy the age in which he is living. Historical knowledge arises out of a constant exchange in which present and past shed light on each other. As the past is a source of knowledge of the present, so the present is a source of knowledge of the past.

6. Hänggi-Pahl 250.

7. Ibid., 294. For the author, see E. Renaudot, *Liturgiarum orientalium collectio* (2 vols.; Paris, 1716; second, more accurate edition: Frankfurt and London, 1847), 2:433f.

8. VSC 48.

9. Vatican II, *Schemata constitutionum et decretorum* (Rome, 1962), 175.

10. *Acta synodalia sacrosancti Concilii oecumenici Vaticani secundi*, Periodus I, Pars II (Rome, 1970), 1:22.

11. *VSC* 48 (Flannery 16).

12. A. Cuva, "Il mistero eucaristico," in the collective work, *La Costituzione sulla sacra liturgia* (Turin, 1967), 503.

CHAPTER ONE

1. *GIRM* 54.

2. The earliest attestation is in *Didache* 9 (Hänggi-Pahl 66).

3. For a good survey of the names for the eucharistic prayer, see M. Righetti, *Manuale di storia liturgica* 3, 3d ed. (Milan, 1966), 342–45. See also Jungmann 2:101ff.

4. A quick and superficial examination of the structure of the Roman Canon does not recall the classic Anaphoras of Chrysostom, Basil, and Mark. To detect structural similarities, we would have to take a very sophisticated approach to the Alexandrian anaphoras; the task would be difficult but not impossible.

5. Ex 20:24. Careful attention must be paid to the cultic context of the verse, which refers to the altar and the offering of sacrifice; account must also be taken of

the broader context, which is the making of the covenant. See also Dt 12:5–7, 11–12; 14:22–23, on the theology of the name in a cultic context.

6. Jl 3:5 (2:32). The passage is not speaking of the place where God makes his name dwell, but of Jerusalem as place of salvation; Jerusalem contains, of course, the temple which is the dwelling place of God's holy name.

7. Rom 10:10–13; Jl 3:5 is also cited in Acts 2:21.

8. Acts 4:12. See also: "And it is the name of Jesus which, through our faith in it, has brought back the strength of this man whom you see here and who is well known to you" (Acts 3:16 JB).

9. Hänggi-Pahl 358–372.

10. On this text, see A. Gerhards, *Die griechische Gregoriosanaphora. Ein Beitrag zur Geschichte des eucharistischen Hochgebets* (to be published in the LQF series).

11. Hänggi-Pahl 375–380. See W. Macomber, "The Oldest Known Text of the Anaphora of the Apostles Addai and Mari," *OCP* 32 (1966): 335–371.

12. W. Macomber, "The Maronite and Chaldean Version of the Anaphora of the Apostles," *OCP* 37 (1971):55–84; see also idem, "A History of the Chaldean Mass,"*Wor* 51 (1977): 107–120, 523–536.

13. The anaphora in the *Testamentum Domini* also has parts which are addressed to the Son (Hänggi-Pahl 220–222). In this instance, the phenomenon may be due because the text is a fusion of the Anaphora of Hippolytus with some morning hymns of the Syrian liturgy (see L. Ligier, "L'anaphore de la *Tradition apostolique* dans le *Testamentum Domini,* " in B. D. Spinks, ed., *The Sacrifice of Praise. Studies on the Themes of Thanksgiving and Redemption in the Central Prayers of the Eucharistic and Baptismal Liturgies. In Honour of Arthur Hubert Couratin* [Rome, 1981], 91–106).

14. The Anaphora of James in particular shows this transition. In the opening praise and thanksgiving, it is the Church that exalts and adores God, "the creator of all creatures, visible and invisible." But, the list of things made by God suddenly stops and makes way for a list of the heavenly choirs that sing his praises. A kind of "negative theology" is at work here; that is, human beings begin to thank God and to list the reasons for praising him but then they break off at a certain point, as though incapable of praising him directly, and substitute for their own thanksgiving the cosmic praise offered to God by the heavenly choirs, the sun, moon, and stars, the earth and sea and all that is in them, the heavenly Jerusalem, and all the martyrs, prophets, holy men and women, apostles, etc. Once the Sanctus is finished, nothing further is said about those offering praise, and the prayer calmly takes up once more the theme of the motives for praise, that is, the list of God's works.

After the Sanctus, the list of works begins with the creation of human beings. It thus begins precisely at the point where it had broken off in order to absorb the Sanctus with its introduction.

In assessing this awkward insertion, we must have recourse to the Greek redaction of the anaphora, since the Syriac and Armenian texts have already introduced corrections aimed at smoothing out the transitions; these texts thus show themselves to be later than the Greek text in Codex Barberini Vat. gr. 2282 (to be found in Hänggi-Pahl 244ff.). For an analysis of the text, see A. Tarby, *La prière eucharistique de l'Eglise de Jérusalem* (Paris, 1972), 77–80. Our analysis is not in complete agreement with his, but his book is nonetheless indispensable.

15. Hänggi-Pahl 348.

16. Ibid., 246.

17. Anaphora of John of Bostra (ibid., 293).

18. Ibid., 221.

19. Ibid., 102.

20. Ibid., 81. The English translation of the Anaphora of Hippolytus is from L. Deiss, *Springtime of the Liturgy. Liturgical Texts of the First Four Centuries*, trans. M. J. O'Connell (Collegeville, MN, 1979), 131.

21. Hänggi-Pahl 376. This development is confirmed by the Anaphora of Theodore of Mopsuestia: "We offer praise, glory, thanksgiving and adoration to you, Father and Son and Holy Spirit" (ibid., 382); see also the Anaphora of Nestorius, ibid., 388. In the Syro-Malabar Anaphora of the Apostles Addai and Mari, the text is the same as in the Chaldean anaphora, except that it is the Trinity which creates.

22. Ibid., 221. The source of the *Testamentum Domini* at this point is the resolutely theocentric Anaphora of Hippolytus.

23. Ibid., 352. In all probability, it is from this passage that the present-day Roman anaphora derives the text for the acclamation to the Son.

24. Ibid., 412. For the original text (and Latin translation), see J. M. Sauget, *Anaphora S. Petri Apostoli Tertia*, in A. Raes, ed., *Anaphorae siriacae, Quotquot in codicibus adhuc repertae sunt*, II, fasc. 3 (Rome, 1973), 301.

25. Our language here is theologically inaccurate; we use it simply because it reflects the historical situation. Properly speaking, we do not see the Lord's body when we look at the host, since the real presence of that body in the sacramental species cannot be seen by any created eye but only by the intellect enlightened by grace), whose proper object is the essence and substance of things. This is so because in the Eucharist there has been a change of substance or a "transubstantiation"; it is under this rubric that the problem is treated by St. Thomas Aquinas, who lived at the time when a spirituality based on the elevation was predominant (see *Summa theologiae* III, 76, 7c).

26. William Durandus of Mende, *Rationale divinorum officiorum* IV, 41, 50. The elevation of the chalice did not become common practice until about the middle of the fourteenth century.

27. In the Eastern anaphoras, the words "thank" or "give thanks" never occur in isolation; they are always accompanied by a series of verbs which often include "adore"; this, along with "confess," "bless," "praise," and "exalt," is one of the classic eucharistic terms.

28. See note 37 of no. 38. The vote on Schema I on the Mass was taken at the plenary session of the Consilium held on October 21, 22, and 26, 1965; the result of the vote was revealed during the meeting at Treviri on March 2, 1967.

Among the questions proposed for a vote was (1c): "After the consecration of the bread and wine should there be a single genuflection as a sign of adoration of Christ's body and blood, or some other sign of adoration determined by popular custom and the authorities of the area?" There were 22 yeas and 11 nays. That is why note 37 of Schema 218 proposes a single genuflection by way of experiment.

29. Hänggi-Pahl 250.

30. P.-M. Gy discussed this question at the Saint-Serge Liturgical Week (Paris) in 1983. It is expected that the papers of this meeting will be published.

31. J. P. Audet, "Esquisse du genre littéraire de la 'bénédiction' juive et de l' 'eucharistie' chrétienne," *RBib* 65 (1958): 371–339; idem, *La Didachè. Instruction des apôtres* (Paris, 1958), 372–403; idem, "Genre littéraire et formes cultuelles de l'Eucharistie. Nova et Vetera," *EL* 80 (1966):353–385.

32. Audet speaks of a "state of soul" or interior attitude of which persons are con-

scious and which they consciously ratify; the fact that this state is spontaneous and unmediated should not lead us to think of it as an emotion or enthusiasm inspired by momentary feelings.

33. *Jubilees* 25, 11–15, trans. R. H. Charles, revised C. Rabin, in *The Aprocryphal Old Testament*, ed. H. F. D. Sparks (Oxford, 1984), 81.

34. T. J. Talley, "De la 'berakah' à l'eucharistie: Une question à réexaminer," *LMD* 125 (1976):11–39.

35. C. Giraudo, *La struttura letteraria della preghiera eucaristica. Saggo sulla genesi letteraria di una forma: Toda veterotestamentaria, Beraka giudaica, Anafora cristiana* (Analecta biblica 92; Rome, 1981), 3.

36. Our concern is, in fact, to show the connection between the earliest texts and how the origin of the form and structures of later anaphoras can be explained in light of this connection.

37. X. Léon-Dufour, *Le partage du pain eucharistique selon le Nouveau Testament* (Paris, 1982), 345ff. (see 103ff. and 161ff.). The subject is treated here with great care and precision.

38. See L. Ligier, "Textus liturgiae Tudaeorum," in Hänggi-Pahl 5ff., 15.

39. 1 Cor 10:16.

40. Hänggi-Pahl 9ff.

41. We refer you to the three classic works: I. Elbogen, *Der jüdische Gottesdienst in seiner geschichtlichen Entwicklung* (Hildesheim, 1962); J. Heinemann, *Prayer in the Talmud: Forms and Patterns*, trans. R. S. Sarason (Studia Judaica: Forschungen zur Wissenschaft des Judentums 9; Berlin-New York, 1977); and L. A. Hoffman, *The Canonization of the Synagogue Service* (Notre Dame, IN, 1979).

42. The *Seder* of Rav Amraan Gaon I is from the ninth century and the *Siddur* of Rav Saadia Gaon is from the tenth; see Hänggi-Pahl 10.

43. For example, a fragment of the *Birkat ha-mazon* was discovered during the excavations at Dura Europos; see C. B. Wells, R. O. Fink, and J. F. Gilliam, *The Excavations at Doura Europos. Final Report* V, Part I (New Haven, 1959), 74–75.

44. L. Finkelstein, "The Birkat ha-mazon," *Jewish Quarterly Review* 19 (1928–29): 211–62.

45. More details will be given in Chap. Four when examining the second anaphora of the new Missal.

46. *Jubilees* 22, 6–9 (*The Apocryphal Old Testament* [n. 33], 71).

47. Giraudo 249.

48. E. Mazza, "Didache IX–X: Elementi per una interpretazione eucaristica," *EL* 92 (1978): 393–419.

49. We have analyzed the Anaphora of Hippolytus along these lines in *EL* 97 (1983): 409–81.

50. See J. Doresse and E. Lanne, *Un témoin archäique de la liturgie copte de S. Basile,* with an Appendix by B. Capelle, "Les liturgies basiliennes et saint Basile" (Louvain, 1960).

51. Hänggi-Pahl 81–94.

52. Funk 1:410–14.

53. In *Didache* 9 there are: (1) the eucharist over the cup; (2) the eucharist over the bread; and (3) the prayer for the unity of the Church.

54. Funk 1:412.

55. See E. Mazza, "La *Gratiarum actio mystica* del libro VII delle *Costituzioni apostoliche.* Una tappa nella storia della anafora eucaristica," *EL* 93 (1979): 123–37.

288

56. See E. Mazza, "L'anafora di Serapione: Une ipotesi di interpretazione," *EL* 95 (1981): 510–28.

57. Hänggi-Pahl 224; to be considered together with the Anaphora of the Twelve Apostles (ibid., 265).

58. H. W. Beyer, "*Eulogeō*," *TDNT* 2:762.

59. We cannot accept Beyer's view of the relation between this prayer and the Our Father, since the latter expresses the relation of the disciples to the Father, not that of Jesus himself. The Our Father represents the teaching of Jesus on how the disciples should pray, and does not convey his own way of praying.

60. *Didache* 10, 2.

61. We have shown this derivation especially in our article on the Anaphora of Hippolytus in *EL* 97 (1983): 409–81.

62. If the Last Supper had been a Passover meal, repetition of it would have been an added difficulty: since the Passover is an annual rite, how could it have been celebrated every Sunday or even at every "breaking of bread"? The Church would have faced a complex problem.

The *Birkat ha-mazon* for Passover is not very different from that of any Jewish meal: it is simply somewhat enriched. We may think that every thanksgiving after eating was influenced by Christ's command: "Do this in memory of me."

The anamnesis of every prayer was altered in a Christocentric direction and, therefore, every meal taken by the disciples echoed the Last Supper of Jesus and resembled the model he had given. Certainly the Easter meal which the disciples celebrated annually was in a special relationship to the Last Supper, but that did not mean that Jesus' command was not obeyed in every eucharistic liturgy.

63. The most classic and best known example of such a statement by theologians is that of Thomas Aquinas, *Summa theologiae* III, 50, 1c. Thomas appeals to Augustine who had explained sacraments as "sacred signs" (*De civ. Dei* X, 5 [PL 41:282]).

64. For this terminology of "functives" and "sign-function" (rather than "sign"), see U. Eco, *A Theory of Semiotics* (Bloomington, 1976), 48ff.

65. Here is a passage that will help us locate the Last Supper in the world of signs as developed by U. Eco: "A sign-function is realized when two *functives* (expression and content) enter into a mutual correlation; the same functive can also enter into another correlation, thus becoming a different functive and, therefore, giving rise to a new sign-function. Thus, signs are the provisional result of coding rules which establish *transitory* correlations of elements, each of these elements being entitled to enter—under given coded circumstances—into another correlation and thus form a new sign. . . . One can thus say that it is not true that a code organizes signs; it is more correct to say that codes provide the rules which *generate* signs as concrete occurrences in communicative intercourse" (ibid., 49).

EXCURSUS

1. "Concelebration whereby the unity of the priesthood is appropriately manifested has remained in use to this day in the Church both in the East and in the West" (*VSC* 57; Flannery 19; Latin text in Alberigo 831).

2. This expression describes the actual practice of concelebration rather than the norm, since the Missal says that the concelebrants are to speak their parts "in a low voice (*submissa voce*) and in such a way that the voice of the celebrant is clearly heard by all the people, who should be able to understand the texts easily" (*GIRM* 170).

3. Andrieu, *OR* 2:131.

4. *OR* I belongs to the first half of the eighth century; *OR* III is a supplement to *OR* I, but composed for a special occasion, so that its date cannot be closely determined. The document as a whole was completed before the end of the eighth century; the first part, which contains the rubric for concelebration, may be regarded as contemporary with *OR* I (Andrieu, *OR* 2:127 and 51).

5. Hippolytus, *Traditio apostolica* 4 (Botte 11).

6. Two recensions of this *Ordo* have come down to us. Ms. Sangallense 614 is the only ms giving the short or older recension. It says: "When they have finished, the pontiff alone arises for the Canon (*surgit pontifex solus in canone*)." The long recension is identical at this point, except that it adds "and enters (*et intrat*): the pontiff arises alone and enters into the canon" (Andrieu, *OR* 2:95, no. 88).

7. Ibid., 2:131, no. 1.

8. See ibid., 2:96, no. 91, note a.

9. The time is a little after *Ordo* III: the last decades of the eighth century but not later than 800 (ibid., 2:136).

10. Ibid., 2:163, no. 52.

11. *Ordo* III was known to the compilers of *Ordo* IV, and there are no traces in it of this rubric on concelebration, as Andrieu, *OR* 2:140 notes.

12. See B. Neunheuser, "La concelebrazione nella Chiesa occidentale," in *Concelebrazione. Dottrina e pastorale* (Brescia, 1965), 9: "It must be said that the already existent unity of priestly action sought still clearer expression in a sharing of the spoken word."–Same interpretation in B. Botte, "Note historique sur la concélébration dans l'Eglise ancienne," *LMD* 35 (1953): 20.

13. Andrieu, *PR* 2:365, no. 34.

14. Ibid., 2:349, no. 34.

15. E. Dekkers, "La concélébration. Tradition ou nouveauté?" in *Mélanges liturgiques offerts au R. P. Bernard Botte* (Louvain, 1972), 112.

16. A. Franquesa, "La concelebración a los 16 años de su restauración," in P. Jounel, R. Kaczynski, and G. Pasqualetti, eds., *Liturgia opera divina e umana (Studi in onore di A. Bugnini)* (Brescia, 1965), 187.

17. A. Franquesa, "La concelebrazione nelle communità sacerdotali," in *Concelebrazione* (n. 12), 187.

18. See B. Botte, *Le mouvement liturgique. Témoignages et souvenirs* (Paris, 1973), 106–9.

19. B. Botte, "Note historique" (n. 12), 9–23; A. Raes, "La concélébration eucharistique dans les rites orientaux," ibid., 24–47.

20. Botte, *Le mouvement liturgique,* 107–9.

21. Address of September 22, 1956. For the point in question, see *AAS* 48 (1956): 718.

22. E. Lanne, "La concelebrazione nella tradizione delle Chiese orientali," in *Concelebrazione* (n. 12), 31.

23. E. Dekkers, "La concélébration" (n. 15), 109.

24. Lanne, ibid., 18.

25. *VSC* 57, 1.

26. Lanne, ibid., 21.

27. Ibid., 20.

28. Ibid.

29. GIRM 153.

30. R. Taft, "Praise in the Desert: The Coptic Monastic Office Yesterday and Today," *Wor* 56 (1982): 536; see the same author's "*Ex Oriente lux* ? Some Reflexions on

Eucharistic Celebration," *Wor* 54 (1980): 308–25; and "The Frequency of the Eucharist Throughout History," in M. Collins and D. Power, eds., *Can We Always Celebrate the Eucharist?* (Concilium 152; New York, 1982).

31. GIRM 153.

32. See the 1965 Decree *Ecclesia semper* on the Rite of Concelebration and of Communion under Both Kinds (*DOL* no. 1792).

33. It is the moment of communion that manifests this equality, this horizontal unity among priests (Lanne, ibid. [n. 22], 25).

34. Ibid., 19.

35. Botte,"Note historique" (n. 12) 21.

36. See above, n. 17.

CHAPTER TWO

1. Jungmann 2:106–7 and n. 36. For the *Hanc igitur* at the consecration of a bishop, see *Gr* 25; for the formula for the blessing of grapes during the Canon, ibid., 630; for the *Communicantes* of the Mass *in cena Domini*, ibid., 330, in the apparatus (reference to ms. Ottoboni lat. 313 in the Vatican Library).

2. Jungmann 2:107, n. 37.

3. Ibid. 2:107. We do not understand why Jungmann says "before the whole assembly" instead of "before God."

4. C. Mohrmann, "Sur l'histoire de *praefari-praefatio*," in her *Etudes sur le latin des chrétiens* 3 (Rome, 1965), 292f.

5. Ibid., 293.

6. Ibid., 295–96.

7. Ibid., 297.

8. "Summing up the results of these preliminary studies, we may say that all the texts in which *praefari* is used without any definite sense of anteriority are relatively late: *praefari = pronunce* is due to a secondary development. . . . In religious language it is chiefly the verb *praefari* that acquires a technical meaning; when the substantive *praefatio* occurs, it is usually a true *nomen actionis*" (ibid., 298–99).

9. Cyprian, *De dominica oratione* 31 (CCL 3A:109). It is clear that the word *praefatio* here has no suggestion of anteriority, since the indication of temporal position is conveyed by the words "before the [eucharistic] prayer."

10. See, e.g., the exorcism of the oil of catechumens in *Gel* 617. On this point we disagree with Mohrmann who regards this case as completely different from the preceding.

11. *Ep. de castitate* (cited in Mohrmann 301f.).

12. Andrieu, *OR* 2:433.

13. Ibid., 2:437.

14. Mohrmann 303.

15. *Gr* 1515. In its notice that Pope Gelasius "composed prefaces and prayers for the mysteries (*sacramentorum prefationes et orationes*)," the *Liber pontificalis* seems not to give the word *prefatio* a technical sense since it puts *sacramenta* in the genitive plural; see Duchesne, *LP* 1:255.

16. E. Dekkers, "*Propheteia-Praefatio*," in *Mélanges C. Mohrmann* (Utrecht, 1963), 190. We had already completed our research of the question when we became aware of Dekker's article, which is now included in our discussion. Using practically the same texts, we had reached the same conslusion independently. This coincidence confirms the validity of the approach taken.

17. Augustine, *C. Faust.* XIII, 1 (PL 42:281).

18. Isidore, *Etymolog.* VII, 8 (PL 8:283)

19. Tertullian, *Apol.* 18, 5 (CCL 1:118). We need to bear in mind how widely known this work was in the early Church.

20. Dekkers 193.

21. W. Rordorf, "The *Didache,* " in R. Johanny, et al., *The Eucharist of the Early Christians,* trans. M. J. O'Connell (New York, 1978), 6.

22. *Didache* 10, 7; see W. Rordorf and A. Tuillier, eds., *La doctrine des douze apôtres* (SC 24; Paris, 1978), 182.

23. *Didache* 9, 1 (SC 248:174). The noun *eucharistia* may here refer either to the text of the thanksgiving or to the entire celebration. In Justin, the noun refers without any doubt to the formulary of thanksgiving (*Apol. I* 67, 5; Hänggi-Pahl 70). The mention of Justin is especially relevant since he, like the *Didache,* is still in the period of textual improvisation and creativity. The president is to pray as best he can; in this respect, he is certainly the heir of the "prophets," and the Eucharist is an act of prophecy. We should bear in mind that "already in the Old Testament the prophets are great men of prayer. . . . In primitive Christianity, too, there is a direct connection between prayer and prophecy, for both are in a special sense works of the Spirit. . . . Prophecy and prayer are not the same, but they belong very closely together" (G. Friedrich, "*Prophētēs,*" *TDNT* 6:852–53).

24. After the Montanist crisis, prophecy seems to have become alien to the ecclesial body. Against this background, E. Cothenet shows that there can be no opposition in principle between prophetism and the institutional Church; see the interesting conclusions in his article, "Prophétisme," *DBS* 8:1335–36.

25. *Constitutiones Apostolorum* VII, 26, 6 (Funk 1:414).

26. Tertullian, *De exhort. cast.* 7, 3 (CCL 2:1024f.).

27. *Didache* 13, 3 (see SC 248:190).

28. Ibid, 15, 1 (SC 248:192). The passage strongly underscores the fact that the liturgy which had been celebrated by prophets was now celebrated by bishops and deacons. This would mean that the priestly role of the prophets passed to their direct heirs, the bishops and deacons (at this period the function of the deacon was not what it is today, but closely resembled that of the bishop; see Acts 6:2–6; 8:5–40; 21:8f.).

29. *Didache* 15, 2 (SC 248:194).

30. Tertullian, *De exhort. cast.* 7, 4 (CCL 2:1025).

31. Ibid., 7, 3 (ibid.).

32. Ibid., 7, 5 (ibid.).

33. For the comparison to be fully relevant, we would have to say, instead of "a varying one," a text marked by "free composition" or by parts in which creative freedom is exercised. But, in a liturgy dominated by fixed texts, such as the Roman liturgy became, there was no such thing as free composition, i.e., on the part of the celebrant. All texts were determined in advance; the only difference was that for some of the predetermined texts there were no alternatives, while for others there were alternatives depending on the liturgical season. In such circumstances, the only creativity allowed was in the "variable" parts, where one text could be replaced by another that was, however, no less determined in advance.

34. We are certainly not saying that the Roman preface is simply an introduction to the Canon. Without thanksgiving there is no eucharistic prayer; the preface is, therefore, a necessary part of the Canon if the latter is to be in fact a eucharistic prayer.

35. See the passages from Cyprian and the *LP* that are cited in Jungmann 2:102, n. 6.

36. "Be thankful (*eucharistoi ginesthe*)" (Col 3:15).

37. Eph 5:20. See also Col 3:17: "And whatever you do in word or deed, do everything in the name of the Lord Jesus, giving thanks to God the Father through him."

38. 2 Cor 9:11–12.

39. Botte-Mohrmann 74, n. 1.

40. *Aequum,* along with *iustum est,* appears in the acclamations at the election of the emperor in 237 and 238 (Botte-Mohrmann 74, note a).

41. See Chap. Six, on the Fourth Eucharistic Prayer.

42. In Christian Latin, words borrowed from the language of law even replaced the more usual words of everyday speech and, being more solemn, lost something of the realism of the latter. Thus, *iustitia,* which is found even in the scriptures, is sometimes replaced by the more solemn *aequitas;* see C. Mohrmann, "Notes sur le latin liturgique," in her *Etudes sur le latin des chrétiens* 2 (Rome, 1961), 105.

43. P. Frabre, "La religion romaine," in M. Brillant and R. Aigrain, eds., *Histoire des religions* 3 (Paris, 1955), 406.

44. Ibid., 359.

45. T. Corbishley, "La religione dei romani," in F. König, ed., *Cristo e le religioni del mondo* (Turin, 1967), 121.

46. 2 Cor 4:15.

47. We must bear in mind that precisely in this part of the text the anaphora itself is a profession of faith.

48. Rom 10:10 (JB).

49. J.-P. Audet, *La Didachè. Instruction des apôtres* (Paris, 1958), 381. See also E. Lanne, "La liturgia eucaristica in oriente e in occidente," in the collective work, *Liturgia e vita* (Turin, 1980), 25–28.

50. The Latin Missal of 1969 has 82 prefaces; the Missal of 1975 adds four more. The English Missal (1974) has 84.

51. M. Mauss, *The Gift. Forms and Functions of Exchange in Archaic Societies,* trans. I. Cunnison (New York, 1967).

52. "The potlatch, so unique as a phenomenon, . . . is really nothing other than the gift-exchange" (ibid., 33). The word "potlatch" means "gift," at least among the Chinook (41).

53. Ibid.,18.

54. "The obligation to receive . . . is no less constraining. One does not have the right to refuse a gift or a potlatch" (ibid., 39).

55. Ibid., 11.

56. "The obligation to give . . . is the essence of potlatch" (ibid., 37). This necessity can be easily translated into biblical terms: it is the necessity of the theophany as a saving event, since, if there is no theophany, human beings cannot respond to God. According to J.-L. Declais, "Mosè sul monte di Dio," in *Parola per l'assemblea festiva,* no. 13 (Brescia, 1972), 19, "a theophany is never described as though it were an end in itself; it always introduces a message, a mission, or an act of judgment."

57. Mauss 40–41.

58. In the preface of the Roman liturgy, *aequum* underscores that the human position is not one of inferiority and that the relationship with God is in balance.

59. "A gift necessarily implies the notion of credit" (ibid., 35).

60. Ibid., 37–41. Mauss sums up nicely: "If things are given and returned it is precisely because one gives and returns 'respects' and 'courtesies.' But in addition, in giving them, a man gives himself, and he does so because he owes himself—himself and his possessions—to others" (44–45).

61. Ibid., ch. 3.

62. Ibid., 36.

63. Ibid., 35.

64. "Antithetical operations are expressed by the same word" (ibid., 31).

65. To this system belong all the Roman prayers containing the word *commercium*, which is usually translated as "exchange." Here is one prayer from among many: "We celebrate, Lord, this glorious exchange: we offer to you what you have given to us, so that we may deserve to receive your very self [*Exercemus, Domine, gloriosa commercia: offerimus quae dedisti, ut te ipsum mereamur accipere: per*]" (*Ver* no. 89).

66. Mauss 10.

67. Third Anaphora of The Apostle Peter, in Hänggi-Pahl 412. There is a comparable passage in the Anaphora of the Apostles Addai and Mari, which is parallel to the Third Anaphora of the Apostle Peter; a critical edition of the latter by J. M. Sauget is in A. Raes, ed., *Anaphorae siriacae. Quotquot in codicibus adhuc repertae sunt* II, fasc. 3 (Rome, 1973), 285ff.

68. Anaphora of the Apostles Addai and Mari, in Hänggi-Pahl 377 [but, we do not find the passage here—Tr.].

69. Férotin 196.

70. The use of words from the juridical order is not due solely to the acceptance of Roman culture by the liturgy. Even the potlatch of primitive peoples shows an interdependence of religious, legal, and moral orders. See Maus 18ff., 31ff., and especially 34: "In any society it is in the nature of the gift in the end to bring its own reward." This implies a legal system that over time governs gifts and exchanges, which eventually give rise to barter and contracts (34f.) Once the concept of "obligation" (which belongs to the very nature of potlatch) acquires a place in society and in a series of many-sided relationships, it ultimately produces a legal and contractual system. On the other hand, potlatch is much more than a legal phenomenon; it is one of those phenomena which Mauss calls "total" (36).

71. Human beings are saved by grace, but this does not mean that they are completely passive in the process of justification; their active role is to be seen chiefly in the gratitude by which the gift of God is actually accepted. Gratitude finds expression in words and becomes a profession of faith. Human beings are justified by faith. If gratitude is offered to God, the human acceptance of his gift is by that very fact also offered. In the Christian Eucharist, the gestures of offering the bread that has been blessed and the cup of salvation give visible expression to this interior attitude.

72. Férotin 213.

73. Fourth Preface for Weekdays, Latin text: "*Quia cum nostra laude non egeas, tuum tamen est donum quod tibi grates rependamus, nam te non augent nostra praeconia, sed nobis proficiunt ad salutem, per Christum Dominum nostrum.*"

74. St. Clement of Rome, *Ep. ad Corinth.* 34, 6; text with French translation in A. Jaubert, ed., *Clément de Rome. Epître aux Corinthiens* (SC 167; Paris, 1971), 154–56. After the citation of Is 6:3 in combination with Dn 7:10, the passage continues: "And so we, too, being dutifully assembled with one accord, should, as with one voice, cry out to Him earnestly" (34, 7; trans. J. A. Kleist, in Ancient Christian Writers 1 [Westminster, MD, 1946], 30). The reference is certainly to a liturgical assembly since "assembled with one accord" (or "in one place") renders the Greek *epi to auto* and *synachthentes*, both of which are technical terms for the liturgical activity that has a congregation as a constitutive element. On this passage of Clement, see W. C. Van Unnik, "1 Clem. 34 and the Sanctus," *Vigiliae christianae* 5 (1951): 204–48.

75. P.-M. Gy, "Le Sanctus romain et les anaphores orientales," in *Mélanges liturgiques offerts au R. P. Bernard Botte* (Louvain, 1972), 167–74.

76. *Libellus de Spiritu sancto* IV, 2; see L. Chavoutier, "Un *Libellus* pseudoambrosien sur le saint Esprit," *SE* 11 (1960): 149. The pamphlet is certainly later than the *De Spiritu sancto* of Ambrose and earlier than the Nestorian crisis. Chavoutier gives good reasons for dating it around 400, during the debates caused in the West by Rufinus' translation (399–402) of Origen's *De principiis*.

77. Cyril of Jerusalem, *Catecheses mystagogicae* V, 6; text and French translation in A. Piédagnel, ed., *Cyrille de Jérusalem. Catéchèses mystagogiques* (SC 126; Paris, 1966), 154.

78. Theodore of Mopsuestia, *Homiliae catecheticae* 16; text and French translation in R. Tonneau and R. Devreesse, *Les homélies catéchétiques de Théodore de Mopsueste* (Vatican City, 1949), 533–49.

79. See the anaphora in the *Euchologion* of Serapion (Funk 2:174).

80. Gy, "Le Sanctus romain," 167.

81. Ibid., 169.

82. B. Botte, "*Maiestas*," in Botte-Mohrmann 111–13.

83. On the problem of the Christological or trinitarian meaning of the Sanctus, see A. Gerhards, "Le phénomène du Sanctus addressé au Christ. Son origine, sa signification, sa persistance dans les anaphores de l'Eglise d'Orient," in the collective work, *Le Christ dans la liturgie* (Rome, 1981), 65–83.

84. *Gr*, no. 1733. Other examples: the Mass of Sts. Achilles and Nereus (no. 1611); the Mass for the fourth Sunday before the octave of Easter (no. 1610); the Mass for the feast of Sts. Marcellinus and Peter (no. 1622).

85. G. Mercati, *Antiche reliquie liturgiche ambrosiane e romane. III. Con un excursus sui frammenti dogmatici ariani del Mai* (Studi e testi 7; Vatican City, 1902), 52–53; "*Per Iesum Christum Dominum, et Deum nostrum, per quem petimus et rogamus.*" Mercati points out that the words *petimus et rogamus* suggest an ensuing text like our *Te igitur*. He refuses, however, to say more than "it appears as if . . ." (see his n. 33), and he gives the reason for his uncertainty: in view of L. Duchesne's statements, it is difficult to believe that at this period the preface could have lacked a Sanctus. The text of the preface is also printed in Hänggi-Pahl 422.

86. Gregory the Great, *Ep. 12 ad Joannem Syracus. episc.* (PL 77:955–58).

CHAPTER THREE

1. Botte-Mohrmann 18.

2. C. Vagaggini, *The Canon of the Mass and Liturgical Reform*, trans. edited by P. Coughlan (Staten Island, NY, 1967), 85.

3. A. Piolanti, *Il mistero eucaristico* (Florence, 1958), 435.

4. Council of Trent, Session XXII, Cap. 4, trans. in Neuner-Dupuis, no. 1550. Latin text in DS 1745.

5. *VSC* 48: "The Church, therefore, earnestly desires that Christ's faithful, when present at this mystery of faith, should not be there as strangers or silent spectators. On the contrary, through a good understanding of the rites and prayers they should take part in the sacred action, conscious of what they are doing, with devotion and full collaboration" (Flannery 16).

6. B. Botte, *Le mouvement liturgique* (Paris, 1982), 180.

7. Ibid.

8. Vagaggini, *The Canon*, 84–107. He concluded: "Any attempt to revise the present Canon merely by way of arranging it, cutting it, or simply patching it up, will in-

evitably lead to an awful mess. And what is more, this sort of approach does not solve the problem of its intrinsic shortcomings and defects, to which we are rightly becoming more and more sensitive today" (122).

9. Ibid., 76–79.

10. Ibid., 79–83.

11. L. K. Mohlberg, ed., *Missale Gothicum* (Rome, 1961), 4, no. 4: *"Vere sanctus, vere benedictus dominus noster Iesus Christus filius tuus, manens in caelis, manifestatus in terris, ipse enim."*

12. This excision is historically justified, since the Amens were added only in the ninth century; see B. Botte, *Le canon de la messe romaine, Edition critique, introduction et notes* (Textes et études liturgiques 2; Louvain, 1935), 57. See also P. Salmon, "Les 'Amen' du canon de la messe," *EL* 42 (1928): 496–506.

13. As early as 1951, during a meeting at Maria Laach, J. A. Jungman had offered suggestions for emending the Canon and reforming its structure. One proposal was to remove the intercession for the Church and the pope from the *Te igitur*, since the same theme had already made its appearance in the prayer of the faithful; see Botte, *Le mouvement liturgique*, 178f.

14. See Bugnini, ibid., 338–41.

15. The papal answer to the Consilium is cited in J. Wagner, "Zur Reform des *Ordo Missae*. Zwei Dokumente," in P. Jounel, R. Kaczynski, and G. Pasqualetti, eds., *Liturgia opera divina e umana. Studi in onore di A. Bugnini* (Rome, 1982), 289.

16. Gregory the Great, *Ep. 12 ad Joannem Syracus* (PL 77:957). G. Morin tells us that in the writings of Gregory, a *scholasticus* is often a lawyer; he suggests that the *scholasticus* in question may have been Firmicius Maternus, author of the *Mathesis* (334–337) and later on, after becoming a Christian, of the *De errore profanarum religionum* (343–347); see G. Morin, "Die *Consultationes Zacchaei et Apollonii*," *HJ* 37 (1916): 230–266.; idem, "Depuis quand un canon fixe à Milan? Restes de ce qu'il a remplacé," *RBén* 51 (1939): 101–108. B. Capelle defended Morin's view against P. Batiffol in a review of the latter in *Bulletin d'ancienne littérature chrétienne* 1 (1921–28): 53.

17. Sure evidence is not easy to find. We do know, for example, that the inscriptions on papal tombs are in Latin beginning with that of Pope Cornelius (d. 253); see Jungmann 1:50.

18. Ambrosiaster cites: "that which your great priest Melchisedech offered to you, a holy sacrifice and a spotless victim." He argues that "great" or "high" (*summus*) refers to God, not to Melchisedech; this would in fact be a possibility in the Greek text. See Ambrosiaster, *Quaestiones Veteris et Novi Testamenti* 109; *De Melchisedec* (PL 35:2329).

19. *LP* 1:239.

20. Jungmann 1:55.

21. Ambrose, *De sacramentis* IV, 21–227; see B. Botte, ed., *Ambroise de Milan. Des sacrements; De mystères* (SC 25bis; Paris, 1961), 114–116.

22. When the differences between the two documents are viewed in this perspective, it must be admitted that the *De sacramentis* is a valuable witness to the extraordinary fixity of the Roman Canon.

23. C. Callewaert, "Histoire positive du canon romain," *SE* 2 (1949): 103–110. C. Mohrmann offers important linguistic and stylistic observations in her *Etudes sur le latin des chrétiens* 3 (Rome, 1965), 227–244.

24. In the ms, this title is from another hand. See L. Eizenhöfer, ed., *Canon missae romanae, Pars prior. Traditio textus* (Rome, 1954), 25; G. F. Warner, ed., *The Stowe Missal* (London, 1905–1916).

25. Ambrose, *De sacramentis* III, 5 (SC 25bis:94). See G. Morin, "Depuis quand un canon fixe à Milan? Restes de ce qu'il a remplacé," *RBén* 51 (1939): 101–108. For a discussion of the entire question, see P. Borella, "La messa ambrosiana," in Righetti 3:659–661.

26. The prayer says: ". . . which is a *figura* of the Lord's body and blood" (*De sac.* IV, 21 [SC 25bis:114]), whereas the catechesis uses the word *similitudo* (ibid., IV, 20 [SC 25bis:112]). But when Ambrose coins a technical term to express the transformation of the bread and wine, he takes the liturgical text as his point of reference and derives *transfigurare* from *figura* (*De fide* IV, 10, 124 [CSEL 78:201]). On the meaning of this term, see R. Johanny, *L'eucharistie centre du salut chez saint Ambroise de Milan* (Paris, 1968), 97–104.

27. B. Botte regards the *igitur* as unimportant, since "in fourth-century Latin *igitur* is no stronger than the Greek *de*" (Botte-Mohrmann 75, n. 9). We think Jungmann is correct in saying that "it is the same *igitur* which forms the transition between the first section of the Holy Saturday *Exultet*, the *laus cerei*, with the oblation that follows" (Jungmann 2:148–149).

28. The word *commendatio* is equivalent to *recommendatio* and is the technical term for a prayer that asks the acceptance of a sacrifice. It seems clearly to originate in the letter which Pope Innocent I wrote in 416 to Decentius, bishop of Gubbio: "Above all, the offerings are to be recommended (*commendandae*) and then the names of those who have supplied the offerings are to be read" (PL 20:533f.).

29. Righetti 3:370.

30. Jungmann 2:150.

31. Botte-Mohrmann 74, note e.

32. Latin: "*ut accepta habeas et benedicas haec dona, haec munera, haec sancta sacrificia illibata.*"

33. Andrieu, *OR 2:*

34. J. Brinktrine, *Die heilige Messe* (Paderborn, 1931), 155.

35. Hänggi-Pahl 108.

36. It was a very ancient custom to bring and therefore also to offer, in addition to bread and wine, various other gifts such as first fruits, oil, and cheese; see Hippolytus, *Traditio apostolica* 51 (Botte 18).

37. C. Mohrmann, "*Illibatus*," in Botte-Mohrmann 115.

38. Gn 4:4–5.

39. Samuel says that God rejects the outward worship of those who disobey him (1 Sm 15:22); Amos (5:21–26) and Isaiah (1:11–20; 29:13) say the same. In the very temple itself, Jeremiah openly asserts the emptiness of the cult celebrated there and denounces the corruption of hearts (7:4–12, 21ff.).

40. Justice "is more acceptable to God than the offering of sacrifices (*hostias*)" (Prv 16:5 Vg.). The expression "*accepta habeas*" in the *Te igitur* is paralleled in Tb 12:5 (Vg.): "They asked him [Raphael] to accept (*acceptam habere*) half of all that they had brought back."

41. A Georgian document of the tenth century contains a translation of the Roman Canon into which it inserts an epicletic, pneumatological section; there is no evidence that this represents a correct interpretation of the original meaning of the Canon. According to this interpolation, the divine acceptance takes the form of the sending of the Spirit. For the Georgian text, see H. W. Codrington, *The Liturgy of St. Peter* (Munster, 1936), 158.

42. See the *Deprecatio Gelasii* (in *EEFL*, p. 476, no. 742) or the great prayer of intercession in the Gallican liturgy for Good Friday (ibid., p. 1026, no. 2355). Here is the

text used in the Roman Good Friday liturgy: "that our God and Lord will bestow peace on his holy Church, preserve her unity and protect her throughout the world (*ut etiam Deus et dominus noster pacificare, adunare, et custodire dignetur per universum orbem terrarum*)" (*Gel*, no. 400).

43. See, e.g., *Didache* 9, 4; 10, 5 (SC 248:176 and 180); *Constitutiones Apostoloroum* VII, 25, 3 and 26, 4 (Funk 1:410–414); Strasbourg Papyrus (Hänggi-Pahl 116); Anaphora of Hippolytus (Hänggi-Pahl 81).

44. Botte-Mohrmann 75, n. 11.

45. E. Lanne, "L'Eglise une dans la prière eucharistique," *Irén* 50 (1977): 514. See also J. Gribomont, "*Ecclesiam adunare*," *RTAM* 27 (1970): 20.

46. Thus, B. Capelle, "*Et omnibus orthodoxis atque apostolicae fidei cultoribus*," in *Miscellanea historica Alberti de Meyer* 1 (Louvain, 1946), 137–50; reprinted in Capelle, *Travaux liturgiques* 2 (Louvain, 1962), 261.

47. Ibid., 262.

48. Botte-Mohrmann 77, n. 2.

49. *Ibid*. B. Capelle adds that *fidei* (or *religionis*) *cultor* implies an active zeal for the faith against heterodox deviations. This implication also helps date the text to the period of the great heresies (Capelle, "*Et omnibus orthodoxis . . .*" [n. 46], 267).

50. See P. Labriolle, "*Papa*," *Bulletin du Cange* 4 (1928): 65–75.

51. It is difficult to determine the date when this happened. Jungmann notes (2:156, n. 25) that the ms of the older Gelasian Sacramentary (first half of the eighth century?) have *et antistite nostro illo episcopo*.

52. The Sacred Congregation for Divine Worship in its decree *Cum de nomine* of October 9, 1972 (*DOL* 247, nos. 1970–1974) gives a list of those who must or may be mentioned. The following *must* be mentioned: (a) the bishop of the diocese; (b) a bishop who has been transferred to another see but retains administration of his former diocese; (c) an apostolic administrator (whether the see is vacant or not), with a temporary or a permanent appointment, if he is a bishop and exercises his office fully, especially in spiritual matters; (d) a vicar and prefact apostolic; (e) a prelate and an abbot *nullius* having jurisdiction over a territory not attached to any diocese. The following *may* be mentioned: coadjutor bishops, auxiliary bishops, and other bishops who really help the Ordinary to govern the diocese.

53. The words are already in *Didache* 10, 5 (mnēsthēti kyrie tēs ekklēsias sou) and in the following anaphoras: Mark (see also Strasbourg Papyrus gr. 254), Basil (Byzantine), John Chrysostom (Greek), James (Greek), and Gregory of Nazianzus (Alexandrian). While the Anaphoras of Basil and Gregory retain the archaic "Remember your Church," the other texts agree with the Roman Canon in speaking of "offering for" the Church, while "remembering" those who are to be specially mentioned in the eucharistic celebration (for the texts, see Hänggi-Pahl 66, 102, 116, 228, 238, 250–252, and 366–368).

54. See F. Cabrol, "Diptyches," *DACL* 4/1:1045–1094. See also Righetti 3:373f.

55. The Latin has *famulorum famularumque tuarum* ("your servants and handmaidens"), a phrase attested in Dt 12:12: "you and your sons and your daughters, your menservants and your maidservants [*famuli et famulae* in the Vulgate]." "Servant" (Latin: *famulus*) is the usual title given to Moses (Jos 1:13, 15; 8:31, 33; 11:12). The implication of the word becomes clear in Heb 3:5 where Moses is again called "servant," but with the significant addition of "faithful." In the Roman Canon, the mention of servants is immediately followed by a reference to their faith which is known to God; we can, therefore, conclude that here, as in the case of Moses, fidelity to God is the specific characteristic of a "servant." We should bear in mind that

famulus, unlike the Greek *Pais*, never refers to the children of the family but only to the servants (Greek: *doulos*); see Botte-Mohrmann 77, n. 3. Saul's immediate followers are called his *douloi* (Latin: *servi*), and the term applies even to Saul himself until he becomes king. All of the people have an obligation to *doulein* (*servire*) the king. 1 Kgs 12:7 has an interesting play on words: Rehoboam, the new king, is advised to be a *doulos* (servant) of the people; if he is, he will be assured of receiving in return a willing and spontaneous *douleia* (service). Perhaps we may give this passage a typological interpretation and see it as referring to Jesus who at the Last Supper acts as a *doulos* by washing the feet of his disciples, who must in their turn act as *douloi* (but the parallel must not be pushed too far). In the LXX, the word *doulos* is always used of the relation between subjects or subalternates to the sovereign, whereas *doulos* and its derivatives never express a comparable relationship of the sovereign to his subjects. This means that the words, in their transferred sense, usually presume the acceptance, free or forced, of the claim of another to dominion. It is clear that in these circumstances the proven ability to make the claim effective is extremely important. See K. H. Rengstorf, *"Doulos," TDNT* 2:261–280.

56. See Jerome, *In Jeremiam* II, cap. 11, v. 15, no. 16 (PL 24:755): "Then comes the public recitation of the names of the offerers; here the celebration that is a ransom for sin turns into a commendation of sinners." The text dates from about 420, but the custom must be older since Jerome had uttered the same complaint in 411 in his *In Ezechielem* VI, cap. 18, v. 5, nos. 6ff. (PL 25:175). We owe these references to Father Jean Gribomont.

57. See below, Chap. Five, on the Third Eucharistic Prayer of the Missal.

58. The identification of *vota* and *sacrificium laudis* is also suggested by this passage from Cassiodorus, *In Psalmos* 65, 3 (PL 70:456): "I will proclaim my promises [*vota mea*] to you; that is, I will continually sing your praises [*laudes tuas*] and will constantly utter [*edicam*] a hymn to your mercy, together with the angels and powers, the thrones and dominations." The same juxtaposition is also in Augustine, *Enarr. in ps*. 49, 21 (PL 36:578): "Offer to God the sacrifice of praise [*sacrificium laudis*] and present your prayers [*preces tuas*] to the Most High." The basis for the coupling of the two is certainly to be found in Ps 49:14 Vg, which reads *"Immola Deo sacrificium laudis et redde Altissimo vota tua."*

59. Righetti 3:375.

60. See Cyprian, *De mortalitate* 26 (CCL 3A:31): "The throng in Paradise . . . sure of their safety [*de incolumitate sua*]."

61. In the Codex Ottobonianus 313 (Gregorian Sacramentary). See *Gr*, p. 87, n. 6 of the critical apparatus.

62. See *Gel*, no. 195: "In the Canon, after the words: 'Be mindful [*memento*], O Lord, of your servants and handmaidens [*famulorum famularumque tuarum*] who will take charge of your chosen ones for the holy grace of baptism, and of all here present,' you stop speaking, and the names of the men and women who will assume this responsibility are read. Then you continue: 'whose faith is known to you.' "

63. In the collective work *Anamnesi. Eucaristia. Teologia e storia della celebrazione* 3 (Casale Monferrato, 1983), 243.

64. Jungmann 2:171. The difficulty was felt both in the East and in the West as can be seen from a letter of Pope Leo to Anatolius, Bishop of Constantinople (*Ep*. 80, 3 [PL 54:914–915]).

65. Pope John XXIII had such devotion to his own patron, Joseph, that he appointed him patron of the Council and introduced his name into the Canon: "May the Immaculate Virgin be ever with us, and Joseph, her most chaste spouse and the

patron of the Ecumenical Council, whose name will from this day forward shine [*refulget*] in the Canon of the Mass" (Address at the Closing of the First Session of the Council, December 8, 1962); the text is in *Acta synodalia Concilii oecumenici Vaticani II*, Vol. I, Periodus I, Pars IV (Rome, 1971), 648. The authoritative decree of the Congregation of Rites, *De S. Ioseph nomine Canoni Missae inserendo*, was dated November 13, 1962 and published in *AAS* 54 (1962): 873.

66. Christmas and its octave, Epiphany, Holy Thursday, Vigil of Easter to the Second Sunday of Easter, Ascension, Pentecost.

67. For an appraisal of the practice, see Jungmann 2:177f.

68. See what was said earlier about the *Te igitur*.

69. The example Jungmann gives is the *Hanc igitur* of the scrutinial Mass on the third Sunday of Lent, to which reference was made above in n. 62.

70. *LP* 1:312; see also n. 5 there.—The same passage of the Mass is recorded in Bede's *Historia ecclesiastica* II, 1, but instead of "etc." the rest of the text is given, that is, "spare us from eternal damnation and help us to be numbered among those whom you have chosen" (PL 95:80).

71. I.e., the words *"nos servi tui, sed et plebs tua sancta."* On the whole question of the *Hanc igitur*, see also S. Marsili, "Per la storia del Canone. '*Hanc igitur oblationem*,' " *RivLit* 23 (1936): 146–150; idem, "Nota sull'*Hanc igitur* del giovedì santo," *RivLit* 24 (1937): 60–62.

72. It is difficult to determine why Pope Gregory revised this prayer; perhaps it was to introduce order into the practice of embolisms (the Verona Sacramentary has over fifty), so that the *Hanc igitur* might end with a general intention which is suited to the entire community and with an emphasis on the ultimate intention for which human beings pray, namely, their admission into the flock of the elect.

73. *Ver*, no. 958.

74. Note the justified prudence with which L. Della Torre reports this interpretation in his *Pregare l'eucaristia* (Brescia, 1982), 81.

75. See W. Grundmann, "*Dynamis*," *TDNT* 2:312: "As power and might belong essentially to Christ [who is the Christ precisely because he possesses the power of God], the concept of power is linked indissolubly with that of Spirit." A typical passage is 1 Cor 2:5, where the Spirit is the "power of God."

76. "Grant us . . . that this offering may be approved, spiritual, pleasing, because it is a figure of the body and blood of our Lord Jesus Christ." Latin: *"Fac nobis . . . hanc oblationem scriptam, rationabilem, acceptabilem, quod est figura corporis et sanguinis Domini nostri Iesu Christi"* (*De sacramentis* V, 21 [SC 25bis:114]).

77. "Deign to make blessed, ratified, and spiritual their offering which is the image and likeness of the body and blood of Jesus Christ your Son and our redeemer." To facilitate a comparison with Ambrose, here is the Latin original: *"Quorum oblationem benedictam, ratam, rationabilemque facere digneris que est imago et similitudo corporis et sanguinis Ihesu Christ Filii tui ac Redemptoris nostri."* The prayer is the *Post pridie* of the Mass for "those who offer their promises to the Lord on the anniversary of the martyrs"; text in Férotin, *Le Liber ordinum en usage dans l'Eglise wisigothique et mozarabe d'Espagne du cinquième au onzième siècle* (Paris, 1904), 322. The same text occurs again in the Mass for the Fifteenth Sunday *de quotidiano*; see Férotin, *Liber mozarabicus*, 641.

78. There is a general consensus on this point, and it is no longer necessary to offer proof. In Ambrose, the prayer asks that the offering become *scriptam, rationabilem, acceptabilem*, while the prayer in the Spanish liturgy asks that it be *benedictam, ratam, rationabilemque*. Both use three adjectives, and the only one used by both is *rationabilis*. Moreover, the place of this word differs in the two: it is second in Am-

brose but last in the *Liber ordinum*. It can be said that both documents expand upon their common source, which contained at least the adjective *rationabilis*.

Instead of three adjectives, the Roman Canon has five: *benedictam, adscriptam, ratam, rationabilem, acceptabilemque*. It has simply combined those used by Ambrose and the Spanish book. Here in parallel columns are the three adjectives used by each of these two documents, with the common term *rationabilis* on the same line:

	benedictam
scriptam	
	ratam
rationabilem	*rationabilemque*
acceptabilem	

The columns show a sequence of five adjectives that is identical with that found in the Roman Canon, which has therefore simply combined the two original texts without any concern to revise their terms. The Latin *facere digneris* ("be pleased to make") in the Canon is closer to the *Liber ordinum*, but *quam oblationem* seems closer to Ambrose. It is impossible to tell from the rest of the text whether the writer of the prayer in the Canon was giving priority to Ambrose over the Spanish text or vice versa. He seems to have regarded both as traditional sources and to have respected both equally.

79. For the better known data, see A. Wilmart, *"Transfigurare," Bulletin d'ancienne littérature et d'archéologie chrétienne* 1 (1911): 282–292 (an article still full of interest); V. Saxer, *"Figura corporis et sanguinis Domini," Rivista di archeologia cristiana* 49 (1971): 65–89; idem, "Tertullian," in R. Johanny, ed., *The Eucharist of the Early Christians*, trans. M. J. O'Connell (New York, 1978), 132–155.

80. See A. Gerken, *Teologia dell'eucaristia* (Alba, 1977), 69–80.

81. In his commentary on the text in question, Ambrose uses language and concepts closer to our own than to the text on which he is commenting. He has already left behind the earlier patristic theology of the sacrament as *figura* (even though he uses the term) and moved increasingly in the direction of what would become our modern theology, which is substantially identical with that of the great Scholastics. On the use of this vocabulary in Ambrose, see Johanny (n. 26), 97ff.

82. We shall not discuss the question of whether the concepts of *oblatio* and *sacrificium* are identical, as they are usually said to be. Nor shall we take a position on the subject, since it has not been studied sufficiently to allow certainty.

83. See Chap. Nine, section IIIC.

84. On the question of whether or not a first epiclesis is required in the anaphora, see also Chap. Eight, at the beginning of section VA.

85. We are not interested in inquiring whether this approach to translation is legitimate, since the very concept of "liturgy in translation" is under review. This much can be said: it is not possible to recover the original Latin by way of the Italian translation; this means that the latter is no longer a translation but an interpretation.

Some may respond to our remark by saying that if we were forced to translate the Canon without alterations, such as the one in question, none of the faithful would be able to grasp anything of it; in fact, the entire language and theology of the Canon are too far removed from the people of our day. Perhaps, then, the correct position is that what is untranslatable should not be translated.

All this shows how difficult it is to translate the Canon. One point may be added. The difficulty is so great, that a translator is constantly forced to make choices among the various possible versions; all of them are legitimate, yet they differ greatly among themselves since one translator gives a privileged status to one element, another to another. This being so, only one course is open: to establish a criterion of choice for oneself. This has been done—but is the criterion correct? The question is naive since every criterion necessarily chooses one point of view from among many, thereby excluding others; if this were not the case, it would not have been necessary to choose a criterion at all.

86. Botte-Mohrmann 117–122

87. The particle -que is never used with a longer series of words, as it would have been in classical Latin; in this case, -que is replaced by et (ibid., 120).

88. "Acceptable" and "spiritual" also occur together in 1 Pt 2:5: "spiritual sacrifices acceptable to God [spirituales hostias acceptabiles Deo]."

89. A similar interpretation, though reached by a different route, is given by J. B. Reus, "De natura orationis canonis: Quam oblationem," EL 58 (1944): 23–41.

90. We use the word "sacrifice" to mean "cultic or ritual sacrifice" and not "renunciation," "mortification," etc.

91. In the rest of this section, we are indebted to R. J. Daly, Christian Sacrifice: The Judeo-Christian Background before Origen (Washington, DC, 1978), 70–84.

92. Lv 4:31, cited in Daly 73. The latter argues on solid grounds that this verse of Leviticus is an intrusion and that therefore the distinction between "acceptance" and "propitiation" seems even more assured.

93. Ibid., 75.

94. Ibid., 76.

95. The text is notoriously corrupt, but if we take v. 7 to be in continuity with the story in vv. 4–6, that is, with the story of the sacrifice, we can conclude that right living is God's criterion for accepting sacrifices. The conclusion cannot be based on this passage alone, but flows from the entire biblical theology of the "acceptance" of sacrifice and especially from the prophetic attack on the cult (ibid., 79).

96. Eph 5:2.

97. Thus, the Roman Canon fits in nicely with the development of eucharistic doctrine in the Latin Fathers. The latter, unlike the Greek Fathers, were less interested in evolving a theory of the sacraments and preferred to focus on the real experience of the participants and on their commitment to a life that is consistent with the sacrament. Ambrose, for example, opts for "a priority of the ethical over the ontic in his teaching on the Eucharist" (Gerken [n. 80], 94).

98. If viewed in this proper framework, the petition in our Canon that God would be pleased to accept the sacrifice is a sufficient antidote to and repudiation of the defective theology that interprets the Tridentine term ex opere operato as a synonym of mechanical and unconditional efficacy.

99. Some ninth-century mss add "the venerable nativity," a variant that is not retained in the critical text. The addition is found, according to J. Deshusses, in the Sacramentary of Noyon (see Gr, no. 11, in the critical apparatus). In 1971, Deshusses dated the Sacramentary of Noyon in 870 (ibid., p. 41), but he subsequently opted for 869; see his "Chronologie des grands sacramentaires de St. Amand," RBén 87 (1977): 230–237. He also cites the Sacramentary of Essen (Gr, no. 11 in the apparatus), which dates from the first quarter of the ninth century.

The East has showed the same reserve, for few texts mention the nativity in the anamnesis. One is the Coptic Anaphora of Catholicos Gregory (d. 1285 according to E. Renaudot): "Let us rejoice and be glad at all that has been done for our salvation . . . the Annunciation that gave hope of salvation, your merciful sojourn in the womb, your birth from the Virgin, your lying in the manger, etc." (Renaudot 2:459). Such a detailed review of all that has been done for our salvation is evidently more appropriate in the opening thanksgiving (especially since Gregory's list here is preceded by words indicating praise) than in the anamnesis.

To this anaphora may be added that of Ignatius which mentions the nativity and the baptism (ibid., 2:216) and the Syriac Anaphora of Mark, which mentions the conception, the nativity, and the baptism (ibid., 2:178).

100. See A. Tarby, *La prière eucharistique de l'Eglise de Jérusalem* (Paris, 1972), 61–63.

101. See n. 99. The new eucharistic prayers of the Roman Missal add the eschatological theme, which is not part of the tradition represented by the Roman Canon. The choice of this theme is evidently the result of comparison with the liturgies of the Eastern Churches. Mention of the nativity could have been included only if it had been decided to make the eucharistic prayer a mirror of popular devotion.

102. The *De sacramentis* of Ambrose, which is the source of our present text, has: "Mindful therefore of his most glorious passion" ("*Ergo memores gloriosissimae eius passionis*"; SC 25bis:116). Even the original meaning of *unde* as indicating local motion can be fitted in here: the local motion would be figurative, and the point of departure would be the Last Supper with its institutive mandate. That is the "place" of origin of our celebration, which consists in commemorating the blessed passion, resurrection from the dead, and glorious ascension of Christ. Consequently, the objection that *unde* cannot be translated as "therefore" will not stand up to analysis.

103. Obviously through inadvertence.

104. In this case, and precisely because of its literary expression, the liturgical tradition is rich in theological meaning and value. The *unde* says that our celebration has as its norm the work of Christ at the Last Supper. From this it follows that the Eucharist of the Church is rightly called a "sacrifice" or, more accurately, a "relative sacrifice." There are two reasons for the qualification "relative": (1) its content is not new but depends entirely on the Last Supper and the words of Jesus: "Do this in memory of me," and (2) the anamnesis describes the content of the Last Supper, which consequently is also the content of the Church's Eucharist, namely, the passion and resurrection. The conclusion is unavoidable that the anamnesis should begin with a consecutive or conclusive particle such as *ergo, unde* or *igitur*.

105. This fact is not without value for the pastoral life. Pastors could well use the various Roman formulations of the anamnesis as definitions of the eucharistic celebration.

106. In his address to the International Congress at Assisi on September 22, 1956, Pius XII made himself the spokesman for this theology. After saying that "the liturgy is the work of the church in its entirety" (*AAS* 48 [1956]: 713), he went on to say: "And so the celebrating priest, who acts in the person of Christ, celebrates the sacrifice (*sacrificat*), and he alone: not the people, not the clergy . . . even though all these others can and do have an active part" (716). The Council of Trent, Session XXII, ch. 1, is much closer to the Roman Canon than is this important papal address, since Trent says that the sacrifice is "to be offered by the Church through her priests (*per sacerdotes*)" (DS 1741; Neuner-Dupuis 1546). According to Trent, therefore, the priest is only the "means" the Church uses in order to celebrate; for Pius XII he, and he alone (*isque solus*), is the celebrating subject. The difference betweeen Pius XII and Trent is clear, and it is because that "Church" had in practice become the same as "hierarchy." Then to say that Church celebrates is to say that the hierarchy, or the priest, celebrates.

107. See Vatican II, Dogmatic Constitution *Lumen gentium* on the Church, 26: "This

Church of Christ is really present in all legitimately organized local groups of the faithful, which, in so far as they are united to their pastors, are also quite appropriately called Churches in the New Testament. For these are in fact, in their own localities, the new people called by God, in the power of the Holy Spirit and as a result of full conviction" (Flannery 381; Latin in Alberigo 870).

108. For this reason, the second typical edition of the *Missale Romanum* (1975) altered the 32 passages in which, in the first edition, the term "celebrant" had been applied without qualification to the presiding priest. In the second edition, the proper term is "celebrating priest" or simply "priest." The reason for the change was given in an internal document (May 24, 1966) meant for the guidance of the experts who were charged with drafting the texts. They were told: " 'Priest' is always to be used instead of 'celebrant,' which is a holdover from the 'private' Mass. It is appropriate that the priest who presides over the assembled people should be called by his proper title and that in this way his role, which is priestly in the narrow sense, should be made clear" (Consilium, *Schemata*, no. 170, *De missali* 23, p. 1, n. 2).

In light of this development and given the objective difficulty of always maintaining care in observing these principles, it is understandable that part of the address of Pius XII cited above (n. 96) should have been taken over by Vatican II. But, the passage cited is not from the most restrictive part of the address; moreover, it is set in a broader context in Vatican II. As a result, it becomes more homogeneous with the thought of the Council and ceases to cause problems.

Also, the two theologies differ not so much in their content as in their approach to the question. One considers the Eucharist as an action of the minister; the other, without denying the competence of the various ministers, looks at the Eucharist from the vantage point of the Church and sees it as an ecclesial celebration in which the assembly is necessarily the basic constitutive sign.

109. Hippolytus, *Traditio apostolica* 35 (Botte 82).

110. See E. Cattaneo, *Il culto cristiano in occidente. Note storiche* (Rome, 1978).

111. "*Unde et memores . . . offerimus.*" In the earliest witnesses to the Canon, the sentence is constructed differently, with two coordinated verbs. See *Gel*, no. 1250: "*Unde et memores sumus, domine, nos servi tui et plebs tua sancta Christi filii tui domini dei nostri tam beatae passionis nec non et ab inferis resurrectionis sed et in caelos gloriosae ascensionis: offerimus. . . .*" From the standpoint of textual development, we see a change from "to be mindful," as a consequence of Christ's mandate, to "to offer," as the principal action called for by the mandate.

112. Irenaeus, *Adversus haereses* IV, 18, 5–6, ed. A. Rousseau, *Irénée de Lyon. Contre les hérésies* (SC 100/2; Paris, 1965), 611, 613.

113. "*De tuis donis ac datis*," parallel to the Greek "*ta sa ek tōn sōn*," which is found, e.g., in the Byzantine Anaphora of Basil (Hänggi-Pahl 236).

114. Chr 29:14; see v. 16. The text of the LXX is especially close to the phrasing found in the Greek anaphoras. It is likely that the Latin phrasing was derived from Greek liturgies and thus only indirectly from the biblical text. The passage cited from 1 Chronicles does not appear in the first volume of the *Biblia Patristica* (Paris, 1975, 216), which covers the period from the beginnings to Tertullian; nor is it cited in the second and third volumes (Paris, 1977, 225; 1980, 219), which cover the entire third century, including Origen. Neither is it cited in the *Supplément*, which is devoted to Philo (Paris, 1982).

115. Botte shows that we must wait for the sixth century to find *maiestas* as a regular title for the emperor, whereas *maiestas* as a divine title, at least in the *Supplices*,

antedates St. Leo. The word had already been part of the Christian vocabulary for some time. See Botte, *"Maiestas,"* in Botte-Mohrmann 111.

116. Ibid., 112.

117. See A. Rousseau in SC 100/1:246.

118. In the Vulgate, the word applied to sacrifice is not so much *purus* as *mundus*, which occurs in Mal 1:11, the key biblical text for the patristic theology of sacrifice. *Mundus* is associated with *immaculatus* in Jas 1:27 Vg., which describes a holy life as the worship acceptable to God.

119. Such a translation is suggested by parallel texts. For example, Ambrose, *De sacramentis* IV, 17 (SC 25bis:116), has: "We offer you this spotless, this spiritual, this bloodless *hostia*, this holy bread and cup of eternal life." We leave the Latin word to show the reader the term actually used by Ambrose; but the meaning is certainly "sacrifice" rather than "victim," since "spiritual" and "bloodless" are technical descriptions of sacrifice and apply to the victim only in a transferred sense.

A similar text that suggests "sacrifice" or even "worship and sacrifice" as the translation of *hostia* is in the Anaphora of St. Mark: "We offer spiritual and bloodless *latreia* [worship, sacrifice]" (Hänggi-Pahl 102). Like Ambrose's early text of the Roman Canon, this passage has the two descriptive adjectives, "bloodless" and "spiritual." Instead of a Greek equivalent of *hostia*, however, it has *latreia* which, as can be inferred from the immediately following citation of Mal 1:11, is here regarded as equivalent to "sacrifice." The ancient form of the Anaphora of Mark, as preserved for us in the Strasbourg Papyrus, has *thysia* (sacrifice) with "spiritual" and *latreia* (worship) with "bloodless" (Hänggi-Pahl 116). The ensuing citation from Mal 1:11 then describes the sacrifice as *kathara* (pure).

120. The Latin text has simply *Supra quae*, i.e., "[Look] upon these things"; the reference is to the sacred bread of everlasting life and the chalice of eternal salvation, which were mentioned a moment before.

121. See Daly (n. 91), 75. The formulation of the theme in our Canon makes it even clearer that the acceptableness of a sacrifice is not an objective quality in the offering but depends on the supremely free decision of a kind and faithful God.

122. Rom 4:11ff.

123. See P. E. Bonnard, "Melchizedek," in Léon-Dufour 348–349.

124. B. Botte, "Abraham dans la liturgie," *Cahiers Sioniens* 5 (1951): 90.

125. Daly 265.

126. The following passage from a preface in *Ver*, no. 1250, is a good illustration of this theological vision: ". . . that we should constantly offer you the sacrifice of praise, the type of which was established by Abel the just man, represented by the lamb prescribed by the Law, celebrated by Abraham, and shown forth by Melchizedek, but fulfilled by the true Lamb, the eternal high priest Christ, who is born today."

127. Do not mistake our meaning. What we have been saying makes it clear that acceptance depends on the sincerity and consistency of the life of the offerer. On the other hand, the theological quality or, better the theological character of the sacrifices of Abel, Abraham, and Melchizedek comes from the relationship of prefiguration between them and the sacrifice of Christ. According to Thomas Aquinas, our sacrifice stands in the same relationship as theirs to the sacrifice of Christ, with this difference that ours is commemorative instead of prefigurative.

The objective value of our sacrifice, then, depends on the sacrifice of Christ, while the free acceptance of it by God depends on the coherence and sincerity of our human actions. "The value of our sacrifice," as we have been using the phrase here, is not a translation of *ex opere operato;* the "value of sacrifice" to which *ex opere operato* refers is the objective value deriving from the saving work which Christ accomplished once and for all. The perfection of that work did not necessarily entail appropriate behavior on our part nor, therefore, the acceptance of our sacrifice by God. There is thus room and reason for the petition that the Father would be pleased with our sacrifice and accept it.

128. *LP* 1:239. See also 241, n. 12, where the editor, L. Duchesne, suggests that these words were added to assert the holiness of the gifts offered by the King of Salem, as against the Manicheans who (he says) refused to use wine in the eucharistic liturgy.

129. Botte-Mohrmann (181–83, n. 4. See also B. Botte, *Le canon de la messe romaine* (n. 12), 43 and 65.

130. The words remain in the Latin text of the Canon.

131. Ambrose, *De sacramentis* IV, 27 (SC 25bis:116): "We offer you this spotless, this spiritual, this bloodless sacrifice, this holy bread and cup of eternal life, and we pray and beseech you to accept this offering, on your altar on high, from the hands of the angels, as you deigned to accept the gifts of your servant, Abel the just, the sacrifice of our patriarch Abraham, and that which the high priest Melchizedek offered to you."

132. J. Daniélou, *The Theology of Jewish Christianity*, trans. J. A. Baker (Chicago, 1964), 117–146.

133. B. Botte, "L'ange du sacrifice et l'epiclèse de la messe romaine au moyen âge," *RTAM* 1 (1929): 285–308.

134. See the Anaphora of Mark (Hänggi-Pahl 108) and especially the plural in the Anaphora of Serapion (ibid., 132), which has characteristics showing it to be even older than the Anaphora of Mark.

135. Dom Botte gives no references in support of this claim.

136. G. Kittel, "*Angelos*," *TDNT* 1:82. [We have slightly altered the translation as it stands in *TDNT*. There the opening words are: "They speak on behalf of God" (for the German: "Sie üben Fürsprache vor Gott").—Tr.]

137. "Let the sweet fragrance ascend in the sight of your divine majesty from your altar on high through the hands of your angel" (Férotin 262).

138. Rv 8:3–4. The allusion is to the altar of incense. See P. Prigent, *L'Apocalypse de saint Jean* (Lausanne-Paris, 1981), 131: "It was the altar of incense rather than the altar of holocausts that lent itself to the spritualization of cult which is to be seen almost everywhere at this period."

139. "When you and your daughter-in-law Sarah prayed, I brought a reminder of your prayer before the Holy One."

140. "Let my prayer be directed like incense before you" (Ps 140:2 LXX). See Sir 35:6.

141. Ficker, "Mesagero," in E. Jenni and C. Westermann, eds., *Dizionario teologico dell'Antico Testamento* (Turin, 1978) 1:777f.

142. Mishnah, Tractate Berakoth 13a.

143. Irenaeus, *Adversus haereses* IV, 18, 6 (SC 100/2:614).

144. It is not necessary to follow the Mozarabic interpretation of this passage (Férotin 262) in which "blessing and grace" become "the Holy Spirit"; this is the only case we have of a pneumatological epiclesis in the Western liturgies.

145. Botte-Mohrmann 24.

146. The reason for this is explained by M. Andrieu, *OR* 2:276: at Rome it was for-

bidden to commemorate the dead in Sunday Masses; such commemorations were permitted only on weekdays.

147. Canon 39, in Monumenta Germaniae Historica, *Concilia* 2:81.

148. We may cite Basil of Caesarea, who in the third book (III, 5) of his *Contra Eunomium* (the fourth and fifth are by Didymus of Alexandria) says: "Baptism is the seal [*sphragis*] of faith, and faith is an assent to God" (PG 29:665).

149. See L. Hertling, *Communio: Church and Papacy in Early Christianity*, trans. J. Wicks (Chicago, 1972), 19–20: "The most frequent formula occurring in inscriptions on early Christian tombs is 'in peace'. . . . Sometimes 'in peace' can be interpreted in the modern sense as tranquility or the absence of strife. . . . This, however, does not hold for the most commonly occurring phrase, *depositus in pace*. . . . It is clear that here *pax* means 'a community, the communion of saints,' that is, the Church. *Vixit in pace* means that the person lived in the unity of the faith and of the sacraments of the Church. *Obiit in pace* means the same, namely, that he died in the community of the Church." These remarks may be applied to the interpretation of the passage in the Canon, since Augustine uses the same expression and language in *Serm.* 172, 2 (PL 38:936) in describing the intercession for the dead during the eucharistic prayer: "The Church observes these practices which have been handed on by the Fathers: it prays for those who have died in communion with the body and blood of the Lord, when they are commemorated during the [eucharistic] sacrifice at the proper moment."

150. Jungmann 2:249–250.

151. Ibid.

152. The theme would later undergo excessive development when *apologiae* were introduced even into the Canon. For an example of these, see *EEFL*, nos. 3270–3282c. On the origin and historical significance of the *apologiae*, see A. Nocent, "Les Apologies dans la célébration eucharistique," in the collective work, *Liturgie et rémission des péchés* (Rome, 1975), 179–196.

153. Hänggi-Pahl 375ff.; trans. in Deiss 159–163.

154. There is a critical edition by J. M. Sauget, *Anaphora s. Petri apostoli tertia* in A. Raes, ed., *Anaphorae siriacae. Quotquot in codicibus adhuc repertae sunt* II/3 (Rome, 1973), 285ff.

155. Funk 1:510; trans. in Deiss 235.

156. As you may know, the Canon is closely related to this Alexandrian anaphora. Here is a Latin translation of the latter to better appreciate the parallel: "*Memento, Domine, nostri quoque peccatorum et indignorum servorum tuorum, et peccata nostra deleto, ut bonus et benignus Deus*" (Hänggi-Pahl 109).

157. See P. T. Camelot, ed., *Ignace d'Antioche—Polycarpe de Smyrne. Lettres. Martyre de Polycarpe* (SC 10; Paris, 1969), 228.

158. J. Doresse and E. Lanne, *Un témoin archaïque de la liturgie copte de S. Basile*, with an appendix by B. Capelle, "Les liturgies basiliennes et saint Basile" (Louvain, 1960), 20–22. Text also in Hänggi-Pahl 353.

159. The Anaphora of Mark contains a similar statement: "Grant us a share and inheritance with the noble fellowship of your holy prophets, apostles, and martyrs" (Strasbourg Papyrus, in Hänggi-Pahl 119).

160. Doresse-Lanne 24–26; Hänggi-Pahl 357. See also E. Lanne, "Les anaphores eucharistiques de saint Basile et la communauté ecclésiale," *Irén* 55 (1982): 321.

161. For a discussion of *mneiais* (memorials) instead of *chreiais* (needs) see M.-J. Lagrange, *Epître aux Romains* (Paris, 1922), 304, n. 13.

162. Ibid., 305 (still in n. 13).

163. *Partem aliquam et societatem.*

164. Jungmann 2:260. In his article, "La grande conclusion du canon romain," *LMD* no. 88 (1966): 107, Jordi Pinell opts for a eucharistic interpretation of this formula of the Canon: "In the doxology of the Canon the eucharistic gifts are not the subject but the complement of the verb *vivificas.* The meaning must therefore be that God, through Christ, endows the gifts with life-giving power so that, in accordance with what St. Paul says, we may receive life in Christ from them. *Vivificas* cannot refer to the fruits of the earth, which are the object of a simple blessing. Therefore I see no reason based on internal criticism that prevents us from giving a clearly eucharistic meaning to the *Per quem haec omnia.*"

165. Though they have different origins, such words as "beseech," "pray," "praise," and "glorify" are to be considered equivalents to the "invoke" of Jl 3:5, at least according to A.-M. Besnard, *Le mystère du nom* (Paris, 1962), 147. It seems, therefore, that Jl 3:5 can be properly applied to the theology expressed in the final doxology of the Canon.—The text of the doxology does not change from one to another of the several Roman eucharistic prayers.

CHAPTER FOUR

1. Hippolytus, *Traditio apostolica* 4 (Botte 11–17). The original text has been lost but ancient versions of it have survived. Of these, the Latin is important because of its antiquity (end of the fourth century; the manuscript is from the fifth); the manuscript, a codex in the Capitular Library of Verona, was edited at the beginning of the century by E. Hauler in his *Didascaliae apostolorum fragmenta ueronensia latina. Accedunt Canonum qui dicuntur apostolorum et aegyptiorum reliquiae* (Leipzig, 1900). The codex is now practically illegible due to the chemicals Hauler used to clarify the text. This information came in a conversation with B. Botte who assures us that in the parts still legible, Hauler's decipherment of the text is reliable.

Botte attempted a reconstruction of the original text; his work, regarded as the basic edition for a scientific study of the text, was also the direct source for the composition of the second anaphora in the new Missal.

[Throughout this chapter, we shall be using our translation in Deiss 130–131, with some slight modifications as called for by the discussion.—Tr.]

2. No one any longer doubts the validity of the attribution. What remains in doubt is the identity of Hippolytus. Among other things: Was he a presbyter? Was he a bishop of Rome (in which case he would have been a kind of antipope)? On this, see also B. Botte, *Hippolyte de Rome. La tradition apostolique* (SC 11bis; Paris, 1968), 14–17.

There is also doubt whether the works attributed to Hippolytus are all by the same author or whether there were two authors named Hippolytus. On this complex question, see the collective work *Ricerche su Ippolito* (Rome, 1977); V. Loi, "L'omelia *In sanctum pascha* d'Ippolito di Roma," *Augustinianum* 17 (1977): 461–484; and, for a summary, A. Grillmeier, *Christ in Christian Tradition* 1. *From the Apostolic Age to Chalcedon (451),* trans. J. Bowden (2d rev. ed.; Atlanta, 1975), 113ff.

3. In saying this, we do not mean to prejudge the question of whether the name "eucharistic prayer" can be given to other texts which are certainly older than Hippolytus. We are saying only that the text in Hippolytus is the first that displays all the familiar characteristics of an anaphora.

4. P. Cagin, *L'eucharistia. Canon primitif de la messe ou formulaire essentiel et premier de toutes les liturgies* (Rome-Paris-Tournai, 1912); idem, *L'anaphore apostolique et ses témoins* (Paris, 1919).

5. "Anaphora of Our Lady Mary, Mother of God, composed by Abba George" (Hänggi-Pahl 200); "Anaphora of Our Lord Jesus Christ" (ibid., 150).

6. Text in I. H. Rahmani, ed., *Testamentum Domini nostri Iesu Christi* (Mainz, 1899), 39–45; see Hänggi-Pahl 219.

7. J. Doresse and E. Lanne, *Un témoin archaïque de la liturgie copte de S. Basile*, with an appendix by B. Capelle, "Les liturgies basiliennes et saint Basile" (Louvain, 1960).

8. Funk 1:495–514.

9. B. Botte, *Le mouvement liturgique. Témoignages et souvenirs* (Paris, 1973), 184.

10. In Hippolytus, the account of institution is part of the "preface" or thanksgiving, into which it fits perfectly as one of the motives for gratitude. Once the Sanctus is inserted, the account of institution becomes a section apart, cut off from the preface.

11. Second Eucharistic Prayer: "*Vere sanctus es, Domine, fons omnis sanctitatis*"; Third Eucharistic Prayer: "*Vere sanctus es, Domine, et merito te laudat.*"

12. This will be discussed in the commentary on the Fourth Eucharistic Prayer; see Chap. Six, section VII.

13. For example: ". . . to be saved through sanctification by the Spirit" (2 Thes 2:13). The broader biblical foundation of this conception is found in Luke: "The Holy Spirit will come upon you, and the power of the Most High will overshadow you; therefore the child to be born will be called holy" (1:35). The parallel between the consecration of the Eucharist and the human nature of Christ as united to his divine nature is a familiar one in the patristic period. For example, Cyril of Alexandria, *Adversus Nestorium* IV, 5 (PG 76:193): "Since the body of the Word is lifegiving which he made his own [*idion*] in a union that we can neither grasp nor express, we who share his holy flesh and blood are completely vivified because the Word abides in us in a divine manner through the Holy Spirit and in a human manner through his holy flesh and his precious blood."

14. Primitive Christological reflection, which took place in a Jewish-Christian context, often presented the Trinity with the help of angelology. In this view, the Father is God, while Christ and the Spirit are two angels. Elsewhere, all three divine persons may be represented as angels. Thus, there are Byzantine icons, even modern ones, that show the three Persons as three angels; the subject is the *Philoxenia* or Hospitality of Abraham (based on Gn 18:2ff.), which is viewed as traditional but, at the same time, is not free of theological problems.

But, as early as the second century, and outside the Jewish-Christian environment, difficulties were raised against the application of the title "angel" to Christ. The title was therefore systematicallly abandoned, with the exception of "angel of great counsel" (Is 9:5 LXX), an expression also to be found in the Anaphora of Hippolytus. On this whole subject of angel-christology, see Grillmeier (n. 1), 1:46–53.

15. The ultimate basis for the text is in Dn 2:28; 10:4; 1 Tm 4:1; 1 Pt 1:20.

16. *Jubilees* 1, 23–26, trans. of R. H. Charles, rev. by C. Rabin, in H. F. D. Sparks, ed., *The Apocryphal Old Testament* (Oxford, 1984), 13.

17. This comparison with *Jubilees* is not irrelevant. We have shown in "Omelie pasquali e Birkat ha-mazon: fonti dell'anafora di Ippolito," *EL* 97 (183): 109–181, that the very structure of the Anaphora of Hippolytus is to be compared, via intermediate texts, with *Jubilees* 22, 6ff.

There is still another point of comparison. Hippolytus has "because you counted [or: made] us worthy to stand before you and serve you," and *Jubilees* 30, 18 has: "The descendants of Levi were chosen for the priesthood, and to be Levites, that they might minister before the Lord (as we do) continually; and Levi and his sons are blessed forever" (Sparks 94).

18. "*Filium dilectionis tuae*" (Anaphora II, inspired by Col 1:13), which corrects the "*dilectum puerum (= Pais) tuum*" of Hippolytus.

19. The Latin differs slightly in the two documents: "*per quem omnia fecisti*" (Hippolytus) and "*per quod cuncta fecisti*" (Anaphora II).

20. Again a slight difference: "*ex Spiritu sancto et uirgine natus*" (Hippolytus) and "*incarnatum de Spiritu Sancto et ex Virgine natum*" (Anaphora II).

21. These words ("When . . . suffering") are not taken over at this point in Anaphora II, but have been transferred to the beginning of the account of institution: "When he was about to hand himself over freely to his passion. . . ." ("Qui cum passioni voluntarie traderetur. . .").

22. Hippolytus includes the birth of Christ. The Easter Homilies of the second century adopt the same perspective and include a commemoration of the Lord's birth; thus, the birth is celebrated again at Easter.

23. The theme of the resurrection remains implicit, as it does in Jn 13:1.

24. Jn 12:32–33. It is a fact, nonetheless, that the *doxa* (glory) of Christ is fully manifested only at the moment of the ascension. The session at the Father's right hand is the crown upon Christ's Easter glory; see Grillmeier 1:75.

25. This heavy emphasis on the saving efficacy of Christ's death is not well understood today because we have lost the ability to read the scriptures typologically; thus, it is not easy to understand how the Passover lamb is a "type" of Christ. For us, the lamb is simply an allegorical image.

On the other hand, we realize the theological importance of the resurrection, but we then project this view back into the early centuries and pass an utterly uncritical judgment on the heritage transmitted to us by the early Church. The facts are quite different. As a result of etymologies based on sound, the word *pascha* was connected with the Greek *paschein* (to suffer), and the Fathers inevitably linked *pascha* and *passio*. Thus, Irenaeus writes in *Epideixis* 25: "The name of this mystery is 'passion,'" which is the cause of our deliverance"; see L. M. Froidevaux, ed., *Irénée de Lyon, Démonstration de la prédication apostolique* (SC 62; Paris, 1969), 71–72.

O. Casel claimed that in the Fathers there is, in substance, a balance between the death and the resurrection; for a critique of this view, see R. Cantalamessa, *La pasqua nella Chiesa antica* (Turin, 1979), XV.

26. From the theological standpoint, the two form a single mystery. There has always however, been a tendency to break down the one mystery of salvation into various mysteries of salvation, until finally, in the theology of the *Devotio moderna*, reflection on the resurrection as a mystery of salvation ceased and the death of Christ alone came to be regarded as salvific.

27. Latin: "*Memores igitur mortis et resurrectionis eius.*" The Italian Missal translates this as: "celebrating the memorial of your Son's death and resurrection." The translation really translates not the text but the theology of the text or, more accurately, the theology of commemoration which a modern thinker believes should be in the text.

28. Jn 15:1; 6:35, 58.

29. Latin: "*Gratias agentes quia nos dignos habuisti astare coram te et tibi ministrare.*" The text of Hippolytus evidently continues to exist in the Latin Missal.

30. Latin of Hippolytus: "*Et petimus ut mittas Spiritum tuum sanctum in oblationem sanctae ecclesiae: in unum congregans des omnibus qui percipiunt sanctis in repletionem spiritus sancti ad confirmationem fidei in ueritate.*" This might be translated: "And we

310

pray you to send your Holy Spirit on the offering of your holy Church, to bring together in unity all those who receive of the holy things. May they be filled with the Holy Spirit who strengthens their faith in the truth" (Deiss 131, slightly modified). See Hippolytus, *Traditio apostolica* 4 (Botte 16).

31. Latin: *"Et supplices deprecamur ut corporis et sanguinis participes a Spiritu Sancto congregemur in unum."* It is likely that the opening words were chosen so that the prayer might be parallel with the *Supplices te rogamus* of the Roman Canon.

32. *"In sancta ecclesia tua"* ("in your holy Church"). This detail comes from Eph 3:21 and is characteristic of Hippolytus (it occurs in five doxologies out of seven), but it also appears in other documents, e.g., the Anaphora of Addai and Mari (Hänggi-Pahl 380).

33. See the parallels in Mk 1:11; 9:7; Eph 1:6.

34. E. Lohse, *Colossians and Philemon*, trans. W. R. Poehlmann and R. J. Karris (Philadelphia, 1971), 38.

35. Ibid., and see n. 43: "The 'rule' of Christ is 'as it were, an already present, representative "forerunner" of the *Basileia tou theou* (rule of God) and is exercised by the exalted Christ' " (Lohse is citing H.-A. Wilcke).

36. Lk 22:29–30. The eschatological aspect of the reign of God is strongly emphasized in the eucharistic texts of *Didache* 9–10.

37. Hippolytus, in a typical phrase, speaks of "your Word inseparable [from you]." This has been properly omitted in Anaphora II.

38. This translation is based on the Byzantine Anaphora of Basil, which speaks of *Logos zōn* (Hänggi-Pahl 232). Behind this in turn is Heb 4:12: "The word of God is living and active."

T. Schnitzler, *I tre nuovi canoni ed i nuovi prefazi* (Rome, 1970), 22, has this very relevant remark: "The Christ who helps us give thanks to the Father is not some Christ of faith or a mythological Christ but the Christ of the gospel which we hear at Mass. Eucharist and Gospel are one in Christ."

39. The words: *"Verbum tuum per quem omnia fecisti,"* are a clear allusion to the gospel of John. This theme, so characteristic of the Anaphora of Hippolytus, reappeared not only in the creeds but also in the Alexandrian Anaphora of Basil: "Through whom you made all things, visible and invisible" (Hänggi-Pahl 348), and, in a more prolix form, in *Constitutiones apostolorum* VIII: "You brought all things from nothingness into being through your only-begotten Son" (Hänggi-Pahl 82).

40. Jn 8:29. The verse emphasizes the three themes in Hippolytus: oneness with the Father, carrying out the Father's will, and mission. Interestingly enough, v. 30 adds that because of these words of Jesus many believed in him. So too, what is being commemorated at this point in the anaphora is the work of salvation as it attains its purpose: the faith of human beings in Christ.

41. The unity characteristic of the process of salvation is found not only in its descending phase, in which the father sends the Son, but also in its ascending phase, in which human beings respond to God in Christ: "Whoever receives me receives him who sent me" (Lk 9:48).

42. See Pseudo-Hippolytus, *In sanctum pascha* 45, cited in R. Cantalamessa, *I piu antichi testi pasquali della Chiesa*, 74: "He did not place the burden of our salvation on an angel or an archangel; in obedience to the Father's command, he, the Word, took completely upon himself the struggle in our behalf." The Jewish Passover Haggadah says: "The Lord did not bring us forth from Egypt by the hand of an angel or a seraphim or a messenger; the Holy One—blessed be he!—brought us forth himself and

by his own majestic power" (Hänggi-Pahl 20). The source for this passage seems to be Is 63:9 LXX: "It was not an ambassador or an angel but the Lord himself who saved them because he loved them" (Cantalamessa, ibid., 117, n. 63). See also U. Neri, ed., *Il canto del mare. Midrash sull'Esodo* (Rome, 1976), 103.

43. In Tertullian, the verb "send" is used in undertaking a doctrine on the distinction between the divine Persons: sender and sent are distinct (see *Adversus Praxean* 9, 2 [CCL 2:1168]). The basis of the argument is in Jn 8:42; 6:57; 14:24. On "envoy" as a Christological title, see R. Cantalamessa, *L'omelia "In s. pascha" dello Pseudo-Ippolito di Roma* (Milan, 1967), 147ss.

44. Jn 3:17. See also 17:13; Acts 3:26; 1 Jn 4:9–10.

45. See also Mk 12:6 where the verb "send" is connected with "beloved Son."

46. Is 53:6; 1 Pt 2:24.

47. Acts 13:26; see 11:14.

48. Acts 5:31; see 13:23.

49. Acts 4:9–12; see 14:3.

50. Mt 1:11.

51. Lk 2:11.

52. Heb 5:9.

53. C. Lesquivit and P. Grelot, "Salvation," in Léon-Dufour 518–522.

54. Mt 9:21; Mk 3:4; 5:23; 6:56.

55. Ti 2:13.

56. Acts 2:21; Gal 3:5.

57. Lk 9:56; 19:10.

58. Is 12:27; 14:13.

59. S. Lyonnet, "Redemption," in Léon-Dufour 481.

60. Is 19:5; Dt 26:18.

61. According to S. Lyonnet, "Redemption," in Léon-Dufour 481, in the New Testament "the term *redemption* serves not only to designate the work performed by Christ on Calvary (Rom 3, 24; Col 1, 14; Eph 1, 7); it equally applies to what He will accomplish at the end of time, therefore in consequence of the *parousia* and the glorious resurrection of the body (Lk 21, 28; Rom 8, 23; Eph 1, 14; 4, 30; prob. 1 Col 1, 30)."

62. It cannot be said, however, that this eschatological conception of salvation is in our new anaphora, since the final coming of Christ is not commemorated even in the anamnesis; the case is different in the third and fourth anaphoras of the Missal.

63. E. Lanne, "La liturgia eucaristica in oriente e in occidente," in the collective work *Liturgia e vita* (Turin, 1980), 25–28.

64. Euchologion of Serapion (Hänggi-Pahl 128).

65. For the Bible, the "name" is the very person as revealed and with all that is known of him or her (information about the person, value judgments passed on the person). "Name" signifies the "refulgence" of the person in our eyes, the refulgence being not a subjective illusion on our part but rather the climactic form of an objective knowledge. "Name" also implies that special interpersonal relationship that is expressed in the biblical word for "knowledge," a term that connotes communion and intimacy.

66. G. Couturier, "Le sacrifice d'action de grâce," *Eglise et théologie* 13 (1982): 18ff.

67. Rom 8:39.

68. Only at a later period do we see Christ's work of salvation being broken into its component parts, that is, the individual actions and episodes in which he carried

out the Father's will. This seems due to the influence of, if not directly caused by, the popular religious outlook of the third century, when mentality and attitudes were formed by the "mystery religions." In the latter, the celebration of salvation focused on various episodes in the life of the particular god.

The saving work of Christ was now parceled out, as it were, and subdivided into its various phases and stages. This is the remote basis for the process that eventually produced the liturgical year. Hippolytus precedes this whole development. For him, it is always the complete work of Christ that is commemorated, and this singleness and wholeness is especially evident at Easter. Today, it would be odd to think of celebrating the entire mystery at Easter, since it is a somewhat complicated matter to bring out the paschal character of the nativity.

69. D. Mollat, "Le discours eucharistique," in his *Etudes johanniques* (Paris, 1979), 119.

70. E. Jacquemin and X. Léon-Dufour, "Will of God," in Léon-Dufour 654.

71. This focus is not something peculiar to Hippolytus, since the Bible speaks quite clearly of the passion of Christ as the object of God's will: "This Jesus, delivered up according to the definite plan and foreknowledge of God . . ." (Acts 2:23; see 4:28; 20:27). In addition, there is Lk 22:42: "Not my will, but thine, be done."

According to the gospel of John, Jesus lives by the will of him who sent him, and the obedience of the Son consists in being in communion with the Father's will. Standard texts are Jn 5:30 and especially 10:17f.: "For this reason the Father loves me, because I lay down my life, that I may take it up again. No one takes it from me, but I lay it down of my own accord. I have power to lay it down, and I have power to take it up again; this charge I have received from my Father." This verse of John is biblical justification for the emphasis Hippolytus places on the voluntariness of Christ's suffering.

72. From the historical standpoint, this is a very interesting phenomenon since it marks the meeting, as it were, of two soteriologies: the transition from a soteriology that lists and describes the fruits of salvation to a soteriology that lists and describes the events of salvation. The first type is the older (see *Didache* 9–10 and the eucharistic texts in the apocryphal literature); the second is more recent and is developed in the Easter Homilies, where it enters the Anaphora of Hippolytus and all of catechesis.

73. N. Füglister, *Il valore salvifico della pasqua* (Brescia, 1976), 141. [German original of Füglister's book: *Die Heilsbedeutung des Pascha* (Studien zum Alten und Neuen Testament 8; Munich, 1963).]

74. "Holy people" is from Dt 7:6; 14:2. The New Testament does not use the phrase but speaks simply of "people." The only problem is the literary source from which the anaphora derives the phrase; the concept as such is contained in the following New Testament texts, among others: "Jesus also suffered . . . in order to sanctify the people" (Heb 12:13); "You are . . . a holy nation, God's own people" (1 Pt 2:9).

In a similar way, the attribute "holy" is applied to the Church. In this context, we should not forget the apocryphal *Book of Jubilees* 33, 20: "Israel is a holy nation to the Lord its God, and a special nation of his own, and a priestly and royal nation for his possession" (Sparks 104).

75. Lv 19:2; 20:26.

76. Hos 11:9.

77. Jn 1:14 (literal translation).

78. "In order to . . . enlighten the just." This is a baptismal theme, applied to the salvation of those already deceased. Their salvation is thus made to be of the same order and kind as that of the living. See Grillmeier 1:73–75.

79. Irenaeus, *Epideixis* 38 (SC 62:92).

80. Latin: "*ut mortem solveret et resurrectionem manifestaret*" ("to do away with death and manifest [or reveal] the resurrection"). The words still carry the flavor of the source. The Italian translation, on the other hand, no longer keeps to the source but is couched in terms that appeal directly to the faithful of today. Since liturgy is not an exercise in archeological fidelity, the Italian translation is successful despite, or perhaps precisely because of, its lack of fidelity to the original.

81. We shall not ask whether this theological principle is sufficiently correct to justify the theological approach adopted in the second and third centuries, according to which Christ's assumption of a soul redeemed the human soul and his assumption of a body redeemed the human body.

82. Ps 33:21; Am 2:7; see Ex 3:14.

83. In regard to the relation between preface and Sanctus, it is possible to say more than simply that they belong together. Using the semiological categories of U. Eco, we can describe the Sanctus as a "sememe" and the preface as a "text." He says in his book *Lector in Fabula* (Milan, 1979), 23: "A sememe must be seen as a virtual text, and a text as simply the expansion of a sememe (in fact it results from the expansion of many sememes, but it is theoretically possible that it can be reduced to the expansion of a single central sememe)."

By way of clarification, it can be said further that a sememe is "a hierarchical tree of possible interpretants of a cultural unit. . . . A sememe is produced by the sum total of the references which the cultural unit actuates along certain axes or in certain fields" (U. Eco, *Segno* [Milan, 1973], 153).

84. It is not the Spirit who sanctifies; the Father sanctifies by pouring out his Spirit.

We are evidently far removed from the various liturgical sequences that invoke the Spirit directly (*Veni Sancte Spiritus*, "Come, Holy Spirit") and thus attribute a certain independence to each of the divine Persons, though not to depart from the orthodox confessions of faith promulgated by the great councils.

85. In the following two passages from Joel and Zechariah, the "day of the Lord" is marked by the outpouring of the Spirit: "[On that day] I will pour out on the house of David and the inhabitants of Jerusalem a spirit of compassion and supplication" (Zec 12:10); "You shall know that I am in the midst of Israel. . . . And it shall come to pass afterward that I will pour out my spirit on all flesh" (Jl 2:27–28). The second of the two passages is cited in Acts 2:17 and applied to the apostles who are preaching the risen Christ. For holiness as a fruit of the eschatological Spirit, see Ez 36:27: "And I will put my spirit within you, and cause you to walk in my statutes."

86. "You are holy, O King of the ages and Lord and Giver [*dator*] of all holiness" (Hänggi-Pahl 245). Anaphora II has: "*Vere sanctus es, Domine, fons omnis sanctitatis*" ("You are holy indeed, Lord, fountain of all holiness"). Both have "Lord," but the "Giver" of James is replaced by "fountain." In P. Jounel's report, the source of the expression "fountain of all holiness" is given simply as the *Liber mozarabicus sacramentorum*, without further indication of place. The report was simply a working paper, and slips can occur in such drafts. In his published commentary of 1968, "La composition des nouvelles prières eucharistiques," *LMD* no. 94 (1968): 48f., Jounel says: "The expression *fons omnis sanctitatis* is not as common as one might expect. It

occurs only once in the *Missale Romanum*, in the *oratio super oblata* for the Mass of St. Ignatius Loyola (July 31)."

87. The *Post-Sanctus* is indebted at this point to the Old Spanish or Mozarabic liturgy. Jounel gives a reference to no. 271 of the *Missale Gothicum*. Here is the passage: "We ask you to bless this sacrifice with your blessing and to pour over it the dew of your Spirit (*et Spiritus Sancti tui rore perfundas*)"; the prayer is the *Post-Sanctus* for the Mass of the Easter Vigil; see L. K. Mohlberg, ed., *Missale Gothicum* (Rome, 1961), p. 69, no. 271. Other Mozarabic texts also compare the Holy Spirit with dew; e.g.: "Extinguish with the dew of the Holy Spirit the vices that incite us (*Extingue Sancti Spiritus rore nostrorum incentiva vitiorum*)" (Férotin 120). Here are some other less relevant examples from the same source: in the Mass of St. Agnes the head of the virgin was "covered with heavenly dew" (Férotin 105), and the Mass of St. Lawrence speaks of "the dew of your love" (ibid., 391). Closer to our text, the Roman liturgy has: "Pour the dew of your blessing over their minds and bodies" (*Ver*, no. 642).

88. H. Lesêtre, "Rosée," *DB* 5/1:1208.

89. Ibid., 1209.

90. Hos 14:5.

91. Is 55:10–11. It is inappropriate here to cite Is 45:8, because the liturgy applies the latter to the incarnation, and the liturgy itself is not a new incarnation. For a different view, see T. Schnitzler, *I tre nuovi canoni* (n. 38), 33.

92. The innovation must have been well received, since it has been extended to the three anaphoras in Masses for Children. The practice is not widely found in the tradition. P. Jounel cites only two instances: first, in the Mone Masses from the seventh century (in Mohlberg's ed. of *Missale Gothicum*, p. 78, no. 282); second, in the Mozarabic liturgy (Férotin 494, no. 1082). But the practice is not equally rare in the Eastern liturgies where the Sanctus commemorates the great liturgy unfolding in heaven. The saints are thus always included even if not explicitly mentioned.

93. In 1933, Dom H. Leclercq published a list of 85 accounts of institution from various anaphoras, not one of which was content simply to reproduce one of the four New Testament accounts; see H. Leclercq, "Messe," *DACL* 9/1:730–750. An analysis of the differences among the various anaphoras on this point is given in J. M. Hanssens, *Institutiones liturgicae de ritibus orientalibus* 3/2 (Rome, 1932), 412–447.

94. "de nous tenir devant toi et de te servir comme prêtres" (Botte 17).

95. Ibid., 17, n. 3.

96. See B. Botte, "Adstare coram te et tibi ministrare," *QL* 63 (1982): 225: "This is not an ordinary Mass but an ordination Mass. The bishop thanks God for having been judged worthy to celebrate the eucharistic sacrifice."

97. We are not competent to go into the question of whether the distinction between clergy and laity is the result of historical circumstances or is by divine law a constitutive element of the Church. This is the well-known question (on which Anglicans and Catholics take opposite sides) of whether the episcopate is a divine institution or simply a historical phenomenon.

Without trying to prejudice the answer, we will cite Tertullian (160–ca. 240), who says in his *De exhortatione castitatis* 7, 3 (CCL 2:1024f.) that "the distinction between clergy (*ordo*) and laity (*plebs*) has been established by the authority of the Church." This statement shows (a) that Tertullian already knows the distinction between *ordo* and *plebs*, and (b) that the distinction cannot have been of long standing, since he is able to suggest the interpretation he does, namely, that the distinction depends on the authority of the Church.

98. D. H. Tripp, "The Thanksgiving: An Essay by Arthur Couratin," in B. D. Spinks, ed., *The Sacrifice of Praise. Studies on the Themes of Thanksgiving and Redemption in the Central Prayers of the Eucharistic and Baptismal Liturgies. In Honour of Arthur Hubert Couratin* (Rome, 1981), 30.

99. Botte, "Adstare coram te . . ." (n. 96), 224: "There is no doubt about it: the object of the thanksgiving is the eucharistic sacrifice, the priestly action."

100. Ibid., 225.

101. Hippolytus, *Traditio apostolica* (Botte 8). The Greek text is from the *Epitome* of the *Constitutiones apostolorum*.

102. Botte, "Adstare coram te . . . ," 225.

103. Ibid.

104. Ibid.

105. Jounel takes a similar position in his article, "La composition des nouvelles prières eucharistiques" (n. 86), 50f.: "a properly priestly action, the joint action of priests and the royal priesthood of the faithful to which the Roman Canon explicitly refers when it speaks of 'we your servants and with us your holy people.' It is for this ministry (the Ethiopic version says 'priesthood') that the prayer in Hippolytus gives thanks."

106. This soteriology is well explained in N. Füglister, *Il valore salvifico della pasqua* (n. 73), 125.

107. The LXX says: "*parestanai enanti Kyriou, leitourgein,*" which is to be compared with the Vg: "*separavit tribum Levi ut . . . et staret coram eo in ministerio.*"

108. LXX: "*Stēnai enantion autou leitourgein kai einai autō leitourgountas kai thumiontas.*" Vg: "*Filii mi . . . vos elegit Dominus ut stetis coram eo et ministretis illi, colatis eum et cremetis incensum.*" A comparison of the two texts enables us to see the precise biblical basis for this point in the Anaphora of Hippolytus. See also *Jubilees* 18, 18, cited above in n. 17.

109. Ex 6:12; 6:30 (both in the LXX).

110. Lv 3:1; 1 Chr 16:1; 2 Chr 7:4.

111. See, e.g., Dt 12:18; 14:26; 27:6–7. H. Cazelles points out that in covenant sacrifices "before God," the divinity becomes a witness, as in Gn 31:49–54; see "Le sens de la liturgie dans l'Ancien Testament," in the collective work, *La liturgie: Son sens, son esprit, sa méthode* (Rome, 1982), 48.

112. 1 Kgs 22:21; Tb 12:15; Lk 1:9.

113. See, e.g., the fine description in 1 Chr 16:4–6; 1 Kgs 8:62, 66.

114. Jn 1:14. Keep in mind the possibility of this verse having a double meaning: *en hēmin* can mean either "among us" or "in us." Thus, the classic theme of God coming to dwell in the world becomes the theme of God dwelling in the hearts of human beings so that these are temples wherein he abides and is present.

115. Jn 2:19–22.

116. Col 2:9.

117. F. Amiot, "Temple," in Léon-Dufour 596–597.

118. H. Cazelles, "Le sens de la liturgie" (n. 111), 51f.

119. Hänggi-Pahl 92. The Coptic version of Basil is older, at least at this point, than the Clementine anaphora. It reads: "and make ('show') them holy among the holy things. Make us all worthy to participate in your holy mysteries"; text in Doresse-Lanne (n. 7), 20, and in Hänggi-Pahl 352.

120. This epiclesis of Basil, which is based on Hippolytus, was to become in turn the source of the epiclesis in the Fourth Eucharistic Prayer of the Missal.

121. The new anaphora is influenced by the Pauline text rather than being strictly dependent on it. Among other things, the Pauline text makes a clear distinction not made in our text: the distinction between "participate" and "communicate" or "be in communion." In modern theological terms, these two are synonyms, in the sense that we can say either "communicate in the eucharistic bread" and "communicate in the body of Christ" or "participate in the eucharistic bread" and "participate in the body of Christ." This terminological equivalence is seen in fourth-century writings, and therefore we need not be surprised to see it appear in the Missal of Paul VI. In 1 Cor 10, on the other hand, the distinction is clearly made and has a quasitechnical character. One participates in the eucharistic bread, but one communicates in the body of Christ. "Participate" or "share" relates to the sacrament; "communicate" relates to Christ. The two terms and two actions are linked, so that one who participates in the sacramental bread has communion with Christ. But, the two levels on which the action unfolds are not to be confused. The first level is that of participation in the sacrament; if the participation is fruitful, the person advances to the second level, that of communion with Christ.

122. 1 Cor 12:13: "By one Spirit we were all baptized into one body—Jews or Greeks, slaves or free—and all were made to drink of the one Spirit."

123. See 1 Cor 10:7; 10:2–4.

124. We regard this point as certain on the basis of the analysis given in *EL* 97 (1983): 109–181.

125. See Council of Trent, Session XIII (1551), cap. 8 (DS 1649; Neuner-Dupuis 1524); Vatican II, Decree *Unitatis redintegratio* on Ecumenism 2: "the wonderful sacrament of the Eucharist by which the unity of the Church is both symbolized and brought about" (Flannery 453; Latin in Alberigo 908).

126. This statement follows from Pauline teaching on the divine gifts bestowed on every baptized person. The individual's charisms, works, ministries, and virtues are the fruit of the one Spirit who gives them for the common good; the individual has nothing that is not for the common good (1 Cor 12:7).

127. The epiclesis shows a crescendo culminating in the work of the Spirit. See T. Schnitzler, *I tre nuovi canoni* (n. 38), 47: "By means of the bread and wine we communicate in the body and blood of Christ and receive the grace of the Holy Spirit; the work of the Spirit consists in uniting the communicants among themselves. . . . The Latin verb *congregemur* is derived from *grex*, 'flock'; we are reminded thus of the Good Shepherd who brings all together in one sheepfold." And ibid., 48: "The images of the flock and the mother hen give the prayer for unity a note of tender kindness that makes a strictly juridical interpretation less likely."

128. The epiclesis of Anaphora II envisages directly only those who share in the body and blood of Christ, that is, the communicants, the "we" who are the subjects of the verbs. Nonetheless, this prayer for unity is not without its ecumenical dimension. Ecumenism cannot be restricted to the top of the ladder, to the hierarchies of the various Churches, since final unity is projected to be the result of a deeper union of each subject—individual or Church—with Christ.

129. *Didache* 10, 5: "Lord, remember your Church and deliver it from all evil; make it perfect in your love and gather it from the four winds, this sanctified Church, into your kingdom which you have prepared for it" (Deiss 76; text in Hänggi-Pahl 66).

130. See E. Lanne, "L'Eglise une dans la prière eucharistique," *Irén* 50 (1977): 328, 331; idem, "L'intercession pour l'Eglise dans la prière eucharistique," in the collective work, *L'Eglise dans la liturgie* (Rome, 1980), 206.

131. The goal of "perfection" or completeness in love does not represent an escape from the real in the name of a mystical dream, but is rather a project for real life, since "whoever keeps God's word, in him truly love for God is perfected" (1 Jn 2:5).

132. Hänggi-Pahl 428.

133. L. Eizenhöfer, *Canon missae romanae. Pars altera. Textus propinqui* (Rome, 1966). We refer you to no. 261, from Optatus of Milevis, as the most important.

134. The embolism used for inserting the names of the dead to be remembered is an almost verbatim citation of Rom 6:5, which deals with salvation through baptism, the sacrament of Christ's death.

135. Doresse-Lanne (n. 7), 22.

CHAPTER FIVE

1. L. Bouyer, *Eucharist. The Theology and Spirituality of the Eucharistic Prayer*, trans. C. U. Quinn (Notre Dame, IN, 1968), 448. Idem, "La terza preghiera eucaristica," in the collective work, *Le nuove preghiere eucaristiche* (Brescia, 1969), 39. Same view in L. Della Torre, *Pregare l'eucaristia* (Brescia, 1983), 85.

2. It is Dom Botte who tells of the decision to compose a text inspired by the Gallican liturgy; see his *Le mouvement liturgique. Témoignages et souvenirs* (Paris, 1973), 184.

3. A. Nocent, "Le nuove preghiere eucaristiche," in the collective work, *Anamnesis 3/2. Eucaristia* (Casale Monferrato, 1983), 253.

4. For a description of these texts, see Bouyer, *Eucharist* 315ff. Above all, see J. Pinell, in *Anamnesis 2. La liturgia. Panorama storico generale* (Casale Monferrato, 1978), 62–88. Also very worthwhile is Pinell's article, "Anámnesis y epíclesis en el antiguo rito galicano," *Didaskalia* 4 (1974): 3–130.

5. The two parallels had been pointed out by P. Jounel, "La composition des nouvelles prières eucharistiques," *LMD* no. 94 (1968): 57f. and had been cited even earlier by C. Vagaggini in his amply documented proposal for new anaphoras; see Vagaggini, *The Canon of the Mass and Liturgical Reform*, trans. edited by P. Coughlan (Staten Island, NY, 1967).

6. H. Wegmann, "Deux strophes de la prière eucharistique III du missel romain," in H. G. Auf der Maur, L. Bakker, A. van de Bunt, and J. Waldram, eds., *Fides sacramenti sacramentum fidei. Studies in Honor of Pieter Smulders* (Assen, 1981), 318.

7. T. Schnitzler, *I tre nuovi canoni ed i nuovi prefazi* (Rome, 1970), 62.

8. See P. Marini, ed., "Elenco degli 'Schemata' del 'Consilium' et della Congregazione per il Culto divino," *Notitiae* 18 (1982): 654–664.

9. See above, n. 5.

10. Schnitzler (n. 7), 63. In his memoirs, *La riforma liturgica (1948–1975)* (Rome, 1983), 205, n. 3, A. Bugnini recalls defending this anaphora against the accusation that it had been composed in collaboration with the Protestant observers accredited to the Consilium. To clear away any doubt, he notes that "the draft of the *schema* that was the basis for the third anaphora was composed in three working months (summer, 1965), in the library of the Abbaye du Mont-Cesar, Louvain, by one of the most capable consultors of the Consilium, now a member of the International Theological Commission, a man whose great theological competence and rare knowledge of the liturgy are acknowledged by all."

11. The reference is to the official report of Johannes Wagner, delivered at Nemi on March 17, 1967.

12. "O Father, truly holy, praise be yours from every creature!"

13. "In the demonstration of the Spirit and power." The Vulgate has *"Spiritus et virtutis"* (see also Acts 1:8). The words "Spirit and power" can be taken as a hendiadys, i.e, "power of the Spirit"; see C. K. Barrett, *The First Epistle to the Corinthians* (New York, 1968), 65–66.

14. Latin: *"Spiritus Sancti operante virtute."*

15. The Christocentrism of this cosmic vision is based on the fact that Christ is the firstborn of all creation and that in him all things in heaven and on earth were made (see Col 1:15–21). If we add the theology of John, we can also explain the words "you enlivened . . . all things," since "all things were made through him" (Jn 1:3) and "in him was life" (1:4).

16. The connection between the birth of the people (a people whose end is to worship God), the gift of the Spirit, and Passover as deliverance from Egypt is very clear in *Jubilees:* "create in them an upright spirit. . . . For they are thy people and thine own possession, whom thou hast delivered with thy great power from the hands of the Egyptians. Create in them a pure heart and a holy spirit, and let them not be ensnared in their sins, now or ever" (1, 20–21; Sparks 12). Another relevant passage is *Jubilees* 16, 17–18: "One of Isaac's sons would become a holy seed, and not be reckoned with the Gentiles: he would become the Most High's portion, and all his descendants settled in that land which belongs to God, so as to be the Lord's special possession, chosen out of all nations, and to be a kingdom of priests and a holy nation" (Sparks 58). The New Testament shows full continuity with these ideas: "Like living stones be yourselves built into a spiritual house, to be a holy priesthood, to offer spiritual sacrifices acceptable to God through Jesus Christ"(1 Pt 2:5). For the relation between Passover and the deliverance of the people as a constitutive theme of the rite, see R. Cantalamessa, *La pasqua della nostra salvezza* (Turin, 1971), 23–27.

17. Session XXII, Doctrine and Canons on the Holy Sacrifice of the Mass, ch. 1 (DS 1739–1742; Neuner-Dupuis 1546–1547).

18. Dogmatic Constitution *Lumen gentium* on the Church, 17 (Flannery 368f.; Latin in Alberigo 862).

19. Heb 13:15–16. The passage is given in full because v. 16a is a necessary part of the argument. In the view of the prophets, cult (of whatever kind, including praise) is acceptable to God only if the life of the offerer is consistent with the logic displayed in worship. It follows that God is pleased with those sacrifices that combine an "acknowledgment of his Name" with doing good and sharing.

20. Latin: *"Ut haec munera quae tibi sacranda detulimus, eodem Spiritu sanctificare digneris."* Note the abrupt way in which the word "sacranda" introduces the theology of consecration into this anaphora. The Italian translation is smoother: "to sanctify these gifts," although the repetition of "sanctify" (see "sanctify all things" in the immediately preceding prayer) is not felicitous.

21. Before the reform of Paul VI, not much attention was paid to the prayer of offering that follows the anamnesis, because the "offertory" rite preceding the anaphora was so overdeveloped.

22. "Preparation of the gifts" is the new name for what the Missal of Pius V called the "offertory." See especially *GIRM* 49, where the language resembles that of the epiclesis in the third anaphora: "At the beginning of the liturgy of the Eucharist the gifts which will become the Lord's body and blood are brought [*affere*; the epiclesis uses the verb *deferre*] to the altar."

23. *Ver,* no. 139: *"Ne . . . munera delata despicias"* ("Do not . . . refuse the gifts we have brought").

24. A. Rodenas, " *'Eso no es comer la cena del Senor'* (1 Cor 11, 20b)," *Salmanticensia* 22 (1975): 551–561. Rodenas offers an accurate interpretation of the verse.

25. Exegetes usually speak of "disorders at table" in the Corinthian community and say that Paul's censure refers to these. But, if we look closely at the text, it is easy to see that v. 21, which contains the reproach directed at disorders at table, is simply a description of fact and is not the accusation Paul is making. The accusation is in vv. 18–19 (lack of unity); this lack is the basis of his claim that the supper of the Corinthians is not the Lord's Supper. We need only keep an eye on the sequence "In fact—therefore—in fact" in Paul's argument: he does not commend the Corinthians, because they assemble for the worse, not for the better (v. 17); "in fact" (Greek: *gar*), and there follows the indictment for a lack of unity (vv. 18–19); "therefore" (Greek: *oun*), Paul concludes, theirs is not the Lord's Supper (v. 20); "in fact" (*gar*), and the situation or event which has broken unity is described (v. 21).

At this point the accusation of vv. 18–19 has been substantiated, but we should not confuse the accusation with the evidence for it. V. 21 is intended as a proof of what is said in vv. 18–19 and not of what is said in v. 20, which is a conclusion from the argument given in vv. 17–19. In summary: first there is the argument, which is rendered complete in itself by the conclusion in v. 20; only then, in v. 21, does Paul speak of the fact which motivated his accusation. It is a very serious matter to say that the supper of the Corinthians is no longer the Lord's Supper, and therefore Paul dwells on the fact, bringing out its seriousness and its implications, since the link between the eating of one's own meal and the breaking of the unity required by the Lord's Supper might not have been clear. It is precisely the formal opposition between *idion deipnon* (one's "own meal") and *kyriakon deipnon* (the "Lord's Supper") that shows how the lack of unity (the category in which the eating of one's "own meal" is put) destroys the *veritas* (truth) of the Lord's Supper.

26. V. 17: "When you come together."

27. In fourth-century Latin, *igitur* was not much stronger than Greek *de* and consequently, according to Botte-Mohrmann (75, n. 9), there is no need to take account of it in the translation. But, in our modern anaphora, *igitur* is used as a synonym of *unde* or *ergo*, which even in the fourth century had a precise meaning and function.

28. Latin: *"Memores igitur, Domine, eiusdem Filii tui salutiferae passionis, necnon mirabilis resurrectionis et ascensionis in caelum. . . ."*

29. In Latin, "salvation" is an attribute of the passion or suffering of Jesus: *"salutifarae passionis,"* in keeping with the ancient patristic conception of *passio/Pascha* ("suffering" = the "passing over" of Christ and, therefore, of his people). In the Italian, the *Christus passus* concept prevails, with the resurrection and ascension tacked on after the manner of a loosely connected appendix.

30. J.-M. Guillaume, *Luc interprète des anciennes traditions sur la résurrection de Jésus* (Paris, 1979), 217–218: "As the events recede into the past, tradition expands and the appearances of the risen Jesus become more extensive. In the beginning . . . no distinction is made between the resurrection and the ascension. The one or the other name can be used to refer to the same reality: this is the period of the first Easter formulas. . . . Next come statements in which a distinction is made purely at the level of ideas (and without any temporal reference) between resurrection and ascension. In the third stage of development, a temporal separation is posited between the two 'phases' of the Easter event."

John sheds the most light on the theological aspect. Here is the analysis offered by R. Schnackenburg, *The Gospel According to John* 3, trans. D. Smith and G. A. Kon

(New York, 1982): "Can resurrection, 'ascent,' and glorification be separated from one another? Is there a peculiar in-between state between coming out of the tomb and return to the Father? All these questions are wrongly posed. We must rather probe what intention the evangelist is pursuing with these forms of expression, and seek to understand the text according to this intention" (318). His conclusion: "The risen Jesus still has a task to fulfill for the disciples: to mediate for them, as the one who has returned home to the Father, the full fellowship with the Father. To that belong the sending of the Spirit (cf. 14:16f.), the hearing of prayer (14:13), the achievement of greater works (14:12), the experiencing of God's love (14:23), in short, everything which is the fruit of Jesus' completed work. Jesus is, as the risen one, already 'in the course of ascending' " (319). "For him [John], the crucifixion is already 'lifting up' and leads directly to his [Jesus'] 'glorification.' For himself everything is compressed into Jesus' 'hour,' therefore, it is not really possible to dissect the event into death, resurrection, lifting up, and installation in heavenly glory" (ibid.).

31. C. Vagaggini, *The Canon* (n. 5), 148–150. The concern for Latin *cursus* passed, of course, from the texts composed by Vagaggini into the Latin texts of the anaphoras in the new Missal. [*Cursus* is prose rhythm and, specifically, the cadences or concluding words (*clausula*) of the sentence.—Tr.]

32. "Looking forward to [or awaiting] his second coming."

33. [The translation—see the beginning of the chapter—is very awkward and un-English with all its participles; but, as you can see, such a very literal translation brings out the author's points.—Tr.]

34. [For the author's argument, we are giving our own translation of Vagaggini's original Italian. The translation in *The Canon*, 126, is different and, of course, superior as English.—Tr.]

35. [In the Appendix to Chap. Five, the draft of Anaphora III, with its four proposals for the anamnesis and epiclesis, is translated, again in a literal manner.—Tr.]

36. The expression *hostia salutaris* occurs twice in the Vulgate: in 2 Mc 3:32 and Lv 10:14.

37. Schemata 218 (= *De missali* 34, Addendum).

38. See the Appendix.

39. VSC 48 (Flannery 17); see also the Dogmatic Constitution *Lumen gentium* on the Church 11 (Flannery 361–363).

40. The words "pleasing to you," which are added in the Italian translation ("May he make of us a perpetual sacrifice that is pleasing to you"), do not occur in the draft or in the definitive text. They seem, nonetheless, an excellent interpretation (and, therefore, a legitimate development) of the Latin *tibi* (to you).

41. See the Appendix to Chap. Five.

42. "Anamnesis" is the prayer that begins "Mindful therefore, Lord" and ends with "this living and holy sacrifice." The "recommendation of the sacrifice" is the prayer that begins "Look, we pray" and leads into the commemoration of the saints.

43. This description of the gifts we offer is to keep alive our awareness that everything is from God and that we cannot give him anything that does not already belong to him. This concern was meaningful in the past; is it still meaningful today?

44. *The Canon*, 169–172.

45. Here are the two Latin versions: "*Agnosce victimam cuius voluisti intercessione placari*" (criticized by Vagaggini), and "*Agnoscens hostiam cuius voluisti immolatione placari*" (final redaction).

46. [Again, a literal translation of Vagaggini's Italian; see *The Canon* 127.—Tr.]

47. See Hänggi-Pahl 384: "We offer . . . this living and holy and acceptable sacrifice . . . by which you were appeased and reconciled [*placatus et reconciliatus*], for the sins of the world."

48. *The Canon*, 174.

49. Rom 12:1. To better appreciate the similarity, here is the Vulgate version of Rom 12:1: "*Ut exhibeatis corpora vestra hostiam viventem, sanctam, Deo placentem, rationabile obsequium vestrum.*" *Hostia* here stands for the Greek *thysia* and may therefore be correctly translated as "sacrifice." See also 1 Pt 2:5.

50. Once again, R. Taft who in his article, "The Frequency of the Eucharist Throughout History," in M. Collins and D. Power, eds., *Can We Always Celebrate the Eucharist?* (Concilium 152; New York, 1982), 20, very politely refers to the unavoidable distinction, made by the entire tradition, between the sacrifice of Christ as a historical event that occurred once and for all, and its sacramental celebration: "A common tradition . . . shows, I think, that only the sacrifice of Christ has absolute value. Attempts to assign the same value to its sacrament are vain."

51. *The Canon*, 176.

52. Here is the Latin text (Férotin 271): "*Hec est hostia que pependit in ligno; hec est caro que resurrexit de sepulcro. Quod pro nobis obtulit sacerdos noster in ueritate, hoc conferimus in panis et uini suauitate. Cognosce precamur, omnipotens Deus, uictimam qua intercedente placatus es, et suscipe in adoptionem quibus Pater per gratiam factus es*" (*Postpridie* prayer of the Mass for the Fourth Sunday of Easter).

Vagaggini cites another text that brings out clearly this theology according to which the victim is now being immolated: "For this spotless victim [*hostia*] still lives, and living, is continually sacrificed. This is the only victim which could appease God, since it is itself God" (*Post nomina* prayer of the Mass for Christmas, in Férotin 55; trans. in *The Canon*, 176).

53. See Session XXII, cap. 1–2 (DS 1739–1743; Neuner-Dupuis 1546–1548). The manner of offering (*offerre* or *immolare*) is different in that on the cross it was by bloodshed while in the Mass it is without bloodshed; but the victim in both cases is a blood victim, that is, *Christus passus*. This is sufficient to legitimate the use of the terminology of the blood sacrifice, even if modern theology regards it as unacceptable, as Vagaggini has persuasively argued.

54. Gregory I, *Dialogorum libri quattor* IV, 58 (PL 77:425). In Latin, the closing words are: "*iterum in hoc mysterio sacrae oblationis immolatur.*"

55. "Relative" means that the rite is sacrificial by reason of its relation to the cross of the Lord; "absolute," applied to the Eucharist, would mean that it is a sacrifice in and of itself, independently of the Lord's cross.

56. *Ver*, no. 1302; in Latin: "*Suscipe, Domine, sacrificium, cuius te uoluisti dignanter immolatione placari, et praesta, quaesumus, ut huius operatione mundati bene placitum tibi nostrae mentis offeramus affectum.*"

57. Latin: "*Suscipe, Domine, propitius hostia: quibus et te placare voluisti et potenti pietate restitui.*"

58. *Ver*, no. 879: "*Munera tua, Deus, institutor, inlustra, et per has hostias quibus te placari uoluisti, sanctifica misericors immolantes.*"

59. "Recognizing the 'victim' (*hostia*) . . ."

60. G. Wegman, "Deus strophes . . ." (n. 6), 314.

61. This definition of "*metanoia*" or conversion of heart is from the new Rite of Penance, Introduction, 6a, trans. in *The Rites of the Catholic Church* 1 (New York, 1976), 345.

62. J. Guillet, "Spirit of God," in Léon-Dufour 575.

63. "As yet the Spirit had not been given, because Jesus was not yet glorified" (Jn 7:39).

64. "Being therefore exalted at the right hand of God, and having received from the Father the promise of the Holy Spirit, he has poured out this which you see and hear" (Acts 2:33).

65. In Latin, the anaphora has *"Spiritu eius Sancto repleti."* The glorification of Christ consists in the giving of this fullness: "He will glorify me, for he will take what is mine and declare it to you" (Jn 16:14).

66. "for the sanctification of soul, body, and spirit, so that we may become one body and one spirit" (Hänggi-Pahl 352). The source of this part of the Anaphora of Basil (archaic text) is the Anaphora of Hippolytus which, instead of "for the sanctification of soul, body, and spirit," has "may be filled with the Holy Spirit." This last is also what we find in Anaphora III. For the archaic text of the Anaphora of Basil, see J. Doresse and E. Lanne, *Un témoin archaïque de la liturgie copte de S. Basile,* with an appendix by B. Capelle, "Les liturgies basiliennes et saint Basile" (Louvain, 1960), 20.

67. Wegman, "Deux strophes" (n. 6), 314.

68. See E. Mazza, "Omelie pasquali e Birkat ha-mazon. Fonti dell'anafora di Ippolito," *EL* 97 (1983): 109–181.

69. See, e.g., the Greek text of the Anaphora of John Chrysostom (Hänggi-Pahl 228).

70. Rom 12:1.

71. See L. Maldonado, *Vers une liturgie secularisée* (Paris, 1971), 34: "Jesus Christ is greater than the temple because he is himself the temple (Mt 12:5; Jn 2:19). In the same way, the liturgy transcends the limits set for it by the walls of a building."

72. See J.-P. Audet, "Le sacré et le profan. Leur situation en christianisme," *NRT* 79 (1957): 33–61; Y. Congar, "Situation du 'sacré' en régime chrétien," in the collective work, *La liturgie après Vaticane II* (Paris, 1967), 385–403.

73. "Gather it from the four winds, this sanctified Church, into your kingdom which you have prepared for it" (*Didache* 10, 5; Deiss 76 and Hänggi-Pahl 66–68).

74. *Constitutiones apostolorum* VII (Funk 1:414).

75. The words *"ipse nos tibi perficiat munus aeternuma"* are almost verbatim from *Ver,* no. 216: "*Propitius, domine, quaesumus, haec dona sanctifica, et hostiae spiritalis oblatione suscepta nosmet ipsos tibi perfice munus aeternum*" ("Lord, graciously sanctify these gifts and, by accepting the offering of our spiritual sacrifice, make us an eternal gift for yourself").

76. Vagaggini's Latin text is in *The Canon,* 136. A literal version of his Italian: "May he make us an everlasting gift to you so that we may obtain a heavenly inheritance with your saints."

77. Latin: "*Quorum intercessione perpetuo apud te confidimus adiuvari.*" In the draft version, the text was even fuller: "*Quorum meritis et intercessione perpetuo apud te confidimus adiuvari*" (see the Appendix).

78. Anaphora of John Chrysostom (Hänggi-Pahl 228). See also the Anaphora of Mark (ibid., 106). To explain these texts it is not necessary to fall back on elements in early Christian eschatology, especially since the texts are still in use and are therefore regarded as compatible with eschatology as it has continued to evolve. See C. Vogel, "Prière ou intercession? Une ambiguïté dans le culte paléochrétien des martyrs," in B. Bobrinskoy, et al., *Communio sanctorum. Mélanges offerts a Jean-Jacques von Allmen* (Geneva, 1982), 284–290.

79. A similar expression is in the prayer over the offerings for the octave Mass of

Christmas in *Ver*, no. 1265: "*Oblatio . . . qua . . . nostrae reconciliationis processit perfecta placatio*" ("Offering . . . by which . . . our reconciliation is made complete"). The most direct conjunction of "sacrifice" (*hostia*) and "reconciliation" seems to be in the Anaphora of Serapion: "By this sacrifice (*thysia*), O God of truth, be reconciled (*katallagethi*) to all of us and be propitiated (*hilastheti*)" (Hänggi-Pahl 130). Finally, this phrase from the third anaphora is cited in the Introduction (no. 2) of the new Rite of Penance; see *The Rites of the Catholic Church* (n. 61), 342, where the translation in the new Roman Missal is used: "the sacrifice which has made our peace with you."

80. Jn 6:51, where "world" has the same meaning as in the anaphora.

81. Hänggi-Pahl 81.

82. Ibid., 132.

83. Deiss 76 (text in Hänggi-Pahl 66).

84. Eph 4:15–16.

85. For discussion of this ecclesiology which was introduced by N. Afanasieff in his *L'Eglise du saint Esprit* (Paris, 1975), see P. C. Bori, "L'unité de l'Eglise durant les trois premiers siècles," *RHE* 65 (1970): 56–68. See also N. Koulomzine, "L'ecclésiologie eucharistique du père Nicolas Afanasieff," in the collective work *La liturgie: Son sens, son esprit, sa méthode* (Rome, 1982), 113–127. Whatever the problems raised by a eucharistic ecclesiology, it is regrettable that Catholic theologians have paid so little heed to Afanasieff's theology, especially when, as O. Rousseau observed in his preface (1972) to Afanasieff's book: "we consider that his name was cited in the discussion at Vatican II. In the collection of documentation that was made for the private use of the Council Fathers and distributed to them in 1964 for purposes of discussion, reference was made, as to a worthwhile source, to Father Afanasieff's book, *L'Eglise qui préside dans l'amour*. In addition, Chapter 3 of Vatican II's *De ecclesia*, no. 26, contains a doctrine like his, permitting us to think that he exercised some influence here. While the arguments he adduces may be open to disagreement, it seems that his basic intuition recaptured an ancient component of traditional ecclesiology. We must acknowledge the service he performed in rescuing it from oblivion" (8).

86. Heb 13:14. It may be an irrelevant coincidence, but the next verse (15) speaks of offering God a sacrifice of praise that is the fruit of lips which acknowledge his name. This is a profoundly eucharistic theme that finds expression in the anaphora.

87. K. Rahner, "The Sinful Church in the Decrees of Vatican II," in his *Theological Investigations* 6, trans. K.-H. and B. Kruger (Baltimore, 1969), 274.

88. *Didache* 10, 5 (Hänggi-Pahl 66).

89. The Latin says, in fact, "and [with] the *entire* people you have won," thus emphasizing the point that the list of roles in the Church is not meant to be exclusive of others not mentioned.

90. Dogmatic Constitution *Lumen gentium* on the Church, 26 (Flannery 381). On the whole question of the relation between the universal Church and its particular embodiments, see B. Neunheuser, "Chiesa universale e Chiesa locale," in G. Barauna, ed., *La Chiesa del Vaticano II* (Florence, 1965), 616–641.

The Latin of Anaphora III is more reserved than the Italian and other translations, in that it does not directly identify "family" and "Church." It speaks only of "this family which you willed should stand before you." The expression is reminiscent of the Anaphora of Hippolytus and refers directly to the cultic activity of the congregation.

91. This is the perspective that informs the description of the last judgment in Mt 25:31–46. It was thus a sensitivity to eschatology that inspired the composers of our anaphora in restoring this part of the intercession.

92. P. Prigent, *Apocalypse et liturgie* (Neuchâtel, 1964). See his more recent *L'Apocalypse de saint Jean* (Lausanne-Paris, 1981).

CHAPTER SIX

1. M. Arranz, "L'économie du salut dans la prière du Post-Sanctus des anaphores de type antiochien," *LMD* no. 106 (9171): 46–75.

2. P.-M. Gy acknowledges that the insertion of this first epiclesis is not fully in accord with the structure of the anaphora; see his "L'eucharistie dans la tradition de la prière et de la doctrine," *LMD* no. 137 (1979): 88.

3. For the terminology used here, see L. Ligier, "Célébration divine et anamnèse dans la prière de l'anaphore ou canon de la messe orientale," *Greg* 48 (1967): 225.

4. J.-P. Audet, "Esquisse historique du genre littéraire de la bénédiction juive et de l'eucharistie chrétienne," *RBib* 65 (1958): 371–399; L. Ligier, "La benedizione e il culto nell'Antico Testamento," in the collective work *Il Canone* (Rome, 1968), 9–21; T. J. Talley, "De la 'berakah' a l'eucharistie: Une question à réexaminer," *LMD* no. 125 (1976): 11–39.

5. At the beginning of the praise of God; during the anamnesis of the history of salvation; at the beginning of the Christological section of this anamnesis; at the beginning of the account of institution. In the pneumatological section that introduces the first epiclesis, the title "Father" occurs without any qualifying adjective, but, nonetheless, in a context of sanctification: "He [Christ] sent from you, Father, as the first fruits for believers, the Holy Spirit who would finish his work in the world and bring all holiness to completion." The invocation "merciful Father" (*clemens Pater*) appears in the intercessions for the living. Jungmann 2:126 makes the point that "holy Father" in the Roman preface corresponds to "most merciful Father" in the *Te igitur* of the Canon. The title "Lord" appears four times in the fourth anaphora, three of the occurrences coming after the account of institution. Therefore, the title "holy Father" is characteristic of the thanksgiving and the section before the account of institution, while "Lord" is characteristic of the section after the account of institution.

6. Jungmann 2:115.

7. Deiss 161; Hänggi-Pahl 337.

8. This expression, which is typical of the Roman prefaces (and of Anaphora II), is based on Mal 1:11 ("in every place incense is offered to my name") and Eph 5:20 ("always and for everything giving thanks in the name of our Lord Jesus Christ to God the Father"). When we add Heb 13:15 ("Let us continually offer up a sacrifice of praise to God, that is, the fruit of lips that acknowledge his name"), we have all the basis for speaking of the cultic and sacrificial value of the thanksgiving contained in the anaphora.

9. Rom 4; Gal 3:6–9.

10. E. Lanne, "La relazione dell'anafora eucaristica alla confessione di fede," *Sacra Doctrina* 47 (1967): 383–396.

11. A. Hamann, "La confession de la foi dans les premiers actes des martyres," in J. Fontaine and C. Kannengiesser, eds., *Epektasis. Mélanges patristiques offerts au Cardinal Jean Daniélou* (Paris, 1972), 99–105; idem, "Du symbole de la foi à l'anaphore eucharistique," in P. Granfield and J. A. Jungmann, eds., *Kyriakon. Festschrift Johannes Quasten* (2 vols.; Munster, 1970), 2:835–843; B. Bobrinskoy, "Confession de foi

trinitaire et consécrations baptismales et eucharistiques dans les premiers siècles," in *La liturgie expression de la foi* (Rome, 1979), 57–67.

12. Lanne (n. 10), 383.

13. See Lanne 395, n. 14, for an explanation of how this identity was weakened in the course of history.

14. Hamann, "Du symbole . . ." (n. 11), 840–841.

15. Ibid., 838.

16. L. Ligier, "Dalla cena di Gesù all'anafora della Chiesa," in the collective work *Liturgia Eucaristica* (Turin-Leumann, 1967), 33.

17. This view eliminates the problem posed during the Protestant Reformation: Justification by faith and/or justification by sacrament (understood as a "good work")? In the Eucharist, in fact, the anaphora, which is a profession of faith, would be the "form of the sacrament."

18. Hence the pastoral importance of active participation of the faithful through the acclamations that are provided; these call for an *interior* participation that is fervent and fruitful.

19. J. de Vaulx, "Holy," in Léon-Dufour 236.

20. On the fully eucharistic character of these passages, see E. Mazza, "*Didache* IX–X . . . ," *EL* 92 (1978): 393–419. Keep in mind that the study is not yet complete.

21. I. de la Potterie, *La vérité dans saint Jean* (2 vols.; Analecta Biblica 73–74; Rome 1977), 2:724.

22. Ibid., 2:734.

23. V. 17 ("sanctify them in the truth") is parallel to v. 11 ("keep them in thy name") and to v. 21 ("that they may all be one") (ibid., 1:78).

24. Ibid., 2:751.

25. The parallelism is only thematic and not verbal, given the different Greek verbs for "know": *gnōrizo* and *gignōsko*.

26. J. T. Forestell, *The Word of the Cross. Salvation as Revelation in the Fourth Gospel* (Analecta Biblica 57; Rome, 1974), 103–146.

27. "All who call upon the name of the Lord shall be delivered" (Jl 2:32 [3:5]).

28. The process of sanctification in Christ is finely expressed in the simple apothegm: "Those who are constantly mindful of Jesus are in the truth"; see J. Gouillard, *Petite philocalie de la prière du coeur* (Paris, 1953), 35. Divine sonship/daughterhood is revealed, i.e., given, in the mystery of Jesus. The invocation "holy Father" expresses and proclaims our acquisition of divine sonship/daughtership as a mystery of salvation that is revealed, i.e., given, in Christ. To proclaim the saving mystery of divine sonship/daughterhood is to live it and therefore to be redeemed.

29. Dt 6:4; 1 Cor 8:4; especially the doxology in Jude 25, as well as Eph 4:6, which was part of the primitive kerygma. See the Byzantine Anaphora of Basil: "You alone are God" (Hänggi-Pahl 230).

30. Rom 9:26 (Hos 2:1); Mt 16:16; Heb 10:31; 12:12; Acts 14:15; 1 Pt 1:23; Rv 4:10; 7:25.

31. Jn 17:3; Jgs 8:19; 1 Kgs 17:1; 1 Sm 17:26–36; 2 Kgs 19:16; Ex 34:6; Rv 3:7; etc. The adjective also occurs in the prayer of Polycarp which, as you may know, reproduces the eucharistic anaphora and applies it to martyrdom; see *Le martyre de Polycarpe* in SC 10 (Paris, 1969), 226–228. "God of truth" is also found in the Alexandrian Anaphora of Basil (Hänggi-Pahl 348).

32. Rom 1:21; Jn 4:22; 1 Jn 4:7–16.

33. Heb 1:8; 1 Pt 5:10; Rv 15:7.

34. "Who . . . dwells in unapproachable light" (1 Tm 6:16). The verse in Paul is di-

rected against worship of human beings and against any claim to plumb the nature of God.

35. 1 Jn. 1:5.

36. For this theme, see the Roman prefaces for Christmas and Epiphany.

37. Lk 18:19 reserves the qualification "good" for God alone (see also Ti 3:4). This theme is treated with some breadth in the Chaldean anaphora in Cod. Brit. Mus. Add. 14669 (Hänggi-Pahl 398). The vocative, "O good One," is used in the Byzantine Anaphora of Basil (ibid., 234) and the Greek Anaphora of James (ibid., 246).

38. Gn 1; Ps 36:10; Acts 17:25. The description "fountain of life" is in the anaphora of the *Euchologion* of Serapion (Hänggi-Pahl 128) and in the Anaphora of James (ibid., 244), while the anaphora in Book VIII of the *Constitutiones Apostolorum* has "giver [*chorēgos*] of life" (ibid., 88).

39. As early as Gn 14:19–22, God's relation with human beings is described as that of a creator; note that the description occurs in a prayer.

40. "That you might fill your creatures with your blessings." The Italian translation has "that you might pour out your love on all creatures." (ICEL: "to fill your creatures with every blessing.") "Love" instead of "blessings" is somewhat arbitrary, but it nonetheless conveys perfectly the meaning of the divine activity and improves the text. In the story of creation, God blesses the creatures of sea and sky (Gn 1:22), then human beings (1:28), and finally the sabbath (2:3). The patriarchs—Noah and his sons (9:1), and Abraham (12:2f.)—are blessed, and, in Abraham, all the nations. Paul extends this blessing to all when he says that in Christ the blessing bestowed on Abraham passes to the pagans (Gal 3:9–14). The Italian translation may have been inspired by the anaphora in Book VIII of the *Constitutiones Apostolorum*, which says: "who fill every living thing with *eudokia*" (Hänggi-Pahl 90; the Latin translation, ibid., 91, has "blessing"). For the sources: Ps 145:16; 136:25.

41. J. Mouroux, *Do This in Memory of Me*, trans. S. Attanasio (Denville, NJ, 1974), 21.

42. A. Tarby, *La prière eucharistique de l'Eglise de Jérusalem* (Paris, 1972), 114.

43. In presenting this theology of grace, the anaphora adopts the Eastern perspective which does not acknowledge an opposition between natural and supernatural, since dialogue with God is the historical condition in which human beings are created.

44. On this theme see O. Clément, "Le dimanche et le jour éternel," *Verbum caro* 20 (1966): 113 (cited in Tarby 114, n. 20).

45. Tarby 117.

46. The two Anaphoras of Basil and the Anaphora of James resemble each other very closely, so much so that the text of James may be thought to depend on the Alexandrian Anaphora of Basil, while being influenced also by Byzantine Basil. In thematic approach and in wording, the fourth anaphora is very close to Alexandrian Basil; in its underlying theology, however, it depends more on the Anaphora of James. In the passage we are considering, we can point to a mediating link between the theology of James and the fourth anaphora; we are referring to Vagaggini's Project C; see *The Canon of the Mass and Liturgical Reform*, trans. ed. P. Coughlan (Staten Island, NY, 1967), 130ff.

47. P.-M. Gy, "Le Sanctus romain et les anaphores orientales," in *Mélanges liturgiques offerts au R. P. Bernard Botte* (Louvain, 1972), 167–174.

48. Peter Chrysologus, *Serm.* 170 (PL 52:644).

49. *Ver*, no. 1544.

50. Gy, "Le Sanctus romain," 168f.

51. In the Antiochene rite, the Sanctus always has a trinitarian reference, while in the Alexandrian rite, it is always theological. A Sanctus addressed to the Son is characteristic of the Greek Anaphora of Gregory of Nazianzus (Hänggi-Pahl 358–372).

52. Gy, "Le Sanctus romain," 174.

53. The Latin text of Anaphora IV makes the Sanctus a confession of the divine name (see the introductory words: "We too . . . joyously confess your name, singing. . . . ."). This was a treasured theological theme in the worship and soteriology of the Old Testament, but the Italian translation legitimately drops it as no longer easily understood.

54. *VCS* 48: "Christ's faithful, when present at this mystery of faith, should not be there as strangers or silent spectators. On the contrary, *through a good understanding of the rites and prayers* they should take part in the sacred action, conscious of what they are doing, with devotion and full collaboration" (Flannery 16; italics added).

55. The Roman prefaces listed only four orders, as compared with nine in the Ambrosian rite which, on this point, agrees with the Anaphoras of Basil and James. On the theological significance of the angelic choirs, see E. Lanne, "Cherubim et Seraphim," *RSR* 43 (1955): 524–535.

56. Rv 7:15.

57. Mt 18:10.

58. The Latin text makes it clear that the glorification of God flows from the vision of the divine glory ("*vultus tui gloriam contemplantes te incessanter glorificant*").

59. 1 Cor 13:12.

60. P. Prigent, *Apocalypse et liturgie* (Neuchâtel, 1964); E. Cothenet, "Earthly Liturgy and Heavenly Liturgy According to the Book of Revelation," in the collective work, *Roles in the Liturgical Assembly*, trans. M. J. O'Connell (23d Liturgical Conference Saint Serge; New York, 1981), 115–135.

61. The theme of union with the heavenly liturgy is not to be confused with another that has been very dear to devotees of the Eucharist: the participation of the angels in worship of the Blessed Sacrament. In our present context, the angels do not take part in our liturgy; rather we join with them in theirs.

62. There are some slight differences from the Old Testament formulas: "your glory" instead of "his glory," "heaven and earth" instead of simply "earth." See Hb 3:3.

63. In early Christology *ho erchomenos* (he who is to come) is a very important messianic title.

64. Compare with Rv 4:8 and Ez 3:12.

65. Tertullian, *De oratione* 3.

66. It is from here that the "day and night" of our prayer comes.

67. In the thanksgiving after communion in *Constitutiones Apostolorum* VII, 26, 5 (Funk 1:414), we find: "Hosanna to the Son of David! Blessed is he who comes in the name of the Lord, our Lord God who manifests himself to us in the flesh." If we remove the clause about the incarnation, we are left with a citation of Mt 21:9, which has an inherently eschatological orientation. That is how it is used in the intercessions for the dead in a Coptic anaphora published in 1958, in E. Lanne, *Le Grand Euchologe du Monastère Blanc* (PO 28:303).

68. This expanded form occurs very often in Revelations and, according to E. Cothenet (n. 60), 126, has its basis in targumic usage.

69. The Latin text has *confiteri*.

70. The Second Eucharistic Prayer has a very simple transitional phrase that introduces the theme of the first epiclesis. In the Third Eucharistic Prayer, the theme is

the praise that rises up from every creature because of God's enlivening and sanctifying action, the ecclesiological aspect which is immediately specified: the formation of a people who will offer perfect worship and so fulfill the prophecy in Mal 1:11. See the Anaphora of Mark (ms Vat. gr. 1970; Hänggi-Pahl 102).

71. "Greatness" is a divine attribute that emphasizes God's transcendence even in his self-manifestation. For this reason, "great" can be the definition God gives of himself: "My name is 'Great' " (Mal 1:11; see Mal 1:5; Lk 9:43 where the Greek word is *megaleiotes*).

72. Prv 3:19; Ps 136:5.

73. Ps 8:5–10.

74. This theme is highly developed in the Chaldean Anaphora in Cod. Brit. Mus. Add. 14669 (Hänggi-Pahl 399–400).

75. "Man was made 'to the image of God,' as able to know and love his creator, and as set by him over all earthly creatures that he might rule them, and make use of them, while glorifying God (Sir 17:3–10)" (Pastoral Constitution *Gaudium et spes* on the Church in the Modern World 12; Flannery 913). "The achievements of the human race are a sign of God's greatness and the fulfillment of his mysterious design" (ibid., 34; Flannery 934).

76. This theme is one of the most widespread in the anaphoras; see the Anaphora of Mark (Hänggi-Pahl 102); Strassburg Papyrus (ibid., 116); Coptic Anaphora of Cyril (ibid., 135); Byzantine Anaphora of Basil (ibid., 232); Anaphora of James (ibid., 246).

77. Tarby (n. 42),127.

78. All creatures are beautiful, but only one is made in the image of God, according to Cyril of Jerusalem, *Catecheses baptismales* 12.

79. See what was said earlier about "through us every creature under heaven" and the dominion of human beings over the rest of creation.

80. A created god, a "god by grace"; see V. Lossky, *The Mystical Theology of the Eastern Church* (London, 1957). 117.

81. Ibid., 114–115.

82. P. Evdokimov, *L'orthodossia* (Bologna, 1965), 107–119; Lossky 117–118.

83. The definition of sin as a loss of friendship with God is also used in the Introduction (no. 5) to the new Rite of Penance: "Every sin is an offense against God which disrupts our friendship with him" (*The Rites of the Catholic Church* 1 [New York, 1976], 344).

84. Tarby 130.

85. Anaphora of James (Hänggi-Pahl 246). The Byzantine Anaphora of Basil makes the theme Christocentric: "in order to conform us to the image of his glory" (Hänggi-Pahl 234). See also Vagaggini (n. 46), 130ff.

86. When sin is described as disobedience, the reference is not to an impersonal violation of a law, for in such classic texts as Rom 5:19 and Heb 2:2 the Greek word that is translated as "disobedience" means a "not hearing," a "refusal to hear." Consequently, even when defined as disobedience, sin is still a rupture of a personal relationship.

87. Neh 9:17.

88. See Acts 17:26–27: "And he made from one every nation of men to live on all the face of the earth, having determined allotted periods and the boundaries of their habitation, that they should seek after God, in the hope that they might feel after him and find him. Yet he is not far from each one of us." On the nearness of God to us see also Rom 10:8 (Dt 30:14) and Jas 4:8.

89. 1 Tm 2:4–5.

90. The idea that God does not turn his gaze from human beings despite their sin is expressed through various verbs and in varying degrees of intensity in the Anaphora of Mark (Hänggi-Pahl 102), the Byzantine Anaphora of Basil (ibid., 234), the Alexandrian Anaphora of Basil (ibid., 348), and the Anaphora of James (ibid., 246).

91. Sir 18:10–14.

92. See the Alexandrian Anaphora of Gregory of Nazianzus: "As my good shepherd you ran after me when I had gone astray; as a true father you had compassion on me when I fell. . . . You arise as light for the straying; you are always present to help the ignorant" (Hänggi-Pahl 362). The author of this anaphora was not Gregory, but an unknown writer who drew extensively on the works of the Cappadocians.

93. On the theme of "hoping for salvation" as taught by the prophets, see Is 35:1-10, which is subsequently completed by Rom 8:24, where hope itself is a locus of salvation in Christ.

94. The Anaphora of James develops the theme by separating it into two parts: "You called us through the Law and formed us (*paideuō*) through the prophets" (Hänggi-Pahl 246). The theme reappears in the epiclesis, this time with the divine activity as the work of the Spirit: "You spoke in the Law, the prophets, and the New Testament." This treatment emphasizes the unity and continuity of the various stages and modes of the divine pedagogy. Biblical sources: Acts 3:21; Rom 3:21–22.

95. Therefore, the covenants are said to belong to Israel (Rom 9:4).

96. "The covenant he [Christ] mediates is better" (Heb 8:6; see Eph 1:10).

97. "Cup of . . . the . . . covenant, which shall be shed for you and for the many" (see Is 55:5).

98. Is 40:8; Tob 14:4; Nm 23:19; Is 25:1; Mal 3:6.

99. The prayer reflects the patience of God, which is never weakness but a call to conversion that respects the varying times and degrees of individual maturation (see 1 Pt 3:20; Rom 9:22–26). It is difficult to find a passage in scripture that expresses fully the patience of God toward each human being, but the Book of Hosea, taken as a whole, is the best source. On seeking God with a sincere heart, see the Conciliar Constitution *Lumen gentium* on the Church 16.

100. See also Mk 1:15; Eph 1:10; Rom 1:3.

101. Mention of the incarnation brings the first reference to the Holy Spirit. Note that apart from the doxology, the four references to the Holy Spirit are all in function of Christ and his saving work. This is a very Johannine approach to the Spirit and confirms the interpretation of the second epiclesis that we shall give below. The description of the incarnation at this point in Anaphora IV is from the Alexandrian Anaphora of Basil (Hänggi-Pahl 388f.).

102. See also Rom 8:3; Phil 2:7–8. This theme does not occur frequently, but it may be found in the Anaphora of Epiphanius of Salamis (Hänggi-Pahl 262) and the Armenian Anaphora of Gregory of Nazianzus (ibid., 238), although with a different nuance. Byzantine Basil prefers to cite Rom 8:3 and omit Heb 4:15.

103. Lk 4:18

104. Eph 1:10; 3:9.

105. See the Anaphora of John Chrysostom: "Having brought to fulfillment (*plērōsas*), the entire economy (undertaken) for us" (Hänggi-Pahl 226). See the Syrian Anaphora of the Twelve Apostles (ibid., 226), which was the source of the Anaphora of Chrysostom.

106. For the biblical basis, see 2 Tm 1:10. See the Chaldean Anaphora in Cod. Brit.

Mus. Add. 14669: "He advanced to his passion and death that by his passion he might deliver us from our passions, and by his death might give us eternal life, and in his resurrection might raise us with him from the dead" (Hänggri-Pahl 401). This passage is simply a rather heavy reworking of the felicitous words found in the Anaphora of Hippolytus: "He stretched out his hands in suffering to free from suffering . . ." (ibid., 81).

We say in the text that the literary formulation of this sentence on death and life is quite successful, but it must also be acknowledged that this is true only of the written text, since when it is proclaimed, one has the impression of a play on words that does not help convey the meaning in an incisive way. The same remark holds for the citation from 2 Cor 5:15 that follows immediately.

107. St. Basil, *Regulae brevius tractatae* 172 (PG 31:1195); *Moralia* 21 (PG 31:739).

108. *Moralia* 80, 22 (PG 31:870).

109. As everyone knows, the Greek of Jn 19:30 (*"paredōken to pneuma"*) has a double meaning: to hand over the spirit in the sense of dying, and to hand over the spirit in the sense of bestowing the Spirit (note the definite article before *pneuma*).

110. Rom 8:14.

111. See the Anaphora of Basil: "He sanctified us with your Spirit" (Hänggi-Pahl 350).

112. I. de la Potterie, "Parole et Esprit dans saint Jean," in M. De Jonge, ed., *L'Evangile de Jean. Sources rédaction, théologie* (Bibliotheca ETL 44; Gembloux, 1977), 177–201. See also H. Schlier, "Il concetto di Spirito nel Vangelo di Giovanni," in his *Reflessioni sul Nuovo Testamento* (Brescia, 1969), 341–350.

113. The theme of any anaphora is precisely remembrance of the work of salvation which Jesus brought to completion. Such remembrance presupposes a true understanding of Jesus as the Truth sent to us by the Father; it is the Spirit who will lead (*hodēgēsie*) us to the entire truth (Jn 16:13) and teach (*didaxei*) and make us remember (*hypomnēsei*) all that Jesus said (Jn 14:26). Without the activity of the Spirit, there can be no thanksgiving and human beings cannot celebrate the anaphora; without the action of the Spirit, neither eucharist nor life in Christ exists.

114. Rom 8:23.

115. A. George has shown interesting points of convergence between the pneumatology of John and that of Luke; see his "L'Esprit Saint dans l'oeuvre de Luc," *RBib* 85 (1978): 500–542.

116. If we are correct in our analysis of this part of the anaphora, wherein the title "holy Father" helps to interpret all the stages of salvation that are described, and if we are correct in our interpretation of the work of the Spirit as final explicitation of the "holy Father" theme, then we must conclude that the fourth anaphora takes a more decidedly pneumatological approach than even the Byzantine Anaphora of Basil and the Anaphora of James. But, the discussion deals solely with a basic texture that hardly emerges in the proclamation of the anaphora.

117. We are evidently unduly schematizing the difference between East and West, inasmuch as the difference exists only in a prevailing diffuse mentality and not in the liturgical texts.

118. The anaphora uses the traditional liturgical term *sanctificare* instead of the technical theological term *consecrare*; the same term should be used in catechesis. Retention of the word "sanctify" helps to highlight the close continuity between the action of the Holy Spirit on the bread and wine and his action on the faithful in eucharistic communion.

119. We are not rejecting a possible epicletic interpretation of the prayers *Quam oblationem* and *Supplices* in the Roman Canon, although these pose various problems for the exegete.

120. The genesis of the structure of the Alexandrian anaphoras is a complex subject, since this structure betrays Antiochene influences which prevent us from saying what the anaphoras were like before they underwent these influences. In any case, the Alexandrian anaphoras have two epicleses: the first flows out of the Sanctus and leads into the account of institution; the second comes after the anamnesis and leads directly into the doxology.

The theologians have developed an interesting distinction between consecratory epiclesis and sanctificatory epiclesis, depending on whether the epiclesis asks for the consecration of the bread and wine or for the sanctification of the faithful who share in the bread and wine. The distinction is strictly applicable, however, only to the anaphoras in our Missal, since in the Alexandrian tradition, the second epiclesis is always both consecratory and sanctificatory.

The first epiclesis remains to be explained. Eight texts must be taken into account: (1) the Anaphora of Mark, (2) Rylands Library Papyrus 465, (3) the Dêr-Balizeh Fragment, (4) the Anaphora of Serapion, (5) the fragment of Louvain Coptic Cod. 26, (6) the Anaphora of Thomas the Apostle (ed. E. Lanne in PO 28:31), (7) the Anaphora of Matthew (PO 28:349), and (8) the Anaphora of Cyril (= Coptic redaction of the Anaphora of Mark). Of these eight "first epicleses," only two are in fact consecratory, namely the Dêr-Balizeh Fragment and the Louvain Fragment, but the latter is mutilated and we do not know whether there was a second epiclesis and what its content was. The Dêr-Balizeh Fragment is also mutilated, but contains some lines which are the conclusion of a second epiclesis, although we can say nothing about its nature. In summary, of the eight texts in question, only one—the Dêr-Balizeh Fragment—shows a first, consecratory epiclesis which is followed, after the anamnesis, by a second epiclesis of unknown content. This is certainly very little on which to base the theology of the two epicleses, one consecratory and the other sanctificatory. In this case-study, we have not taken into account the Ethiopian anaphoras, which are late and the results of an encounter of various traditions.

121. A few examples will suffice. For the Latin Fathers, see St. Ambrose, *De mysteriis* 9, 53–54 (SC 25bis:187–188). For the Syrian Fathers, see E. Pataq-Siman, *L'expérience de l'Esprit par l'Eglise* (Paris, 1871), 193–202, 222–224. See also the interesting Jacobite texts cited by I.-H. Dalmais, "L'Esprit Saint et le mystère du salut dans les epiclèses eucharistiques syriennes," in the collective work *L'Esprit Saint dans la liturgie* (Rome, 1977), 55–64.

122. C. Vagaggini, *Theological Dimensions of the Liturgy. A General Treatise on the Theology of the Liturgy*, trans. L. J. Doyle and W. A. Jurgens (Collegeville, MN, 1976), 30ff., 602.

123. It is worth noting that Thomas Aquinas discussed the problem of miraculous eucharistic visions in which it is not the glorious Christ but "flesh or a child" that appears; see *Summa theologiae* III, 76, 8.

124. V. Palashkovsky, "La theologie eucharistique de Saint Irenée, évêque de Lyon," in *Studia Patristica* II/2 (Texte und Untersuchungen 64; Berlin, 1952), 277–281.

125. Tertullian, *Adversus Marcionem* IV, 40 (CCL 1:656). It is clear that a modern reader must think of "sacrament" wherever the word "figure" occurs.

126. G. Martelet, *The Risen Christ and the Eucharistic World*, trans. R. Hague (New York, 1976), 143.

127. See H. de Lubac, *Corpus mysticum: L'Eucharistie et l'Eglise au moyen âge. Etude historique*, 2d Ed. (Théologie 3; Paris, 1949), 297–339.

128. See A. Gerken, *Teologia dell'eucaristia* (Rome, 1977), 158ff.

129. See E. Dumoutet, *Le Christ selon le chair et la vie liturgique au moyen âge* (Paris, 1932), 149–150.

130. Radbert could say without hesitation that the Eucharist really gives us the very same Christ who was born of the Virgin, died, was buried, and rose, and not simply an *umbra* (shadow = sacrament in the language of the time). In his position, sacramentality seems essentially to diminish as well as to guarantee the real presence. Radbert represents an exaggerated realism which in the name of the real presence ends up denying the sacramentality of that presence. See Martelet 132–133.

131. Y. Congar, "Pneumatologie ou Christomonisme dans la tradition latine?" *ETL* 45 (1969): 397.

132. All the epicleses ask for the transformation of the bread and wine into the body and blood of the Lord, but they do so in a direct way, not via the concept of sacrament as found in one or other explicit theology. An interesting exception, though not of any great significance since it depends on 1 Cor 10:16, is the First Ethiopian (Alexandrian) Anaphora of Cyril: "May the Holy Spirit bless and sanctify this bread and wine that it may become a participation in the body and blood of your beloved Son" (Hänggi-Pahl 197).

133. "When Jesus knew that his hour had come to depart out of this world to the Father, having loved his own who were in the world, he loved them to the end" (Jn 13:1). "Father, the hour has come; glorify thy Son that the Son may glorify thee" (Jn 17:1).

134. *Post-Pridie* for *Feria V in authentica* (*seu in Cena Domini*) (Hänggi-Pahl 453).

135. Comparable expressions lead into the account of institution in various anaphoras; the question arises whether these were not an archaic summary of the theology of the institution which by their development generated increasingly full and complete forms of the account of institution. Some examples of these introductory expressions are found in the Byzantine Anaphora of Basil: "He left us reminders [*hypomnēmata*] of his saving passion, and these we celebrate [*protetheikamen*] according to his commands. For when he was about to go forth to a voluntary . . . death" (Hänggi-Pahl 234); and in the Chaldean Anaphora in Cod. Brit. Mus. Add. 14669: "He left us this awe-inspiring mystery and gave us this good likeness [*demut*], in order that we must constantly do what he did and live by his mysteries" (ibid., 402).

136. In Paul's intention, the story of the institution offers a model for celebration that will eliminate from the Corinthian Eucharist the incongruities (divisions, v. 18) arising from disorders at table (v. 21) during the eucharistic meal.

137. "Of the Lord" = "belonging to the Lord"; see M. Zerwick, *Analysis philologica Novi Testamenti graeci* (Rome, 1953) on this passage.

138. See A. Rodenas, " 'Eso no es comer la Cena del Senor' (1 Cor 11, 20b)," *Salmanticensia* 22 (1975): 555–561.

139. On the origin of the concept of sacramental "validity," see P.-M. Gy, "La notion de validitè sacramentelle avant le Concile de Trente," *Revue de droit canonique* 28 (1978): 193–202.

140. "The faithful of Christ, gathered at the altar, offer sacrifice through the hands of the priest, who acts in the name of Christ and represents the community of God's people as they join in professing a single faith" (*De admissione ad communionem eucharisticam* 2).

141. DS 1741; Neuner-Dupuis 1546.

142. The relevant documents are listed in E. Mazza, "Messa dei fanciulli o messa con i fanciulli?" *RivLit* 64 (1977): 629, n. 23.

143. This means that the celebrant is the sacrament of Christ, a point which Pope John Paul II brings out well in his Letter *Dominicae Cenae* to all the Bishops on the Mystery and Veneration of the Eucharist (February 24, 1980), II, 1; trans. in *The Pope Speaks* 25 (1980): 150. B. D. Marliangeas, *Clés pour une théologie du ministère* (Paris, 1978) is required reading on this subject.

144. Jungmann 2:194ff.

145. These words are from 1 Cor 11:24 according to the Vulgate (Lk 22:19 in the Vg has *datur*, "is given"). Instead of "which will be given up for you," the Italian translation has "[this is my body] offered in sacrifice for you." This is already an interpretation, and we have to ask whether it is pastorally meaningful or even whether it is meaningful at all (see Chap. Nine).

146. This point was proposed to the 1967 Synod of Bishops for a consultative vote.

147. J. A. Jungmann, *La messa del popolo di Dio* (Turin, 1974), 79; this change into an acclamation was a personal decision of Paul VI.

148. The possibility of introducing acclamations was subsequently extended to the three anaphoras of Masses with Children. The pastoral result has been very positive, especially when the acclamations are sung.

149. Redemption interpreted as service is a familiar concept; it is used in interpreting the washing of feet in Jn 13. It should be noted, however, that *proslambanō* (receive, accept) is also used once for redemption in the New Testament (Rom 15:7).

150. Ps 15:10; Acts 2:27; 2:31; 13:34–37.

151. 1 Cor 11:26. The word "this" should be emphasized.

152. H. Schürmann, *Comment Jésus a-t-il vécu sa mort?* (Paris, 1977), 83–117; J. Jeremias, *The Eucharistic Words of Jesus*, trans. N. Perrin (London, 1966), 204–262; A. Deschamps, "Les origines de l'eucharistie," in the collective work, *L'eucharistie, symbole et réalité* (Paris, 1970), 92–125. For the approaches to the problem, see T. Süss, *La communion au corps du Christ* (Neuchâtel, 1968), 205–256, especially 211 on E. Schweizer. See also F. J. Leenhardt, *Le sacrement de la sainte cène* (Neuchâtel-Paris, 1948), 29–38.

153. The modern concept of "sacrament" is not different from or opposed to the "real symbol" which various authors are now retrieving from the patristic period, even though the word "symbol" arouses an immediate distrust in some minds. The important thing is to move beyond terminology to its theological content.

154. The Latin texts have: *unde* (Roman Canon and Anaphora IV), *igitur* (Anaphoras II and III; Anaphoras I and II for Children), or *quapropter* (Anaphora III for Children). The Italian translation omits the conjunction in every case.

155. See the classical work of O. Casel, *Faites ceci en mémoire de moi* (Lex orandi 34; Paris, 1962).

156. Sacred Congregation for Divine Worship, *Introduction* to the *Eucharistic Prayers for Masses with Children and for Masses of Reconciliation* (November 1, 1974), no. 19, in *DOL* 2017.

157. Ibid., no.3 (*DOL* 2001).

158. A "memorial" causes one to remember; the word, therefore, refers not to the object being commemorated and remembered, but to the means that produces remembrance; we may, therefore, speak of "objective remembrance." See J.-M. R. Tillard, "Le mémorial dans la vie de l'Eglise," *LMD* no.106 (1971): 24–25.

159. "The whole Prayer of Thanksgiving is, in substance, a memorial prayer, particularly the Christological portion" (Jungmann 2:219).

160. Ibid., 2:218–219.

161. In the recent reform, the Roman liturgy acquired an element previously missing: the mention of the *parousia* or final coming of the Lord. The change is highly significant not only theologically but pastorally, since this theme plays little part in Christian life, which consequently lacks the important element of expectation. It hardly needs saying that eschatological expectation is not to be identified with fear of death and divine judgment, even if there is some connection, as can perhaps be seen from the Anaphora of James.

163. The passage is inspired by the primitive kerygma; see Acts 2:22–36.

164. It is easy to show a definite influence of the creeds on the anamneses of ancient liturgies.

165. B. Botte, "Problèmes de l'anamnèse," *JEH* 5 (1954): 19.

166. See Eph 5:2 and Heb 10. For the Fathers, see J. de Watteville, *Le sacrifice dans les textes eucharistiques des premiers siècles* (Neuchâtel, 1966).

167. "Cross" is used as a name for the entire paschal mystery, which is a single mystery even if it is described by means of the various historical events that comprise it. So, too, the "sacrifice" includes not only the Lord's death but also his resurrection and ascension into heaven, as well as his sitting at the Father's right hand, his sending of the Spirit, and his own second coming. The anamnesis in the anaphora has for its function to provide this list and then to define *this* memorial as a "sacrifice." "Sacrifice" applies, therefore, both to the paschal mystery as a single entity and to the phases of its historical reality. We cannot speak of the Eucharist as sacrificial without going on to define the meaning and scope of the sacrifice in light of the Eucharist itself.

168. W. Rordorf, "Le sacrifice eucharistique," *TZ* 25 (1969): 335–353. The modern theology of sacrifice has been enriched with a further patristic datum that entered directly into the anaphoras. We are referring to the use of citations from Heb 13:15; Mal 1:11; and Zep 3:9, which speak of the prayer of praise as the only sacrifice acceptable to God. From this follows the sacrificial character of the anaphora, which in some liturgies is the object of *offerre* along with the bread and wine. One example is the Anaphora of Serapion: "Accept also the thanksgiving of your people and bless those who have offered the gifts and the thanksgivings" (Hänggi-Pahl 132). See also the Armenian Anaphora of Gregory of Nazianzus: "We offer blessing and praise" (ibid., 329). This perspective is not easy to include in a summary theological synthesis, but it provides a very useful basis for better understanding the sacrificial perspective of the Council of Trent. See Gerken (n. 128), 139–176, who offers a very radical approach to the theology of Trent; for an analysis of the Tridentine texts, see H. Holstein, "La cène et la messe dans la doctrine eucharistique du concile de Trente," in his *Humanisme et foi chrétienne* (Paris, 1976), 649–662.

169. Heb 9:14.

170. Heb 10:14.

171. The "sacrifice that is acceptable to you" is Christ himself as in Eph 5:2 and Heb 10. The idea of "a source of salvation for the world" seems to come from the anamnesis in the Anaphora of Theodore of Mopsuestia: "By which a great salvation has come to the entire human race" (Hänggi-Pahl 383). See also the Greek Anaphora of James (ibid., 246).

172. Vagaggini, *The Canon* . . . (n. 46), 126. [Again, we translate Vagaggini's Italian

text in a literal manner; for a different translation of the Latin, see the passage in *The Canon*. . . . —Tr.]

173. Here is a series of passages from the anaphoras: "We offer this awe-inspiring and bloodless sacrifice" (Greek and Syriac Anaphoras of James; Hänggi-Pahl 248 and 271); "We offer this spiritual and bloodless worship" (Anaphora of John Chrysostom according to Cod. Barb. 336; Hänggi-Pahl 267); "We offer you this spiritual sacrifice" (Syriac Anaphora of the Twelve Apostles; Hänggi-Pahl 267); "Offering in your sight this mystery of the saving body and blood of your only-begotten Son" (Armenian Anaphora of Athanasius; Hänggi-Pahl 322); "I offer you the symbols. . . . You have given me this mystical (= sacramental) participation in your flesh in bread and wine" (Alexandrian Anaphora of Gregory of Nazianzus; Hänggi-Pahl 362); "We have offered you this living sacrifice, this bloodless oblation. We have offered you this bread, the likeness (= sacrament) of the body of the Only-begotten. . . . We have also offered the cup, the likeness of the blood" (Anaphora of Serapion; Hänggi-Pahl 130).

174. Ethiopian Anaphora of John, Son of Thunder (Hänggi-Pahl 157).

175. The anaphoras do not permit us to distinguish between the real presence of the Lord's body and blood and the real presence of his sacrifice, that is, of his death and resurrection. The "sign" is the same for both, namely, the sacramental bread and wine. The theology at work in the anaphora makes the two presences one and the same, and it is impossible to see how they could be opposed.

Among the terms used for the eucharistic bread and wine is not only the classical "eucharist," but also "sacrifice." See, e.g., these passages from the Bobbio Penitential, nos. 43 and 44, in E. Martène, *De antiquis Ecclesiae ritibus* (Antwerp, 1736), 1:710: "If anyone loses the sacrifice through negligence, he is to do penance for a year"; "And anyone who neglects the sacrifice and allows it to be eaten by worms is to do penance for half a year." The Bobbio Penitential dates from the years 700–725 according to C. Vogel, *Les "Libri Paenitentiales"* (Trunhout, 1978), 74. Furthermore, from the *Iudicia* of Pope Gregory III, ch. 28 (Martène 1:711): "If anyone loses the eucharist, that is, the sacrifice, through negligence, he is to do penance for a year or for three Lents." And *Ex pervetusto codice S. Vitonis Virdunensis* (Martène 1:712): "If the sacrifice falls to the ground from the hands of the offerer . . . " For a better understanding of the historical context of these documents, see the codicological study of A. M. Martimort, *La documentation liturgique de dom Eduard Martène* (Rome, 1978), 323–324.

176. Jungmann, *La messa del popolo di Dio* (n. 147), 20.

177. L. Deiss, *It Is the Lord's Supper. The Eucharist of Christians*, trans. E. Bonin (New York, 1976), 69.

178. See Deiss 91–92: "Two deviations imperil a proper understanding of the Church's participation in her Lord's sacrifice. The first emphasizes man's offering almost to the point of substituting it for—or at least overshadowing—Christ's. The offertory, with its mystique blown out of proportion, afforded ample scope for the expression of such errors. Lest the faithful seem to be approaching God empty-handed, they would offer him whatever might symbolize human joy and suffering. There were touching excesses. . . . Where the first deviation sins by excess in regard to man's offering, the second sins by defect. Since we cannot offer God anything—outside of Christ—which is worthy of his glory, some conclude that they need not offer him anything at all. This attitude launches a disintegrative process in which the sacrificial meaning of the Eucharist is rapidly lost."

179. Third Eucharistic Prayer.

180. "Look, Lord, upon the sacrifice which you have prepared for your Church."

181. The beginning of the epiclesis in Anaphora IV is quite different from the beginning in Anaphora III. In the latter, the text was based on a passage in the Old Spanish liturgy: "Recognize the victim by whose intercession you have been reconciled" (Férotin 645). The beginning of the epiclesis in Anaphora IV is a mosaic of biblical texts: "*Look upon* the face of thine anointed" (Ps 84:9); "The day of the Lord is at hand; *the Lord has prepared a sacrifice*" (Zep 1:7). The combining of these texts is inspired by a typological interpretation of the sacrifice of Isaac: "God will provide himself the lamb for a burnt offering" (Gn 22:8).

182. The term "encounter" is inappropriate, but has become accepted. Keep in mind 1 Cor 10:16: "The cup of blessing which we bless, is it not a participation [or: communion] in the blood of Christ? The bread which we break, is it not a participation [or: communion] in the body of Christ?"

183. We are drawing directly on the fine exposition in Tarby (n. 42), 141–143, 155–159.

184. The two phases reflect the rite of atonement (*kippur*) which also had two stages: (1) the immolation of the victim, and (2) the entrance of the high priest into the Holy of Holies.

185. The expression of the theme would be improved by adding the enthronement at the Father's right hand, which is found in the sources: Byzantine Anaphora of Basil (Hänggi-Pahl), Alexandrian Anaphora of Basil (ibid., 352), Greek Anaphora of James (ibid., 248), etc.

186. Heb 9:24.

187. Heb 7:25.

188. Heb 12:24.

189. See de la Potterie (n. 21), 2:1012–1013: "If 'the Spirit is the truth' (1 Jn 5:7), he is so in relation in Christ. . . . The action of the Spirit of truth has therefore a trinitarian structure: the Spirit of truth leads to Christ, who is the truth, and through him to the Father."

190. P. Evdokimov, *Lo Spirito Sano nella tradizione ortodossa* (Rome, 1971), 117.

191. The Eucharist is, therefore, only apparently Christocentric. In its very Christocentrism, the Eucharist is an epiphany or manifestation of the Spirit to the faithful and the entire Church.

192. Tarby (n. 42), 156.

193. "Grant . . . that, being gathered into one body by the Holy Spirit. . . ."

194. For the distinction between "one" (*unus*) and "unique" (*unicus*), see E. Lanne, "L'Eglise une dans la prière eucharistique," *Irén* 50 (1977): 326–344, 511–519. On the creeds, ibid., 46–58.

195. Augustine, *In evangelium Joannis tractatus* 26, 13 (PL 35:1613).

196. An exception is the Byzantine Anaphora of Basil, which is the source of the epiclesis in Anaphora IV: "Bring together in the communion of the one Holy Spirit all of us who share in one bread and cup" (Hänggi-Pahl 238). See also the Alexandrian Anaphora of Basil (ibid., 352).

197. See D. Marzotto, *L'unità degli uomini vel Vangelo di Giovanni* (Brescia, 1977); M. L. Appold, *The Oneness Motif in the Fourth Gospel* (Tübingen, 1976); F. M. Braun, "Quatre signes johanniques de l'unité chrétienne," *NTS* 9 (1962–1963): 147–155. For a better formulation of the problem with a view to the application of Johannine theology to the primitive eucharistic liturgy, see R. E. Brown, *The Community of the Beloved Disciple* (New York, 1979); E. R. Goodenough, "John, a Primitive Gospel," *JBL* 64 (1945): 145–182.

198. Marzotto 64–67.

199. Jer 30–31.

200. Jer 31:3.

201. Jer 31:1.

202. Jer 31:9–10.

203. Ez 20:44.

204. Ez 34:23.

205. *Didache* 9, 2.

206. Ez 37, 28.

207. It is likely that the influence of Second Isaiah on these Christian texts was exercised through the *Ahabhah Rabbah*: "Gather us into peace from the four corners of the earth and bring us as free men into our own land . . . where we may constantly praise you and your oneness out of love" (Hänggi-Pahl 38).

208. Jn 4:27–42; 6:1–15; 10; 11:45–54; 12:20–36; 17; 19:23–42.

209. An actualization of Is 52:13, which the early Church applies to the ascension, while John applies it directly to the cross.

210. Marzotto (n. 197), 150.

211. Chapters 10 and 17 of John suggest the equivalence between "having life" and "being one."

212. Jn 12:23–32.

213. Jn 4:22–24.

214. Jn 11:49–52.

215. See sec. III of this chapter on "Holy Father."

216. Marzotto 189.

217. Note the widening scope of the prophecy: "the nation . . . the children of God.

218. This passage is the basis for the intercessions in the second anaphora.

219. Source of the "inheritance in heaven" idea in the intercessions of Anaphora IV; the Italian translation is fuller: "an everlasting inheritance in your kingdom."

220. *Didache* 10, 5 (Deiss 76).

221. Jn 17:21–23.

222. Lk 22:29–30.

223. Jn 4:22–24.

224. "That they may become in Christ a living sacrifice for the praise of your glory" (combination of Rom 12:1 and Eph 1:14).

225. "That, being gathered . . . they may become [*perficiantur*]. . . .

226. Rom 12:1–2.

227. 1 Cor 16:15; Rom 12:1.

228. L. Maldonado, *Secolarizzazione della liturgia* (Rome, 1972), 30–31.

229. Phil 2:16–17; Rom 1:9; 15:15–16; 2 Tm 2:4–6; Phil 4:18.

230. In fact, our text is not reducible to the Constitution on the Liturgy 48.

231. See the collective work *Anamnesis* 1 (Turin, 1974), 49.

232. In the Chaldean and Alexandrian liturgies, the epiclesis is not followed by the intercessions, but leads directly into the final doxology. The doxology is not an independent prayer, but is introduced by an "in order that" which links it to the epiclesis which it concludes. The doxology also concludes the epiclesis in the Anaphora of Hippolytus, which is the source of our Second Eucharistic Prayer. We take the name "Chaldean liturgy" (instead of "Eastern Syrian liturgy") from W. F. Macomber, "A History of the Chaldean Mass," *Wor* 51 (1977): 107–20, 523–36.

233. The words over the cup ("shed *for you* and *for the many* for the forgiveness of

sins") are the real basis of the theology of the intercessions when the latter are placed after the anamnesis and epiclesis.

234. In the Greek Anaphora of James, the intercessions are "for" various classes (the saints, etc.; Hänggi-Pahl 250), while in the two texts of the Anaphora of Basil, the petitioners join themselves "with" the saints (ibid., 238, 354). At this point, then, our fourth anaphora is closer to the Anaphora of James than to the two Anaphoras of Basil.

235. See the Roman Canon.

236. In the fourth anaphora, the intercessions continue and render explicit the "Church" theme of the epiclesis. From a theological standpoint, the join is complete; it is less from a literary standpoint.

237. The intercession for the episcopal order is traditional; see, e.g., the intercessions in the Anaphora of James (second redaction) in which commemoration is made of the 318 Fathers of the Council of Nicaea, the 150 of Constantinople, the 200 of Ephesus, the 630 of Chalcedon, the 604 of the Fifth Council, and the 189 of the Sixth (Hänggi-Pahl 259).

238. We assume that the *offerentium* are the priestly celebrants.

239. 1 Pt 2:10; the term refers to the Church and becomes programmatic in Vatican II.

240. Jer 29:13–14.

241. Jn 12:32.

242. The words "who have died in peace of your Christ" are from the Syriac Anaphora of James; but "the faith of Christ" of the original (*"qui in fide Christi obdormierunt"*: (Hänggi-Pahl 275) has been replaced by "the peace of Christ" from Col 3:15.

243. The context in Col 3:15 suggests this expansion of the "peace of Christ."

244. See the Byzantine Anaphora of Basil: "You [Lord] know the age and name of each; you know each one from their mother's womb. . . . You know each and their petitions, their dwellings, their every need" (Hänggi-Pahl 240).

245. Tm 2:19; Nm 16:5.

246. Jn 10:14.

247. T. Schnitzler, *I tre nuovi canoni ed i nuovi prefazi* (Rome 1970), 149.

248. See the Anaphora of Ignatius of Antioch: "the heavenly kingdom as our heritage" (Hänggi-Pahl 291). See also 1 Pt 1:4; Rom 8:17.

249. See the Byzantine Anaphora of Basil: "Lead us into your kingdom" (Hänggi-Pahl 357). See Lk 22:29–30, where Jesus tells his disciples at the Last Supper that he will prepare a kingdom for them as his Father has prepared one for him.

250. Rom 8:21. The liberation of creation is here linked to the operation in us of the Spirit who is given as first fruits.

251. Rom 8:19–24.

252. Rom 8:30.

253. Or: "sing your praises."

254. See the Byzantine Anaphora of Basil: "For you have given everything to us [*panta gar edōkas hēmin*]" (Hänggi-Pahl 242).

255. The text of the doxology is from the Roman Canon and is the same in all the anaphoras. For a commentary, see Jungmann 2:264–74.

256. In the anaphoras just listed, the epiclesis becomes a doxology and the Spirit is poured out that he may open the mouth of the Church to glorify God. The same theme finds moving expression, independently of the doxology, in the Anaphora of Serapion (Hänggi-Pahl 128).

257. *Ibid.*, 242.

258. Anaphora of Addai and Mari (ibid., 380).

259. Anaphora of Serapion (ibid., 130). See also Ambrose, *De sacramentis* IV, 20 (SC 25bis:112). On the biblical meaning of the term, see U. Vanni, "Omoioma in Paolo," *Greg* 58 (1977): 321–45, 431–70.

CHAPTER SEVEN

1. Sacred Congregation for Divine Worship, *Preces eucharisticae pro Missis cum pueris et de reconciliatione* (Rome, 1974). The text was not printed but mimeographed. The Introductions to the two sets of Masses are in *DOL* 1999–2023 and 2024–27.

2. Decree of promulgation (November 1, 1974), signed by James Cardinal Knox and A. Bugnini; text in *DOL* 1994–98. The norms set down in this decree were ratified by Paul VI in an audience of October 26, 1974, when he approved the experimental use of the new texts.

3. *DOL* 1996.

4. "Preces eucharisticae pro missis de reconciliatione," *Notitiae* no. 202 [1983]: 270. This is not a decree and is not signed. It is simply a note of presentation and is to be attributed to the editors of the periodical, which is published by the Sacred Congregation for the Sacraments and Divine Worship (Section for Divine Worship). It follows from this that no change has been made since the booklet of November 1, 1974; we shall therefore use the text of that booklet.

5. See Chap. Eight where the criterion of creativity as applied to the anaphoras for children is discussed.

6. *DOL* 1997

7. *DOL* 2024.

8. Italian Episcopal Conference, *Preghiere eucaristiche della riconciliazione* (Vatican City, 1977), *Premesse* 3. By "proper preface" is meant "preface of the day"; therefore, these anaphoras can be used when a seasonal preface is prescribed. This is a general principle which the Italian Episcopal Conference rightly regarded as needing clear explication. — The note introducing the (unchanged) Latin text in *Notitiae* no. 202 (1983): 270 takes a different approach: "Even though these anaphoras have their own prefaces, they can also be used with other prefaces if the latter refer to repentance and conversion (as is the case, for example, with the prefaces of Lent)."

9. A. Cuva, "Le nuove preghiere eucaristiche," *Liturgia* 12 (1978): 82–89.

10. "It is truly right, holy Father, that we should thank you, truly just that we should glorify you."

11. The Italian translation weakens the thought by translating *provocare* as "call." (ICEL: "invite us.")

12. The Italian has "in your infinite mercy"; this smacks of courtly rhetoric and is unusual as a translation of genitives ("God of goodness and mercy"), which may be translated more simply as adjectives ("good and merciful").

13. Hos 11:7–9. F. Brovelli, "Le 'preghiere eucaristiche della riconciliazione,' " *RivLit* 65 (1978): 360, gives the following biblical references for the opening lines of the anaphora: Ps 86:15; 103:8; 111:14; 145:8.

14. "You offered many covenants to human beings."

15. The two texts are alike based on the Alexandrian and Byzantine Anaphoras of Basil, the Anaphora of James, and the Alexandrian Anaphora of Mark (see Hänggi-Pahl 348, 234, 246, 102, respectively).

16. H. Schürmann, *Comment Jésus a-t-il vécu sa mort?* (Paris, 1977), 114.

17. The text alludes to classical passages in the New Testament. "Proclaim the ac-

ceptable year of the Lord" (Lk 4:19) is a prophecy (Is 61:2) which Jesus applies to himself to signal the coming of the final times, the beginning of the messianic and eschatological era. There is question here of *kairos*, not of *chronos*. The *kairos* (favorable [or: acceptable] time) in question is coextensive with the entire messianic age; if it were simply one part of that age, it would be *chronos*. When Lk 4:19 is applied to a *chronos* (segment of time), that is, to the Holy Year, the text is not being taken in its literal and proper sense or even in a typological sense; it is simply being given an "accommodated" sense.

18. The Italian translation—"from the beginning of the world you make us sharers in your loving plan, so as to make us holy as you are holy"—has literary value but lacks the incisiveness of the Latin. (ICEL: "Father, from the beginning of time you have always done what is good for man so that we may be holy as you are holy.")

19. Gn 1:26f.

20. The basis of the statement is a combination of two biblical texts: Mt 5:48 and Lv 11:44f.

21. The Italian translation is more specific: "(united) around you."

22. The Introduction to the anaphoras says that the structure of the texts is the same as that of Anaphoras II–IV of the Roman Missal (*DOL* 2026).

23. The Italian translation: "When we were dead because of sin" is, in our opinion, an improvement over the Latin *"cum vero perissemus"* ("when we had perished"), which is excessively terse and does not clearly bring out the special character of the destruction caused by sin. (ICEL: "When we were lost.")

24. The title "just" is given to Christ in Acts 3:14: "But you denied the Holy and Righteous One, and asked for a murderer to be granted to you, and killed the Author of life." The context in the anaphora and in Acts is the same: Christ's death on the cross.

25. P. Béguerie and J. Evenou, *Eucharisties de tous pays* (Paris, 1975), 82.

26. Irenaeus, *Demonstratio* 45 (SC 62:104); *Adversus haereses* IV, 24, 1 (SC 100/2:698–700. See R. Tremblay, "La fonction salvifique de la passion et de la mort de Jesus Christ et son rapport à la résurrection selon s. Irénée de Lyon. Esquisse," in M. Benzerath, A. Schmid, and J. Guillet, eds., *La pâque du Christ, mystère de salut (Mélanges offerts au P. F.-X. Durrwell)* (Paris, 1982), 280.

27. Brovelli (n. 13), 362.

28. "And through him to reconcile to himself all things, whether on earth or in heaven, making peace by the blood of his cross" (Col 1:20).

29. Brovelli 363.

30. *Rite of Penance* 5, in *The Rites of the Catholic Church* 1 (New York, 1976), 344.

31. The anaphoras of the Syriac family prefer to describe Christ's final coming as "glorious"; see the Anaphora of John Chrysostom (Cod. Barberini gr. 336; Hänggi-Pahl 226). See also the Syriac Anaphora of the Twelve Apostles (ibid., 267).

32. God has destined us for salvation (1 Thes 5:9), but this salvation is an inheritance that will not be revealed until the end of time (1 Pt 1:5). See C. Lesquivit and P. Grelot, "Salvation," in Léon-Defour 522: "Salvation, then, in the strongest sense of the word, is to be considered eschatologically as the day of the Lord (1 Cor 3:1ff; 5:5). . . . Christ will come to present us with salvation (Heb 9:28). We also await this final manifestation of the Savior, who will complete His task in transforming our body (Phil 3:20f); and it is in this respect that our salvation is an object of hope (Rom 8:23ff)."

33. Eph 2:14.

34. The Italian translation of the offering is clearer than the Latin: "We offer to

you, O truly faithful God, this sacrifice which reconciles the entire human race to you." (ICEL: "Therefore we offer you, God ever faithful and true, the sacrifice which restores man to your friendship.")

35. The language of Anaphora IV of the Missal is almost the same at this point.

36. These words are followed in Hippolytus by a request that "all who participate in the holy (mysteries) may be filled with the Holy Spirit" (Hänggi-Pahl 81).

37. Ibid., 222.

38. The Italian translation uses two synonyms: division and discord.

39. "You grant them . . . new life in Christ, and the power to serve all human beings by entrusting themselves more fully to the action of the Holy Spirit."

40. The Italian translation is redundant but more poetical: "We thank you . . . for the marvelous signs which you have worked in the world through Christ our Lord."

41. Latin: "*Experiendo cognoscimus.*"

42. Jer 5:23; 7:24; Lev 26:41; Hos 10:2.

43. Jer 31:31–34; Ez 36:25–28.

44. The Italian translates as "stubborn hearts."

45. The Italian weakens the Latin by translating *virtus* as "good will."

46. Beguérie and Evenou (n. 25), 87.

47. Is 2:4. See also: "I will cut off the chariot from Ephraim and the war horse from Jerusalem; and the battle bow shall be cut off, and he shall command peace to the nations" (Zec 9:10).

48. The Italian translation has: "the way that leads us to peace."

49. "Word," "hand," and "way" all refer to interpersonal relations and thus continue the theme of Christ's mediation.

50. In Luke, Christ dies as a martyr or witness; see A. George, "Le sens de la mort de Jésus pour Luc," *RBib* 80 (1973): 186–217.

51. Ez 36:24–28. We include v. 24 because it contains a reference to unification, that is, to the theme that immediately precedes the epiclesis.

52. The same thought is implicit in the introduction to the account of institution in Anaphora II for Masses with Children: "On the day before he suffered, he manifested your infinite love for . . ."

53. "With jubilation we have received from tradition this figure [*typum*] that comes from you" (Hänggi-Pahl 380).

54. Fourth Eucharistic Prayer.

55. Third Eucharistic Prayer.

56. See the Appendix to Chap. Five.

57. This unity is not to be confused with the unity of the congregation that is requested in the epiclesis.

58. The reference is not simply to obstacles to ecumenical unity, but to everything that is a sign of division and discord in any and every area of life.

59. 1 Cor 15:24–28.

60. *DOL* 1975ff.

61. On the origin of this eucharistic prayer, see W. Von Arx, "Das Hochgebet für die Kirche in der Schweiz," *Zeitschrift für Schweizer Kirchengeschichte* 71 (1977): 279–293.

62. S. Marsili, "Una nuova preghiera eucaristica per la Chiesa italiana," *RivLit* 67 (1980): 465–478.

63. J. Baumgartner, "Ambigua per la Chiesa italiana la nuova preghiera eucaristica? Una replica," *RivLit* 68 (1981): 82–94.

64. Marsili 472.

65. Baumgartner 87.

66. Marsili 478.

67. Baumgartner 86.

68. Preface A. [Our translation of the anaphora is from the Italian text, the only one of three originals available to me.—Tr.]

69. "You constantly sustain us on our journey" (the *Post-Sanctus* is the opening part of the invariable section).

70. See the translation, above.

71. Ibid.

72. Ibid.

73. "May they . . . journey in faith and hope."

74. "Make us open and available to the brethren whom we meet on our journey, so that we . . . may advance with them on the path of salvation."

75. Mt 6:33. See R. Guelly, G. Lagon, P. J. Labarrière, A. Vergote, and J. P. Jossua, *La prière du chrétien* (Brussels, 1981), 118.

76. Preface D.

77. See our commentary on the preface of Anaphora II of the Missal (above, Chap. Four, sec. IV B).

78. Intercessions A.

79. Invariable part of the Intercessions.

80. Lk 15:11ff.

81. Intercessions A.

82. Rom 3:28; 8:24.

83. This is the theme of the parable of the Good Samaritan.

84. Intercessions B.

85. Rom 12:15.

86. Jn 14:6.

87. Prayer of offering (in the invariable section).

88. W. Michaeis, "Hodos," *TDNT* 581.

89. Marsili (n. 63), 476; Baumgartner (n. 64), 91f.

90. G. W. H. Lampe, ed., *A Patristic Greek Lexicon* (Oxford 1961), 1334.

91. Hänggi-Pahl 81.

92. Marsili 474.

93. Invariable section (introduction to the first epiclesis).

94. F. X. Durrwell, *L'eucharistie, sacrement pascal* (Paris, 1981), 48.

95. J. Dupont, "Les disciples d'Emmaus (Lc 24, 13–35)," in *La pâque du Christ* (n.26), 184.

96. C. Perrot, "Emmaus ou la rencontre du Seigneur (Lc 24, 13–35)," in ibid., 163.

97. Dupont 186ff.

98. Perrot 166.

99. Ibid., 164.

100. Dupont 167.

101. Perrot 165.

102. Ibid., 164.

103. Dupont 192.

104. Ibid.

105. Perrot 165.

106. Dupont 195.

CHAPTER EIGHT

This chapter is a revision of an article published in *RivLit* 69 (1982): 663–657.

1. "De liturgia in prima synodo episcoporum," *Notitiae* 3 (1967), 368.

2. A. Bugnini, *La riforma liturgica (1948–1975)* (Rome, 1983), 431.

3. Ibid., 470: "At the insistence of the Congregation for the Doctrine of the Faith the problem was set aside for future consideration."

4. *Directory for Masses with Children*, no. 52 (*DOL* 2185. The entire document is in *DOL* 2134–2188).

5. Bugnini 470.

6. Ibid., 471, n. 42.

7. Ibid., 472.

8. *VSC* 36, 1: "The use of the Latin language, with due respect to particular law, is to be preserved in the Latin rites" (Flannery 13).

9. Ibid., 36, 4: "Translations from the Latin for use in the liturgy must be approved by the competent territorial ecclesiastical authority already mentioned" (Flannery 13).

10. Vatican II did not necessarily require such a procedure. According to G. Venturi, "Evoluzione della problematica relativa alla traduzione liturgica," in *Mysterion. Miscellanea liturgica in occasione dei 70 anni dell'abate Salvatore Marsili* (Turin, 1981), 309, the text of the liturgical constitution "when read carefully, does not say that vernacular texts used in the liturgy must be the result of translation from the Latin; it says only that translated texts must be approved by competent authority."

11. Sacred Congregation of Rites, Instruction *Inter Oecumenici* on the Orderly Carrying Out of the Constitution on the Liturgy, no. 40a (*DOL* 332).

12. According to Bugnini 265, "adaptation" calls for "immersing oneself in the reality of each people and nation. It is the principle of adaptation that has given rise down the centuries to the various Rites in the Church."

13. *VSC* 37–40; also 24, 62, 65, and 68.

14. Bugnini 267–274.

15. F. Kabasele, "Zaïre," in J. Levesque, ed., *A travers le monde. Célébration de l'eucharistie* (Paris, 1981), 465–47. Similar remarks on the anaphora allowed for India in 1972: "In 1975 Rome issued a decree prohibiting the use of the Indian anaphora and of readings taken from nonchristian sacred books" (J. N. M. Wungaards, "Inde," in ibid., 96). See Bugnini 267, n. 9; and N. Manca, "Polemiche sulla liturgia indiana," *Mondo e missione* April, 1976, 228–230. This anaphora proclaims the wonderful deeds of God not only in Israel but in India and throughout the world. See D. S. Amalorpavvadass, "A Fresh Start in Liturgical Renewal and Inculturation," *Word and Worship* 2, no. 2 (1978): 50–82. For further discussion of the Indian anaphora, see B. D. Spinks, "The Anaphora for India. Some Theological Objections to an Attempt at Inculturation," *EL* 95 (1981): 529–549.

16 *VSC* 23: "Any new forms adopted should in some way grow organically from forms already existing" (Flannery 10).

17. See *Directory* 3 (*DOL* 2136).

18. Only this Introduction has been officially published: Sacred Congregation for Divine Worship, "Preces eucharisticae pro missis cum pueris et de reconciliatione," *Notitiae* 11 (1975): 4–12; trans. in *DOL* 1999–2027.

19. Introduction (to the Eucharistic Prayers for Masses with Children) 10 (*DOL* 2008).

20. Ibid., 11 (*DOL 2009*).

21. J. Gelineau, "Une technique à retrouver: le bon usage d'un modèle dans les prières eucharistiques," *LMD* no. 114. (1973): 85–96.

22. Introduction 11: "In this case the Latin text is not intended for liturgical use" (*DOL* 2009).

23. Ibid.: "These principles are all the more pertinent in the case of languages that are far removed from Latin, expecially non-Western languages."

24. Cited in Bugnini 472, n. 46.

25. "The committee of translators should always remember that in this case the Latin text is not intended for liturgical use. Therefore it is not to be merely translated. The Latin text does determine the purpose, substance, and the general form of these prayers and these elements should be the same in the translations into the various languages. Features proper to the Latin (which never develop a special style of speaking with children) are never to be carried over into the vernacular texts intended for liturgical use: specifically, the Latin preference for compound sentences, the somewhat ornate and repetitious style, and the so-called cursus. The style of the vernacular text is in every respect to be adapted to the spirit of the respective language as well as to the manner of speaking with children in each language concerning matters of great importance. There principles are all the more pertinent in the case of languages that are far removed from Latin, especially non-Western languages. An example of translation for each eucharistic prayer in one of the Western languages is provided as a possible aid to the translator" (*DOL* 2009).

26. "Hieratic and solemn" is Mazzarello's version of the Latin *"ornatus et redundans"*; see S. Mazzarello, *I fanciulli alla messa* (Padua, 1977), 91.

27. No. 4 reads: "Each of the three eucharistic prayers for Masses with children contains, with a very few exceptions, all those elements that, according to the General Instruction of the Roman Missal, no. 55, make up the eucharistic prayer" (*DOL* 2002).

28. First anaphora: "Holy Father . . . grant that they [the bread and wine] may become the body and blood of your beloved Son." Third anaphora: "Father, in your goodness sanctify these gifts of bread and wine so that they may become for us the body and blood of your Son, Jesus Christ." These petitions before the account of institution may be described as epicleses in a broad sense.

29. As a result, the trinitarian structure of the eucharistic prayer becomes more evident.

30. Mazzarello (n. 26), 118, n. 4.

31. This statement depends directly on the *General Instruction of the Roman Missal*, no. 55f.

32. See Rom 12:1 and parallel passages.

33. See J. A. Jungmann, *La messa nel popolo di Dio* (Turin, 1974), 9: "In antiquity the emphasis was on the *offerimus*. Clement of Rome . . . calls Christ himself the high priest 'of our oblations.' " See also ibid., 20: "It must be admitted, indeed, that *offerre* (and its noun, *oblatio*) was not a sacrificial term in prechristian texts. Even in the liturgy the word was used initially with the generic meaning of 'bring,' 'present.' "

34. "Proclaiming his death and resurrection, we offer you the bread of life and the cup of salvation."

35. "He leads us to you: receive us, we pray, together with him."

36. Irenaeus of Lyons, *Adversus haereses* IV, 18, 1 (SC 100/2:596).

37. (a) "Heaven and earth are full of your glory. Hosanna in the highest!" This

part of the Sanctus concludes the first part of the thanksgiving, which focuses on God's work in the world: on creation and the divine "philanthropy" (love of human-kind). (b) "Blessed is he who comes in the name of the Lord. Hosanna in the high-est!" Conclusion of the Christological section. (c) "Holy, holy, holy Lord God of hosts. Hosanna in the highest!" Conclusion of the ecclesiological section (where com-memoration is made of the people of God, the Church, the pope, the bishop, Our Lady, the saints, and the angels).

38. "What Jesus Christ told us to do we now do; and, proclaiming . . ."

39. See *Feria V in authentica* in the Ambrosian liturgy: "This we do, this we cele-brate, in obedience to your command, O Lord" (Hänggi-Pahl 452). And in the Celtic liturgy: "Recalling, therefore, and obeying the precept of the only-begotten Son . . ." (ibid., 493).

40. The following Gallican text seems to be the direct source for this passage of the anaphora: "This we do, therefore, Lord; in obedience to this command; we proclaim the suffering of this sacred body" (ibid., 491).

41. The Eucharist as proclamation is discussed in Chap. Nine.

42. N. Afanassieff, *L'Eglise du Saint-Esprit* (Paris, 1975).

43. The connection between Church and present kingdom is concisely expressed by Vatican II; see the Dogmatic Constitution on the Church 3: "The Church—that is, the kingdom of Christ already present in mystery . . ." (Flannery 351 [slightly al-tered]; Latin text in Alberigo 850).

44. Introduction to the anaphoras for children, 3: "Before the words *Do this in mem-ory of me* a sentence has been introduced, *Then he said to them*, in order to make clearer for children the distinction between what is said over the bread and what re-fers to the celebration's being repeated" (*DOL* 2001).

45. Introduction 19: "The place for the acclamation by the faithful at the end of the consecration has been slightly changed. This is done for pedagogical reasons. That the children may clearly understand the connection between the words of the Lord, *Do this in memory of me*, and the anamnesis by the priest celebrant, the acclamation, whether of memorial or of praise, is not made until after the anamnesis has been re-cited."

46. "Therefore, holy Father, we stand before you, remembering with joy what Je-sus Christ did for our salvation. In this holy sacrifice which he entrusted to his Church we recall his death and resurrection." This passage seems to reflect the Chal-dean (East Syrian) anaphoral tradition; see the Anaphora of the Apostles Addai and Mari: "We . . . have gathered in your name and now stand before you at this mo-ment and have received with jubilation . . . , celebrating this . . . mystery of the pas-sion, death, burial, and resurrection of the Lord and Savior, Jesus Christ" (Hänggi-Pahl 380). See also the Anaphora of Nestorius (ibid., 391).

47. See the translation of the third anaphora.

48. See, e.g., the Anaphora of Nestorius: "Mighty Lord, God the Father, we com-memorate the salvation accomplished for our sake. Above all, we believe and con-fess . . . his marvelous plan which was carried out by means of our humanity and brought to fruition for our salvation: the cross and passion, the death . . ." (Hänggi-Pahl 391).

49. In the time of Irenaeus, the symbol, or creed, had not found the definitive form familiar to us today.

50. The anaphoras transmitted from the past are varied and heterogenous in con-tent. It is not clear why the Alexandrian anaphoras give pride of place to the work

346

of creation (text based on Genesis), whereas the Anaphora of Hippolytus focuses exclusively on redemption in Christ and has only a passing remark on creation: "Through whom you have created everything."

51. J. Scherer, *Entretien d'Origène avec Héraclide* (SC 67; Paris, 1960). This is a report of a synod (ca. 244–249) on which we have very little information. Origen asks for a decision on inserting the word "God" into the anaphora as an attribute of the Son, the intention being to oblige Heraclides to the faith in question. The text shows that this was a time when the text of the anaphora was being improvised; on the other hand, churchmen were also becoming aware that an orthodox text was required in the anaphora as a vehicle of ecclesial orthodoxy. See also the *Apostolic Tradition* of Hippolytus (ca. 220): the principle of free composition is asserted, but the author adds (in chap. 28) that the prayer must be sound by orthodox standards (Botte 28).

52. First anaphora: "You sent us your beloved Son to save us." Second anaphora: "Jesus whom you sent . . ." and "you give us your Son Jesus."

53. Second anaphora: "He came to show us. . . .He came to remove from human hearts. . . ." Third anaphora: "In his goodness he came into the world." At a later point, the coming of the Son takes eschatological form: "At the end he will come in glory."

54. First anaphora: "He leads us to you." Second anaphora: "So that he may lead us to you"; "the sacrifice that draws us to you."

55. R. Cantalamessa, *La pasqua della nostra salvezza* (Turin, 1971), 140.

56. First anaphora.

57. "You loved us so much that you created this vast and beautiful world for us."

58. Though this theme does not become a structural part of the third anaphora, it is present there as well: "You are . . . kind to all of us, and you show your mercy to all human beings."

59. Evil has a negative place here: it "prevents friendship." Hatred—one form of evil—"keeps us from being happy."

60. "For this, Father, we are glad and we thank you . . . we rejoice and praise you, saying . . ." The closest parallel is the Maronite Anaphora of St. Peter the Apostle (Hänggi-Pahl 415).

61. "You created us to live for you while loving one another. It is by your gift . . . that we can share. . . ."

62. "We thank you above all for your Son, Jesus Christ."

63. "That we might recognize one another as brothers and sisters, and you as Father of us all."

64. Another allusion to the theme of unity may be seen in the formula of offering: "Accept us, we pray, *together with* your beloved Son." This formula clearly derives from Vatican II's Decree on the Ministry and Life of Priests (*Presbyterorum ordinis*), no. 5 (Flannery 870ff.), but the anaphora brings out the theme of unity more clearly.

65. The other two anaphoras conclude quite differently. Anaphora III says nothing about praise in the sentence before the doxology, but asks only that we may dwell in heaven with Christ. Anaphora II does speak of praise, but it is praise offered to God in the heavenly liturgy. In Anaphora I, which we have been analyzing, the praise is offered here and now by this particular assembly in this particular anaphora.

66. See Bugnini (n. 2), 265: "In the area of liturgical reform the great problems of adaptation that are acknowledged in the Constitution on the Liturgy have hardly been touched as yet. A decisive attack on them is left for the third stage of the reform, after the general revision of the liturgical books which provide the structural

foundation as a basis that takes into account the data of tradition, the general principles laid down in the Constitution, and the pastoral needs of today's faithful." See also C. Braga, "Un problema fondamentale di pastorale liturgica: Adattamento e incarnazione nelle varie culture," *EL* 89 (1975): 5–39.

67. A. Bouley, *From Freedom to Formula. The Evolution of the Eucharistic Prayer from Oral Improvisation to Written Texts* (Washington, DC, 1981).

CHAPTER NINE
1. Cardinal Mercati: 1866–1957. Cardinal Prefect of the Vatican Library from 1936.
2. P. De Puniet, "Les paroles de la consécration et leur valeur traditionnelle," *RHE* 13 (1911): 34–72.
3. Gregory I, *Ep.* IX, 2 (PL 77:956–957).
4. De Puniet 64. The reprint: Reggio Emila, Biblioteca del Seminario, B. 5. 53. 12.
5. Cyprian, *De oratione dominica* 31 (PL 4:539). V. Grossi, ed., *Tertulliano—Cipriano—Agostino. Il Padre nostro* (Rome, 1980), 30, comments: "In Cyprian [*oratio*] is equivalent to *prex*. But after him *prex*, which had a sacrificial connotation, came to be used for the Eucharist, while *oratio* was used for the Our Father. Originally, however, *oratio* did not have this limited scope in either Tertullian or Cyprian."
6. Tertullian, *De oratione* 9, 9 (CCL 1:263).
7. John Chrysostom, *Homilia* 82, 30, on Mt 26:26 (PG 58:740).
8. Justin, *Apologia I* 66, 2 (Deiss 92; text in Hänggi-Pahl 70).
9. G. J. Cuming, "Di'euchēs logou," *JTS* 31 (1980): 80–82.
10. A distant echo of this ancient teaching is still audible in our habit of referring to the consecrated bread and wine as "the Eucharist": they are "eucharist" because they have been "eucharistified." When we refer to them as "eucharist" are we not equivalently saying that they have been consecrated, i.e., that they have had the thanksgiving or "eucharist" spoken over them?
11. The first passage is from *Adversus haereses* IV, 18, 8 (SC 100/2:610); the second and third are from ibid., V, 2, 3, (SC 153/2:35).
12. A. Rousseau uses "eucharistified" both in his translation of *Adversus haereses* IV, 18, 4, and in his retroversion into Greek of the Latin: "*Quomodo autem constabit eis eum panem in quo gratiae actae sint corpus esse Domini sui. . . .*" (SC 100/2:609). A justification of this translation is given in SC 100/1:244f.
13. Tertullian, *De oratione* 1, 3 (CCL 1:257). Compare this with Ambrose who makes a distinction in the eucharistic prayer between the words of the Lord and those of the priest and applies the adjective "heavenly" only to the explanatory words: "Do you want to know which heavenly words effect the consecration? . . . It is the evangelist who says everything down to 'Accipite' (the body and the blood); from that point on the words are those of Christ" (*De sacramentis* IV, 21 [SC 25bis:114]).

It is quite clear that for Ambrose the words of consecration as such are "heavenly words"; indeed, they have consecratory power precisely because they are "heavenly." In Ambrose's usage, *caelestis* designates the origin of the words, namely, Jesus as God; their divine character alone gives the words the same effectiveness as the words that created the world. For confirmation, see *De sacramentis* IV, 14–15 (SC 25bis:108–110): "What words, then, effect the consecration, and whose words are they? They are the words of the Lord Jesus. . . . What is the character of the words of Christ? They are the words by which all things were made. The Lord commanded, and the heavens were made; the Lord commanded, and the earth was made. . . . Consider, therefore, how effective Christ's words are. If, then, there is such power in the words of the Lord Jesus . . ."

14. D. Van den Eynde, " 'Eucharistia ex duabus rebus constans': St Irénée," *Adv. haereses* IV, 18, 5,: *Antonianum* 15 (1940): 26f. See also K. Gamber, "Das Eucharistiegebet als Epiklese und ein Zitat bei Irenäus," *Ostkirchliche Studien* 29 (1980): 301–305.

15. The term "eucharist" is perhaps now so closely associated with the eucharistified bread and wine that it would be confusing to apply it to the prayer of thanksgiving.

16. Basil, *De Sancto Spiritu* 27, 66 (SC 17bis:480).

17. Y. Congar, *I Believe in the Holy Spirit* III, trans. D. Smith (New York, 1983), 238.

18. Ibid., 246. It might be prudent to say that the teaching authorities of the Church have never defined anything in this area, not even in Session XIII of the Council of Trent (Chap. 3). The doctrine in question is commonly accepted and taught by the Church in the exercise of its ordinary teaching office; theologians qualify it as "Catholic doctrine." This theological qualification as such leaves freedom for further study and describes a proposition that is reformable if there are sufficiently strong reasons.

19. Thomas Aquinas, *Summa theologiae* III, 75, 7c: "*Substantia corporis Christ . . . non suscipit magis neque minus.*" See ibid., 75, 2c.

20. Ibid., III, 78, 2c and 1c. According to Thomas, the entire eucharistic prayer is not required for the consecration, but only the "words of insititution." In support of his position, he cites Ambrose (a. 1, *sed contra*) and the fact that the eucharistic prayer is not the same in all Churches or at all peroids (a. 1, ad 4).

21. P. Cagin, *L'Eucharistie. Canon primitif de la messe ou formulaire essentiel et premier de toutes les liturgies* (Rome-Paris-Tournai, 1912), 70; 142–143,

22. S. Salaville, "Epiclèse," *DTC* V/1 (Paris, 1924), 203.

23. See J. Doresse and E. Lanne, *Un témoin archaïque de la liturgie copte de S. Basil*, with an Appendix by B. Capelle, "Les liturgies basiliennes et saint Basil" (Louvain, 1960).

24. Y. Congar, "Pneumatologie ou 'Christomonisme' dans la tradition latine?" *ETL* 45 (1969): 394–416.

25. See H. A. J. Wegman, "Généalogie hypothétique de la prière eucharistique," *QL* 61 (1980): 263–278.

26. G. Martelet, *The Risen Christ and the Eucharistic World*, trans. R. Hague (New York, 1976), 151–152.

27. J.-M. R. Tillard, "L'eucharistie et le Saint-Esprit," *NRT* 90 (1968): 363–387.

28. M. Jugie, "L'epiclèse et le mot 'antitype' de la messe de saint Basile," *Echos d'Orient* 9 (1906): 198.

29. Hänggi-Pahl 364–366.

30. P.-M. Gy, "L'eucharistie dans la tradition de la prière et de la doctrine," *LMD* no. 137 (1979): 81–102, n. 18.

31. Isidore says that the consecration is effected by the *Oratio sexta*, which is the part of the anaphora between the Sanctus and the Our Father. For an example of this *Oratio sexta*, see the formulary for the *Missa omnimoda* in M. Férotin, *Le Liber ordinum en usage dans l'eglise wisogothique et mozarabe d'Espagne du cinquième au onzième siècle* (Paris, 1904), 237.

32. Isidore, *Etymologiarum libri* VI, 38 (PL 82:255).

33. John Chrysostom, *In traditionem Judae homilia* 1, 6 (PG 49:380).

34. Ambrose, *De mysteriis* 54 (SC 25bis:188); *De sacramentis* IV, 14–15 (ibid., 108–110).

35. Ambrose, *De sacramentis* IV, 14 (SC 25bis:108).

36. P.-M. Gy, "Les paroles de la consécration et l'unité de la prière eucharistique selon les théologiens de Pierre Lombard à saint Thomas d'Aquin," in *Lex orandi lex credendi* (*Miscellanea C. Vaggagini*) (Rome, 1980), 189–201.

37. Thomas Aquinas, *In quattuor libros Sententiarum* IV, d. VIII, qu. 1, art. 4, gla. 3, especially the *expositio textus*.

38. *Constitutiones Apostolorum* VII, 25 (Funk 1:410).

39. E. Mazza, "L'anafora di serapoine: Una ipotesi di interpretazione," *EL* 95 (1981): 510–528. See also our article, "La 'Gratiarum actio mystica' del libro VII delle Costituzioni apostoliche. Una tappa nella storia del anafora eucaristica," *EL* 93 (1979): 123–137.

40. A. Chavasse, "L'epiclèse eucharistique dans les anciennes liturgies orientales," *Mélanges de science religieuse* 3 (1946): 197–206.

41. The solution would therefore hold for every type of anaphora, independently of the problem of the epiclesis in relation to the account of institution.

42. Chavasse 197.

43. Ibid., 198. We have to be very cautious in suggesting this either-or. The alternatives are on different levels, and an interior intention can never replace the literary text of the Canon or vice versa. In baptism, for example, can the minister's intention make up for an inadequate form? Obviously not. The same holds for the Canon: if the text does not suffice for applying the words of Jesus at the Supper to the present bread and wine, the interior intention of the minister cannot make up for the deficiency. See n. 45, below.

44. Y. Congar, *I Believe* (n. 17), 239–240.

45. Chavasse 200. In the period when the Canon was composed, the problem of ministerial intention did not exist. It is a later problem and typical of a later theology that had lost sight of the implications of the sign character of the sacraments. We are not casting doubt on the importance of the minister's interior situation in achieving a proper obedience to the command of Christ; we take that for granted. In the verb "do," we include all the interior requisites for which the Lord's Supper calls: faith, unity, following of Christ, and so on. The Greek *poiein* in particular seems to have sacrificial connotations; for the patristic period, see A. G. Martimort, "L'intention requise chez le sujet des sacrements," *Année canonique* 24 (1980): 85–108.

46. John Chrysostom, *In traditionem Judae homilia* 1, 6 (PG 49:380).

47. Congar, *I Believe* III, 233.

48. We use the word "create" to retain the perspective of John Chrysostom.

49. Heb 9:26, 28, 12. These texts deal specifically with the death of Christ, but they are evidently applicable to the entire work of redemption and therefore to the events in the upper room. The Last Supper is not a first Mass that is followed by many others; it is the only Mass and will be present in all the Masses celebrated by the Church.

50. Congar, *I Believe* III, 233.

51. Is 40:8.

52. The anaphora, being a prayer of thanksgiving, is a good expression of the return to God of the divine word that has borne its fruit. His word that effects human salvation elicits human words in response: the confession of faith and thanksgiving. It is in this dialogue that salvation reaches its completion; God's saving action is incompatible with a total human passivity. Since Jesus is the Word of the Father and

since it is he who works our salvation, a human response of gratitude must necessarily take shape in commemoration of the Lord. If the work of salvation is rightly called a sacrifice, then our grateful response will necessarily be a commemoration of that sacrifice.

53. A. Feuillet and P. Grelot, "Word of God," in Léon-Dufour 666–667.

54. L. Deiss, *It's the Lord's Supper. The Eucharist of Christians*, trans. E. Bonin (New York, 1976), 81.

55. Ibid., 82.

56. X. Léon-Dufour, *Le partage du pain eucharistique selon le Nouveau Testament* (Paris, 1982), 184.

57. Cited in A. Gerken, *Teologia dell'eucaristia* (Alba, 1977), 216.

58. H. Schürmann, "Jesus' Words in the Light of His Actions at the Supper," in P. Benoit, R. E. Murphy, and B. van Iersel, eds., *The Breaking of Bread* (Concilium 40; New York, 1969), 128–129.

59. Léon-Dufour, *Le partage*, 162.

60. Ibid., 64.

61. Schürmann, "Jesus' Words," 126. For greater detail, see idem, *Comment Jésus a-t-il vécu sa mort?* (Paris, 1977), 99f.

62. Léon-Dufour, *Le partage*, 231.

63. Ibid., 137.

64. Ibid., 282.

65. A.-L. Descamps, "Cénacle et calvaire. Les vues de H. Schürmann," *RTL* 10 (1979): 344.

66. Ibid., 345.

67. Schürmann, *Comment Jésus*, 103ff.

68. Schürmann, "Jesus' Words," 130–131.

69. Léon-Dufour, *Le partage*, 80.

70. Ibid., 221.

71. Schürmann, *Comment Jesus*, 112. And again, on 113: "It must be admitted that the symbolic action performed by Jesus at the Supper was already efficacious." The future is realized in the present, says Descamps in his analytical commentary on Schürmann's views, but it not clear whether he has fully grasped the point in question; see Descamps (n. 65), 345.

72. Léon-Dufour, *Le partage*, 221.

73. R. Taft, "The Frequency of the Eucharist throughout History," in M. Collins and D. Power, eds., *Can We Always Celebrate the Eucharist?* (Concilium 152; New York, 1982), 20.

74. A. Gerken (n. 57), 69–91.

75. Ibid., 70.

76. Ibid., 84.

77. F. X. Durrwell, *The Eucharist: Presence of Christ*, trans. S. Attanasio (Denville, NJ, 1974), Chap. 4.

78. Léon-Dufour, *Le partage*, 141.

79. Ibid., 142.

80. 1 Cor 11:24.

81. Lk 22:19.

82. Léon-Dufour, *Le partage*, 143.

83. Ibid., 143–147.

84. See ibid., 146: "One consequence must be made clear. In these words Jesus is

not proclaiming that he is going to his death as to a 'means' of salvation; rather he is announcing that, faithful unto death to God and the human race, he will be present among his own by becoming their food and giving them life through himself."

85. 1 Cor 16:17.

86. Jn 11:52.

87. Lk 22:19.

88. Jn 8:28; 12:32f.; 3:14; 19:30, 34, 37.

89. Mk 10:38ff.

90. Mk 14:36.

91. Rv 14:10.

92. The exception is the Anaphora of Hippolytus and texts that follow it more directly, as, for example, the Clementine Anaphora (Hänggi-Pahl 81 and 92).

93. 1 Cor 10:16.

94. L. Finkelstein, "The Birkat ha-mazon," *Jewish Quarterly Review* 19 (1928–29): 211–262.

95. Jn 19:30.

96. Jn 7:39; 16:7, 20, 22ff. The Spirit leads human beings back to Christ by reminding them of what he said and did enabling them to understand it (Jn 14:26).

97. See Jer 31:31–34.

98. See B. Cooke, "Synoptic Presentation of the Eucharist as Covenant Sacrifice," *Theological Studies* 21 (1960): 1–44.

99. Léon-Dufour, *Le partage,* 168.

100. Ibid., 169.

101. Mt 9:2–6.

102. Lv 17:11, 14; Dt 12:23. See C. Spicq and P. Grelot, "Blood," in Léon-Dufour 52–53.

103. J. Behm, *"Haima,"* TDNT 1:173.

104. Jn 10:18.

105. Mt 5:23ff.; Mk 12:33.

106. We deliberately contrast ritual sacrifice and personal sacrifice. In the latter, the relation of communion with God is established not by a rite but by the life the person lives: a life of obedience to God and fulfillment of his will. Because of its relation to the cross, the Last Supper is not a ritual sacrifice but a personal sacrifice. The consequences of this truth for the Church's Eucharist are evident: a nonritual worship should not give rise to a ritualistic liturgy on the part of the Church.

There is a further conclusion to be drawn: if we are dealing with a personal sacrifice, it is useless and hopeless to look to the ritual sacrifices of the Old Testament for a definition of sacrifice that can be applied to the Eucharist. If the redemptive work of Christ follows the logic of personal sacrifice, we can never have a "definition" of sacrifice but only a "description" that narrates the saving events; see F. Clark, *Themata selecta de sacrificio eucharistico* (for private use; Rome, 1964–65). The anaphora shows forth the sacrificial logic at work in the Eucharist.

Because of its prophetic mode of proclamation, the Last Supper of Jesus is not a rite; it is the cross, and nothing less ritual than the cross has ever existed.

107. Léon-Dufour, *Le partage,* 178–179.

108. Is 53:10.

109. Léon-Dufour, *Le partage,* 179.

110. Schürmann, *Comment Jesus* (n. 61), 107.

111. Ibid.

112. This identity results from our faithful carrying out of the command. The case

is no different than when a person today speaks the parable of the Prodigal Son. The parable was originally spoken two thousand years ago by someone else in a different language and with different words; but, if it is spoken now with the same faith and outlook that Jesus had and in a way that is conformed to his will, it is still the same parable of Jesus and has the same effectiveness it had then; it will, therefore, communicate the mercy of God in the same way. In fact, it is really not "another" parable. Now, if this is true of the word of God, there should be no problem in saying that the bread and wine on our altar are the very bread and wine of the Lord's final meal. The word of God guarantees this relation. Note that we say "identity," which is much more than presence, meaning, purpose, value.

Select Bibliography

I. SOURCES

Acta synodalia Concilii oecumenici Vaticani II, Volumen I, Periodus I, Pars IV. Rome, 1971.

Alberigo, J., ed. *Conciliorum oecumenicorum decreta*. 3d ed. Bologna, 1973.

Andrieu, M. *Les Ordines Romani du haut moyen âge*. Spicilegium Sacrum Lovaniense 11, 23, 24, 28, 29. Louvain, 1931ff.

———. *Le Pontifical Romain au moyen âge*. Studi e Testi 86–89. Vatican City, 1938–1941.

Béguerie, P., and J. Evenou. *Eucharisties de tous pays*. Paris, 1975.

Botte, B. *La Tradition apostolique de saint Hippolyte. Essai de reconstitution.* LQF 39. Münster, 1963.

Della Torre, L., ed. *Pregare l'eucaristia. Preghiere eucaristiche di ieri et di oggi per la catechesi e l'orazione.* Brescia, 1982.

Deshusses, J., ed. *Le sacramentaire grégorien. Ses princiales formes d'après les plus anciens manuscrits.* Spicilegium Friburgense 16. Fribourg, 1971; 2d ed., 1979.

Documents on the Liturgy, 1963–1979. Conciliar, Papal, and Curial Texts. Collegeville, MN, 1982.

Doresse, J., and E. Lanne, eds. *Un témoin archaïque de la liturgie copte de S. Basile*, with an Appendix by B. Capelle, "Les liturgies basiliennes et saint Basile." Louvain, 1960.

Duchesne, L., ed. *Le Liber pontificalis*. 2 vols. Paris, 1886–92; 2d. ed., 1955–1957.

Eizenhöfer, L., ed. *Canon missae romanae. Pars prior Traditio textus.* Rome, 1954.

———. *Pars altera. Textus propinqui.* Rome, 1966.

Férotin, M., ed. *Le Liber ordinum en usage dans l'Eglise wisogothiqwue et mozarabe d'Espagne du conquième au onzième siècle.* Monumenta Ecclesiae liturgica 5. Paris, 1904.

————. *Le Liber mozarabicus sacramentorum et les manuscrits mozarabes.* Monumenta Ecclesiae liturgica 6. Paris, 1912.

Flannery, A., ed. *Vatican II. The Conciliar and Postconciliar Documents.* Collegeville, MN, 1975.

Funk, F. X., ed. *Didascalia et Constitutiones Apostolorum. 2 vols. Paderborn, 1905.*

Hänggi, A., and I. Pahl, eds. *Prex eucharistica. Textus e variis liturgiis antiquioribus selecti.* Spicilegium Friburgense 12. Fribourg, 1978.

Hauler, E., ed. *Didascaliae apostolorum fragmenta ueronensia latina. Accedunt canonum qui dicuntur apostolorum et aegiptiorum reliquiae.* Leipzig, 1900.

Jaubert, A., ed. *Clément de Rome, Epître aux Corinthiens.* SC 167. Paris, 1971.

Kaczynski, R. *Enchiridion documentorum instaurationis liturgicae.* Turin, 1976.

Lesley, A., ed. *Missale mixtum secundum regulam beati Isidori dictum Mozarabes.* Rome, 1755.

Lodi, E. *Enchiridion euchologicum fontium liturgicorum.* Rome, 1979.

Mercati, G. *Antiche reliquie liturgiche ambrosiane e romane, Con un excursus sui frammenti dogmatici ariani del Mai.* Rome, 1902.

Macomber, W. "The Oldest Known Text of the Anaphora of the Apostles Addai and Mari." *OCP* 32 (1966): 335–371.

Missale Romanum. Ex decreto sacrosancti Concilii Tridentini. Rome, 1962.

Missale Romanum. Ex decreto sacrosancti concilii oecumenici Vatican II, Rome, 1970.

Mohlberg, L. K., et al., eds. *Liber sacramentorum romanae aecclesiae ordinis anni circuli.* Rome, 1960.

————. *Missale Francorum.* Rome, 1957.

————. *Missale gallicanum vetus.* Rome, 1958.

————. *Missale gothicum.* Rome, 1961.

————. *Sacramentarium veronense.* Rome, 1956.

Neuner, J., and J. Dupuis, eds. *The Christian Faith in the Doctrinal Documents of the Catholic Church.* Rev. ed. Staten Island, NY, 1982.

Ordo missae. Rome, 1969.

Piédagnel, A., ed. *Cyrille de Jérusalem. Catéchèses mystagogiques.* SC 126. Paris, 1966.

Raes, A., ed. *Anaphorae siriacae. Quotquot in codicibus adhuc repertae sunt.* Rome, 1939–1973.

Rahmani, I. H., ed. *Testamentum Domini nostri Iesu Christi.* Mainz, 1899.

Renaudot, E. *Liturgiarum orientalium collectio.* Paris, 1716; rev.ed. in 2 vols., Frankfurt, 1847.

The Rites of the Catholic Church. 2 vols. New York, 1976–1980.

Roman Missal. The Sacramentary. Collegeville, MN, 1974.

Rordorf, W., and A. Tuilier, eds. *La doctrine des douze apôtres.* SC 248. Paris, 1978.

Sparks, H. F. D., ed. *The Apocryphal Old Testament.* Oxford, 1984.

Tonneau, R., and R. Devreesse. *Les homélies catéchétiques de Théodore de Mopsueste.* Vatican City, 1949.

Wagner, J., "Zur Reform des Ordo Missae. Zwei Dokumente," in P. Jounel, R. Kaczynski, and G. Pasqualetti, eds., *Liturgia opera divina e umana (Studi in onore di A. Bugnini)* (pp. 263–289). Rome, 1982.

Wells, C. B., R. O. Fink, and J. F. Gilliam. *The Excavations at Doura Europos.* Final Report V, Part I. New Haven, CT, 1959.

II. STUDIES

Anamnesis 3. Eucaristia. Teologia e storia della celebrazione. Casale Monferrato, 1983.

Audet, J.-P. "Esquisse du genre littéraire de la 'bénédiction' juive et de l' 'eucharistie' chrétienne." *RBib* 65 (1958): 371–399.

———. *La Didachè. Instruction des apôtres.* Paris, 1958.

———. "Genre littéraire et formes cultuellles de l'Eucharistie. Nova et vetera." *EL* 80 (1966): 353–385.

———. "Le sacré et le profan. Leur situation en christianisme." *NRT* 79 (1957): 33–61.

Baumgartner, J. "Ambigua per la Chiesa italiana la nuova preghiera eucaristica? Una replica." *RLit* 68 (181): 82–94.

Benzerath, M., A. Schmid, and J. Guillet, eds. *La pâque du Christ, mystère du salut (Melanges offerts au P. F.-X. Durrwell).* Paris, 1982.

Botte, B. "La seconda preghiera eucaristica." In the collective work *Le nuove preghiere eucaristiche* (pp. 27–33). Brescia, 1969.

———. *Le mouvement liturgique. Témoignages et souvenirs.* Paris, 1973.

Botte, B., and C. Mohrmann. *L'Ordinaire de la Messe. Texte critique, traduction, et études.* Etudes liturgiques 2. Paris-Louvain, 1953.

Bouyer, L. *Eucharist. The Theology and Spirituality of the Eucharistic Prayer.* Translated by C. U. Quinn. Notre Dame, IN, 1968.

———. "La terza preghiera eucaristica." In the collective work *Le nuove preghiere eucaristiche* (pp. 39–50). Brescia, 1969.

Brillant, M., and P. Aigrain, eds. *Histoire des relitions* 3. Paris, 1955.

Bugnini, A. *La riforma liturgica (1948–1975).* Rome, 1983.

Cantalamessa, R. *L'omelia "In. s. pascha" dello Pseudo-Ippolito di Roma.* Milan, 1967.

———. *La pasqua della nostra salvezza.* Turin, 1971.

Capelle, B. "Et omnibus orthodoxis atque apostolicae fidei cultoribus." In his *Travaux liturgiques* 2. Louvain, 1962.

Cattaneo, E. *Il culto cristiano in occidente. Note storiche.* Rome, 1978.

Congar, Y. "Situation du 'sacré' en régime chrétien." In the collective work *La liturgie après Vaticane II* (pp. 385–403). Paris, 1967.

———. *I Believe in the Holy Spirit* 3. Translated by D. Smith. New York, 1983.

Cooke, B. "Synoptic Presentation of the Eucharist as Covenant Sacrifice." *Theological Studies* 21 (1960): 1–44.

Daly, R. J. *Christian Sacrifice. The Judaeo-Christian Background before Origen.* Washington, DC, 1978.

Dix, G. *The Shape of the Liturgy.* London, 1945.

Durrwell, F.-X. *The Eucharist: Presence of Christ.* Translated by S. Attanasio. Denville, NJ, 1974.

———. *L'eucharistie sacrement pascal.* Paris, 1981.

Eco, U. *A Theory of Semiotics.* Bloomington, IN, 1976.

Fuglister, N. *Il valore salvifico della pasqua.* Brescia, 1976.

Gelineau, J. "Le acclamazioni anafore." In the collective work *Le nuove preghiere eucaristiche* (pp. 35–37). Brescia, 1969.

———. "La quarta preghiera eucaristica." In the collective work *Le nuove preghiere eucaristiche* (pp. 51–68). Brescia, 1969.

Gerhards, A. "Le phénomène du Sanctus adressé au Christ. Son origine, sa signification, sa persistance dans les anaphores de l'Eglise d'Orient." In the collective work *Le Christ dans la liturgie* (pp. 65–83). Rome, 1981.

Gerken, A. *Teologia dell'eucaristia.* Alba, 1977.

Giraudo, C. *La struttura letteraria dell preghiera eucaristica. Saggio sulla genesi letteraria di una forma. Toda veterotestamentaria, Beraka giudaica, Anafora cristiana.* Analecta biblica 92. Rome, 1981.

Grillmeier, A. *Christ in Christian Tradition I. From the Apostolic Age to Chalcedon (451).* 2nd. ed. Translated by J. Bowden. Atlanta, 1975.

Gy, P.-M. "Les paroles de la consécration et l'unité de la prière eucharistique selons les théologiens de Pierre Lombard à S. Thomas d'Aquin." In G. J. Bekes and G. Farnedi, eds., *Lex orandi lex credendi (Miscellanea in onore di P. Cipriano Vagaggini)* (pp. 221–233). Rome, 1980.

Heinemann, J. *Prayer in the Talmud: Forms and Patterns.* Translated by R. S. Sarason. Studia Judaica: Forschungen zur Wissenschaft des Judentums 9. Berlin-New York, 1977.

Hanssens, I. M. *Institutiones liturgicae de ritibus orientalibus* 3/2. Rome, 1932.

Hoffman, L. A. *The Canonization of the Synagogue Service.* Notre Dame, IN, 1979.

Houssiau, A. "L'anafora alessandrina di S. Basilio." In the collective work *Le nuove preghiere eucaristche* (pp. 69–88). Brescia, 1969.

Johanny, R., ed. *The Eucharist of the Early Christians.* Translated by M. J. O'Connell. New York, 1978.

Jounel, P. "La composition des nouvelles prières eucharistiques." *LMD* 94 (1968): 38–76.

Jungmann, J. A. *The Mass of the Roman Rite: Its Origins and Development (Missarum Sollemnia).* 2 vols. Translated by F. A. Brunner. New York, 1951–1955.

Kittel, G., ed. *Theological Dictionary of the New Testament.* Translated by G. Bromiley. Grand Rapids, MI, 1964ff.

König, F., ed. *Cristo e le religioni del mondo.* Turin, 1967.

Lampe, G. W. H., ed. *A Patristic Greek Lexicon.* Oxford, 1961.

Léon-Dufour, X. *Dictionary of Biblical Theology.* 2nd ed. Translated by J. Cahill, E. M. Stewart, et al. New York, 1973.

———. *Le partage du pain eucharistique selon le Nouveau Testament.* Paris, 1982.

Ligier, L. "Les origines de la prière eucharistique." *QL* 53 (1872): 181–202.

Marili, S. "Una nuova preghiera eucaristica per la Chiesa italiana," *RLit* 67 (1980): 465–478.

———. "Per la storia del Canone. *Hanc igitur oblationem,*" *RLit* 23 (1936): 146–150.

———. "Nota sull'*Hanc igitur* del giovedi santo." *RLit* 24 (1937): 60–62.

Martelet, G. *The Risen Christ and the Eucharistic World.* Translated by R. Hague. New York, 1976.

Mauss, M. *The Gift. Forms and Functions of Exchange in Archaic Societies.* Translated by I. Cunnison. New York, 1967.

Mazza, E. "La *Gratiarum actio mystica* del Libro VII delle *Costituzioni apostoliche.* Una tappa nella storia della anafora eucaristica," *EL* 93 (1979): 123–137.

———. "L'anafora di Serapione: Una ipotesi di interpretazione." *EL* 95 (1981): 510–528.

Mohrmann, C. "Sur l'histoire de *praefare-praefatio.*" In her *Etudes sur le latin des chrétiens* 3 (pp. 291–305). Rome, 1965.

———. "Notes sur le latin liturgique." In her *Etudes sur le latin des chrétiens* 2 (pp. 93–107). Rome, 1961.

Pinell, J. "Anámnesis y epíclesis en el antiguo rito galicano." *Did* 4 (1974): 3–130.

Righetti, M. *Manuale di storia liturgica* 3. *La Messa.* 3d ed. Milan, 1966.

Schnitzler, T. *I tre nuovi canoni ed i nuovi prefazi.* Rome, 1970.

Schürmann, H. *Comment Jésus a-t-il vécu sa mort?* Paris, 1977.

Spinks, B. D., ed. *The Sacrifice of Praise. Studies on the Themes of Thanksgiving and Redemption in the Central Prayers of the Eucharistic and Baptismal Liturgies. In Honor of Arthur Hubert Couratin.* Rome, 1981.

Talley, T. J. "De la 'berakah' à l'eucharistie. Une question à réexaminer," *LMD* 125 (1976): 11–39.

Tarby, A. *La prière eucharistique de l'eglise de Jérusalem.* Paris, 1972.

Thurian, M. "De novis precibus eucharisticis." *QL* 53 (1972): 252–254.

Vagaggini, C. *The Canon of the Mass and Liturgical Reform.* Translated and edited by P. Coughlan. Staten Island, NY, 1967

Wegman, H. A. J. "The Rubrics of the Institution-Narrative in the Roman Missal 1970." In P. Jounel, R. Kaczynski, and G. Pasqualetti, eds., *Liturgia opera divina e umana (Studi in onore di A. Bugnini)* (pp. 319–328). Rome, 1982.

———. "Deux strophes de la prière eucharistique III du Missel Romain." In H. G. Auf der Maur, L. Bakker, A. van de Bunt, and J. Waldram, eds., *Fides sacramenti sacramentum fidei. Studies in Honour of Pieter Smulders* (pp. 300–320). Assen, 1981.

Index

Acceptance, prayer for, 79–83
Account of institution, 2, 3, 7,
    8, 9, 10, 11, 15, 20, 21,
    22–29, 56, 68, 91, 92, 98,
    110, 170, 201, 257, 258,
    259, 260, 261, 262, 279
  for the Eucharistic Prayers
    for Masses with Children,
    243, 246
  for the First Anaphora of Re-
    conciliation, 199
  for the Fourth Eucharistic
    Prayer, 158, 164, 173–176
  for the Roman Canon, 110–
    111, 210
  for the Second Eucharistic
    Prayer, 110–111, 210
  for the Third Eucharistic
    Prayer, 125–128, 130, 131,
    139
Aquinas, Thomas, 256, 261
Addai and Mari, Apostles,
    Anaphoras of. See
    Anaphoras of Addai and
    Mari, Apostles
Afanassieff, N., 243
Alcuin, 84
Alexandrian anaphora, 19, 164,
    171, 183, 211. See also
    Anaphora of Basil,
    Anaphora of Gregory of
    Nazianzus
Alexandrian Anaphora of
    Basil. See Anaphora of
    Basil

Alexandrian Anaphora of
    Gregory of Nazianzus.
    See Anaphora of Gregory
    of Nazianzus
Alexandrian liturgy, 45, 91,
    158, 242
  of St. Mark, 129
  of Serapion, 129
Alexandrian Sanctus, 163
Ambrose, 47, 58, 68, 69, 70,
    71, 72, 81, 260, 261
Ambrosian liturgy, 173
Ambrosiaster, 57
Amon, K., proposal for reform
    of the Roman Canon, 56–
    57
Anamnesis, 3, 8, 11, 69, 92, 98,
    111–118, 124, 129, 134,
    135, 136, 173, 178, 181, 182,
    201, 212, 242, 244, 264
  Christocentric character, 7
  for the Eucharistic Prayers
    for Masses with Children,
    240, 241, 243
  for the First Anaphora of Re-
    conciliation, 202–203
  for the Fourth Eucharistic
    Prayer, 138, 158, 164–170,
    177
  as a profession of faith, 74
  purpose of, 75
  for the Roman Canon, 74–
    79, 111–118
  for the Second Anaphora of
    Reconciliation, 210–211

for the Second Eucharistic
Prayer, 74–78, 111–118
for the Third Eucharistic
Prayer, 131–137
trinitarian character, 7
Anaphora. *See* Anaphora for
the Swiss Synod, Eucha-
ristic Prayers for Masses
with Children, First
Anaphora of Reconcilia-
tion, First Eucharistic
Prayer, Fourth Eucharistic
Prayer, Second Anaphora
of Reconciliation, Second
Eucharistic Prayer, Third
Eucharistic Prayer
Anaphora of Addai and Mari,
Apostles, 5, 7, 8, 85, 159,
189, 210, 258
Anaphora of Basil, 6, 8, 19, 21,
48, 65, 86, 90, 119, 122,
136, 142, 144, 165, 185,
190, 199, 202, 255, 257
Anaphora of John Chrysostom,
22, 48, 136, 163
Anaphora of Clementine, 19,
113, 119
Anaphora of Cyril, 136, 189
Anaphora of the East, 2, 136,
145, 175, 186, 202
Anaphora of Gregory of Nazianzus, 4
Anaphora of Hippolytus, 7, 19,
21, 30, 47, 56, 90, 91, 93,
94, 97, 98, 99, 100, 102,
103, 104, 105, 107, 108,
110, 111, 112, 113, 114,
115, 116, 118, 119, 120,
121, 159, 189, 257, 258
compared with Anaphora II,
95–96
Anaphora of James, 6, 7, 11,
12, 19, 21, 48, 74, 109,
162, 165, 202, 258

Anaphora of St. Mark, 7, 19,
21, 59, 62, 85, 136, 189,
202
Anaphora of St. Peter the
Apostle, 8, 85
Anaphora of Serapion, 19, 21,
146, 262
Anaphora for the Swiss Synod,
124, 218, 213–224
doxology, 215–216
intercessions, 216, 218, 219
intercessions, invariable,
215–216
intercessions, variable, 214–
215
origin of, 216
Post-Sanctus, 218
prefaces, 216, 218, 219, 222
prefaces, invariable, 214
prefaces, variable, 213–214
text, 218–224
Anaphora in the Syriac tradition, 46
Anaphora of Theodore of Mospuestia, 137
Angelology, 81–83
Antiochene anaphora, 4, 19,
54, 90, 91, 121, 211
Antiochene liturgy, 11, 130
of St. James, 65
Antiochene rite, 162
Apostolic Constitutions, 19, 20,
21, 40, 85, 90, 112–113,
119, 144, 160, 262
Apostolic See, 177, 192, 235, 238
Apostolic Tradition, 90, 112, 113,
114, 134, 159
Apuleius, 37
Metamorphoses of, 36
Arranz, M., 158
Ascension of Christ, 74, 75,
132, 133, 181, 182, 184
Assembly, cultic, 118
Aulet, J.-P., 12, 13, 14, 15
Augustine, 38

Baptism, 160
  theology of, 168
Basil, Anaphora of. *See* Anaphora of Basil
Baumgartner, J., 217, 218, 221
Béguerie, P., 200
Berengarius, 171
Bessarion, C., 259
Birth of Christ, 104
Blessing, 23
  cultic, 15, 16
  cup of, 17, 20, 275
  Jewish. *See* Jewish blessing
  of offerings, 61
  spontaneous, 15
Blood
  cup of, 270
  and life, 277–278
  sacrifice of, 139
Bobbio Missal, 84
Body and blood of Christ, 1, 7, 68, 70–71, 98, 119, 130, 170, 179, 200, 273–274, 280. *See also* Bread and wine of Christ
Bouyer, L., 124
Book of Jubilees, 14, 18, 95
Botte, Dom B., 32, 35, 42, 55, 63, 72, 78, 81, 84, 112, 113, 114, 115
Bread, 3
  breaking of, 224
Bread and cup of Christ, 8, 21
Bread and wine of Christ, 1, 2, 4, 7, 8, 70–71, 76, 79, 98, 99, 130, 170, 177, 179, 181, 200, 256, 257, 260, 265, 269, 280
  consecration, 170, 174
  as God's gift, 45
  sanctification of, 11, 266
  transformation, 266
  See also Body and blood of Christ
Brinktrine, J., 59

Brovelli, F., 201
Bugnini, A., 237

Cagin, P., 257
Callewaert, C., 58
Calvary, 270
Canon, *See* Roman Canon
Canon law, 54
Canon of Gelasius, 58
Canon of Paul VI, 125
Capelle, Dom B., 36, 63
Cargin, P., 90
Carolingian period, 36
Catholic Church, 256
Cuva, A. 193
Celebration
  of God in the Fourth Eucharistic Prayer, 158, 161–162
  of redemption, Eucharist is a, 175
Celtic countries, introduction of the Roman Canon to, 53
Chaldean Anaphora of Addai and Mari. *See* Anaphora of Addai and Mari
Chaldean Church, 258
Chalice, 10, 201
  elevation of, 8, 9
  preface for consecrating, 38
  of reconciliation, 201
  of salvation, 3, 79
Chavasse, Antoine, 28, 210, 257, 262–266, 280
Chavoutier, L., 47
Church
  Catholic, 256
  Chaldean, 258
  Eastern, 4, 32, 34
  Roman, 42
Chrysologus, Peter, 162
Chrysostom, John, 5, 252, 259, 260, 264, 265, 271
  Anaphora of. *See* Anaphora of John Chrysostom

Clementine, Anaphora of, *See* Anaphora of Clementine
Clementine liturgy, 119
Cleric, preface for making a man a, 38
Coetus X, 90, 125, 135. *See also* Commission X
Coming of Christ, 93–94
Commemoration, 75, 84–86, 111
  of Christ, 23
  of the Church, 143
  of the dead, 83–84, 240
  of the holy apostles, 121
  of the living, 64, 188
  of Mary, virgin Mother of God, 121, 242
  of the saints, 121–122, 240, 242
  of sinners, 84–87
Commission at Nemi, 137
Commission X, 149. *See also* *Coetus* X
Communicantes in the Roman Canon, 65–66, 242
Communion, 37, 141
  with Christ, 169, 220
  of the dead, 188
  Eucharistic, 203
  with God, 166, 277
  with the Lord, 182
  of saints, 65, 66
  of the universal Church, 242
Communion epiclesis, 92
Concelebration, 29
  ceremonial, 34–35
  and ordination of priests, 31, 33
  sacramental, 34–35
Confession of faith, 159–160
Congar, Y., 172, 255, 256, 258, 263, 264, 265, 266
Congregation for Divine Worship, 216, 235

Congregation for the Sacraments and Divine Worship, 192
Consecration, 172, 261, 264
  prayer for, 266
  theory of, 265
Consecratory epiclesis, 92
Consilium, 57
Constitution on the Church, 146
Constitution on the Liturgy, 29, 33, 163, 236
Consubstantiation, 172
Coptic Anaphora of Basil. *See* Anaphora of Basil
Coptic Anaphora of Cyril. *See* Anaphora of Cyril
Cosmic cross, theme of, 201
Council at Lyons, 259
Council of Trent, 54, 127, 139, 172, 174, 182
Couratin, A., 113
Covenant, 22, 24, 25, 106, 159, 167, 183, 184, 198, 208, 276, 277, 279
  cup of the, 276
Creation, 161–162, 165
Cross
  of Christ, 280
  cosmic theme of the, 201
  sacrament of the, 250
  sign of the, 27, 266
Crucifixion, 181
Cultic assembly, 118
Cultic sacrifice, 186
Cuming, G., 253
Cup, 275–276
  of blessing, 17, 20, 225
  of blood, 278
  and bread, order of, 20, 21
  and bread and cup, order of, 20
  of the covenant, 276
  of life, 278

Cyril, 162
  Anaphora of. *See* Anaphora
    of Cyril
Cyprian, St., 37, 251, 252, 260

Daly, R. J., 73
Damasus, pope, 57
Dead
  commemoration of the, 83–
    84, 240
  intercessions for, 121
  Mass of the, 48
Death and ressurrection of
    Christ, 3, 8, 11, 69, 103,
    104, 107, 111, 146, 177,
    181, 182, 184, 202, 242,
    244, 270, 280
Dekkers, E., 31, 38, 40
De Puniet, Dom, 250, 251
De sacramentis, 81
Der-Balizeh Papyrus, 21
Didache, 18, 19, 21, 23, 30, 39,
    40, 41, 45, 120, 121, 127,
    144, 146, 147, 160, 182,
    183, 185
Dialogues, 139
Diptych, 64
*Directory for Masses with Chil-
    dren*, 235, 237
Disciples at Emmaus, 222–224
Doxology, 1, 3, 4, 5, 7, 11, 16,
    36, 56, 87, 91, 99–100,
    122, 124, 188
  for the Anaphora for the
    Swiss Synod, 215–216
  for the Eucharistic Prayers
    for Masses with Children,
    248
  for the Fourth Eucharistic
    Prayer, 158, 189–190
  for the Second Anaphora of
    Reconciliation, 212
  for the Second Eucharistic
    Prayer, 99–100

for the Third Eucharistic
    Prayer, 149
  trinitarian, 190
Durandus of Mende, William,
    9, 63
Durrwell, F. X., 222, 272

East Syrian Church, 258
Easter, 37, 104, 223
Easter Homilies, 19, 94, 96,
    104, 106
Eastern anaphoras, 2, 136, 145,
    175, 186, 202
Eastern Churches, 4, 32, 34
Eastern epiclesis, 170
Eastern liturgies, 2, 143, 264
Egyptian family of anaphoras,
    258
Egalitarian formula in the Ca-
    non, 8
Eizenhöfer, L., 121
Embolisms, 23
Emmaus, disciples at, 222–224
England, introduction of the
    Roman Canon to, 53
Epiclesis
  communion, 92
  comparison of Hippolytus
    with Anaphora II, 118
  consecratory, 92
  Eastern, 170
  for Eucharistic Prayers for
    Masses with Children,
    240, 241, 246
  first, 2, 4
  first, of the Fourth Eucharis-
    tic Prayer, 158, 169
  first, of the Third Eucharistic
    Prayer, 128–131
  for the First Anaphora of Re-
    conciliation, 203–204
  for the Fourth Eucharistic
    Prayer, 170–173
  for the Roman Canon, 68–72

sanctificatory, 92
second, 3
second, for the Fourth Eucharistic Prayer, 158
second, for the Second Eucharistic Prayer, 99
for the Second Eucharistic Prayer, 118–120
for the Third Eucharistic Prayer, 140–142
for unity, in the Fourth Eucharistic Prayer, 180–186
Ethiopian liturgies, 90
Eucharist
  anaphora as form of the, 250
  mystical, 262
  as sacrament of unity, 120, 203
  as sacrifice, 178–179
Eucharistic communion, 203
Eucharistic meal, 77
Eucharistic concelebration. *See* Concelebration
Eucharistic Prayer
  of Hippolytus, 12
  theocentricity of the, 4,
  trinitarian address, 5
  See also Eucharistic Prayers for Masses with Children, First Eucharistic Prayer, Fourth Eucharistic Prayer, Second Eucharistic Prayer, Third Eucharistic Prayer
Eucharistic Prayers for Masses with Children, 225–249
  account of institution, 243, 246
  anamnesis, 240, 241, 243
  contents of texts, 244–248
  doxologies, 248
  epiclesis, 240, 241, 246
  ICEL translation of Prayer I, 225–228
  ICEL translation of Prayer II, 229–231

  ICEL translation of Prayer III, 232–235
  introduction to, 235–236, 248
  Latin texts as model, 239–240
  literal translation of Prayer I, 225–228
  literal translation of Prayer 11, 229–231
  literal translation of Prayer III, 232–235
  Post-Sanctus, 246
  Sanctus, 243, 245, 246, 248
  trinitarian theology, 245
Evenou, J., 200
Exorcism, preface of, 38
Expiation, sacrifice of, 278

Faith
  anamnesis as a profession of, 74
  confession of, 159–160
  mystery of, 242
  prayer of, 62
  profession of, 3, 159
Faithful
  commemoration of the living, 64
  sanctification of the, 170
Fastidius, 37
Final coming of Christ, 189
Finkelstein, 18
First Anaphora of Reconciliation
  account of institution, 199
  anamnesis, 202–203
  Christological expansion, 200–202
  epiclesis, 203–204
  intercessions, 204
  offering, 202–203
  Post-Sanctus, 199–200
  Sanctus, 197–199
  thanksgiving, 197–199

First epiclesis
  of the Fourth Eucharistic
    Prayer, 158, 169
  of the Third Eucharistic
    Prayer, 128–131
First Eucharistic Prayer, 2
Fourth Anaphora. *See* Fourth
  Eucharistic Prayer
Fourth Eucharistic Prayer, 11,
    21, 42, 75, 91, 125, 127,
    154–190, 197, 203, 211
  account of institution, 158,
    164, 173–176
  anamnesis, 177
  anamnesis in the narrow
    sense, 138, 158
  anamnesis of salvation, 158,
    164–170
  celebration of God, 158, 161–
    162
  doxology, 158, 189–190
  epiclesis, 170–173
  epiclesis for unity, 180–186
  first epiclesis, 158, 169
  ICEL translation of, 154–157
  intercessions, 158, 186–189
  introduction to the Sanctus,
    158
  literal translation, 154–157
  offering, 158, 179–180
  opening dialogue, 158
  paschal mystery, 178–179
  Post-Sanctus, 198
  praise of God, 161–162
  prayer for the Holy Spirit,
    169–170
  as a profession of faith, 158–
    160
  Sanctus, 158, 162–164, 187,
    188
  second epiclesis, 158
  structure, 158
  trinitarian doctrine, 170
Florus of Lyons, 63
Forgiveness of sins, 277

Frankish territory, introduction
  of the Roman Canon into,
  53
Franquesa, A., 31, 35
Füglister, N., 106

Gallican anaphora, 123
Gallican liturgy, 37, 123
Gelasian Sacramentary, Old,
  38, 65
Gelasius, Pope, 58
*General Instruction of the Roman
  Missal*, 240, 243
Genuflection to the sacrament,
  8, 10
Gerken, A., 272, 273
Giftgiving, *see* Potlatch
Gifts, 78, 126, 180–181
  bread and wine as God's, 45
  offering, 77
  preparation of, 129
Giraudo, C., 15, 16, 18
Grapes, preface of, 38
Greek Anaphora of Basil. *See*
  Anaphora of Basil
Greek Anaphora of St. Mark.
  See Anaphora of St. Mark
Gregorian Sacramentary, 36,
  38, 41
Gregory the Great, Pope, 48,
  53, 57, 67, 139, 250, 251,
  252, 262
Gregory of Nazianzus, Anaph-
  ora of. *See* Anaphora of
  Gregory of Nazianzus
Gy, P.-M., 47, 48, 162, 163,
  260, 261

Hamann, A., 160
Hippolytus, 7, 12, 19, 31, 90,
  92, 96, 113, 134, 203, 221,
  257

Anaphora of. *See* Anaphora of Hippolytus
departures from, in Second Eucharistic Prayer, 91–100
doxology of, 100
Eucharistic Prayer of, 12
Holy apostles, commemoration of, 121
Holy Father, 160, 161, 169, 197
Holy See, 191
Holy Spirit, 208
invocation of, 3
prayer to, 4, 169–170
in work of salvation, 169
Holy Year, 191, 201
Holzherr, Abbot G., 217
Host, 10
elevation of 8, 9

ICEL translations
epiclesis for the Third Eucharistic Prayer, 140–141
First Anaphora of Reconciliation, 194–196
first epiclesis for the Third Eucharistic Prayer, 128–129
Fourth Eucharistic Prayer, 154–157
intercessions for the Third Eucharistic Prayer, 142–143
Prayer I of the Eucharistic Prayers for Masses with Children, 225–228
Prayer II of the Eucharistic Prayers for Masses with Children, 229–231
Prayer III of the Eucharistic Prayers for Masses with Children, 232–235
sacrifice of the Third Eucharistic Prayer, 134
Second Anaphora of Reconciliation, 205–207

Second Eucharistic Prayer, 88–90
See also Literal translations
Immolation, 139
Impanation, 171, 172
Incarnation-death-resurrection of Christ, 104, 172
Innocent III, pope, 63
Institution, Account of. *See* Account of Institution
Intentions, 66–68
Intercessions, 2, 3
of the Anaphora for the Swiss Synod, 216, 218, 219
for the Church, 146–147
for the congregation, 148–149
for the dead, 121
of the First Anaphora of Reconciliation, 204
of the Fourth Eucharistic Prayer, 186–189
invariable, of the Anaphora for the Swiss Synod, 215–216
for the living, 121
of the Second Anaphora of Reconciliation, 211–212
of the Second Eucharistic Prayer, 91–92, 120–122
of the Third Eucharistic Prayer, 124, 142–149
variable, of the Anaphora for the Swiss Synod, 214–215
Invocation, 15
to God, 170
of the saints, 145
Irenaeus, St., 78, 82, 136, 171, 241, 253, 255, 256, 260
Isidore of Seville, 38, 260
Israel, 25, 184
Isŏ'yahb III, 5
Italian Church, 217
Italian Missal, 101, 128

James, St.
Anaphora of. *See* Anaphora
of James, St.
Antiochene liturgy of, 65
Jewish blessing, 12, 13, 14, 15,
16, 17–21, 22, 23, 158, 159
Jewish ritual meal 17, 22, 24,
25. *See also* Passover
John XXIII, Pope, 66
Jounel, P., 110
Jubilee Year of Redemption
(1983–1984), 192
Jubilees, 23
Jugie, M., 259
Jungmann, J. A. 36, 37, 59,
65, 66, 67, 84, 85, 178, 180
Justin, 253, 254, 255, 260

Kerygma, 74, 159
Küng, H., proposal for reform
of the Roman Canon, 56–
57

Lanne, E., 32, 33, 34, 62, 159
Last Supper, 1, 5, 7, 9, 16, 17,
19, 20, 21, 22, 23, 24, 25,
26, 27, 28, 29, 69, 70, 83,
98, 99, 100, 101, 110, 111,
118, 130, 131, 141, 144,
171, 173, 174, 175, 176,
177, 180, 181, 210, 223,
239, 242, 246, 250, 251,
252, 253, 257, 258, 259,
262, 263, 264, 265, 266,
267, 269, 270, 271, 272,
276, 280
Latin liturgy, 8, 121
Leo the Great, St., 47, 48, 58,
80, 162
Leonine Sacramentary, 38
Léon-Dufour, X., 267, 269, 270,
271, 274
Levcaro, C., 235

Liber pontificalis, 67
Life, cup of, 278
Literal translations
epiclesis for the Third Eucha-
ristic Prayer, 140–141
First Anaphora of Reconcilia-
tion, 194–197
first epiclesis of the Third
Eucharistic Prayer, 128–
129
Fourth Eucharistic Prayer,
154–157
intercessions for the Third
Eucharistic Prayer, 142–
143
Prayer I of the Eucharistic
Prayers for Masses with
Children, 225–228
Prayer II of the Eucharistic
Prayers for Masses with
Children, 229–231
Prayer III of the Eucharistic
Prayers for Masses with
Children, 232–235
sacrifice of the Third Eucha-
ristic Prayer, 134
Second Anaphora of Recon-
ciliation, 205–207
Second Eucharistic Prayer,
88–90
Liturgies
Alexandrian, 45, 91, 158, 242
Alexandrian, of St. Mark,
129
Alexandrian, of Serapion,
129
Ambrosian, 173
Antiochene, 1, 11, 130
Antiochene, of St. James, 65
Clementine, 119
Eastern, 2, 143, 264
Ethiopian, 90
Gallican, 37, 123
Latin, 8, 121
Old Spanish, 71

Mozarabic, 37, 46, 68, 69, 70, 71, 81, 124, 138, 139
Roman, 1, 8, 32, 36, 37, 41, 43, 47, 71, 74, 85, 92, 100, 124, 140
Syrian, 90
Western, 91, 109
Living, intercessions for the, 121
Livy, 36
Lombard, Peter, 261
Lord's Prayer, 22, 105, 251, 252. *See* also Our Father, Prayer of thanksgiving
Lord's Supper. *See* Last Supper

Macomber, W., 5
Mai, A., 48, 162
Mark, St.
Alexandrian liturgy of, 129
Anaphora of. *See* Anaphora of St. Mark,
Marsili, Abbot S., 217, 218, 221, 222
Martelet, G., 172
Martin, St., 37
Mary, Mother of God, 66
commemoration of, 121, 242
Mass
of the Dead, 48
relation with Supper, 70
Masses
with Children, 177, 191, 192, 225–249
of Reconciliation, 191–212
Mauss, M., 44, 45
Memento
of the living, 67
for the Roman Canon, 64–65, 83–84
Memory of the saints, 66
Mercati, Giovanni Cardinal, 250, 251
Metamorphoses of Apuleius, 36

Metz, J. B., 145
Missal
Bobbio, 84
Italian, 101, 128
of Paul VI, 21, 74, 90, 104, 119
of Pius V, 10, 140
Roman, 97, 98, 171, 216
Missale Gothicum, 56
Moghila, Peter, 32
Mohrmann, C., 36, 37, 38
Morin, G., 58
Mother of God, commemoration of, 242
Mozarabic liturgy, 37, 46, 68, 69, 70, 71, 81, 123, 124, 138, 139
Mysteries of Christ, 178
Mystery of faith, 242
Mystical Eucharist, 262
Mystical prayer, 260

Nemi, Commission at, 137
New Testament, 3, 4, 11, 15, 24, 25, 61, 78, 102, 106, 111, 117, 127, 138, 175, 179, 186, 250, 262, 273, 279
Nocent, A., 65, 123

Oblation, 177
Offering, 1, 3, 98, 99, 186
blessing, of, 61
for the First Anaphora of Reconciliation, 202–203
for the Fourth Eucharistic Prayer, 179–180
of gifts, 77
prayer of, 134
for the Second Anaphora of Reconciliation, 210–211
for the Second Eucharistic Prayer, 98–99
theme of, 129

Old Testament, 3, 12, 15, 16, 60, 61, 72, 73, 74, 78, 79, 80, 81, 99, 102, 103, 106, 116, 117, 120, 128, 160, 167, 181, 183, 209, 219, 220, 270, 271, 274, 277

Opening dialogue, 2
  for the Fourth Eucharistic Prayer, 158
Ordination and concelebration, 31, 33
Ordo Romanus I, 29–30, 31, 59
Ordo Romanus III, 29, 30, 31
Ordo Romanus IV, 31
Ordo Romanus XI, 37
Origen, 245
  trinitarian doctrine of, 163
Orthodoxy, 170
Orthopraxis, 170
Our Father, 37–38, 251, 252. *See also* Lord's Prayer, Prayer of thanksgiving

Palashkovsky, V., 171
Palestine, 109
Palms, preface of, 38
Paschal mystery, 178–179
Passion of Christ, 27, 74, 75, 97, 106, 107, 110, 132, 133, 173, 179
Passion of Polycarp, 86
Passover, 17, 24, 96, 98, 103, 104, 105, 106, 127, 176, 201, 202
  Christ as, 202
  See also Jewish ritual meal
Passover lamb, 97
Paul VI, Pope, 57, 235, 236
  canon of, 125
  Missal of, 21, 74, 90, 104, 119
Penance and reconciliation, 191, 192, 201, 202
Pentecost, 11, 56, 102, 181, 182
Peter, St., Anaphora of. *See*

Anaphora of St. Peter the Apostle
Peter the Cantor, 261
Peterson, E., 59
Petition, 15
Prophecy, equivalence to preface, 39–40
Pilgrim on earth, 146
Piolanti, A., 54
Pius V, Missal of, 10, 140
Pius XII, 32
Polycarp, passion of, 86
Pontifical of the Roman Curia, 31
Post pridie, 68
Post-Sanctus, 2, 6, 7
  for the Anaphora for the Swiss Synod, 218
  for the Eucharistic Prayers for Masses with Children, 246
  for the First Anaphora of Reconciliation, 199–200
  for the Fourth Eucharistic Prayer, 171, 198
  for the Second Eucharistic Prayer, 91, 92, 109–110
Potlatch, 44–47
Praise
  of God in the Fourth Eucharistic Prayer, 161–162
  hymn of, 209
  prayer of, 1
Prayer
  for acceptance in the Roman Canon, 79–83
  for acceptance of sacrifice, 141
  of blessing, 12–16
  of consecration, 255, 266. *See also* Thanksgiving
  of the faithful, 62
  for the Holy Spirit in the Fourth Eucharistic Prayer, 169–170

371

mystical, 260
of offering, 134
of praise, 1
sacramental, 260
of thanksgiving, 1, 18, 29,
    252, 253, 262
Preface, 1, 2, 30, 36–48
  for the Anaphora for the
      Swiss Synod, 213–214
      216, 218, 219, 222
  for blessing a virgin, 38
  cleric, for making a man a,
      38
  for consecrating a chalice, 38
  definition, 36–41
  equivalence to prophecy, 39–
      40
  of exorcism, 38
  for the Fourth Eucharistic
      Prayer, 162
  of the grapes, 38
  for ordaining a subdeacon, 38
  of the palms, 38
  and prophecy, 38–40
  for a reader, 38
  Roman, 44
  for the Second Anaphora of
      Reconciliation, 207–208
  for the Second Eucharistic
      Prayer, 108
Priestly Document, 73
Prigent, P., 149
Proclamation of the name of
    God, 3, 4, 159
Profession of faith, 3, 159
  anamnesis as, 74
  anaphora as a, in the Fourth
      Eucharistic Prayer, 158–
      160
Prophets, 167
Prosphora, 1. See also anaphora

Radbert, Paschasius, 172
Reader, preface for a, 38

Reconciliation
  Anaphora for Masses of,
      191–212
  chalice of, 201
  ICEL translation of the First
      Anaphora of, 194–196
  ICEL translation of the Second
      Anaphora of, 205–207
  literal translation of the First
      Anaphora of, 194–197
  literal translation of the Sec-
      ond Anaphora of, 205–207
  mystery of, 193, 200
  sacrifice of, 145
  theme of, 191
Redemption, 104, 185, 189, 209
  Eucharist as a celebration of,
      175
  mystery of, 177, 193
  plan of, 167
  theology of, 102–104
Reggio Emilia Seminary, 250
Remigius of Auxerre, 63
Resurrection of Christ, 27, 74,
      75, 102, 105, 108, 132,
      133, 177, 181, 184, 224
Revelation, work of, 185
Roman Canon, 1, 2, 8, 9, 11,
      12, 21, 22, 29, 30, 31, 35,
      41, 47, 48, 49–87, 98, 99,
      111, 121, 124, 125, 132,
      136, 158, 162, 170, 175,
      179, 189, 202, 211
  account of institution, 110–
      111, 210
  anamnesis, 74–79, 111–118
  commemoration, 84–86
  commemoration of the dead,
      83–84
  composition of, 57–59
  conclusion of, 87
  epiclesis, 68–72
  ICEL translation, 49–53
  introduction to Celtic coun-
      tries, 53

literal translation, 49–53
Memento, 64–65, 83–84
prayer of acceptance of sacri-
    fice, 59–60, 72–74, 79–83
proposals for reform, 55–57
sacrifice, acceptance of, 59–
    60, 72–74, 79–83
schema for altering, 57
text of, 59–87
translations of, 49–53
Righetti, M., 59, 64, 84
Rite of Penance, 191, 201, 202
Roman anaphora, 91, 202
Roman Church, 26, 42, 53, 74,
    91, 111, 128, 129, 130,
    131, 216, 256, 260, 263
Roman liturgy, 1, 8, 32, 36, 37,
    38, 41, 43, 47, 71, 74, 85,
    92, 100, 124, 140
Roman Missal, 97, 98, 171, 216
    General Instruction in the, 33
Roman preface, 44
Roman rite, 8, 158, 175, 237,
    238, 240
Roman Sacramentaries, 38
Rodemas, A., 130
Rordorf, W., 179
Russian Church, 32, 64

Sacrament of the cross, 250
Sacramental prayer, 260
Sacramentary, 85
    Gelasian, 38, 165
    Leonine, 38
    Gregorian, 36, 38, 41
    Roman, 38
    Verona, 38, 67, 129, 140
The Sacraments, 58, 72
Sacrifice, 36, 37, 60, 72–74
    of Abel, 80
    of Abraham, 80
    acceptance of, in the Roman
        Canon, 72–74
    blood, 139

cultic, 186
Eucharist as, 178–179
of expiation, 278
of Melchizedek, 80
of nature religions, 99
prayer of acceptance, in the
    Roman Canon, 59–60
prayer for acceptance, in the
    Third Eucharistic Prayer,
    141
of reconciliation, 145
spiritual, 186
theology of, 241
in the Third Eucharistic
    Prayer, 134–137
Saints
    communion with the, 66
    commemoration of the, 121–
        122, 240, 242
    invocation of the, 145
    memory of the, 66
Salaville, S., 257
Salvation, 4, 22, 28, 41, 42, 43,
    44, 65, 93, 103, 104, 105,
    161, 173, 179, 184, 185,
    188, 189, 219–220, 246
    anamnesis of, in the Fourth
        Eucharistic Prayer, 158
    chalice of, 3, 79
    in Christ, 108, 167–168
    Holy Spirit in work of, 169
    mystery of, 3, 160, 186
    sacrament of, 2
Samaritan woman, 185
Sanctification of the faithful,
    170
Sanctificatory epiclesis, 92
Sanctus, 2, 6, 47–48
    Alexandrian, 163
    for the Eucharistic Prayers
        for Masses with Children,
        243, 245, 246, 248
    for the First Anaphora of Re-
        conciliation, 197–199
    for the Fourth Eucharistic

Prayer, 158, 162–164, 187, 188
for the Second Anaphora of Reconciliation, 208
for the Second Eucharistic Prayer, 83, 91, 92, 108–109, 110
for the Third Eucharistic Prayer, 125–128
See also Post-Sanctus
Savior and redeemer, 94, 102, 104, 167, 220
Schism of 1054, 259
Schnitzler, T., 124, 125
Scholastic theology, 266
Schürmann, Heinz, 199, 269, 270, 271, 279
Second Anaphora. *See* Second Eucharistic Prayer
Second Anaphora of Reconciliation, 200
anamnesis, 210–211
Christological section, 209
doxology, 212
ICEL translation, 205–207
intercessions, 211–212
literal translation, 205–207
offering of, 210–211
preface, 207–208
Sanctus, 208
Second coming, 3
Second epiclesis
for the Fourth Eucharistic Prayer, 158
for the Second Eucharistic Prayer, 99
Second Eucharistic Prayer, 75, 88–122, 158, 209, 220
account of institution, 110–111, 210
analysis of text, 100–122
anamnesis, 74–78, 111–118
departures from Hippolytus, 91–100
doxology, 99–100

epiclesis, 118–120
Hippolytus, departures from, 91–100
ICEL translation, 88–90
intercessions, 120–122
literal translation, 88–90
offering, 98–99
Post-Sanctus, 109–110
preface, 97
Sanctus, 108–109
second epiclesis, 99
source of, 90
thanksgiving in, departure from Hippolytus, 92–97
translations of, 88–90
Semiology. *See* Signs
Serapion
Alexandrian liturgy of, 129
Anaphora of. *See* Anaphora of Serapion
Servant of Yahweh, 278
Severus, Sulpicius, 37
Sicard of Cremona, 63, 261
Signs, 26, 27, 28, 29, 201
of the cross, 27, 266
of the Last Supper, 27
of sin, 183
of unity, 211
Sin
defining, 166
forgiveness of, 277
Sinners, commemoration to, 84–87
Spain, introduction of the Roman Canon into, 53
Spanish liturgy, Old, 71
Spiritual sacrifice, 186
Spiritual worship, 144
Stowe Missal, 58
Subdeacon, preface for ordaining, 38
Suetonius, 36
Suffering Servant, 278, 279
Supper-cross relation, 70, 200, 201, 210, 271, 273–279, 280

Swiss Church, 217, 224
Swiss Synod, 216
　Anaphora for the. *See* Anaphora for the Swiss Synod
Symmachus, 36
Synod, 221
　of Bishops, 235
Syrian liturgies, 90
Syro-Antiochene anaphoras, 158

Tabera, C., 235
Taft, R., 33, 271
Talley, T. J., 14, 16
Tarby, A., 162, 165, 181
Tertullian, 38, 40, 41, 164, 171, 251, 252, 254, 255
Testament of the Lord, 203
Testamentum Domini, 113
Thanksgiving, 2, 15, 17, 22, 23, 24, 25, 39, 41, 42, 43, 44, 46, 47, 91, 92–98, 111, 112, 113, 118, 134, 158, 159, 204, 207, 219, 221, 244–245, 255
　departure from Hippolytus in the Second Eucharistic Prayer, 92–97
　for the First Anaphora of Reconciliation, 197–199
　hymn of, 209
　prayer of, 1, 18, 29, 262
Theodore of Mospuestia, Anaphora of. *See* Anaphora of Theodore of Mospuestia
Theology of baptism, 168
Theology of sacrifice, 241
Tillard, S.-M., 259
Third Anaphora. *See* Third Eucharistic Prayer
Third Eucharistic Prayer, 75, 91, 123–153, 158, 202, 209, 211

account of institution, 125–128, 130, 131, 139
anamnesis, 131–134
anamnesis, four proposals, 135–137
anamnesis, ICEL translation, 131
anamnesis, literal translation, 131
author of the text, 125
doxology, 149
epiclesis, 140–142
epiclesis, ICEL translation, 140–141
epiclesis, literal translation, 140–141
first epiclesis, 128–131
intercessions, 142–149
intercessions, ICEL translation, 142–143
intercessions, literal translation, 142–143
introduction, 123–125
sacrifice, 134–137
Sanctus, 125–128
sources of the text, 137–140
structure, 123–125
translation of the Latin anaphora, 149–153
vere sanctus es, Domine, ICEL translation, 125–126
vere sanctus es, Domine, literal translation, 125–126
Todah, 15, 16
Torah, 220
Translations. *See* Literal translations, ICEL translations
Transubstantiation, 69, 261
Trent, Council of, 127, 139, 174, 182
Triforme corpus Christi, 172
Trinitarian adddress in eucharistic prayers, 5
Trinitarian character of the anamnesis, 7

Trinitarian doctrine
  in the Fourth Eucharistic
    Prayer, 170
  of Origen, 163
Trinitarian doxology, 190
Trinitarian formula in the
    Canon, 8
Trinitarian structure, 11, 159
Trinitarian theology of the Eu-
    charistic Prayers for
    Masses with Children,
    245
Trinity, 6, 7, 8, 81, 172

Unification, work of, 185
Unity, 142, 170, 183, 185, 186,
    213–214
  Eucharist as a sacrament of,
    120, 203
  mystery of, 246

prayer for, 211
principle of, 127
sign of, 211
theme of, 212, 221–222

Vagaggini, C., 55, 125, 133,
    135, 136, 137, 138, 145,
    149, 171, 179, 211
Vatican II, 29, 127, 135, 165,
    174, 236, 237
Verona Sacramentary, 38, 67,
    129, 140
Virgin, preface for a blessing
    of a, 38

Wegman, H., 124, 125, 140
Welte, B., 268
Western liturgies, 91, 109
Worship, 144